Congressional Politics

Roger H. Davidson, Advisory Editor
The University of Maryland

Congressional Politics

Christopher J. Deering, Editor

George Washington University

The Dorsey Press
Chicago, Illinois 60604

For
Priscilla
and the cousins:
Jacob, Michael, Josie, and Mary

Cover photo: UPI/Bettmann Newsphotos

Sponsoring editor: Leo A. W. Wiegman
Project editor: Susan Trentacosti
Production manager: Ann Cassady
Cover design: Hunter Graphics
Compositor: Weimer Typesetting Co., Inc.
Typeface: 10/12 Palatino
Printer: R. R. Donnelley & Sons Company

LIBRARY OF CONGRESS
Library of Congress Cataloging-in-Publication Data

Congressional politics/Christopher J. Deering, editor.
     p.   cm.
  Bibliography: p.
  Includes index.
  ISBN 0-256-05976-4 (pbk.)
  1. United States.   Congress.   I. Deering, Christopher J., 1951-.
JK1061.C589 1989
328.73—dc19   88–15530
                                                             CIP

Printed in the United States of America
1 2 3 4 5 6 7 8 9 0 DO 5 4 3 2 1 0 9 8

Preface

Some years ago during graduate school I was formally introduced to a way of thinking about political phenomena that most people understand intuitively from an early age. This notion, which is firmly ensconced in the canons of international relations theory, is known as the "level of analysis" problem. At its simplest, it merely points out that people look at problems differently and that they come up with different explanations for why things happen. More formally, the levels of analysis identify separate levels of theory by identifying different units of analysis—individuals, institutions, and systems.

A short time after being introduced to that notion which is formally articulated by scholars such as Kenneth Waltz and J. David Singer I ran across a "B.C." cartoon by Johnny Hart. In that particular cartoon Hart's leading character, B.C., is conducting a prehistoric opinion survey of his fellow cave dwellers. In the process he asks of one of his subjects: "What do you think of the world situation?" Accustomed, no doubt, to stock responses B.C. is startled to hear: "I think being located between Venus and Mars puts us in a vulnerable position." Because the answer is so far out of B.C.'s frame of reference he is reduced to muttering as he walks away.

I assume that there are no serious students or teachers of Congress who would explain the operations of the institution in astronomical or even astrological terms. But we do vary widely in how we explain Congress. Some choose to focus on the behavior of members. Others feel that the operation of basic structures and coalitions afford the best explanation. And still others, harking back to Madison perhaps, feel that the interplay of various political institutions provides the most comprehensive approach.

The point is that there is no fixed way to look at the United States Congress. It is an endlessly fascinating and endlessly complex institution. To understand it we cannot look at a single component or be content with a single approach—and that is the theme and message of this collection. Fortunately, utilizing a level of analysis framework does rather little harm to the topical arrangements traditionally displayed in texts and courses on Congress, which means that the approach has already been embraced, at least implicitly, by instructors and students. I simply offer the opportunity to underscore that fact by adding a couple of features to this collection of original essays.

First, without being heavy handed, I asked each of the authors to keep in mind and, where appropriate, to comment upon their particular level of analysis. The essays are not intended and did not turn out to be highly theoretical. But they are not simply nuts and bolts presentations, either. Each of the authors in this book is widely known for his or her scholarship. That is why I asked them to contribute. This is a book for students of Congress. It is written by scholars who also teach about Congress. That basic interaction, I trust, is at the root of what we do. Most of us study Congress because we are fascinated by it. Most of us teach about Congress because we want to communicate that fascination to others. This book is a tool in that process: It allows us to tell students about our work, and it will help students of Congress to understand their subject. (We also hope, of course, that our colleagues will like this book, adopt it, spread fame and glory about the land for us, and therefore enable us to reach a second edition.)

Second, I have never been entirely comfortable with one or two policy chapters at the end of a book or a separate section on Congress's policy outputs. Instructors who like policy probably think such chapters appear too late in the book. Instructors who do not like policy simply skip them. I have tried to take a more integrated approach here by having an output chapter associated with each part and with each level of analysis. It seems to me that—taking a lead from Theodore Lowi , Randall Ripley, and Grace Franklin—process and substance are inextricably intertwined but that reasonably clear patterns of variation can be identified. Hence, those outputs that can be controlled by Congress's entrepreneurs—mostly casework—are presented in Part One. Those outputs that are dominated by the institutional Congress—largely distributive and pork barrel in nature—are presented in Part Two. And those outputs that are the product of interbranch or systemwide competition—fiscal, foreign, and strategic defense policy—are treated in Part Three. The intent is to have outputs discussed at the same point that the institutional characteristics shaping them are discussed: member behavior, institutional behavior, and systemic interactions.

Having said all this it is still true that this is a very traditionally organized book. It treats the subject matter most frequently covered in texts and courses on Congress. It is written in an intelligent and straightforward style. And it raises important questions—of both a philosophical and a technical nature—for students to think about.

The quality of this book is chiefly a tribute to its authors. And I am very grateful to them. They delivered on time, responded quickly to my requests, and cooperated at every turn. At the outset of this project, Chuck Jones told me that legislative scholars tend to be a responsible lot. I am delighted (and of course relieved) to report that the performance of my friends and colleagues here certainly proved him correct.

Roger Davidson also deserves special thanks. As a friend, mentor, and colleague he has supported me in this and many other endeavors over the years. Like my colleagues, I have learned that with remarkable consistency and grace Roger is unfailingly a good citizen, sterling critic, and original scholar. I am very lucky to have his friendship and his support. Thanks also go to Jon Bond, Christopher Bosso, Gary Copeland, Larry Longley, Michael Lyons, and Priscilla Regan whose reading of parts or all of the manuscript contributed many improvements.

Since our first APSA breakfast meeting, Dorsey's Leo A.W. Wiegman has been an enthusiastic supporter of this project. I am very grateful to Susan Trentacosti, at Dorsey, for her excellent work in producing this book. Also with Dorsey, Amy Byer provided very helpful editorial support and helped to avoid many needless errors. And at George Washington University, Bill Briggs, Betty Burton, Kim Marcus, and Marcia Sleight provided valued research and other support along the way.

The proposal for this book and my daughter Mary were conceived at just about the same time. They have both come along nicely in the interim and that is a great joy to me. I now know that Mary can walk; we will see what *Congressional Politics* can do on its own two feet. Meanwhile, family, friends, and colleagues have provided the sort of supportive environment in which good work prospers. But special thanks are due to Priscilla and Michael, Sharon McAdam, and Jim Kent.

Christopher J. Deering

Contents

About the Contributors

Christopher J. Deering is Associate Professor of Political Science at George Washington University. He is coauthor of *Committees in Congress* (1984) and author of a number of articles on legislative politics and Congress's role in foreign and defense policy formation. He has served as an APSA Congressional Fellow (1984–85) and a Brookings Institution Research Fellow (1977–78).

Timothy E. Cook is Associate Professor of Political Science at Williams College. He is the author of a number of articles on congressional representation, political communications, and political socialization that have appeared in the *American Journal of Political Science, Legislative Studies Quarterly,* and *PS*. He has served as an APSA Congressional Fellow (1984–85) and is currently working on a book on media strategies in the House of Representatives.

Roger H. Davidson is Professor of Political Science at the University of Maryland. He is the author of numerous books—which include *The Role of the Congressman* and (with Walter J. Oleszek) *Congress and Its Members* and *Congress Against Itself*—and articles on a wide array of topics in congressional politics and policymaking. He has taught at Dartmouth College, the University of California–Santa Barbara, and Georgetown University and was a Senior Specialist at the Congressional Research Service, Library of Congress.

C. Lawrence Evans is Assistant Professor of Political Science at the College of William and Mary. He is the author of a number of papers and journal articles on committee politics and is currently working on a book on congressional committees.

Patricia A. Hurley is Associate Professor of Political Science at Texas A&M University. She is the author of a number of papers and articles on electoral linkages with Congress which have appeared in the *American Journal of Political Science, Legislative Studies Quarterly,* and *American Politics Quarterly*. She is currently engaged in research on congressional representation and partisan realignment.

John R. Johannes is Professor and Chair of Political Science at Marquette University. He is the author of numerous papers and articles on member-constituent relations and of *To Serve the People* (1984). He also has served on the editorial board of the *American Journal of Political Science.*

Charles O. Jones is Hawkins Professor of Political Science at the University of Wisconsin. He is the author of numerous books and articles on legislative politics and public policy that include *The United States Congress* (1985), *Introduction to the Study of Public Policy* (3rd ed., 1984), *Clean Air* (1975), and *The Minority Party in Congress* (1970). He has served on numerous commissions and boards, on the editorial boards of several journals, and as editor of the *American Political Science Review.*

Lance T. LeLoup is Professor and Chair of Political Science at the University of Missouri–St. Louis. He is the author of numerous papers and articles on Congress and fiscal policy, a leading scholar of budgetary politics, and author of *Budgetary Politics* (4th ed., 1988).

Paul Light is on the staff of the Senate Committee on Governmental Affairs. He is the author of several books on politics and policy: *Artful Work: The Politics of Social Security Reform* (1985); *Vice Presidential Power* (1984); and *The President's Agenda* (1982). He has also served as director of research for the National Academy of Public Administration, a guest scholar at the Brookings Institution, an APSA Congressional Fellow (1982–83), and taught at the University of Virginia.

Walter J. Oleszek is Specialist in American National Government at the Congressional Research Service, Library of Congress. He is the author of numerous articles, of *Congressional Procedures and the Policy Process* (3rd ed., 1988), and (with Roger H. Davidson) of *Congress and Its Members* (2nd ed., 1985) and *Congress Against Itself* (1977). He has served on the staffs of several congressional committees and has taught at Colgate and American Universities, SUNY, and at the University of Maryland.

Glenn R. Parker is Professor of Political Science at Florida State University. He is the author of numerous articles on congressional politics and of two books: *Homeward Bound: Explaining Changes in Congressional Behavior* (1987) and (with Suzanne L. Parker) *Factions in House Committees* (1985).

Lyn Ragsdale is Associate Professor of Political Science at the University of Arizona. She is the author of a number of papers and articles on Congress, the presidency, and electoral politics which have appeared in such journals as *Legislative Studies Quarterly* and *American Journal of Political Science.* She is also author (with Gary King) of *The Elusive Executive: Discovering Statistical Patterns in the Presidency* (1988).

Kay Lehman Schlozman is Professor of Political Science at Boston College. She is the author of a number of articles on interest groups and (with John T. Tierney) of *Organized Interests and American Democracy* (1986).

Barbara Sinclair is Professor of Political Science at the University of California, Riverside. She is the author of *Majority Party Leadership in the House of Representatives* and of numerous other books and articles on congressional politics. She served as an APSA Congressional Fellow (1978–79). She is engaged in continuing research on congressional leadership and has just spent a year in the office of Speaker of the House Jim Wright.

John T. Tierney is Associate Professor of Political Science at Boston College. He is the author of a number of articles on interest-group politics and (with Kay Lehman Schlozman) of *Organized Interests and American Democracy* (1986).

Carl E. Van Horn is Professor of Political Science at Rutgers University and Associate Director of the Eagleton Institute of Politics. He is the author of numerous papers and articles on policy and policymaking and coauthor of *Politics and Public Policy* (1988) and *The Politics of Unemployment* (1985). He has served as an APSA Congressional Fellow (1984–85).

CHAPTER 1

Congressional Politics: An Introduction and an Approach

Christopher J. Deering

In May 1986, seven U.S senators, led by Oregon Republican Robert Packwood, met at a West Virginia mountain retreat not far from Washington, D.C. They were not vacationing. Rather, they had joined together to attempt to revive a sweeping tax reform proposal that appeared to be dead in the water. The glare of Washington attention, House-Senate rivalry, disagreements with the president, and constant lobbying by interest groups had immobilized the tax reform effort. The retreat to West Virginia was a final attempt to escape the distractions and to fashion a workable solution to the impasse. Or, to use a currently popular phrase, the group of seven decided to get outside the "Capital Beltway" and away from distracting and competing political demands. It seems to have worked.

The group of seven returned to Washington with a reworked proposal, presented it to their colleagues on the Senate Finance Committee on Monday morning, and unanimously passed it from the committee by Wednesday. The political process surrounding tax reform was far from over, of course. Months would pass before the House and Senate could agree on a final proposal that would also gain President Ronald Reagan's signature. But the core proposal hammered out in a long weekend of negotiating would remain intact and the most fundamental change in the American tax system since before World War II would be put into place.

The story of the Tax Reform Act of 1986 is unique, but the contending forces behind it, the nature of the process, and many of the qualities of the resulting legislation are not. Consider three components of the legislation finally signed by the president:

- Six million working poor were removed from the rolls of those liable to pay taxes.
- Tax breaks for the oil and gas industry were maintained despite the sweeping elimination of other deductions and exemptions that littered the tax code.
- Large contributors to the Louisiana State University and the University of Texas football programs were exempted from an IRS ruling that

1

would prevent them from deducting the value of their tickets from their taxes as a business expense.[1]

The first of these changes marked a major redistribution of the tax burden borne by American citizens. It is the sort of legislation that Congress passes only very rarely. The second change represents the status quo. Traditional interests well represented in Congress and by lobbyists in Washington prevented any substantial change in the tax law that would be harmful to their industry. This outcome is quite common. The final change represents a very narrow loophole that would benefit only two institutions in the entire country. It was the sole product of two powerful members of Congress who happened to sit on the tax writing committees and also to be alumni of the two universities: Representative Jake Pickle, formerly of the University of Texas, and Senator Russell Long, formerly of Louisiana State University.

Each of these provisions is the law of the land; each provision was accepted by both the House and the Senate; and each was also accepted by the president when the bill was signed. But clearly they differ vastly from one another: the first is one of several provisions that mark this particular bill as a landmark piece of legislation; the second marks an area of change desired by many but compromised away or left untouched to preserve the larger goal of tax reform; and the third is indicative of the narrow benefits—of no particular consequence to overall tax reform, the budget deficit, or the ultimate success of the bill—that individual members of Congress are able to squirrel away in legislation to benefit their communities or particular constituencies within their communities.

Each of these provisions also tells us a little something about how Congress operates and why, for many, Congress is such a difficult institution to comprehend. Changes of the first type are typical of the textbook Congress: A deliberative assembly that meets to discuss important matters and to fashion large-scale public policy through laws. Most of us realize that this is an idealized picture of Congress. In fact, most Americans are more likely to believe that Congress generally produces "outputs" that resemble the second type of provision; namely, legislation that benefits an identifiable group or sector of society represented by a powerful lobby. Accustomed as we are to this pluralistic characterization of Congress, we must also recognize that individual members of Congress can affect the legislative process in identifiable ways and that they too contribute to the outputs, as noted in the football example given above.

Understanding the nature of Congress is quite a challenge—not just for the student but also for the astute and seasoned observer. The United States Congress is a large and multifaceted institution. This is a simple fact. But the result is that no two observers ever see quite the same thing. Hence, descriptions and characterizations of Congress tend to be heavily influenced by which part of the institution is being observed.

The theme of this book is meant to keep those thoughts before you, and the examples above are intended to underscore the point that Congress continuously operates at three levels: at the individual level, at the institutional level, and at the level of the political system. In order to understand Congress in a more comprehensive fashion it is important to keep each of these levels of operation in mind. Moreover, it is useful to note that each level of operation has a distinct effect upon Congress's wide variety of outputs. Stated another way, Congress is best understood by examining three "levels of analysis" and the types of outputs that characterize each level.[2] These levels of analysis are scattered throughout the material that you read about Congress but they are too rarely set in juxtaposition to each other.

THE FIRST LEVEL: MEMBERS OF CONGRESS

Members of Congress control considerable resources. They have sizable staffs, offices in Washington and in their districts or states, travel budgets, access to media, the franking privilege, and enough prestige and clout to enable them to acquire virtually any sort of information they might need to do their jobs. They have varying amounts of status within their parties, among their colleagues, and within their committees. The members also enjoy a great deal of freedom to do their jobs as they see fit. Each has a single vote during committee, party, or floor proceedings and no one—save perhaps their constituents—can tell them how to cast that vote. It is quite proper, therefore, to view representatives and senators as powerful individuals who are very much in control of their own political destinies. And it follows that these same members have considerable ability to influence the legislation and other products that emerge from Congress.

How Do Members Shape Congress?

It is also proper to view members of Congress as rational, goal-oriented individuals. That is, members are likely to engage in behavior or to utilize the resources available to them to achieve their goals. Taken a step further, if members do not have resources that are appropriate to achieve their goals they will try to get them. There are limits, of course. Representatives and senators are not likely to supply themselves with personal executive jets to enable them to fly back and forth to their districts. They are also not likely to amend the Constitution to prohibit anyone from running against them in subsequent elections. But they can and have provided themselves with enough travel expenses to go home virtually anytime they want, and they have passed legislation that makes it more difficult for challengers to mount campaigns against them.

Members of Congress do a lot to shape and to control the political environment within which they operate, and some would insist that reelection is the primary explanation for and means of understanding how the contemporary Congress operates. In a provocative and insightful essay, David Mayhew argues that "the organization of Congress meets remarkably well the electoral needs of its members."[3] He does not say so explicitly, but he clearly means that individual members of Congress have shaped the institution in ways that assist them in achieving their electoral goal. Indeed, Mayhew has argued that members of Congress are "single-minded seekers of reelection" and that they pursue this goal to the virtual exclusion of all others.[4] For Mayhew, to understand Congress we must first understand the individual members of Congress. This can be visualized in the form of a simple diagram:

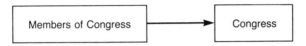

As this diagram suggests, individual legislators are the irreducible components of Congress. They are the players that make up the team. Without them no collective identity can exist. Moreover, as the nature of the membership changes so does the institution. For example, if the bulk of the members are indeed single-minded seekers of reelection the institution will change to reflect that orientation; but if Congress is populated by strongly partisan members an altogether different outcome should result.

Member Outputs

If members are able to shape the institution to their needs it stands to reason that they can also shape Congress's outputs to their needs. Some scholars have argued persuasively that members of Congress are putting less time into legislation and more time into the sort of particularized constituent benefits, called constituent service or *casework*, that helps to ensure their reelection. Morris Fiorina, for example, has suggested that members have altered their traditional mix of activities, which emphasized lawmaking and pork barrel legislation rather than casework, so that casework now comes first.[5] Hence, the lost social security check, trouble with a local bureaucracy, or other problems have become an area for intervention by members of Congress. Indeed, some observers have gone so far as to characterize members as simply ombudsmen for their constituents in Washington. Casework is not the only *individual* level product provided by members of Congress; amendments to existing laws, insertion of language into draft legislation, or even alterations in the official reports that accompany most bills can provide particularized benefits for constituents. The more powerful a member becomes, the more valuable and far-reaching the benefits of such actions become.

Strictly speaking, no member of Congress can produce legislation without the help and consent of the other members. All legislation must be passed in identical form by both chambers and signed by the president. Nonetheless, members can contribute to legislation in individualized ways so that pieces of law, minute though the pieces may be, can effectively become the product of a single member. The tax exemptions for wealthy LSU and UT football boosters (and other "transition rules" that softened the blow of changes in the tax code) are examples of this process.

Some legislative products result largely or exclusively from individual member initiatives such as favors, casework, media messages, and other items wholly within the control of members. Increasingly, they are also the most likely form of contact between members and their constituents—the things members are likely to be best known for in their districts. If, as Burdett Loomis has suggested, we should view congressional offices as small businesses,[6] then it stands to reason that each of these small businesses would also provide various products. The major product, of course, is the member of Congress, but they must advertise and present that product to the consumers in each of the 540 states, districts, and territories that make up the political geography of the United States.

Scholarship on Congress increasingly has adopted this purposive or rationalist approach. The examination of election and reelection success of members, their casework, media orientations, careers, and "home styles" (i.e., the way the legislators interact with their districts) all reflect this framework of analysis. Furthermore, it is argued that the goals and activities of the members help to explain why the House and Senate are decentralized, why parties are weak, and why leaders lack the power they once enjoyed. In this view, Congress is a reflection of the motivations, styles, and activities of the members in the aggregate. The question is whether this is the only means of examining Congress.

THE SECOND LEVEL: CONGRESS AS AN INSTITUTION

Most people who join organizations go through a learning period. New employees learn where to park, where and when to get paid, and where the bathrooms are. New recruits learn the rules, regulations, and standard operating procedures of the military services. And pledges learn the traditions, standards, and rules of the game for their fraternities and sororities. Each organization has some history behind it, and each has a more or less formal organization. Over time, new members learn what the formal procedures are and also "how things are really done." It is no different for Congress and for members of Congress. As a result, some would argue that Congress, as an institution, has a life of its own—a structure, a history, a way of doing things—that is quite independent of what any particular member might want. This is, of course, an *organic* view of the institution: Congress is more than just the sum of its parts. These same analysts would also suggest that members of Congress must adapt to their new surroundings and that, as a result, they are shaped by the institution.[7] This approach may be represented by simply reversing the direction of the arrow which appeared in the previous diagram. Here it is Congress that shapes the behavior of the members rather than vice versa.

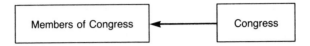

How Does the Institution Shape Members?

From this point of view, members can either adapt to their surroundings, conflict with them and suffer the potential consequences, or work to change the institution. Since no member is in a position to unilaterally alter the institution, the latter option can be achieved only in concert with other like-minded members. Thus, for most members, most of the time, adaptation or exit are the only two options. Once elected, they enter an institution with a strong set of norms, a standing set of rules, an ongoing committee system, a set party structure, and institutionalized leaders. A new member will not immediately chair a committee or be elected speaker or majority leader, and must accept a level of resources which, while generous, has been determined by previous congresses. Put simply, the actions of members of Congress are constrained in numerous ways.

Studies of Congress were once dominated by this institutional approach. Committees, for example, were seen as microcosms of Congress.[8] They recruited like-minded members and forced them to serve apprenticeships while their senior colleagues questioned the witnesses, drafted the laws, and made the floor speeches. Party leaders were noted for their power. The Senate was alleged to be a "club" dominated by a few senior "insiders."[9] Most members were seen as adopting roles within the institution that would allow them to serve productively as members.[10] Distinctions were made between the "show horses" and the "work horses" of each chamber.[11] And, perhaps most important of all, new members were admonished with the phrase: "In order to get along, you've got to go along."

While this approach is no longer the norm, there is a great deal of value in the insights and observations offered by it. And it has by no means disappeared. At its simplest, this institutional approach argues that members of Congress are not free agents but rather are constrained, guided, and shaped by the nature of the institution. This can be brought into sharper focus by considering, as you will throughout this book, the differences between the House and the Senate. No matter what a member's goals or motivations might be, he or she cannot ignore the distinctly different sets of rules and procedures in the two chambers. Members also must come to grips with committee, party, and leadership structures that are distinctly different in the two chambers. In short, they must adapt to the nature of the chamber.

Of course, the reverse is also true. Committees reflect the goals and motivations of the members that make them up. Leaders must cope with weak partisanship and members who are not generally beholden to their parties for their election or reelection. Also, aggressive members may break, bend, or seek to change rules and practices that do not suit them. Nonetheless, a set structure cannot simply be ignored; it is bound to shape the individual behavior of the members.

Institutional Outputs

The stamp of the institution is not restricted to the behavior of the members. Just as there are outputs that are characteristically individual, there are also outputs that are characteristically institutional. Most notably, the institutional Congress tends to produce policies that are distributive or regulatory in nature, incremental, and designed to appeal to identifiable constituencies. This is the Congress of dominant committees and subcommittees and of old fashioned *subgovernments*—the alliance of executive branch agencies, congressional committees, and private sector beneficiaries in a mutually supportive environment.[12] No single member completely controls the policy output; negotiation, compromise, and concerted action are required. The final product is never what a single member would choose to do on his or her own but it is a distinctly legislative product.

These types of outputs are also unlikely to attract wide attention, serious presidential interference, or to be the subject of debate during national election campaigns. Rivers and harbors legislation, agricultural price support programs, certain military projects, or tax breaks for the oil and gas industry (maintained in the 1986 Tax Reform Act) are all examples of this type of uniquely legislative product. No president is likely to be successful in an attempt to invade this congressional turf, as President Jimmy Carter found out when he opposed funding for numerous water projects. Indeed, Carter's critics pointed to this attempt to stem the flow of pork-barrel projects as evidence of his ignorance of Congress's means of doing business. Almost anyone from inside the Beltway would know better than to challenge Congress on something so dear to its collective heart.

The individual and the institutional perspectives each provide important and productive insights to the U.S. Congress. As noted above, neither exists without the other. Absent the membership, the institution quickly ceases to exist, but no single member can supplant this institution with its 200 years of history, experience, and change. But even then, is this a complete view of the institution?

THE THIRD LEVEL: CONGRESS IN THE POLITICAL SYSTEM

By definition, politicians operate within a political system rather than in isolation from it. For members of Congress, the most immediate day-to-day environment is the institution. But they must also operate, separately and jointly, within the larger political system. Thus, while members of Congress and the internal structure of the institution go a long way toward explaining congressional politics, neither operates in a vacuum. The political environment also shapes *how* Congress and its members operate. For convenience, this political environment can be subdivided into two categories: one contains events (of a political, economic, cultural, or other character) sufficiently important to alter routine agendas and the second contains a set of ongoing structural conditions that define the nature of the political system.

Major catastrophes, economic swings, or national security emergencies are bound to affect the institution. The mode of operation for Congress could not be the same during the Civil War or during World War II as it was before either of those two major historical events. Likewise, Congress could not emerge from either of those two great conflicts unchanged or unmindful of the effects they had upon American political institutions. Broadly speaking these events can be said to make up the "nonroutine" congressional agenda, an agenda made up of items of major importance, that are not easily foreseen, and which command the public's attention in an immediate and consuming fashion.

The most important ongoing structural characteristic for American political institutions is the separation-of-powers political system installed by the Founding Fathers. Beyond that, the media, the executive bureaucracy, the federal structure of the American system, public opinion, and the nature of the international system all affect Congress.

How Does the Political System Shape Congress?

In its extreme form, a systemic approach suggests that the most consistent and telling factors which shape the behavior of Congress are external to it.[13] That is, members' goals and ambitions and the internal structure of the institution are but a reflection of the environmental pressures placed upon the institution. Change does not normally originate from within or as a result of inexorable laws of bureaucratic change and evolution but rather as an adaptive response to the political environment.[14] Unlike the two previous diagrammatic representations, which were essentially mirror images of one another, this diagram must be seen as a series of external pressures upon the institution:[15]

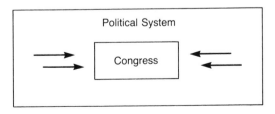

Pressures upon Congress can present a wide variety of problems for the institution. In some cases the institution does not have to change in order to respond; for example, new or intensified issues, such as the energy crisis of the 1970s, may require no substantial structural changes for Congress to respond. In other cases change might very well be in order; the successes of the Progressive movement throughout the United States at the turn of the last century, for example, were reflected by internal democratization and decentralization of Congress. The speaker lost a great deal of power, committees gained power, and a larger number of members gained a share of the policy making power within Congress. It is fair to say that changes in Congress's political environment created pressures for change within Congress as well.[16]

The nature of the separation-of-powers system is among the strongest and most consistent determinants of congressional behavior—precisely as Madison and the Founding Fathers intended it. Each branch, Madison suggested, "should have a will of its own." And that *institutional will*—a sense of identity or esprit de corps—would instill in each branch's occupants a protective quality that would ward off the aggressive or expansionist intentions of the other branches. As Madison wrote in *The Federalist Papers* [No. 51]:

> But the great security against a gradual concentration of the several powers in the same department consists in giving to those who administer each department the necessary constitutional means and *personal motives* to resist the encroachments of the others.[17]

Each branch would be permanently suspicious of the motivations of the others and therefore on the lookout for potential transgressions.

This is most apparent in the relationship between the executive and the legislative branches. Because the Constitution forces Congress and the president to share power the relationship between these two branches is at the heart of our system of government. It is also a perennial issue for politicians, journalists, and academic observers. A president's success is assumed to be conditional on the makeup of Congress. Less obvious, but also true, is the fact that Congress's record is dependent upon the occupant of the presidency.

Systemic Outputs

Finally, it is again worth noting that certain issues are broadly enough defined to be *systemic* in character. Fiscal and foreign policy—guns and butter issues—are the most obvious examples of such issues. To be sure, Congress may act independently around the edges of these issues by trimming defense programs, keeping unwanted military bases open, or legislating new tax loopholes, but the annual budget, arms control, major foreign policy initiatives, or comprehensive tax reform are the joint products of these two institutions, the public, the media, and other interested parties.

Systemic issues arise in part because they represent "high stakes" controversies or nonincremental policy changes—those that are new, large, and require major funding. The characteristics of these policies invite controversy and attention, and therefore almost guarantee competition among the branches. Roosevelt's New Deal, Johnson's Great Society, Carter's energy policies, and Reagan's economic policies all required massive changes in existing federal policy, affected millions of taxpayers, and were at the heart of each president's campaign for election. Thus, they were high-priority items involving significant financial and political stakes for the competitors. Under such circumstances a business-as-usual, low visibility, distributive approach to policymaking could hardly have been possible.

Finally, it is worth mentioning that these issues, or unexpected changes in these issues, can easily dominate the congressional agenda. The effect of this is to crowd out routine agenda items and, at times, even to alter the way those routine matters are handled by Congress. And the most dramatic of these changes—war or depression—are likely to leave lasting and fundamental effects upon all of our political institutions.

CONGRESS: THREE LEVELS OF ANALYSIS

The United States Congress is an endlessly fascinating institution, but it is also fair to describe it as Byzantine. In 1802, the legislative branch of government employed 152 people, a number that included the members of both the House and the Senate, the handful of support personnel, and the vice president. By the early 1980s, the number of legislative branch employees had reached nearly 40,000, including 540 legislators, nearly 14,000 personal and committee staff, and over 25,000 other support personnel. An institution of this size cannot help but be complicated. Even when the outer layer of the legislative bureaucracy is peeled away (i.e., the police, the barbers, and the groundskeepers) a complex institution remains. For example, House Democrats of the One hundredth Congress had a party structure made up of eighty-six different formal positions. In the One hundredth Congress, the House and Senate had more than 50 committees and about 240 subcommittees. And, by the One hundredth Congress there were nearly 100 informal caucuses—groups organized around particular issues or voting blocs—competing for legislators' attention.

Like many bureaucracies, Congress has tended to add rather than to subtract structures during its 200-year history. As a result, the formal structure of the institution has slowly but surely grown more complex as each new layer or substructure is grafted onto the existing institution. In fact, it is not too far from the truth to suggest that, like rings on a tree, the age and history of the Congress may be discerned in these layers and structures. Even though the goal of this book is not chiefly historical, the fact that Congress has developed over a long period of time is worth remembering since it helps to explain some of the anomalies that crop up in legislative structure and procedure. History is but one additional tool that will help you to unravel the mysteries and vagaries of the institution.

Beyond that, however, it is hoped that an appreciation of the three different approaches (or levels of analysis) will provide you with additional analytic tools as you go about your study of Congress. But also remember that none of these three approaches to the study of Congress is complete or completely correct. Each provides important clues to the puzzle that is Congress, but in order to fully understand the institution, we must not only look closely at it but also stand back and take a more comprehensive look. No course on Congress would be complete if it ignored any of the important pieces discussed above. Instead, a composite approach to examining Congress, graphically represented by combining the three previous diagrams, can be presented. Here, it is suggested, we must look at how members shape the institution, how members in turn are constrained and shaped by the institution, and how both individuals and the institution are shaped by external forces.

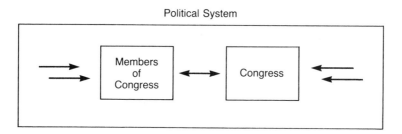

Political System

One final note of caution is in order regarding the various approaches. Each is a compromise. By focusing on details, the individual approach is less able to address the sweep of congressional trends; it is reductionist in nature. At the same time the systemic approach loses sight of important details because of its scope. Thus, the broader an explanation becomes the less able it is to account for details; the narrower an explanation becomes the less able it is to account for broader changes. There is nothing inherently good or bad about this, but it is a factor that must be kept in mind.

This same point can be made by considering once again the example that opens this chapter. By focusing selectively on one piece of the Tax Reform Act of 1986 a case could be made that any one of these three approaches is the best approach to studying Congress. But none of the three can sufficiently account for what happened on that particular piece of legislation; that is, tax breaks for football fans are as difficult to trace to the Constitution as major shifts in the tax burden are to trace to a single member's initiative. Clearly, there is no single best perspective.

The chapters which follow are organized in three parts; these parts roughly correspond to the three levels of analysis. Part One, The Members of Congress, contains a series of chapters on members of Congress; Part Two,

The Institutional Congress, contains chapters on the institution; and Part Three, Congress in the Political System, contains chapters on Congress in the political system. The authors of the chapters do not necessarily adopt a rigid point of view that follows any one of the diagrams presented earlier. But each does offer important and original insights regarding Congress. As you read, you should not only pick up the factual information regarding various phenomena of congressional politics but also puzzle over the various ways in which it is possible to think about Congress, its members, and the political system.

NOTES

1. For background on the Senate Finance Committee's tax bill see Eileen Shanahan, "Finance Panel OKs Radical Tax Overhaul Bill," *Congressional Quarterly Weekly Report*, May 10, 1986, pp. 1007–13. For background on the finished tax bill's effect on American sports see John F. Berry, "Skyboxes, Longhorn Alums and Other Taxing Matters," *Sports Illustrated*, February 9, 1987, pp. 30ff.
2. No claim of originality for the level of analysis approach is intended here. Explicitly and implicitly it appears frequently in the political science literature, but, with one exception, I do not know of any explicit treatment of it where Congress is concerned. See Darrell M. West, *Congress and Economic Policymaking* (Pittsburgh, Penn.: University of Pittsburgh Press, 1987). Good examples of this general approach can be seen in J. David Singer, "The Level-of-Analysis Problem in International Relations," *The International System: Theoretical Essays*, ed. Klaus Knorr and Sidney Verba (Princeton, N.J.: Princeton University Press, 1961), pp. 77–92; and in Kenneth N. Waltz, *Man, the State, and War: A Theoretical Analysis* (New York: Columbia University Press, 1954).
3. David R. Mayhew, *Congress: The Electoral Connection* (New Haven, Conn.: Yale University Press, 1974), p. 81.
4. Ibid., p. 17.
5. Morris P. Fiorina, *Congress: Keystone of the Washington Establishment* (New Haven, Conn.: Yale University Press, 1977), pp. 41–46.
6. Burdett A. Loomis, "The Congressional Office as a Small (?) Business: New Members Set Up Shop," *Publius* 9, pp. 35–55. For a similar line of argument employing this purposive approach see Robert H. Salisbury and Kenneth A. Shepsle, "U.S. Congressmen as Enterprise," *Legislative Studies Quarterly* 6 (November 1981) pp, 559–76.
7. One of the classic examples of this approach is Richard F. Fenno's study of the Appropriations Committee, *The Power of the Purse: Appropriations Politics in Congress* (Boston: Little, Brown, 1966), although it is interesting to note that Fenno's landmark study, *Congressmen in Committees* (Boston: Little, Brown, 1973), takes a much more purposive approach to legislative behavior.
8. Again, see Fenno, *The Power of the Purse*.
9. William S. White, *Citadel: The Story of the U.S. Senate* (New York: Harper & Row, 1956).
10. John C. Wahlke, Heinz Eulau, William Buchanan, and Leroy C. Ferguson, *The Legislative System: Explorations in Legislative Behavior* (New York: John Wiley & Sons, 1962); Donald R. Matthews, *U.S. Senators and Their World* (Chapel Hill:

University of North Carolina Press, 1960); and Roger H. Davidson, *The Role of the Congressman* (New York: Pegasus, 1969).

11. See Chapter 4 and also James L. Payne, "Show Horses and Work Horses in the United States House of Representatives," *Polity* 12 (Spring 1980), pp. 428–56.

12. J. Leiper Freeman is generally credited with originating the notion of policy subsystems in his study of the Bureau of Indian Affairs. See Freeman's *The Political Process: Executive Bureau–Legislative Committee Relations*, rev. ed. (New York: Random House, 1965). But see also, Ernest F. Griffith, *The Impasse of Democracy* (New York: Harrison-Milton Books, 1939), and Douglass Cater, *Power in Washington* (New York: Random House, 1964).

13. Contemporary examples of this approach, at least in any pure form, are hard to come by but several do come to mind that might fit (without in anyway suggesting that the authors themselves would agree to such a classification). Lawrence C. Dodd's well-known essay, "Congress and the Quest for Power," argues that there is a cyclical pattern of power shifts between Congress and the executive that is noticeable throughout American history. The explanation for this is traced to the power-seeking motivations of individual members so the argument might also fit in the first level. But the historical sweep of the argument suggests larger forces at work as well; see Lawrence C. Dodd and Bruce I. Oppenheimer, *Congress Reconsidered* (New York: Praeger Publishers, 1979), pp. 269–307. James L. Sundquist, *The Decline and Resurgence of Congress* (Washington, D.C.: Brookings Institution, 1981) also suggests that the inherent competition between the branches is a root cause of their behavior, at least over the long haul. James Madison's original statements regarding the "machine that would go of itself" remain the classic statement in this regard; but again, even Madison assumed that individual motivations would fuel the institutional interactions.

14. As one example on this point see Peter Swenson, "The Influence of Recruitment on the Structure of Power in the U.S. House, 1870–1940," *Legislative Studies Quarterly* 7 (February 1982), pp. 7–36. Compare it with Nelson W. Polsby, "The Institutionalization of the U.S. House of Representatives," *American Political Science Review* 62 (March 1968), pp. 144–68.

15. Despite the appearance of references to the political system this is not a systems analysis approach. It does not stress inputs, conversions, and outputs, but instead emphasizes the self-perpetuating nature of systems based upon shared power and competition. In this context, systems analysis would be somewhat more appropriate at the institutional level.

16. On this point see Roger H. Davidson and Walter J. Oleszek, "Adaptation and Consolidation: Structural Innovation in the U.S. House of Representatives," *Legislative Studies Quarterly* 1 (February 1976), pp. 37–65.

17. Alexander Hamilton, James Madison, and John Jay, *The Federalist Papers*, ed. Clinton Rossiter (New York: Mentor, 1961). (Originally published 1788.) Emphasis mine.

PART ONE

The Members of Congress

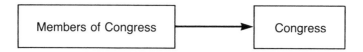

CHAPTER 2

Do Voters Matter?
Democracy in Congressional
Elections

Lyn Ragsdale

Sheldon Clark was an obscure, yet important, figure in the 1986 elections for Congress. A cab driver in Tucson, Clark ran as a Republican candidate in the second congressional district of Arizona against thirteen-term incumbent, and one-time presidential hopeful, Morris Udall. Clark spent nearly $5,000, mostly his own money, but gained scant attention from voters. He did little campaigning and could best be reached by calling the Sunset Cab Company and leaving a message for cab number 174. Udall spent nearly half a million dollars and won 76 percent of the vote. Indeed, after the race the local Udall office reported that he had run unopposed. As for Clark, by election day he had moved on to New Mexico to take a mining job and like scores of other congressional candidates before, during, and since 1986, has not been heard from again.

The Clark story tells of the connections among individual voters, individual members of Congress, and candidates who choose to oppose them. On its face, the story is an amusing anecdote about a congressional campaign that did not get off the ground. But it is more than the campaign that never took off. Sheldon Clark's tale provides a backdrop for a much larger, tattered and faded picture of democracy offered by congressional elections. Clark's overwhelming defeat by Udall is amusing only if the voter-incumbent-challenger connections are observed as a simple electoral exercise: one candidate must win, the other must lose. It is not at all funny when tougher questions are asked about the meanings of those connections as a much more complicated exercise in democracy or its abeyance.

Theories of democracy often run afoul of American elections. In its folk-lore and scholarly lore, America is celebrated as a long-lasting democracy; indeed, the phrase "American democracy" is taken as though the two words were redundant. Yet writers on the subject have typically observed that the normative criteria they establish for voters and elections rarely match either the actual comings and goings of American voters or the electoral races they supposedly decide.

In successive attempts, democratic theorists and election analysts have revised theories of democracy to more closely reflect election day experiences. Theories once demanded that voters in a democracy gather as much information as possible on issues of the day and regularly participate in elections to let their choices be known. But mounting empirical evidence suggested that voters knew little and often participated even less in civic matters. Current theory no longer assumes that fully informed, fully participant voters are required for democracy to exist. While candidates were once assumed to present a clear choice to the electorate, this requirement too has been relaxed, because often such clarity cannot be found in candidates' rhetoric. Yet the theoretical revisions beg the central question about whether the words America and democracy are synonymous. In particular, revising normative theory to match empirical reality leaves unresolved whether American elections are mechanisms for broad, relatively equal, citizen control of the government. A logical fallacy exists in many of the writings on "American democracy": If American election contests do not fit prevailing theories of democracy, it is the requirements of the theories that are too demanding. It is rarely suggested that *the elections,* rather than the theories, are lacking.

This chapter explores the workings or the nonworkings of electoral democracy in America as they unfold in elections to the U.S. House of Representatives and the U.S. Senate. There are some 521,000 elected offices in the United States. Voters usually pay concerted attention to only one, exceedingly atypical, race—that for the U.S. presidency. The remaining one-half million offices share a good deal in common. They take place with limited voter attention, minimal media interest, and sporadically organized campaigns. In this regard, U.S. House elections are archetypal American contests. They are characterized by citizens who are reluctant to take part and candidates who are hesitant to challenge seated incumbents. In Senate races, which usually are better financed and more visible than House contests, voters' attention is greater although not dramatically so. House elections, Senate elections, and the contrasts that can be drawn between them provide ways to discern how contemporary electoral processes help or hinder democratic government.

This chapter begins with an outline of the principal elements of democracy, then discusses several theories of democracy that have been applied to American elections as they attempt to integrate these principal elements. Finally, it considers the degree to which U.S. congressional elections fit the theories, force revisions of the theories, or force American analysts to reassess whether congressional elections are viable democratic exercises.

THEORIES OF DEMOCRACY AND ELECTIONS

In order to appreciate the linkage between notions of democracy and contemporary congressional elections, it is important to grasp the essential elements of democracy and then to see how different theories of democracy weight them. These are treated in turn.

Elements of Democracy

Democracy, as historically conceived, involves a government run by the people who live under it.[1] Theories of democracy generally rest on three distinct, but interrelated, dimensions. First, democracy hinges on citizens' participation in political affairs. Wrote John Stuart Mill, "It is evident that the only government which can fully satisfy all the exigencies of the social state is one in which the whole people participate."[2] This includes their ability to organize political associations, to freely express political opinions, to gain access to varied forms of political information, to select public officials, or to actually be selected as such an official. It is unlike other approaches of governance that discourage or foreclose broad-based participation and settle instead for actions by a few.

Second, as a corollary, democracy involves the equality of the participants. Citizens are equal in their abilities to influence the outcomes of government decisions. This is typically assumed to involve more than the mere technical equality offered by universal suffrage. It extends to equal access to information about the decisions of the government, equal access to the government itself, and equal ability to evaluate its performance.

Third, there is competition among those seeking to influence government decisions. Through the competition, the citizenry is given the right to oppose actions of a government in power and choose among alternative courses of action. This is in contrast to settings in which opponents to a government are suppressed and denied access to the citizenry. Or governmental decisions are presented to the citizenry by sham, false information, or manipulation. In these situations, there is only one obvious choice, but choice itself is illusory.

There are thus three essential conditions for democracy: citizen participation (the people rule), political equality (the people rule equally), and public competition (the people have a choice). Elections are adapted to accommodate these conditions. They establish a mechanism for participation by allowing citizens to express preferences about the operation of the government indirectly through the selection of representatives. Jefferson wrote that "the essence of a republic" is "action by the citizens in person in affairs within their reach and competence, and in all others by representatives chosen immediately and removable by themselves."[3] This electoral participation is designed to lead to equal control of the government since each citizen has a single vote equal (at least in a mathematical sense) to every other person's vote. Competition among candidates and parties seeking these votes provides a way of channeling the right to oppose from such mechanisms as violence, street protest, or overthrow of officials, to elections. Citizens can put honorable leaders into office, but they can also throw the rascals out.

Each of the three conditions must be present for elections to contribute to democracy. If they are not, serious questions are raised about the promise and the performance of democracy. For instance, people may be able to participate through elections, but may not do so equally. American blacks gained the right to participate in elections with the advent of the Fifteenth Amendment (in 1870). Yet black voting continued to be severely hampered by economic circumstances, racial intimidation, and legal impediments, such as grandfather clauses, poll taxes, and literacy tests. For fully a century after the ratification of the amendment, blacks' rights to participate were of little consequence in their ability to act equally with whites. There are also situations in which popular participation through elections is hailed, but no public competition exists. As Robert Dahl put it:

> In fact one of the most striking changes during this century has been the virtual disappearance of an outright denial of the legitimacy of popular participation in government. Only a handful of countries have failed to grant at least a ritualistic vote to their citizens and to hold at least nominal elections.[4]

But the nominal elections involve no contests: one party runs and always wins. People of the USSR, for example, enjoy universal suffrage, but they have no choice in which party is selected to run the government.

Democratic Theories

While various theories of democracy all contain this nucleus of participation, equality, and competition, they diverge in the specific emphases given each and the role elections play in providing for them. Three main theories tie elections to democracy: classical democracy, polyarchy, and marketplace democracy.[5]

Classical democratic theory calls for knowledgeable participation by the greatest number of people. This idealized conception of democracy stems from utilitarianism of the eighteenth and nineteenth centuries. The utilitarians, including Jeremy Bentham, James Mill, and later John Stuart Mill, maintained that the proper end of government is the greatest good for the greatest number. To achieve such a government, citizens engage in political action to communicate to the government what the "greatest good" is and to guarantee that it be implemented. By this view, voters are rational activists. Possessing intelligence, they seek as much information as possible and readily use it to participate in public affairs. They carefully evaluate all evidence and decide their vote on how well the alternatives offered match the evidence available. Possessing virtue, they strive to take as much part in government as they can in order to advance the common good. Possessing equality, all citizens bear responsibility for defining the general good. Elections provide a way to achieve participation, reinforce the equality, and through competition of ideas establish the common good.

The classical doctrine is essentially a normative theory of democracy, prescribing what should be. It establishes very stringent requirements for voters both in the knowledge they are supposed to have and the level of their active engagement. It is criticized by other theorists on three counts. "There is, first, no such thing as a uniquely determined common good that all people could agree on or be made to agree on by the force of rational argument."[6] Second, people are not rational in the way that the theory demands. It is unlikely that people will critically sift through all the information that is before them and correctly interpret what the observations mean. Thus, people are not only unlikely to have a notion of the common good, but they are also unlikely to take well thought-out individual stands on matters that come before the polity. Third, people are not as altruistic as the theory demands. Rather, they are self-interested. Although they may feel a duty to participate in politics, they may act on the feeling only sporadically and, then, in safe, contained, minimal forms of participation—notably voting. The theory thus prescribes human nature in politics—it does not describe it.

A second theory, *polyarchal democracy,* holds that democracy can endure when public participation in politics is minimal rather than maximal. Citizens may be active in government, but are not likely to be too active; they may be informed, but are infrequently well informed. Democracy does not exist in an ideal sense, but is approximated in relatively, but nonetheless incomplete, democratic regimes called polyarchies.[7] Emphasis in this theory shifts from actual participation to the *right* of participation in elections and office seeking. It is much like people who live near a lake, but who never take part in any water activities. Yet, they swear they would never live anywhere else, because "we could always use the lake if we wanted to." For the enjoyment of democracy, as well as the lake, opportunity rather than activity becomes crucial. Or, as Gabriel Almond and Sidney Verba put it: "[A citizen] is not constantly involved in politics, he does not actively oversee the behavior of political decision makers. But he does have the potential to act if there is need. . . . He is not the active citizen: he is the potentially active citizen."[8] Voters adopt a norm to participate, even if they do so only on occasion.

While the classical theory places greatest emphasis on the electorate, the polyarchal theory concentrates on the elected officials. Democracy rests on "public contestation" or the competition among political parties or candidates seeking office, even if levels of knowledge or participation of the electorate are low.[9] Democracy, Almond and Verba tell us, is fostered not by demands from the citizenry, but from elected elites applying the "law of anticipated reactions":

> A good deal of citizen influence over governmental elites may entail no activity or even conscious intent of citizens. On the contrary, elites may anticipate possible demands and activities and act in response to what they anticipate. They act responsively, not because citizens are actively making demands, but in order to keep them from becoming active.[10]

While the theory of polyarchy eliminates the stringent demands for participation and awareness placed on voters by classical theory, polyarchal theory itself has been criticized for its less than flattering characterization of voters. Studies conducted during congressional and presidential elections concluded, consistent with the theory, that voters were unsophisticated in their knowledge of issues, had relatively unformed ideological beliefs, and were oblivious to simple factual matters of politics, such as which party controlled the Congress.[11] Scholars objected to what they saw as a portrayal of voters as near fools. In addition, criticisms were leveled that the theory espoused political stability at the expense of need for political change. Since, in the theory, citizens remain relatively passive unless an issue becomes intense and leaders quietly anticipate public reactions, the status quo is maintained, even if such stability is pernicious.

A third version of democracy, the *marketplace theory*, counters the polyarchal view. Its central premise is that voters are not fools.[12] Rather than the negative connotations attached to voters' lack of interest and participation that at times grew out of polyarchal theory, voters under marketplace theory are actually expected to lack such involvement. Voters are rational individuals, but the theory's view of rationality differs sharply from that offered in the classical theory. While rationality involved the search for full information in the classical theory, here voters are self-interested individuals who seek to minimize the amount and the cost of the information they obtain. Anthony Downs challenges the classical doctrine: "Any concept of democracy based on an electorate of equally well-informed citizens presupposes that men behave irrationally."[13] Democracy is a marketplace within which voters seek information bargains.

Voters, however, often find it difficult to purchase information, because candidates either take ambiguous stands on public policy matters or they do not achieve sufficient visibility to make their message accessible to the average, nonchalant, preoccupied voter. Candidates, themselves, are rational and they strive to take positions and court images that will be acceptable to the broadest spectrum of the electorate. Thus, the impact of candidate competition on participation rights (and rites) inhibits voters' full awareness of political activities and full interest in engaging in them. "Politicians' behavior may affect the extent to which *voters'* behavior fits democratic theories" (emphasis in the original).[14] This essentially gets voters "off the hook" built by both the classical and polyarchal theories. Marketplace theory instead casts the blame on candidates. Surely, voters cannot be blamed for their absence of awareness when presented with lopsided contests like the one between Sheldon Clark and Morris Udall.

How do voters behave? The theory suggests that they need not have well-informed opinions on major national issues or be deeply familiar with the qualifications of candidates. Rather, they practice simple methods of reward and punishment, holding elected officials responsible for the nation's good and bad times.[15] Or they may act somewhat more sophisticatedly, viewing past performance as a predictor of future success.[16] In either case, they vote *retrospectively* based on how well they feel the government satisfies its responsibilities. As perceived by voters, these responsibilities may be anything—war, the economy, a shortage of oil, illness, the loss of a job—and may not always be things over which the government has any control. Equality of participation exists because everyone is able to evaluate government performance relative to citizens' personal or social needs.

The marketplace theory of democracy is presently in vogue in studies of American elections. It is heralded as one that establishes minimal requirements for both voters and candidates and, as such, provides a truly empirical theory of national elections. It states, as does the polyarchal theory, that participation is more important as a right than as an activity. Equality rests on all citizens' abilities to provide sweeping and unspecific evaluations of whether times have been good or bad. Competition pushes candidates to take stands that blur rather than clarify.

Yet, questions can be raised about the soundness of the marketplace theory. As noted above, both the classical and polyarchal theories are criticized in varying degrees for not taking empirical facts sufficiently into account. It may be that the marketplace theory can be criticized for taking empirical facts into account too much and thereby defining democracy backwards: fitting theory to facts, rather than testing the theory on the basis of available facts. How this may take place is examined below as all three theories are tested for how well they can explain congressional elections.

CONGRESSIONAL ELECTIONS: DEMOCRACY AS PASSIVITY

These three theories of democracy accommodate in varying ways the central dimensions of a democracy: participation, equality, and competition. How do the theories fair when they are confronted with real, live elections? The theories have been applied most consistently to American national elections at the presidential level. They have not been scrutinized to any great degree at the congressional level.[17] An intricate jigsaw puzzle of House and Senate elections confronts the theories. The puzzle, which looks nothing like that for presidential elections, is a very difficult one for each of the theories to attempt to solve. It should not be surprising if some, if not all, of the theories fall short. The congressional election puzzle has five interlocking yet erratically shaped pieces.

The Ideal Collapsed

The first piece of the congressional puzzle (depicted in Table 2–1) reveals that *a majority of citizens do not participate*. Indeed, this provides an ironic twist to the concept of majority rule—a majority of the eligible electorate choose not to rule. Both Senate and House elections face the problem of low participation. The extent of participation depends on whether a more visible, more interesting presidential race is also going on. Many citizens find it less than appealing to vote for the House or the Senate just for their own sakes. Turnout for House races is approximately 14 percent lower during midterm elections

TABLE 2–1   Turnout in Presidential and House
Elections, 1952–1986 (percentage of voting
age population)

Year	Presidential Elections	Senate Elections	House Elections
1952	61.6	61.6	57.6
1954	—	39.7	41.7
1956	59.3	56.6	55.9
1958	—	48.1	43.0
1960	62.6	60.0	58.5
1962	—	50.5	45.4
1964	61.9	62.6	57.8
1966	—	35.4	45.4
1968	60.9	58.9	55.1
1970	—	48.4	43.5
1972	55.4	52.7	50.9
1974	—	38.9	36.1
1976	54.4	54.3	49.5
1978	—	35.5	35.1
1980	53.4	49.9	48.1
1982	—	40.5	37.7
1984	53.1	52.6	47.7
1986	—	36.5	29.5

SOURCE: U.S. Bureau of the Census, *Statistical Abstract of the United States,*
108th ed. (Washington, D.C.: Government Printing Office), selected
volumes.

when the presidency is not at stake. There is also a considerable drop-off
between presidential election year turnout and midterm turnout for the Senate, although it is more difficult to make a direct comparison because the
Senate figures only involve the thirty-plus states that hold Senate elections
every other year. This picture of congressional participation appears even
bleaker when one recognizes that since 1972 a near majority of citizens stay
home during presidential elections, too. Even among those that do turn out,
a pattern of *roll off* can be observed: that is, people vote for president, but
choose not to vote for House, Senate, or other candidates in the same election
year. From 1952 to 1986, there was a 5 percent roll off from voting in the
presidential race to voting in contests for the House and a 2 percent roll off
rate for Senate voting. Although voters may already be in the voting booth
making a decision on the chief executive, some nonetheless skip pulling any
levers for the House of Representatives or the Senate.

Low voter turnout in House and Senate races is reinforced by low interest
in congressional campaigns and in their outcomes, even among those who do
vote. Significant numbers of voters during the 1978 through 1986 elections
were not interested in either the campaign or who won it (Table 2–2). Of

TABLE 2–2 Congressional Campaign Interest, Concern, and Knowledge, 1978–1986

	1978		1980		1982		1984		1986	
	All Respondents	Voters Only	All Respondents	Voters Only	All Respondents	Voters Only	All Respondents	Voters Only	All Respondents	Voters Only
Interest in campaign										
Very much	22%	32%	36%	47%	26%	37%	35%	45%	22%	37%
Somewhat	45	51	45	43	44	49	45	43	44	50
Not much	34	17	19	10	30	13	20	12	33	13
Care about election outcome*										
Very much	15	21	18	27	21	30	—	—	18	27
Pretty much	28	37	27	38	35	44	—	—	35	46
Not much	36	32	29	27	29	21	—	—	31	23
Not at all	21	9	13	9	14	6	—	—	16	4
Knowledge of congressional composition†										
House	59	74	62	82	31	68	55	66	33	42
Senate	—	—	—	—	38	54	27	34	17	19

* Question not asked in 1984.
† Based on the question, "Which party had the most members in the House/Senate before the election?" Question not asked for the Senate in 1978 and 1980.

SOURCE: NES/CPS American National Election Studies, 1978–1986.

particular note, an average of 35 percent of voters during that period cared little about the outcome of the election, *yet voted nonetheless*. In addition, individuals have very limited knowledge about the party composition of the House and Senate before the elections. Knowledge that the House of Representatives has been in Democratic hands since 1932 seems to be diminishing over time. People also seem strikingly unaware of the Republican majority held in the Senate prior to the 1982, 1984, and 1986 races.

Congressional elections thus swiftly wreak havoc on the classical theory of democracy. The theory suggests that the greatest number of citizens must participate for democracy to be in place. Yet, low levels of turnout, interest, and concern raise questions about the viability of full citizen participation as it is defined in classical theory. In addition, since equality in the theory rests on the participation of all citizens, this standard too cannot be met. Nor can the common good arise from such skewed participation. What is taken as the "common" good is nothing more than the satisfaction of interests sought by individuals and groups that do participate. Congressional voters are not the rational activists mandated by the theory. Consequently, the rest of the components of the theory collapse.

In the Absence of Competition

The polyarchy theory alleviates the central problem the classical theory encounters by positing limited citizen participation. It thus easily accommodates the first piece of the congressional puzzle and adds a second: *Voters obtain little information and have limited contact with candidates* (see Tables 2–3 and 2–4). Beyond the decision to participate in an election, voters must also decide how much effort they are willing to expend on determining their choices among candidates. Some interest is necessary to gain and select information about the candidates. With the low interest observed above, voters are unlikely to have much information about the candidates or have much contact with their campaigns. When shown the names of congressional candidates, voters typically can recognize House and Senate incumbents seeking reelection, but they are much less likely to be familiar with the names of Senate challengers and, in particular, House challengers. If asked to actually remember the names of the candidates running, voters have even greater difficulty. At least 40 to 50 percent of the voters across the period could not remember the names of the candidates. The contact voters are likely to have with candidates is linked to its ease of availability. If it is something voters must actively seek out, they will not do so. This can be readily seen in Table 2–4 by the small numbers of voters who personally met the candidates in a congressional race, attended meetings to hear them speak, or talked to members of their campaign staffs during elections from 1978 to 1986. If the form of contact is passive, exposure is greater. Sitting home to receive mail, read a newspaper, or turn on the radio or television requires much less initiative and may gain just as much information. Thus, the polyarchal theory adequately accommodates voters' tendencies toward passivity.

TABLE 2-3 Voters' Information about Congressional Candidates, 1978–1986 (incumbent races only)

	1978		1980		1982		1984*		1986	
	Incumbent	Challenger	Incumbent	Challenger	Incumbent	Challenger	Incumbent	Challenger	Incumbent	Challenger
Name recognition†										
House	91%	44%	91%	46%	93%	61%	88%	53%	91%	44%
Senate	96	85	98	80	96	78	—	—	97	74
Name recall‡										
House	47	14	44	17	51	21	40	15	40	10
Senate	60	48	58	38	59	27	—	—	60	40

* Senate data not available for 1984.
† Whether respondent, when presented with the name of a candidate, recognizes the individual.
‡ Whether respondent can actually remember (without prompting from the interviewer) the candidate's name.

SOURCE: NES/CPS American National Election Studies, 1978–1986.

TABLE 2-4 Voters' Contact with Congressional Candidates, 1978–1986 (incumbent races only)

	1978 House		1978 Senate		1980 House		1982 House		1984 House		1986 House	
	Incumbent	Challenger	Incumbent	Challenger	Incumbent	Challenger	Incumbent	Challenger	Incumbent	Challenger	Incumbent	Challenger
Any contact	89%	44%	94%	83%	87%	44%	90%	44%	88%	46%	89%	41%
Met personally	22	4	10	6	18	4	22	7	20	5	20	4
Saw at meeting	19	3	11	6	15	2	18	8	17	3	18	2
Talked to staff	12	2	7	5	12	1	14	6	15	4	16	1
Received mail	69	14	56	38	64	14	72	14	73	25	73	13
Newspaper	70	27	78	76	58	23	69	22	67	38	66	23
Radio	35	13	48	45	28	12	40	35	29	15	36	9
Television	51	20	86	86	48	20	61	18	54	29	59	20

source: NES/CPS American National Election Studies, 1978–1986.

The theory then relies on the competition among parties and candidates as the key to the democratic exercise. Citizens can participate if they want to, but so long as candidates and, in particular, elected officials seeking reelection anticipate the reactions of the voters, democracy survives. Yet, a third piece of the congressional puzzle quickly causes problems for the polyarchy theory: By and large, *congressional elections are not competitive*. The absence of public competition is keenest when incumbent members of the House seek reelection. Surely if one wanted a very safe, well paying, and rather interesting job, retaining a seat in the House fits the bill. Over 90 percent of incumbent House members seeking reelection win, and they do so by comfortable, if not impressive, victory margins of well over 60 percent (Table 2–5). Although Senate elections are more competitive than House elections, Senators are still reelected in high numbers and by safe election margins. Three out of four senators who seek reelection are victorious. Indeed, in eight of the thirteen election years from 1958 to 1986, the number of senators retiring from Congress exceeded the number losing in the general election.

This lack of competitiveness in incumbent races can also be seen in the differences in information voters secure about incumbents and challengers.

TABLE 2–5   Competition in Congressional Elections, 1958–1986

Year	Members Reelected		Average Vote Won by Member		Members Reelected by 60% or More	
	House	Senate	House	Senate	House	Senate
1958	90%	64%	61.2%	57.5%	63.1%	71.3%
1960	93	97	60.6	54.5	58.9	71.8
1962	92	83	62.1	54.8	63.6	40.0
1964	87	85	61.7	60.3	58.5	63.0
1966	88	88	62.7	52.6	67.7	59.3
1968	97	71	64.2	52.9	72.2	58.9
1970	95	77	65.4	56.3	77.3	45.8
1972	94	74	65.6	60.5	77.8	55.0
1974	88	85	64.0	52.5	66.4	47.8
1976	96	64	65.8	50.8	71.9	68.7
1978	94	60	65.8	52.5	78.0	53.3
1980	91	55	66.1	50.1	72.9	56.2
1982	90	93	65.0	58.6	68.9	50.0
1984	95	90	65.6	61.9	75.1	73.0
1986	98	75	69.5	59.1	81.2	71.4
1958–1986 (mean)	93	77	64.4	55.7	70.2	59.0

source: House data for the first and third columns found in Norman J. Ornstein et al., *Vital Statistics on Congress, 1984–1985 Edition* (Washington, D.C.: American Enterprise Institute for Public Policy Research, 1985), pp. 49–50, 53. House average vote taken from Gary Jacobson, *The Politics of Congressional Elections*, 2nd ed. (Boston: Little, Brown, 1987), p. 32. Selected years calculated by the author.

Senate data calculated by the author from *Congressional Quarterly Almanac* and *Congressional Quarterly Weekly Report* (Washington, D.C.: Congressional Quarterly Incorporated, passim).

Although the polyarchal theory suggests that voters' participation and information is low, it does not fully account for the gap in information about incumbents and challengers displayed in Tables 2–3 and 2–4. For instance in 1986, 23 percent fewer people recognized the names of the Senate challengers than recognized the incumbent senators. For House elections the recognition gap was 47 percent.

These results on voter information and election outcomes contradict the notion of competition highlighted in the polyarchal theory. But they are just that—results; they do not shed light on factors contributing to the noncompetitiveness. The fourth puzzle piece helps account for the absence of competition: *Incumbents spend increasingly more money on their campaigns than do challengers.* When seats are *open*—there is no incumbent, that is—money is more plentiful and more equal for the candidates and competition is more intense, as seen in Table 2–6. However, when members of Congress seek reelection, and most of them do, a considerable disparity exists between funds available to them and to their opponents. In 1984, as one example, incumbents from both the House and the Senate spent roughly two dollars for every dollar spent by their opponents. Incumbents often engage in what is known as *preemptive spending.*[18] They raise large amounts of money and spend a portion of it early in the campaign to scare away credible opponents. Consequently, the right to oppose becomes less meaningful. The contests reaffirm the status quo by default, not necessarily by the desires of the electorate. Thus, the two puzzle pieces fit neatly together: It costs money to forestall competition. But the two pieces dilute the validity of the polyarchal theory and its emphasis on candidate competition.

Voters, Fools, and Electoral Inequality

Neither the classical theory nor the polyarchy theory very closely resembles the processes and the outcomes of congressional elections. Classical theory requires full participation; congressional elections involve minimal participation. Polyarchy theory mandates vigorous competition; congressional elections involve minimal competition. By contrast, marketplace theory seems to resolve several deficiencies of the other two theories. First, it recognizes that it is costly for congressional voters to participate. Limited participation is granted so long as all voters can equally provide their assessments of past government performance or future prospects. Since voters are self-interested and principally concerned about their own daily lives, the theory correctly predicts that voters lack interest and concern about congressional elections. Second, for similar reasons of self-interest, the theory also accurately depicts voters' reticence to seek out information about or contact with candidates. Third, the theory recognizes low levels of competition. As rational and self-interested beings, members of Congress secretly desire to run unopposed in every election. They will do everything they can during the election period and the interelection period to meet as little opposition

TABLE 2-6 Congressional Campaign Expenditures, 1974–1984 (in thousands)

	1974	1976	1978	1980	1982	1984
House						
All candidates						
Total expenditures	$44,051	$60,046	$86,129	$115,222	$174,922	$203,400
Mean expenditures	53	73	109	153	228	239
Open seats						
Mean expenditures	90	124	201	202	285	380
Incumbents						
Mean expenditures	57	79	111	165	265	276
Challengers						
Mean expenditures	40	51	75	122	152	119
Challenger money as percent of incumbent money	70	65	68	74	57	43
Senate						
All candidates						
Total expenditures	28,436	38,109	64,696	74,164	114,036	170,400
Mean expenditures	437	595	951	1,107	1,782	1,936
Open seats						
Mean expenditures	402	757	821	1,133	4,143	2,033
Incumbents						
Mean expenditures	556	624	1,342	1,302	1,858	2,486
Challengers						
Mean expenditures	333	453	698	843	1,217	1,307
Challenger money as percent of incumbent money	60	73	52	65	66	53

SOURCE: 1974–1982, Norman J. Ornstein et al., *Vital Statistics on Congress, 1984–1985 Edition* (Washington, D.C.: American Enterprise Institute for Public Policy Research, 1985), pp. 65–66, 69–70; 1984, Federal Election Commission, *FEC Reports on Financial Activity, 1983–1984, Interim Report No. 9* (Washington, D.C.: Government Printing Office, May 1985), p. xi.

as possible. In addition, rational politicians who desire to run for Congress will choose races they have a chance of winning, not ones they are sure to lose. Experienced, well-qualified candidates will wait for a seat to open, rather than oppose a venerable incumbent. Fourth, as a result, incumbents gather incredible treasure chests of campaign money that dwarfs the amounts received by their often less-qualified opponents.

The theory also fits well with the fifth puzzle piece (depicted in Table 2–7): *Political action committees finance increasingly larger percentages of congressional campaigns.* Political action committees (PACs) are the newest incarnation of money in congressional elections. The committees are of two broad types. First, there are *special interest PACs* that serve as the electoral arms of interest

TABLE 2–7   Growth of Political Action Committees, 1974–1984

Type of PAC	1974	1976	1978	1980	1982	1984
Corporate	89	433	784	1,204	1,467	1,682
Labor	201	224	217	297	380	394
Trade/membership/ health	318	489	451	574	628	698
Nonconnected	—	—	165	378	746	1,053
Other	—	—	36	98	150	182
Total	608	1,146	1,653	2,551	3,371	4,009

	Contributions (in millions)					
	1974	1976	1978	1980	1982	1984
Type of PAC						
Corporate	$2.5	$7.1	$9.8	$19.2	$27.4	$34.0
	(20%)	(31%)	(28%)	(35%)	(33%)	(34%)
Labor	6.3	8.2	10.3	13.1	20.2	23.3
	(50%)	(36%)	(29%)	(24%)	(24%)	(23%)
Trade/membership/ health	2.3	4.5	11.5	16.1	21.7	24.6
	(18%)	(20%)	(33%)	(29%)	(26%)	(26%)
Other	1.4	2.8	3.5	6.9	13.9	17.3
	(11%)	(12%)	(10%)	(12%)	(17%)	(17%)
Total PAC contributions	12.5	22.6	35.1	55.3	81.3	100.3
Adjusted for inflation (1984 = 1.00)	26.3	41.2	55.9	69.7	89.4	100.3
PAC contributions as percent of total contributions	(17%)	(23%)	(25%)	(29%)	(31%)	(37%)

SOURCE: Gary C. Jacobson, *The Politics of Congressional Elections*, 2nd ed. (Boston: Little, Brown, 1987), tables 4.1, 4.2.

est groups which involve fairly narrow, particularized concerns of businesses, corporations, labor unions, and trade associations. These PACs give campaign money to candidates who will be receptive to their concerns once in Congress. Second, there are *nonconnected PAC* committees that are not affiliated with any business or association. They are ideologically based, most often conservative, and seek to support candidates who favor similar broad shifts in the direction of the government.[19] Both types of PACs find it advantageous to supply money during the congressional campaign to secure access to the victorious candidate after the election. They influence the campaign in the hope of influencing the legislative process thereafter. Not surprisingly, most PAC contributions go to House and Senate incumbents. The marketplace theory posits that such organized interests are acting strategically as rationally motivated entities. Giving money to incumbents, rather than their opponents, provides the greatest strategic advantage most of the time, particularly for business, trade, and labor groups whose stakes in the legislative process have been mapped out over decades.

Current understanding of congressional voters, candidates, campaigns, and election results seemingly confirms the marketplace theory. Citizens cannot afford the time or effort to obtain full information about politics or participate at every opportunity. Instead, their decisions to participate and their decisions regarding which candidate to select are based on vague impressions and quick snapshots of the recent political past. These decisions are intertwined with decisions made by candidates on how extensively to campaign and what to emphasize in their campaign messages. Voters cannot be considered fools when candidates set out to fool them. In addition, candidates have another pool of interested political activists, including individuals, parties, and PACs, to which they must more clearly respond. The theory seemingly provides an accurate description of "democracy" as it exists in American congressional elections.

PROBLEMS IN THE CONGRESSIONAL MARKETPLACE

Yet marketplace theorists and election analysts still face several obstacles. First, despite appearances, three of the puzzle pieces do not fit tightly together. As observed in Table 2–6, the average total moneys spent on House campaigns has quadrupled from $44 million in 1974 to $175 million in 1984. Nor has this trend been halted in any way. Total campaign spending in the 1986 House elections reached a new high of $239 million. The increase for Senate elections is even steeper—an over seven-fold increase from 1974 to 1986 at which time total Senate expenditures exceeded $211 million. Yet, one wonders what the increasing amounts of money spent on congressional campaigns are designed to purchase. During the same period, congressional races have not become more competitive. In 1972, as seen in Table 2–5, 78 percent of House incumbents were reelected by 60 percent of the major party vote. That figure had not declined by 1986. The number of senators winning by 60 percent or more actually increased in the 1984 and 1986 elections. Nor have the moneys led to greater information being supplied to voters about the candidates, especially the challengers. Across the five elections examined in Tables 2–3 and 2–4, there is no consistent increase in the amount of awareness or contact voters have for either House or Senate candidates.

Is the increase in money, then, simply a matter of the high cost of campaigning going ever higher?[20] Or is it perhaps a matter of rising benefits rather than rising costs? Greater numbers of *political elites*—organized groups and active individuals with a substantial stake in society—may perceive advantages to pursuing their interests through the legislative process to secure favorable legislation, regulations, or allocations of federal funds. In order to secure access to the process, these political elites vigorously participate in congressional campaigns. Indeed the biennial gains in campaign money are occurring across the board, among individuals, political parties, and, most notably, political action committees, as Table 2–7 makes clear. The predominantly policy-specific goals of these political activists are not necessarily served by competition in congressional races. Long-standing relations with incumbents who are supportive of desired programs could be upset if viable challengers entered the races. In addition, elites' desires for legislative access and success can be met regardless of how informed or ill-informed voters' decisions are.

The lack of fit among these three pieces is symptomatic of a second, larger dilemma for the marketplace theory. The theory is precisely empirical in meeting each of the facts regarding congressional election seriatim. Yet when attempting to fit the pieces together, the more general criteria of democracy—equality, competition, and participation—subtly slip away. Congressional elections are mired in a two-edged inequality. Members of Congress and activists interested in the legislative process engage in efforts that foreclose competition, often making the right to oppose an empty gesture. They advance a fundamental inequality among the contestants of congressional elections and, in so doing, may deny that there is more than one choice.

An inequality is also advanced among voters in congressional elections. The theory says that members are anticipating reactions of the voters. But they are more carefully anticipating the reactions of politically active elites who lend them campaign money and support. Voters may be voting retrospectively, but how they evaluate the good and bad times of the nation and the government's relationship to it depends first on how the good and bad times are perceived by activists. Early on in the interelection period, elites discern which contests will be competitive based on existing national conditions and which races they would like to see remain uncompetitive. They funnel money and other resources accordingly.[21] To the extent that large sums of money are funneled into key Senate races, House contests may actually be *less* competitive than they would be otherwise. Elites channel the greatest amounts of money into keenly competitive races—open seat races from both houses and some Senate races. Consequently, the available pool of campaign money is drained from less competitive races such as most incumbent races for the House. Competition thus becomes even more attenuated in these races, which constitute the vast number of congressional contests faced by American voters.

Political action committees in particular seek a quid pro quo of campaign money for access to the members and in so doing create an inequality of participation. Thus, inequalities arise on grounds of superior wealth, superior knowledge, and superior access. Downs acknowledges the irony: "The foundations for inequalities of power are inherent in democratic societies, even though political equality is their basic ethical premise."[22] Yet, this does not seem to bother Downs who simply acknowledges that it operates as a "distortion" in the system.[23]

In addition, even if members wanted to attend to the reactions of the voters, voters have few concrete reactions to give. Voters may not be fools, but they are hardly well informed, especially on activities of the members on the job. They infrequently contact members or their office staffs in between elections, have great difficulty remembering anything special the member has done for the district, and are not apt to have thought about the member's voting record.[24] With such little attention, lopsided contests and the resulting domination of interests in Congress, it is little wonder that turnout declines. Voters participate in congressional elections but act only as intermediaries between members of Congress and active national and local elites. They are not afforded control of the decisions of the government through elections as the general outline of democracy asserts. Rather than being the most important participants in the congressional election process, voters are incidental participants—crucial in keeping the mechanism of choice operating, but not crucial to the choices made.

Thus, congressional elections are characterized by political inequality, weak competition, and the lack of participation of a majority of eligible voters. Taking these three factors together hardly conjures up visions of democracy in the heads of theorists, election analysts, or voters.

And finally, what marketplace theory has in effect done to accommodate so closely the empirical world is strip away any normative obligations of both voters and candidates. It essentially induces a theory from specific empirical facts known about election participants. It starts empirically with a series of unglamorous truths about the self-interest of citizens and elected officials and it ends theoretically by equating democracy with rationality. Yet the theory fails to recognize that rationality is ultimately undemocratic.

David Mayhew asserts a cogent, provocative argument that the central goal of members of Congress is to gain reelection.[25] He argues that members are well equipped to do so and the institution of the Congress helps them meet their unitary goal. As rational actors, members can claim credit for largess sent to the district, advertise their accomplishments in the body, and avoid taking positions on controversial matters that might wake up voters back home. Once considered to be the rituals only of members of the House, service to constituents on matters ranging from veterans' pensions to termite control is now also routinely carried out by senators. The institution of Congress amplifies the members' rationality by allowing them travel, staff, and mailing perquisites, by decentralization through which members can advance parochial policy interests, and by increasing collegial decision making on the floor which permits greater independence of individual members.[26] While other writers have argued that members have multiple goals, the reelection goal has always been among them.[27]

But the primary goal of reelection for members of Congress contradicts rather than promotes democracy. Rational members work to be reelected by the greatest margin possible and attempt to do so by raising the greatest amount of money possible (even if it is unnecessary or if a portion of it goes unspent). These efforts may be admirable for the personal or political well-being of the member. Yet, the all-consuming reelection goal yields a denial of competition that benefits the collective whole. Nor is this an unintended consequence of members' interest in career stability. It is a conspicuously intended consequence of members and politically interested elites who seek the greatest possible access to members and benefit as much as members do from incumbents' reelections. Rational members seek another term, rational active interests seek the rational member, and rational voters seek to avoid too much exposure to politics. Each promotes their own individual calculus only to lose any collective responsibility in the process. American congressional politics "has given way to 'Every man for himself,' and the country is poorer for it."[28] The marketplace theory nicely mirrors the reality of congressional elections. But in so doing, it is no longer a theory of democracy, but one of rationality.

CONCLUSION: ELECTORAL PARTICIPATION, EQUALITY, AND COMPETITION

A theory of democracy could be crafted to maintain that blacks not voting in South Africa is an expression of democracy so long as they are *virtually* represented in elections by whites who favor their cause. Observers would have a hard time suggesting that South African elections or such a theory are democratic. They have an equally hard time giving up the myth that American congressional elections are also democratic. "For the democratic 'myth' to be an effective political force, it cannot be pure myth. It must be an idealization of real behavioral patterns."[29] There seems to be little in the behavioral patterns of voters, members of Congress, or other politically active elites which demonstrate the desires for participation, equality, and competition required for democracy. John Stuart Mill wrote:

> Of what avail is the most broadly popular representative system if the electors do not care to choose the best member of Parliament, but choose him who will

spend most money to be elected. . . . Whenever the general disposition of the people is such that each individual regards those only of his interests which are selfish, and does not dwell on . . . the general interest, in such a state of things good government is impossible.[30]

A proper theory of democracy must, then, assert certain ethical requirements of its participants. The theory, unlike the marketplace approach, must be partly prescriptive because without these prescriptions in the empirical practice of elections and government, democracy does not exist. Governments themselves are the embodiments of prescriptions: People should have free speech, the right to assemble, the right to vote. People should also vote and members of the legislature should also be subject to the possibility of defeat. Theories of democracy can thus afford such prescriptiveness. If they merely mimic the empirical world, it can never be discerned whether democracy exists or whether what exists has simply been defined as democracy. Joseph Tussman notes the inelegant chicanery that people may mistake for democracy if the prescriptions are relaxed:

> It is altogether possible that we may drift increasingly in the direction of ritualistic democracy. We will feel little pain and the portrait of Lincoln will not come crashing from the wall. . . . Without too much imagination we can see the Presidential Sweepstakes becoming the main event, combining the excitement of a national lottery with the thrill of a coronation. We will redouble our efforts and turn out the votes, but the vote will decide less and less as we move deeper into the morass of public relations, the projections of images, and the painless engineering of consent. Perhaps this path is inevitable for us, but it is not democracy—only its tragic parody.[31]

What alternatives exist? Any cry for political awareness, education, and activity among citizens is ultimately hollow. It would require a revolution in Americans' political habits and political communication patterns. It can also not be achieved without fundamental changes in the electoral institutions within which citizens are supposed to participate. In this case, the marketplace theory is absolutely correct: voters should not be expected to participate when members acting rationally seek to foreclose any competition in the race. Changes can be made, however, to achieve greater competitiveness in congressional elections. In this regard, proposals to federally finance congressional campaigns that have been made in the Senate, but roundly resisted in the House, may provide one step. The current Senate proposals call for voluntary campaign spending limits based on state populations and another cap on what candidates can receive from PACs. Those candidates who agree to the limits would obtain federal funds by increasing the amount of the donation the taxpayer could check off on Form 1040.

In the 1972 presidential campaign before the imposition of federal campaign spending limits, George McGovern spent $13 million, only one-third of the $38 million spent by Richard Nixon. Although better known and more strongly supported by his party than Sheldon Clark, George McGovern's candidacy was saddled with an inequality between the candidates that was as obvious as that borne by Clark.

It would be ludicrous to place all bets on reform, but reform would enliven competition. When races are competitive, as with open seats, voter participation is greater, voter information about the candidates is higher, and the opposition has a richer opportunity to challenge the views and accomplishments of members of Congress. This brings us closer to the measures of participation, equality, and competition upon which democracy rests, but which currently cannot be readily observed in congressional elections.

NOTES

1. Other approaches to democracy consider it as much broader than a particular form of government. It is seen as a form of social interaction among individuals that encourages mutual consultation and voluntary agreement. See John Dewey, *The Public and Its Problems* (New York: Holt, Rinehart & Winston, 1927).
2. John Stuart Mill, "Representative Government," in *Utilitarianism, Liberty, and Representative Government* (New York: E. P. Dutton, 1951), p. 281.
3. Thomas Jefferson, letter to Pierre S. du Pont de Nemours, April 24, 1816, in *The Writings of Thomas Jefferson*, vol. 9, ed. Paul Ford (New York: G. P. Putnam's Sons, 1899).
4. Robert A. Dahl, *Polyarchy* (New Haven, Conn.: Yale University Press, 1971), p. 5.
5. There is also a fourth theory of democracy that rests on the competition among political parties. *Responsible party democracy* depends on parties to clearly delineate programs that party candidates then follow in their campaigns and once in office. Candidates are held responsible to the party and the party is held responsible for its programmatic line. Parties become the device by which participation, control, equality, and most especially competition result. Voters can become better informed by virtue of party responsibility. See E. E. Schattschneider et al., "Toward a More Responsible Two-Party System," *American Political Science Review* 44 (September 1950), supplement, and Austin Ranney, "Toward a More Responsible Two-Party System: A Commentary," *American Political Science Review* 45 (June 1951), pp. 488–99. Their viewpoint, however, is more wishful thinking than sound theory, at least as it is applied to American elections. Barring constitutional rearrangements to strengthen political parties in both electoral and governmental arenas, American parties and their standard bearers have always and will always lack such responsibility. The theory is therefore not considered in any depth in this essay.
6. Joseph A. Schumpeter, *Capitalism, Socialism, and Democracy*, 2nd ed. (New York: Harper & Row, 1947), p. 251.
7. Robert A. Dahl, *A Preface to Democratic Theory* (Chicago: University of Chicago Press, 1956).
8. Gabriel A. Almond and Sidney Verba, *The Civic Culture* (Boston: Little, Brown, 1965), p. 347.
9. Dahl, *Polyarchy*, p. 8.
10. Almond and Verba, *Civic Culture*, p. 353.

11. Angus Campbell et al., *The American Voter* (New York: John Wiley & Sons, 1960). Donald E. Stokes and Warren E. Miller, "Party Government and the Salience of Congress," *Public Opinion Quarterly,* Winter 1962, pp. 531-46.
12. V. O. Key, Jr., *The Responsible Electorate* (New York: Vintage Books, 1966), p. 7.
13. Anthony Downs, *An Economic Theory of Democracy* (Chicago: University of Chicago Press, 1957), p. 221.
14. Benjamin I. Page, *Choices and Echoes in Presidential Elections* (Chicago: University of Chicago Press, 1978), p. 5.
15. Key, *Responsible Electorate;* Page, *Choices and Echoes.*
16. Downs, *Economic Theory;* Morris P. Fiorina, *Retrospective Voting in American National Elections* (New Haven, Conn.: Yale University Press, 1981).
17. But see Fiorina, *Retrospective Voting.*
18. Edie N. Goldenberg and Michael W. Traugott, *Campaigning for Congress* (Washington, D.C.: Congressional Quarterly Press, 1984).
19. Larry J. Sabato, *PAC Power: Inside the World of Political Action Committees* (New York: W. W. Norton, 1984).
20. If the inflation rate is taken into account these campaign figures still increase substantially across the period. Campaign expenditures have been rising much faster than the consumer price index. One contributing factor to high campaign costs is the increased use of television commercials for House campaigns, but this alone does not account for the full extent of the rise.
21. Gary C. Jacobson and Samuel Kernell, *Strategy and Choice in Congressional Elections,* 2nd ed. (New Haven, Conn.: Yale University Press, 1983).
22. Downs, *Economic Theory,* p. 237.
23. Ibid., p. 236.
24. As one example, in 1986, 78 percent of voters interviewed said they had not contacted a member of the district or Washington office to express an opinion, ask for help on a problem, or seek information. Seventy-five percent could not remember anything special the member had done for their district. Forty-four percent had not given any thought to the member's voting record.
25. David R. Mayhew, *Congress: The Electoral Connection* (New Haven, Conn.: Yale University Press, 1974).
26. Steven S. Smith, "New Patterns of Decision Making in Congress," in *The New Direction in American Politics,* ed. John E. Chubb and Paul E. Peterson (Washington, D.C.: Brookings Institution, 1985), pp. 203–234.
27. Richard F. Fenno, Jr., *Congressmen in Committees* (Boston: Little, Brown, 1973).
28. Fiorina, *Retrospective Voting,* p. 222.
29. Almond and Verba, *Civic Culture,* p. 351.
30. Mill, *Utilitarianism,* p. 257.
31. Joseph Tussman, *Obligation and the Body Politic* (London: Oxford University Press, 1960), p. 106.

CHAPTER 3

Home Styles—Then and Now

Glenn R. Parker

Constituency service can assume many forms, but whatever shape it takes, the motivation is always the same: Legislators are dedicated to helping their constituents in any way they can. For instance, Lawton Chiles, a Democratic senator from Florida, sent at least six letters to prison and parole officials in an effort to have a constituent serving a federal prison sentence for corruption paroled.[1] And legislators are not the least bit shy about exercising their influence on behalf of their constituents. One of the most brazen expressions of this willingness to seek beneficial treatment for constituents was the effort by Democratic Representative Albert Bustamante of Texas to have Midshipman David Robinson (an unusually gifted seven-foot basketball player from the U.S. Naval Academy) released from his required military duty so he could play for the San Antonio Spurs of the National Basketball Association.[2] Such a request may seem laughable, but certainly not to top U.S. Navy officials, since Bustamante is a member of the House Armed Services Committee.

Whether the matter be a lost social security check or an appeal by district or state interests for help in Washington, the representative or senator is expected to be helpful and effective. Although such attention is important if not essential for longevity in office, many legislators consider the "errand running" aspect of the job extremely demanding. "It's a hard way of making a living. You have closer contact with the people than ever before. Constituents are more inclined to express themselves. We have more errand work than before, and less time to do legislative work."[3] Few would disagree with this legislator's assessment of the constituency service demands associated with the job, but more provocative is his observation that somehow this state of affairs represents a shift in the constituency orientations of representatives and senators. If true, then a change has occurred in how incumbents relate to their constituents—a change in their home styles. This chapter addresses the questions of whether such a change in home styles has occurred, and if so, how and why home styles have changed; attention is also given to the effects of home-style change on the attitudes of constituents and the behavior of House and Senate incumbents.

DEFINING HOME STYLES

Richard Fenno first coined the term *home style* to describe the way in which incumbents cultivate their constituencies: ". . . their object is to present themselves as a person in such a way that the inferences drawn by those watching will be supportive."[4] Recent studies have demonstrated the relevance of home styles to the behavior of members while in their districts[5] and states,[6] the messages incumbents deliver to their constituents,[7] and the electoral safety of incumbents.[8] Fenno has identified three components of home style: presentation of self, explanation of Washington activity, and allocation of resources between Washington and the district. The ultimate purpose of home-style behavior is to engender constituent trust—an essential ingredient for lengthy congressional careers.

According to Fenno, the centerpiece of an incumbent's home style is the presentations that he makes to his constituents. He must project images that generate the trust and electoral support of his constituents: one that assures them that he is qualified to hold office, that he can identify with their attitudes and values, and that he can empathize with their problems. Explanation of Washington activity, the second component of home style, describes the effort of incumbents to rationalize their behavior in Congress by defining, interpreting, and justifying legislative behavior or votes. "A House member will explain any Washington activity that is relevant to winning and holding support at home," Fenno observes, "for the objective of explanation, as of presentation, is political support."[9] The final component, allocation of resources, refers to the decisions made by legislators as to how to distribute resources, such as personal attention, between constituent (district) and legislative (Washington) activities. A congressman, for example, may choose to divert more resources to constituent services and the promotion of district interests, and away from legislative responsibilities.

Not all decisions relating to the allocation of a member's resources are difficult ones. The cost an incumbent may incur in expanding the distribution or the volume of newsletters to constituents, for example, is relatively minor since the task can be relegated to staff, and the costs associated with the development and organization of a newsletter have already been borne in producing past newsletters. Time spent in the constituency, on the other hand, is a nontransferable cost for incumbents: They have to meet face-to-face with their constituents, and cannot avoid the personal interactions they are normally sheltered from in Washington. As Donald Matthews observed with respect to the constituency demands on senators, "While at home, it is hard for a senator to insulate himself from constituent demands on his time and attention."[10] How to spend one's own personal time is one resource allocation decision that poses a dilemma for most members. Simply put, "When he is doing something at home, he must give up doing some things in Washington and vice versa."[11] In short, time spent in the constituency conflicts with legislative (Washington) responsibilities. Such a zero-sum situation makes the allocation of time between Washington and the district or state a critical allocation decision, and one that is not taken lightly by most representatives and senators.

AN HISTORICAL PERSPECTIVE ON HOME STYLES

The three components of home style may well have characterized the behavior of congressmen in even the earliest congresses, and conversely, incumbents in the present Congress probably display home-style behaviors that are similar to those exhibited by members serving in earlier eras. Some of the similarities are evident in the circulars that incumbents mailed to their constituents in the late 1700s and early 1800s.

Circular letters reported on the proceedings of Congress and national affairs, and were periodically sent to constituents by members of Congress, generally those representing southern and western districts. This practice, begun in the First Congress, survives today in the form of slickly produced congressional newsletters and mass mailings. Most congressmen hoped that these circular letters would be regarded by voters as an acceptable substitute for individual, personal letters; at the same time, they expected that a single copy of a circular letter would be read by more than one constituent. "Circular letters therefore provide an indication of what a member wanted his constituents to know and what he thought they wanted to know."[12]

Similarities in Home-Style Messages

As the forerunner for the present-day newsletter sent to constituents, it is not surprising that the messages contained in circulars sound similar to those promulgated through today's newsletters: Diana Evans Yiannakis found that present-day newsletters and press releases tend to emphasize the members' positions on national issues.[13] Circular letters also provided an indication of a legislator's positions on pressing issues, and "a congressman generally presented the most elaborate defense of his position when he suspected that the voters of his district would disagree with him."[14] Circulars, like newsletters, were written to achieve maximum political benefit: Many circulars reminded voters that the incumbent was again a candidate for reelection, and some members managed to have their letters arrive at politically opportune times. Congressman John Clopton from Virginia, for example, explained his inability to write a longer letter to his wife by noting that "I have been so closely engaged in getting circular letters ready to go by this mail to be in time to arrive at the election for New Kent next Thursday that I have barely time to drop you a few lines . . ."[15]

Unlike present-day mass mailings, few circulars were directed toward local concerns,[16] but a trend in that direction became evident by the third or fourth decade of the nineteenth century:

Letters of members from newer areas, mainly western, were significantly more concerned with the matters relating directly to the local interests of their constituents than those of members from the older, largely southern, states. The available circular letters written by territorial delegates suggest that such men tended to look upon themselves largely as lobbyists for their respective territories. The territorial delegate confined his activities in Congress mostly to matters concerned with territories, particularly his own, and his reports to his constituents tended to be an account of how he had looked out for their interests.[17]

These circulars conveyed the same type of home-style messages that congressmen deliver today. For example, Matthew Lyon's April 1808 circular to his Kentucky constituents called attention to his ability to identify and empathize with constituents:

> Whatever advocations I have pursued, I have never ceased to be a farmer, since I have been a man. Very few persons in the district have raised more corn and wheat, and done more labor with their own hands, than I have with mine. No man can better sympathize with, or know the feelings of the laboring man, than myself. Although I do some mercantile business with and for my children, my property is such as is common to the other people of the district. I can have no interest different from yours.[18]

And just like today, early representatives were happy to run errands for constituents. For instance, James Kolbourn of Ohio noted his willingness to help constituents in an 1815 circular: "If any of my constituents have claims upon the government, requiring to be presented at the public offices, they will please to command me, accompanying their accounts, with proper vouchers and instruction, and the best that circumstances will permit, it will be my pleasure to do on their behalf."[19] Such errands covered a multitude of issues, some of which continue to occupy the attention of congressmen and their staffs. John Scott's list of accomplishments addressed to his constituents in the Missouri Territory in the early 1800s is similar in some respect to the problems handled by present-day congressional offices:

> There had been committed to my charge during the last two sessions that I have been the delegate, upwards of one thousand individual applications for redress, composed of soldiers' applications for patents, soldiers and militia pay, applications for pensions by disabled soldiers, and the widows' half-pay pensions, claims on government for supplies furnished troops, for property lost and destroyed during the war, claims growing out of Indian depredations, Indian agencies, Indian treaties and supplies furnished at the same, private applications on land subjects, and other claims on the justice or bounty of the government.[20]

Representatives in the early congresses pursued constituent complaints with the same vigor exhibited by today's congressmen. William Lattimore's 1815 circular to his constituents in the Mississippi Territory is one example of just how tenacious these early legislators could be in handling constituent requests and complaints:

> Having received, too late in the session for legislative relief, a petition from a number of the inhabitants of Wilkinson County, praying to be secured from a forfeiture of their lands, I laid it before the Commissioner of the General Land Office, with a letter of my own stating the circumstances of the territory, and the unsatisfied claims of the people for military services, and soliciting a suspension of the sales of lands which are or soon may be forfeited; and having been afterwards informed that the subject was still under the consideration of the secretary of the treasury, to whom it had been referred, I called on him, and received a very satisfactory expression of his disposition to grant the indulgence solicited, provided he should find that he could do it on legal ground.[21]

Even then the bureaucracy served as a convenient whipping boy for congressmen:

> When I am canvassing my district and I come across a man who looks distantly and coldly at me, I go cordially to him and say, "My dear friend, you got my printed letter last session, of course?" "No, sir," replies the man with offended dignity, "I got no such thing." "No!" I cry out in a passion. "No!! *Damn that post-office!*"[22]

While it is impossible to know how pervasive these themes and messages were in the home styles exhibited by members of earlier eras, it is clear that some incumbents did indeed display the same type of behavior that we associate with the home styles of today. Members of Congress, past and present, appear to picture themselves as qualified, capable of identifying and empathizing with constituents, and worthy of trust; they seem prepared, if not willing, to explain their positions and votes to constituents. Despite such similarities, there is one major way in which the home styles of the early years differed from those of today: the allocation of personal time to the constituency.[23]

Time Spent in the Constituency

As noted earlier, a member's personal time is a precious and carefully guarded resource. The lengthening of legislative sessions, the maintenance of a second home in Washington by many representatives and senators, and the increased attractiveness of Washington's social life suggest that today's legislators spend less time in their constituencies than did members in the earliest congresses. Can the personal attention devoted to today's constituents be expected to rival the attentiveness exhibited by citizen legislators of the past given the complexity and growth of twentieth century government and society? Perhaps not, but the gap may have closed during recent decades.

There is no way of directly calculating exactly how much time legislators in the early congresses spent with their constituents. It seems likely that the time members spent in their districts and states was inversely related to the length of legislative sessions. The members stayed in Washington only as long as they needed to; time not spent in session was normally spent in the district or state (and traveling between the constituency and Washington). "Almost none of the members acquired homes in the capital or established year-round residence there. They merely wintered in Washington, spending more time each year with constituents than with each other."[24] Furthermore, the capital was not a very attractive place to spend time. Washington served as a "magnet for society's idle and society's unwanted: people sick in mind or body, imagining conspiracies against them, imploring help, or bent upon revenge; pleaders for pardons and reprieves; small-time confidence men; needy pamphlet-writers, selling their talents for calumny for the price of a public printing contract; . . . most conspicuously of all it was the indigent who migrated to Washington. . . ."[25] For these reasons, then, the length of early congresses provides an indirect measure of how much time members spent in their constituencies: The longer the legislative session in early congresses, the less time spent with constituents, and vice versa. By this measure, past legislators spent considerably more time in their districts and states than present members of the House and Senate.

Since most members now maintain a second home in Washington, time spent in the district or state means time spent away from their families; therefore, the close of a legislative session does not automatically lead legislators to return to their districts or states as in earlier eras. In fact, today's senators and representatives actually spend less time in their districts and states between legislative sessions and congresses;[26] when Congress is not in session there is no assurance that the time will be spent in the district or state. Unlike the situation in the earliest congresses, then, time not spent in legislative session does not readily translate into time spent with constituents.

Little time was spent in Washington in the early eras, as indicated by the rampant desire of many congressmen to abandon the office:

> The distinguished senators of the First Congress set the early career pattern for that chamber: They fled the Capitol—not yet located in Washington—almost as fast as was humanly possible. . . . Career data on the early Senate is a morass of resignations, short-term appointees, elective replacements, and more resignations. There are *no* notable careers in terms of service.[27]

These part-time senators and representatives spent considerable time in their constituencies, working at their trade or profession; today's legislators find it considerably more difficult to devote similar levels of attention to their districts and states. One of the most obvious reasons for this state of affairs is the expanded scope, complexity, and volume of legislative business. By most measures of legislative activity—hours in session, number of committee and subcommittee meetings, volume of legislation, roll call votes—the legislative workload has grown to a staggering level. The leisurely atmosphere of legislative service in the early years has been replaced by a far more hectic pace:

> For most of its history, Congress was a part-time institution. Before World War II, and even after, Congress remained in session only nine months out of each twenty-four, and the members spent the remainder of their time at home practicing law or attending to private business. In recent decades, legislative business has kept the House and Senate in almost perpetual session—punctuated by district work periods. During the average two-year Congress, the House is in session about 225 eight-hour days. The average senator or representative works an 11-hour day while Congress is in session.[28]

As the workload expanded, legislators found it necessary to spend more time in Washington, and less time in their districts and states. Legislative sessions, however, began to lengthen in the early 1900s, and again in the early 1930s. Until the twentieth century, and with the exception of the First Congress, rarely did the total length of a Congress exceed 400 days. Between the Second Congress (1791–92) and the Sixtieth Congress (1907–1908), more than 400 days were spent in session in only five Congresses (the Twenty-seventh, Fortieth, Fiftieth, Fifty-third, and Fifty-fifth); during the next fourteen years, six of the seven Congresses remained in session for more than 400 days (the Sixty-first through Sixty-third, and Sixty-fifth through Sixty-seventh). After the Seventy-third Congress (1933–34), no Congress lasted *less* than 400 days, and about one-half of the Congresses remained in session for more than 600 days!

The increased time spent in session after 1934 can be partially explained by the growth in the legislative work load: the total number of measures enacted jumped from 843 during the Seventy-second Congress (1931–34) to 1,662 in the Seventy-sixth Congress (1939–40) and remained above 1,000 bills until the 1970s. The number of recorded votes rose during the 1970s, even though the number of bills enacted declined. The shifts in time spent in Washington in the early 1900s appears to reflect two related organizational processes in addition to the growth in the congressional workload: the institutionalization and professionalization of Congress.

The twentieth century represents an important period in the *professionalization* and *institutionalization* of Congress. H. Douglas Price contrasts members of the professional legislature with the part-time amateurs they replaced in the 1900s:

> The "professional" legislature is different. In it disparity of influence among members is generally less. And the professional legislature achieves substantial capability to oversee and influence the bureaucracies of the executive branch in a way that the amateurs never can. But this capability is achieved at the cost of reduced openness to shifting sentiments in the electorate (the motto of the professional legislature might well be, "The incumbent is always right"). In the professional legislature, "representation" is achieved largely by the shifting stands of sophisticated members rather than by physical turnover of

members from presumably homogenous constituencies. The member of a professional legislature faces complex problems of organizational theory, not the simple dilemmas of Edmund Burke.[29]

As membership stabilized and the attraction of a congressional career grew, Congress became a full-time vocation and members devoted more time to their duties.

Attention to duties in Washington also increased with the institutionalization of Congress. An institutionalized organization has three characteristics, according to Nelson Polsby.[30] First, an institutionalized organization has established boundaries that differentiate it from its wider environment. Frequently this implies that it is relatively difficult to become a member of the organization, and leaders in the organization are recruited from within the ranks of the organization. Second, the organization is complex in the sense that its functions are internally separated, with the parts of the organization not wholly interchangeable; roles are specified and there are regularized patterns of recruitment to roles, and of movement from one role to another. Finally, the organization resorts to universalistic criteria rather than discretionary methods for conducting its internal business: precedents and rules replace favoritism, nepotism, and personal preferences as guides to conduct. The institutionalization of Congress served to spread more widely the incentives for senators and representatives to actively participate in legislative policymaking, and to make the institution into a valuable source of gratification, status, and power—an end in itself rather than a vehicle for the pursuit of social policies. In sum, the professionalization and institutionalization of Congress increased the attractiveness of spending time in Washington, and if members needed more reason to do so, the expanding legislative workload provided additional justification.

Significant change in the allocation of personal time to constituent affairs reflects an important modification of a member's home style. While home styles are relatively stable and difficult to change,[31] there is evidence that just such a pronounced change in home styles has occurred on a broad scale.[32] The remainder of this chapter describes how the adoption of more attentive home styles by representatives and senators occurred, explains why members have become increasingly attentive to their constituencies despite the increased pressures of the legislative workload, and discusses some of the effects of this home-style change.

CHANGING HOME STYLES

Prior to the 1960s, high levels of constituency attention were rather unusual and largely structured by a member's position in the seniority hierarchy. Writing in the 1950s, Donald Matthews characterized the attention of senators to their constituencies as following a *political life cycle* based upon seniority:

If the senator survives the first challenge to his position, then he becomes more secure than before. All the advantages he possesses at his first reelection bid are even more compelling now. But with greater seniority and security go additional legislative responsibilities. By the end of his second term, he is, in all likelihood, a senior member of major committees. He is well on the way to becoming an important national figure, increasingly concerned with pressing national and international problems. In the vocabulary of social psychology, his "reference groups" change, he becomes more concerned with Senate, national, and international problems, and devotes less time and attention to the folks back home. The press of legislative duties becomes ever harder to escape. Advancing years make fence-mending trips increasingly onerous.[33]

Although the incentives to spend time in Washington remained, incentives were created during the mid-1960s and early 1970s that caused members to alter their existing home styles and increase their attentiveness to constituent problems and needs. One indicator of this change in home styles was the increase in the time that representatives and senators personally spent in their constituencies. The number of days that House and Senate incumbents spent in their districts and states between 1959 and 1980 is depicted in Figure 3–1.[34]

FIGURE 3–1   Time Spent in the Constituency, 1959–1980

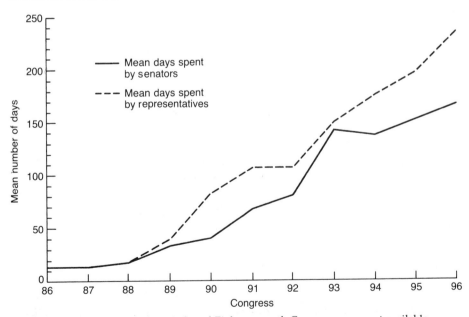

Note: House data for the Eighty-sixth and Eighty-seventh Congresses are not available.

SOURCE: Glenn R. Parker, *Homeward Bound: Explaining Changes in Congressional Behavior* (Pittsburgh, Penn.: University of Pittsburgh Press, 1986), pp. 74–75, 78–79.

Clearly, the amount of time incumbents spend in their constituencies has increased since the mid-1960s. Today's legislators appear to have reversed the trend that had been characteristic of personal contact since the turn of the century: members are spending more time rather than less time in their districts and states. This change was facilitated by Congress in its effort to accommodate members' needs to ensure electoral *safety*, gain political *leeway* for their behavior in Washington, and provide *service* to constituents. Congress accomplished this by reducing the direct costs associated with attention to the constituency. In the process, strong incentives for members to adopt a more attentive home style were established.

Member Goals and Institutional Opportunities

The three member goals that underlie this change in home style are pervasive within Congress, which is one reason why the change has been so widespread. Electoral safety is a primary concern for most members of Congress since it is a "goal that must be achieved over and over if other ends are to be entertained."[35] The pursuit and exercise of power and influence within Congress is a goal that requires members to gain a measure of freedom from their constituents without fear of electoral reprisal; this goal is held by many if not most legislators. Finally, serving constituents has always been an important representational obligation, and one that has grown in significance.[36] Safety, leeway, and service were needs that could be satisfied through diligent attention to the constituency. What made the home-style change so attractive to House and Senate incumbents at every level of seniority is that the adoption of more attentive style could simultaneously satisfy all of them.

While these three needs or goals have probably existed individually and collectively for decades, they assumed unusual importance in the 1960s and 1970s. Morris Fiorina has suggested that constituents' demands reached unusual proportions as a result of the explosion of federal programs during the 1960s.[37] Electoral safety, always a concern for most members, became an even more critical and pervasive problem in the 1960s as a large number of freshmen senators and representatives were elected from areas that were politically atypical of their own partisan and ideological identifications. One indicator of this is the large number of House freshmen who gained office during this period by defeating an incumbent from the opposition party. Figure 3–2 presents data describing the number of congressional seats that changed party control between 1954 and 1980. It is clear from this figure that large numbers of Democrats replaced Republican incumbents in the 1958, 1964, and 1974 elections; Republican candidates, however, regained some of these seats at the next election. Finally, the need to preserve political maneuverability in Washington gained salience because of the increased dividends that such leeway could pay in terms of other legislative goals like power and influence in Congress. That is, the increase in opportunities to exert influence served as an important incentive

FIGURE 3–2 House Seats that Changed Party, 1954–1980

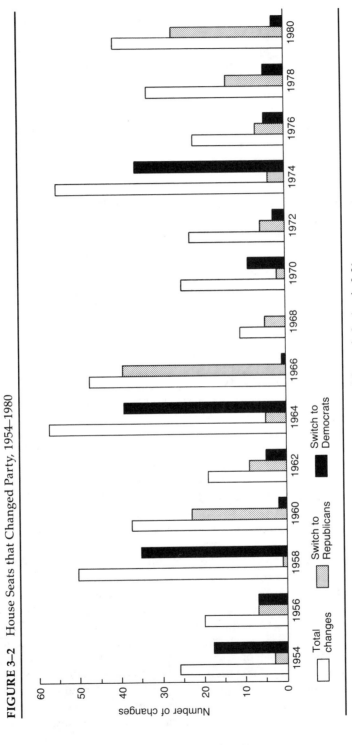

SOURCE: *Congressional Quarterly Almanac* (Washington, D.C.: Congressional Quarterly, Inc.), vols. 2–36.

for members to maximize their freedom from their constituents through diligent attention to their constituencies.

The increased opportunities to exercise influence within Congress are evident. For example, the increased use of unanimous consent agreements for organizing Senate business during the 1960s and 1970s[38] gave individual senators a greater voice in determining the Senate's agenda. Perhaps as important was the decision in the 1950s by the Senate minority leader from Texas, Lyndon Johnson, to guarantee every Democratic senator a choice committee assignment regardless of seniority—the so-called *Johnson Rule*. In the House, members were also gaining bargaining leverage with their leaders and pressing for institutional reforms that would spread power further in Congress. In some respects, the power structure was becoming more permeable: between the Eighty-fourth (1955–56) and Ninetieth (1967–68) Congresses, the proportion of Democrats chairing a standing committee or subcommittee increased from 27 percent to 45 percent.[39] Thus, the needs of incumbents for electoral security, greater freedom in Washington, and service to constituents, together with the expansion of institutional opportunities for exercising congressional power, precipitated a pronounced change in home style: the adoption of a more attentive home style, a major component of which is direct and indirect personal contact with constituents. These needs both necessitated and prompted a response by Congress which produced institutional changes that promoted more attentive home styles.

Institutional Incentives for Home-Style Change

As Congress accommodated the needs of its members to maintain personal contact with their constituents, it facilitated changes in home styles by reducing the direct costs associated with constituency attention. Some of this cost reduction was accomplished by increasing the subsidies for various constituency activities and expanding the perquisites available for maintaining contact with constituents. For example, as the subsidies for constituency travel were increased, representatives and senators spent more time in their districts and states. These changes in attention coincide with increases in the House and Senate travel allowances between 1965 and 1980 (Tables 3–1 and 3–2); in fact, increases in the travel allowance are causally related to the amount of time that representatives and senators spent in their constituencies between 1958 and 1980.[40]

Other costs associated with an attentive home style were made more transferrable by shifting them to staff; office staffs were enlarged and charged with greater responsibility for constituency service. This enabled members to expand their services to constituents without having to absorb the full brunt of the increased contact associated with maintaining an attentive home style. Thus, the use of staff for constituency service helped members to shift the burden of such activities without reducing the level of service to constituents.

TABLE 3-1   Magnitude of Change in Attention to the State

Years of Significant Change in Attention	Increase from Previous Congress		Number of Subsidized Trips
	Days	Percent	
1965–1966	17.9	100	6
1969–1970	27.5	65	12
1973–1974	61.1	74	20

Entries are the mean number of days spent in the state by senators filing travel vouchers.

SOURCE: Glenn R. Parker, *Homeward Bound: Explaining Changes in Congressional Behavior* (Pittsburgh, Penn.: University of Pittsburgh Press, 1986), p. 77.

TABLE 3-2   Magnitude of Change in Attention to the District

Years of Significant Change in Attention	Increase from Previous Congress		Number of Subsidized Trips
	Days	Percent	
1965–1966	23.4	141	4
1967–1968	44.8	112	12
1969–1970	22.6	27	12
1973–1974	43.1	40	18
1975–1976	26.4	18	26
1979–1980	38.3	19	32

Entries are the mean number of days spent in the district by representatives filing travel vouchers.

SOURCE: Glenn R. Parker, *Homeward Bound: Explaining Changes in Congressional Behavior* (Pittsburgh, Penn.: University of Pittsburgh Press, 1986), p. 86.

Another means of reducing the costs attached to maintaining an attentive home style was to structure the legislative schedule to allow members to spend time in their districts and states without detracting from the more appealing demands of their Washington activities (e.g., committee work). By structuring the legislative schedule so that members could spend time with their constituents without jeopardizing legislative interests, Congress helped to reduce the personal costs of such attention. Perhaps the most obvious way in which Congress structures the legislative schedule to reduce these costs is through the proliferation of recess periods. Congress normally conducts no legislative business during recesses; legislators need not worry about forsaking legislative responsibilities while spending time with their constituents. Some recess and holiday periods, such as the one-month recess during August of the first session of every Congress, are dictated by legislative statute. The number of days in which the House and Senate were in recess began to rise after the Eighty-ninth Congress (1965–66), increasing to more than 200 days by the Ninety-sixth Congress (see Figure 3–3). Increases in days of recess translate into more time spent in the district or state.[41]

The legislative schedule has been modified in other ways to facilitate personal contact with constituents. Congress, especially the House, is infamous for operating on a Tuesday through Thursday schedule of business which enables members to spend their weekends in their constituencies—a good time for maximizing contact with constituents. Blocks of time have also been set aside in the legislative schedule for constituency visits and travel (i.e., district work periods). Since most business in the Senate is conducted under unanimous consent agreements, scheduling decisions in the Senate are as accommodative to their members as are those in the House, and also help to reduce conflicts between legislative business in Washington and time spent in the state.

The reduction in the costs of attention to their constituencies brought about by cost subsidization and shifting thus increased the incentives for members to devote greater attention to the affairs of their districts and states and facilitated a change in the home styles of representatives and senators. The result has been the widespread adoption of attentive home styles. This conversion to attentive home styles was not a transitory change produced by electoral insecurities of the moment, or movement through a *political life cycle* (members reduce their attention to constituent affairs as they gain seniority and the legislative power that goes along with it); rather, the change was a permanent one.[42]

Consciously or unconsciously, congressmen played an integral role in promoting the widespread change in home styles. They pressured their leaders to make the legislative schedule more amenable to constituency demands. They established the various federal subsidies that reduced the cost associated with changing home styles, and they consistently supported the expansion of these office perquisites. Even the expansion of the legislative workload and the increase in the constituent demand for services might be construed as occurring at the behest of congressmen.[43] The cumulative effect of these actions was an interlocking and reinforcing set of incentives that made the adoption of more attentive home styles attractive, feasible, and rational. Subsidies for constituency travel, for example, would be useless unless time could be created within the legislative schedule for state and district visits; congressional recesses and the Tuesday–Thursday legislative schedule provided ample opportunities to exploit these travel allocations. Increasing constituency demands makes no sense unless the cost of such expanded service can be absorbed; consequently, increases in staff made the expansion of constituency service viable for many legislators. The interlocking of these incentives was achieved as incumbents modified institutional arrangements to facilitate constituency attention. In the process, incentives for members to adopt more attentive home styles were established and reinforced.

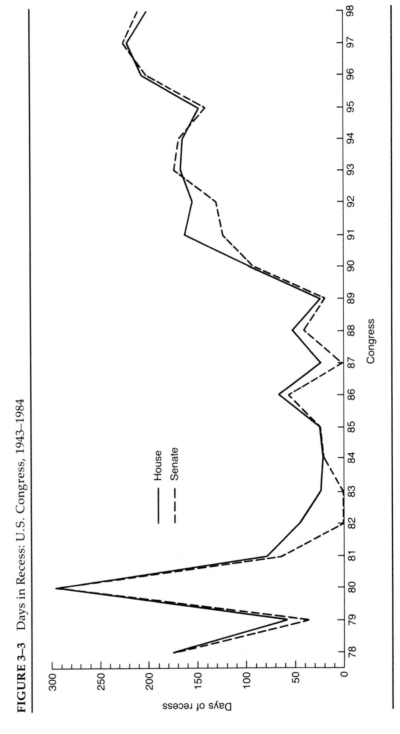

FIGURE 3–3 Days in Recess: U.S. Congress, 1943–1984

SOURCE: *Congressional Directory* (Washington D.C.: Government Printing Office, 1985).

SOME CONSEQUENCES OF HOME-STYLE CHANGE

Members adopted attentive home styles for different reasons and the exact mixture of goals probably varied from member to member. Each goal, however, attracted a sizable and intense group of advocates. The electorally insecure viewed an attentive home style as a mechanism for enhancing their electoral safety. Members from districts and states with constituents heavily dependent on governmental programs viewed the adoption of an attentive home style as the best way to respond to constituent needs; for the politically ambitious, an attentive style provided the leeway necessary to further career, policy, or personal goals. Even if members did not rank these goals in the same order, the satisfaction of one goal often enhanced the realization of others without incurring additional costs.

There are several direct consequences of the adoption of attentive home styles. The adoption of more attentive home styles had the effect of enhancing electoral safety among "marginal" senators and representatives, promoting political leeway for incumbents, and encouraging constituents to view their congressman as capable of resolving all types of constituent problems. The adoption of attentive home styles also indirectly affected the distributions of power in the House and Senate, the individuality of legislators, and the pressures placed on leaders by members for opportunities to exercise power and influence. These indirect consequences result from the effects of attentive home styles in promoting electoral safety and political leeway in Washington; since these effects have been discussed elsewhere,[44] this section will focus on only the direct effects.

Decline of Marginal Districts and States

A peculiar phenomenon in the study of congressional elections is the post-1960 increase in the electoral safety of House and Senate incumbents. One of the first scholars to document this change was David Mayhew. Mayhew documented an unusual decline in the number of congressmen with marginal electoral victories during the 1960s and 1970s.[45] This decline in electorally marginal congressional districts has stimulated considerable research and has generated a variety of explanations. Some have blamed the disappearance on the growth in the federal bureaucracy,[46] the lack of qualified challengers,[47] or the changing behavior of the American electorate.[48] To this list of culprits one can add the names of the incumbents themselves: the adoption of, or conversion to, more attentive home styles has turned marginal congressional seats into safe ones.

The growth in the travel allowances and other perquisites that facilitated legislator-constituent contact and communication during the 1960s and 1970s enabled marginal senators and representatives (incumbents representing areas with a contrasting partisan and/or ideological consensus) to expand their voter coalitions. Unable or unwilling to adopt attitudes more in line with the sentiment of the majority of their constituents, legislators from these areas chose to win over voters with lavish displays of attention. The expansion of subsidies made such demonstrations possible, and at a minimal cost.

During the late 1950s and throughout the 1960s and 1970s, many members were voted into office from areas where the opposition party was normally quite strong. For example, the 1958, 1964, and 1974 elections brought an unusually large number of Democrats to Congress from traditionally Republican districts. As noted earlier, most of these Democrats actually defeated Republican incumbents rather than winning *open seats*—a race where there is no incumbent (Figure 3–2). The nature of turnover during this period led to the election of a large number of representatives and senators from areas where the opposition party was strong, if not entrenched. While party organizations normally serve as the vital core of electoral coalitions, members elected from politically atypical areas found it necessary to expand their voter coalitions beyond the narrow confines of their minority-party supporters. For those members, the party organization was an ineffective base for building a successful voter coalition. By adopting more attentive home styles, many hoped to fashion a successful voter coalition that would transcend the bounds of party loyalties, that is, a personal following.

Thus, incumbents elected from areas with strong opposition party traditions and loyalties found a way to increase their electoral safety without switching parties or subjugating their political positions to the whims of their constituents. The method was quite simple: demonstrate a thorough concern for constituents by emphasizing your attention to their needs and problems. The adoption of attentive home styles—facilitated by reductions in the personal costs associated with such a style—enabled "marginal" members to hold on to their seats. The result was a decline in the electoral insecurity of senators and representatives who would be a priori the most marginal group of incumbents. Indeed, changes in attentiveness on the part of marginal, atypical representatives served to increase their electoral safety in House elections between 1964 and 1980 and similar home-style changes by atypical senators (northern Democratic senators elected from Republican states) helped to enhance their electoral safety between 1964 and 1974.[49]

Political Leeway

It is far more difficult to find systematic evidence that senators and representatives have gained policy or career leeway, especially since representatives and senators have always been an independent lot. There is substantial evidence, however, that the popular images of representatives are heavily influenced by their attention to their constituencies,[50] and rarely are there any hints of policy content in these images.[51] An attentive home style generates positive evaluations that are free of the potentially negative effect associated with issue positions and votes: By emphasizing their service to their districts or states, incumbents divert constituent attention away from those

Washington activities, such as voting, that could be harmful to their images and popularity in the constituency. Further, since an attentive home style promotes political support at home, incumbents gain latitude in their Washington behavior. "He cultivates home support not just because he wants to be reelected. He cultivates support at home, also, because he wants voting (and other) leeway in Washington. It is an incomplete notion to think of constituent support as useful only for reelection purposes. It is important beyond that. Political support at home guarantees the congressman some freedom of maneuver on Capitol Hill."[52]

Constituent Images of Congressmen

One final effect of the adoption of more attentive home styles is that constituents view congressmen as extremely successful manipulators of governmental action. These images and the reported success of incumbents in dealing with constituents' problems have created expectations of service and successful bureaucratic interventions. While few constituents have had any contact with their representative, most feel that if they did have to contact their representative he would help them in some way. Thus, most constituents perceive their legislators to be helpful even though they have never had personal experience on which to base such judgment. These perceptions mirror the home-style messages that incumbents transmit in their interactions with constituents. "House members believe that they can, by their presentations, convey the possibility of access to a larger number than actually take advantage of the opportunity. Directly, there is access; indirectly there is the promise of access."[53]

CONCLUSION: STABILITY AND CHANGE IN HOME STYLES

Home styles seem to be structured along the same lines today as in the past. Legislators in the 1980s seem to engage in the same activities and project the same images as members of the earliest congresses. What seems to have changed dramatically, however, is the amount of time and resources that incumbents personally devote to constituency affairs. This change in home style was facilitated by Congress as it reduced the direct costs to members of adopting an attentive home style by increasing the ceilings on various allowances and office resources, and by adjusting the legislative schedule to minimize conflicts between home and Washington activities. The widespread adoption of attentive home styles occurred because such a change could satisfy salient needs of members and because the costs of adopting such a style were reduced. The adoption of attentive home styles strengthened the electoral safety of the most marginal subsets of representatives and senators, enhanced their reputations as helpful and accessible to constituents, and increased the political freedom and leeway they enjoy.

There is little reason to suspect that the type of widespread modification of home styles that occurred during the mid-1960s and mid-1970s will reappear. Despite continuing advances in technology that enable members to contact more constituents than in the past, effective limits have been reached on a major component of an attentive home style—personal attention to constituency affairs. Incumbents are spending large amounts of time in their districts and states already, and there seems little additional room in their compact schedules for devoting significantly greater amounts of time to constituency affairs: in 1979–80, representatives were spending almost one in every three days in their districts, and senators were spending slightly less than one in every four days in their states.[54]

Even if members of Congress are able to manage additional time for personally courting constituents, can Congress become any more accommodative to the needs of its members for contact with constituents? Congress already operates, at least informally, on a Tuesday–Thursday schedule of business, and any additional constraints on the legislative schedule are certain to slow the legislative process even further. As it stands, Congress rarely finishes more than a modest portion of its scheduled legislative business; additional adjustments that reduce the time that can be devoted to congressional business will make the task even more ponderous.

Perhaps the most important reason for the improbability of further widespread change in home style is that members show little interest in increasing their attentiveness to constituency affairs. Fifty percent of the House members interviewed by the Commission on Administrative Review in 1977, for example, felt that constituents' demands detracted from what they "would ideally like to do as a member of Congress."[55] Thus, there is very little reason to believe that another sustained explosion in attention to the constituency like that which occurred during the 1965–74 period is likely to occur in the near future.

One question remains: Why are House incumbents so much more attentive to their constituencies than senators (Figure 3–1)? The explanation seems to rest in the nature of the two-year congressional term, the size of the different constituencies, and the extent to which personal contact serves the members' best interests. The longer term of senators and the larger size of their constituencies make personal contact less effective and efficient; moreover, it is far more difficult to worry about an election that is six years away from one that occurs every two years. Thus, "Senators up for reelection are most active, and recently elected senators seem to engage in more electorally related activity than senators in the middle of their term."[56] Personal contact may better serve the interests of representatives than senators because, for the latter, even the most extensive personal contact with voters may fail to reach a significant proportion of the electorate. In fact, representatives appear to exploit their resources for maintaining contact with constituents to a larger degree than senators. For example, in 1965–66 House and Senate incumbents were spending similar amounts of time in their constituencies, but House members were receiving only two-thirds of the travel subsidy that senators could claim. With the same level of travel subsidy (twelve round-trips), senators were spending about thirty-five days per session in their states whereas representatives were spending fifty days per session in their districts (1969–70).

NOTES

Author's note: I want to express my appreciation to H. Douglas Price and Richard F. Fenno, Jr., for their comments on an earlier version of this chapter.

1. "Chiles Urged Early Parole for Former County Official," *Tallahassee Democrat,* May 15, 1987, p. 8B.
2. *Sporting News,* June 1, 1987, p. 50, col. 4.
3. Quoted in Roger H. Davidson, *The Role of the Congressman* (New York: Pegasus, 1969), p. 101.
4. Richard F. Fenno, Jr., *Home Style: House Members in Their Districts* (Boston: Little, Brown, 1978), p. 55.
5. Ibid.
6. Richard F. Fenno, Jr., *The U.S. Senate: A Bicameral Perspective* (Washington, D.C.: American Enterprise Institute for Public Policy Research, 1982).
7. Diana Evans Yiannakis, "House Members' Communication Styles: Newsletters and Press Releases," *Journal of Politics* 44 (November 1982), pp. 1049–71.
8. Morris P. Fiorina, *Congress: Keystone of the Washington Establishment* (New Haven, Conn.: Yale University Press, 1977); Glenn R. Parker, *Homeward Bound: Explaining Changes in Congressional Behavior* (Pittsburgh, Penn.: University of Pittsburgh Press, 1986).
9. Fenno, *Home Style,* p. 137.
10. Donald R. Matthews, *U.S. Senators and Their World* (New York: Vintage Books, 1960).
11. Fenno, *Home Style,* p. 34.
12. Noble E. Cunningham, ed., *Circular Letters of Congressmen, 1789–1839,* 3 vols. (Chapel Hill: University of North Carolina Press, 1978), p. xxxv.
13. Yiannakis, "Communication Styles."
14. Cunningham, *Circular Letters,* p. xxxiii.
15. Ibid., p. 429.
16. Diana Evans Yiannakis reported that about 44 percent of the paragraphs in the newsletters she examined made some reference to the district. See Yiannakis, "Communication Styles," p. 1062.
17. Cunningham, *Circular Letters,* p. xiii.
18. Ibid., p. 600.
19. Ibid., p. 906.
20. Ibid., p. 1986.
21. Ibid., p. 936.
22. Ibid., p. xix. Morris Fiorina makes the same characterization of the relationship between congressmen and the bureaucracy in the twentieth century: "The bureaucracy serves as a convenient lightning rod for public frustration and a

convenient whipping boy for congressmen." See Fiorina, *Congress: Keystone of the Washington Establishment*, p. 49.

23. There is another respect in which past and present home styles differ: unlike past legislators, today's legislators do far less (some might say nothing) to promote their own political parties. See Michael Les Benedict, "The Party, Going Strong: Congress and Elections in the Mid-Nineteenth Century," *Congress and the Presidency* 9 (Winter 1981–82), pp. 48–49.

24. James Sterling Young, *The Washington Community, 1800–1828* (New York: Harcourt Brace Jovanovich, 1966), p. 89.

25. Ibid., p. 25.

26. Parker, *Homeward Bound*, chapter 4.

27. H. Douglas Price, "Congress and the Evolution of Legislative 'Professionalism,' " in *Congress in Change*, ed. Norman J. Ornstein (New York: Praeger Publishers, 1975), p. 5.

28. Roger H. Davidson and Walter J. Oleszek, *Congress and Its Members* (Washington, D.C.: Congressional Quarterly Press, 1981), p. 31.

29. Price, "Legislative 'Professionalism,' " pp. 3–4.

30. Nelson W. Polsby, "The Institutionalization of the U.S. House of Representatives," *American Political Science Review* 62 (March 1968), pp. 144–68.

31. Fenno, *Home Style*; Parker, *Homeward Bound*, pp. 45–47.

32. Parker, *Homward Bound*, chapter 3.

33. Matthews, *U.S. Senators*, p. 242.

34. These data were collected from the travel vouchers that incumbents filed with the clerk of the House of Representatives and the secretary of the Senate. See Parker, *Homeward Bound*, pp. 39–45.

35. David R. Mayhew, *Congress: The Electoral Connection* (New Haven, Conn.: Yale University Press, 1974), p. 16.

36. Fiorina, *Congress: Keystone of the Washington Establishment*.

37. Ibid.

38. Walter J. Oleszek, *Congressional Procedures and the Policy Process* (Washington, D.C.: Congressional Quarterly Press, 1978), p. 144.

39. Normal J. Ornstein, Thomas E. Mann, Michael J. Malbin, and John F. Bibby, *Vital Statistics on Congress, 1982* (Washington, D.C.: American Enterprise Institute for Public Policy Research, 1982).

40. Parker, *Homeward Bound*, pp. 58–114.

41. Ibid., chapter 4.

42. Ibid., chapter 3.

43. There is some evidence that the increases in the legislative workload and the demand for constituency services have occurred with the acquiescence, if not the encouragement, of congressmen. See John R. Johannes and John C. McAdams, "The Distribution of Congressional Casework, 1977–1982," paper presented at the annual meeting of the American Political Science Association, Chicago, April 1984; Peter Swenson, "The Influence of Recruitment on the Structure of Power in the U.S. House, 1870–1940," *Legislative Studies Quarterly* 7 (February 1982), pp. 7–36.

44. Parker, *Homeward Bound*, pp. 158–70.

45. David R. Mayhew, "Congressional Elections: The Case of the Vanishing Marginals," *Polity* 6 (Spring 1974), pp. 295–317.

46. Fiorina, *Congress: Keystone of the Washington Establishment*.

47. See Barbara Hinckley, "House Reelections and Senate Defeats: The Role of the Challenger," *British Journal of Political Science* 10 (October 1980), pp. 440–60; Gary C. Jacobson and Samuel Kernell, *Strategy and Choice in Congressional Elections* (New Haven, Conn.: Yale University Press, 1981).
48. See Walter Dean Burnham, "Insulation and Responsiveness in Congressional Elections," *Political Science Quarterly* 90 (Summer 1975), pp. 411–35; John A. Ferejohn, "On the Decline of Competition in Congressional Elections," *American Political Science Review* 71 (March 1977), pp. 166–76.
49. Parker, *Homeward Bound*, pp. 137–49.
50. Ibid., pp. 120–22.
51. Popular images of senators are not as colored by their attention to their states, though attention to the state provides a positive component to the images of senators in the same way as it generates positive evaluations of congressmen.
52. Fenno, *Home Style*, p. 157.
53. Ibid., p. 132.
54. Parker, *Homeward Bound*.
55. U.S. Congress, House Commission on Administrative Review, *Final Report*, 95th Cong., 1st sess., 1977. H. Doc. 95–272. Vol. 2, *Survey Materials*, p. 875.
56. Fenno, *Senate*, p. 33.

CHAPTER 4

PR on the Hill: The Evolution of Congressional Press Operations

Timothy E. Cook

In 1983, the House of Representatives had just passed a resolution calling for a verifiable bilateral nuclear freeze. Susan Trausch of the *Boston Globe* went to interview the representative who triumphantly shepherded the resolution through the House. Far from being exultant, he was surly and out of sorts. As Trausch tells the story,

> "So you must be popping champagne over there," I said naively during a phone interview.
> "Sure," he said, and then there was a silence followed by a sigh. He hesitated, gave a short laugh, and said, "There's just one thing. Now what do I do?"
> The problem had obviously been distressing him so much that he didn't care if he was telling a reporter about it. In fact, he seemed desperate for some sort of media advice.
> "What's next?" he asked. "Is it Central America? Should I take a trip down there? What's your sense of this?"
> "Gee," I said. "You got me."
> Sitting at the other end of the phone with my mouth open, I remember thinking that this had to be some sort of aberration in the process caused by the congressman's being a bit of a nut. But I have since learned that while he may have been a little more panicked than most, he was merely verbalizing what every other elected official in Washington is thinking twenty-four hours a day: please, Lord, send me an issue that will get me on the *Today* show.[1]

Trausch was baffled, but many contemporary observers of Congress in the 1980s would not be so bewildered. Indeed, in the age when a president can be popularly referred to as the "Great Communicator," and in an age where television coverage has become the name of the game in political campaigns, many respected commentators point to a growing preoccupation with publicity throughout Congress and argue that the consequences are far from beneficial.[2] This view of Congress as driven by the relentless search for publicity is shared by scholars, too. In particular, Norman Ornstein and Austin Ranney have contended that the media, particularly television, contribute to the fragmentation of power within Congress, and to its inability to provide leadership in American politics.[3] With the expansion of television news in the 1970s, they argue, the media began paying more attention to individual members than to the institution. In Ornstein's words, "It became possible for any member of Congress to get national coverage and become a nationally recognized figure. Unshackled by norms or rules, aided by staff resources, every member down to the most junior had the opportunity to seize attention."[4] With every member able and willing to pursue media visibility, both Ornstein and Ranney conclude there is little incentive either to conform to internal incentives or to struggle for legislative accomplishments.

An observant visitor to Capitol Hill could not overlook the presence of the media. Television cameras aim at members dressed in telegenic blue shirts in *the swamp,* a section of the Capitol lawn set aside for interviews; interns dash from one press gallery to the next with stacks of press releases; reporters crowd outside a hearing room to receive a committee report or corner a witness. But despite the media's omnipresence on the Hill, one has to wonder: Are members now largely motivated by the desire for publicity? Are they able to garner such national attention? And has public relations been responsible for edging out policymaking in Congress?

CONGRESS ENTERING THE MEDIA AGE: WHAT HAPPENED IN THE SEVENTIES

Members of Congress have always been interested in publicity; they have always been concerned about their portrayal in the national and the local press.[5] Moreover, members long have complained about the media's preference for the "show horse" over the "work horse."[6] What then would have made the institution as a whole more publicity-conscious in the 1970s? Several possibilities come immediately to mind.

First, the personal staffs of members of Congress expanded tremendously in the 1970s. Legislators pursuing publicity could concentrate more completely on getting media attention with the help of a press secretary, a post which became commonplace in virtually every Senate office and in most House offices by the end of the decade (see Figure 4–1).[7] These press secretaries often had backgrounds in the media or in public relations.[8] Most legislators now had in-house experts on winning publicity.

Second, the number of reporters in Washington credentialed to cover Congress grew dramatically after 1960 (see Figure 4–2). Members interested in getting coverage had more potential points of access. Although the increase occurred in all areas, the upswing in electronic media—television and radio—was especially strong.

Third, congressional campaigns became even more dominated by the electronic media. In particular, television advertising was a major contributor to the rising cost of House and Senate campaigns. A new generation was elected which of necessity was comfortable with the new medium.

Fourth, members of Congress and national reporters began to discover each other. In particular, the extraordinarily positive coverage of the House Judiciary Committee hearings in 1974 on the impeachment of President Nixon

FIGURE 4–1   Percent of House and Senate Offices with One or More Full-Time
Press Aides

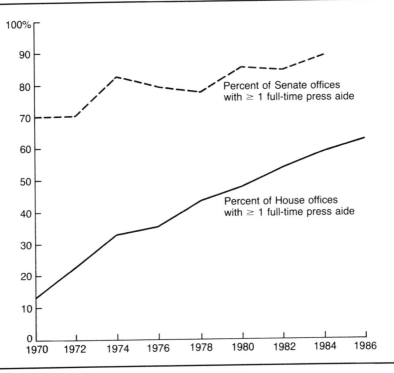

SOURCE: *Congressional Staff Directory*, 1970–1986.

showed representatives what could be done with media attention and gave
reporters an impressive sign of the newsworthiness of the House—the chamber traditionally overlooked in congressional coverage.[9]

Fifth, and perhaps most important, the media had gradually been allowed into congressional proceedings. Television cameras were allowed into
House hearings in 1970, onto the House floor in 1979, and onto the Senate
floor in 1986. According to Michael Robinson's *first law of videopolitics*, "television alters the behavior of institutions in direct proportion to the amount
of coverage provided or allowed: The greater the coverage, the more conspicuous the changes."[10] Robinson concluded in 1975 that Congress so restricted
television that its impact was minimal. With the intrusion of television into
all stages of the legislative process, its impact should have appreciated greatly.

Yet with all these important alterations in the relationship of Congress
and the media, the latter's impact on the Hill has not been as dramatic as
some allege. It is true that members of both the House and the Senate are
becoming more professionalized and sophisticated in their pursuit of public-

FIGURE 4–2 Growth of Congressional Press Galleries, 1960–1976

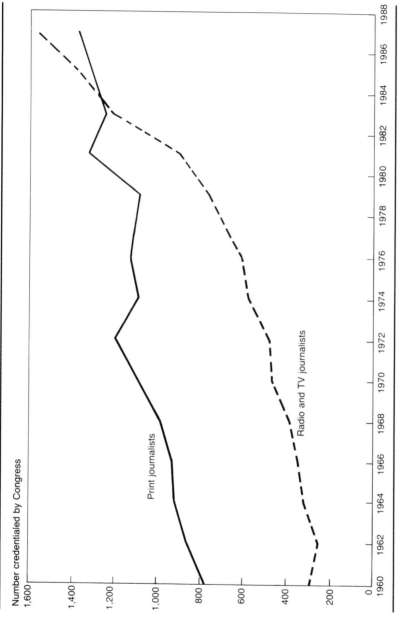

Number credentialed by Congress

Print journalists

Radio and TV journalists

SOURCE: For 1960 through 1976: Michael J. Robinson, "Three Faces of Congressional Media," in *The New Congress*, ed. Thomas E. Mann and Norman J. Ornstein (Washington, D.C.: American Enterprise Institute for Public Policy Research, 1981), figure 3–2, p. 83. For 1977 through 1987: *Congressional Directory* (Washington, D.C.: Government Printing Office).

ity. It is also true that the media, especially network television news, now pay more attention to more members of Congress, even as the time devoted to the institution itself seems to be on the wane. But legislators cannot immediately determine their own publicity with either local or national media. At either level, the legislators' ability to receive media attention is determined by factors beyond their control. The average member of Congress does not receive much attention from the national media, which are more concerned with the activities of individuals they see as important—usually those in positions of authority, such as party leaders and committee chairs. Even back home, where legislators are presumed to be newsworthy on an almost daily basis, the technical demands of television and the failure of television markets to overlap constituency boundaries make the electronic media problematic to use. Consequently, even with the impressive development of PR on the Hill, members of Congress generally pursue media attention the old-fashioned way—at the local level, not at the national level, and with print rather than electronic media.

COVERING THE LEGISLATURE: THE NATIONAL MEDIA'S RULES OF THE GAME

Publicity may be valuable to legislators. But it is not available to all on equal terms, for the simple reason that not everything that they do passes the tests of newsworthiness applied by journalists. These tests are crucial to reporters, because nobody knows for sure what is and what is not news. The news does not reflect the world as it is; it is invariably selective. Reporters are vulnerable to pressures from others—sources, superiors, audiences—who may have divergent ideas about what is newsworthy.

With the incessant need to come up with a story day in, day out, reporters must devise ways to routinize their work. But there are few clear divisions between news and non-news, as discussions with journalists reveal.[11] Instead, news is not defined by the product so much as by the organizational process. Whatever pops out of this process is, almost by definition, news.

The Rules

Two unspoken rules of the game dominate the routines of journalism. The first rule is: *go where news is deemed most likely to happen even before it occurs.* Reporters establish standard "beats," usually marked by institutional locales such as police stations and legislatures. Far from pursuing a "man-bites-dog" story, most reporting accentuates not the unexpected, but the predictable.

Yet sometimes when reporters arrive where news is likely to occur, they are confronted with a vast array of potential newsmakers. This leads to the second rule: *routinely turn to individuals in structured positions of authority who will serve as principal "authoritative" sources.* Journalists thereby assure a daily routine at the news beat that they cover and a steady flow of news copy. They also diminish criticism by focusing on persons that colleagues, editors, publishers, and audiences generally agree to be newsworthy. The process becomes a self-fulfilling prophecy: as individuals or institutions become ever more frequently covered, their apparent importance is confirmed, and more reporters cover their activities. The dynamic works in reverse for those outside positions of authority: they are overlooked, partly because they are presumed to be less important and partly because they are not organized enough to constitute a media beat. Even if accidental news breaks the routines, the dependence on authoritative sources reasserts itself as the event recedes.[12]

This is not to say that the media are merely a mouthpiece for these authoritative sources. There is competition over the shape of the final product, but this competition is bounded. Reporters rarely ask if these sources are worth covering at all, and they seldom challenge the officials' selection and definition of the problem. For example, an evasive president can prevent press conferences from being give-and-take on the issues and instead have them focus on the details of the agenda he has set.[13] Reporters may have a strong sense of independence from editors and sources, because they choose the order of paragraphs, select quotes, and craft the final product but only within guidelines suggested by others.[14]

The Rules Applied

The easiest way for Washington journalists to routinize their work is covering the president. He is presumed to make news day in and day out. This focus serves a journalistic function: it provides a daily piece of the puzzle of the news broadcast or the front page, and the focus on a familiar individual is vital for storytelling. Presidents' near-automatic entrée to the news adds much to their power.[15] Other officeholders and institutions are not so blessed. Indeed, the coverage of the institution of Congress in both television and print has diminished from a position of parity with the president in the 1960s to relative invisibility. When Congress is covered, it is increasingly mentioned only in reaction to presidential initiatives.[16]

The media's relationship with Congress differs from that with the president. The congressional press corps is far more complex and permeable than its White House counterpart. Journalists at the White House resemble a pack, in agreement not only on who is the prime newsmaker (the president) but what is the main story of the day.[17] Such consensus is not found among the congressional press corps, whose members are on the Hill for many different reasons. Some reporters in Washington are *stringers*, Washington bureau representatives for local media interested less in Congress itself (which can be covered through the wire services) than in the activities of their local senators and representatives. Among the media with a national audience,[18] some reporters are full-time congressional correspondents, generalists covering what is going on in the institution itself, much as White House correspondents cover the president's activities. These reporters, comprising less than one hundred, are far outnumbered by the national reporters credentialed to cover Congress, but who would not consider Congress their beat.[19] Many national reporters cover a specific issue—labor, environment, taxes—and pay attention to Congress and its members only as they concern that area. Others cover another institutional beat, such as the presidency or the Supreme Court, and occasionally require congressional reaction to provide a "balanced" story. Congress is attractive to reporters for its accessibility, which allows it to be a superb wellspring of information. Indeed, Stephen Hess goes so far as to say that news from Washington is so dependent upon congressional sources that it reflects a congressional perspective.[20]

Newsworthiness within Congress

Reporters must next decide *who* in Congress should be covered. Unlike the executive in both the White House and the agencies, Congress lacks officially designated spokespersons. Unlike parliamentary systems, opposition parties lack *shadow ministers,* minority party counterparts who would replace party leaders and ministers after a change of government, to react to governmental decisions on a given policy area. The problem was stated in 1970 by Frank Stanton, president of CBS: "Who would speak for an institution not conspicuous for its unanimity of expression even in the rare cases when there is near unanimity of view?"[21]

Reporters thus require rules of thumb to distinguish those who are worth covering from those that are not. Here is one example: since there are only 100 senators as opposed to 435 representatives, one senator out of 100 must be more powerful and important than one representative out of 435. Consequently, national coverage focuses more on individual senators than on individual representatives. Such rules of thumb may have curious consequences: since an institution of 100 newsworthy individuals is presumably more notable than an institution of 435 not so newsworthy individuals, the Senate ends up being more heavily covered than the House.[22]

Within each chamber, national reporters tend to converge on sources perceived as authoritative. National coverage of Congress is not equally open to all members who might want it. The daily routine of newsmaking requires "ultimate spokesmen" in Congress—most often members in designated positions like party leaders and committee chairs.[23] Journalists presume that these individuals' activities are more newsworthy than what an average member of Congress says and does. *What members do,* in either the Senate or the House, is generally less useful for winning national attention than *who they are.* In either television or print, national coverage is dominated by party leaders and senior members.[24]

At the same time, members of the House are far less likely to proceed in anonymity today than they did twenty years ago (see Figure 4–3). In the late 1960s and early 1970s, it was rare for a senator not to be mentioned on the nightly network news, but the reverse was the case with House members.

FIGURE 4–3   Percent of House Members and Senators Mentioned at Least Once in a Given Year on the Nightly Network News, 1969–1986

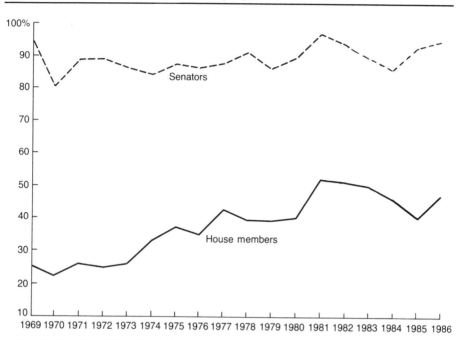

SOURCE: Calculated by author from the Vanderbilt Television News Index.

From 1969 through 1973, approximately three-fourths of the membership of the House failed to get on the air *even once* during a given year. That anonymity began to decline in 1974. House members' apogee of visibility was the ninety-sixth Congress, during the much-publicized budget battles of President Reagan's first term, when twice as many representatives received television coverage as in the Ninety-first Congress twelve years earlier. Still, around one-half of the House members toiled unnoticed by the network news. Other television news outlets, like morning news shows, the "MacNeil/ Lehrer News Hour," or "Nightline," have not provided a forum for many House members. According to calculations made by Stephen Hess, only 145 House members sitting in the Ninety-eighth Congress appeared in these broadcasts from January 1983 through June 1984.[25] Although more members may be receiving some form of coverage in recent years, those in party or committee leadership positions have been obtaining greater coverage than ever before.

As visible as the House and its members have become since the early 1970s, the Senate and its members remain more visible. Even in the days of the *Inner Club*—the 1950s and 1960s where a handful of Senate careerists committed to the norms, folkways, and traditions of the institution—they did not shun external publicity. When the Inner Club disappeared with the influx of liberal activists in the 1960s, the Senate completely embraced the role of "a great forum, an echo chamber, a publicity machine," while the House remained "a highly specialized instrument for passing legislation."[26] Even if senators are now more preoccupied by detail following the expansion of congressional staffs, and even if House members are more inclined to address the large picture, the contrast between the two chambers continues to be acute. One of the main adjustments new senators must make to the institution is to adjust to the media; ex-House members, in particular, can no longer be accustomed to relative anonymity in the national press. Richard Fenno describes such a member:

> . . . A former House member, three weeks into his Senate term, was asked to comment on his party's President's State of the Union address. He called it "dull and forgettable." He found his statement in the next day's *Washington Post*. As his aide recalls, "He had not seen the paper before he went down to meet with the president the next day. When he came back, he said he thought the president was pretty cool to him. Then he saw the *Post*. He said, 'I've got to be careful now. The only paper that used to care what I said was the *Centerville Sun*.' "[27]

Although the overall visibility of the average senator is higher than an average House member, most news in the Senate is, like news in the House, dominated by relatively few individuals. Stephen Hess notes, for example, that half the coverage of senators in 1983 went to only ten members. This figure is inflated because several of those senators were running for president, but the lion's share of national attention in any year studied goes to less than twenty individuals. Moreover, these newsmakers tend to be party or committee leaders or candidates for higher office, just as in the House.[28]

In conclusion, the activities of most members of Congress are generally not publicized by the national media. Do legislators then accept their relegation to virtual invisibility? And if not, how do they work to surmount a system that shuts most of them out?

DEALING WITH THE NATIONAL MEDIA: WHY BOTHER?

Why would members be interested in national publicity? Consider the goals of members of Congress. Reelection, for example, presumed to be the basic goal of all members, who must be reelected in order to get anything else done, is not an incentive for pursuing the national press. Despite allegations to the contrary, there are no indications that national media visibility helps members get reelected. If anything, it may only attract strong challengers (as occurred in 1980) and indirectly create electoral vulnerability.[29]

In the fall of 1984 in response to the question, "Do the national media help in getting the job done?" many of the forty House press secretaries I interviewed were incredulous, some saying that nobody back home read the *Washington Post* or *The New York Times.*[30] Some were suspicious of the national media. As the press aide to a two-term moderate southern Democrat said, "The national media just aren't familiar with it, can't just move into the district and report it. The local media are already savvy about local issues . . . so the local nuances are picked up. You run the risk of being criticized by the national media and then having your opponents use this information." Others felt uncomfortable with the image projected by national media attention that implicitly distances the member from the district. A press secretary to a freshman western Democrat said, "I'm not sure it [network news] can help but I think it can hurt. What the network news does to news is something like what the big screen does to TV movies—it's larger than life, it's not the same story."

To be sure, some House press secretaries pointed out advantages of dealing with the national media. Several noted that national visibility could have a trickle-down effect to the local media and complement local coverage. Moreover, few press secretaries find the national media tough or unfair.[31] But reaching one's constituents through the national media simply is not worth the greater time and resources compared to operating through the accessible local press.

The national media may not be attractive for pursuing reelection, but they can be of great help in furthering two other goals of members of Congress: making policy and wielding influence in Washington. The reasons have relatively little to do with the ability to rouse public opinion to pressure other legislators. Rather, the media provide crucial information on what is going on within each chamber as well as elsewhere in Washington. Even in the 1950s, Donald Matthews found senators turning to the media to find out what they, as a body, were doing:

> [I]t is not so well known that the senators often find out about what is going on in the Senate by reading the papers. Senators are incredibly busy people. Most of them have specialized legislative interests. Most important legislative events take place in the myriad committee and subcommittee hearings occurring all over the Hill. Senators have neither the time nor energy to keep tab on this hundred-ring circus. The newspapers help immeasurably in the senators' never-ending struggle to keep track of what is going on in the Senate. It is ironic but still true that the members of so small a legislative body should find it necessary to communicate with each other via public print, but often they do.[32]

The Senate of the 1950s, of course, was a clubbish, personalized institution. Today's legislators are, if anything, yet more attentive to the media.[33] Given that both chambers are far more complex and fragmented, members must be reliant on the media for cues on what is happening within Congress.

Media Strategies and Legislative Strategies

The media affect the legislative process in three principal ways. First, they can determine the *salience of an issue*. David Price has noted that members of Congress gravitate toward issues that offer the best chance for a payoff at a low cost—those marked by both high public salience and low conflict among interest groups. At the other extreme are the issues that members shun, marked by high conflict and low salience, where a legislator can do little but make enemies.[34] As Price goes on to explain, one way to place an issue on the congressional agenda, even when it generates high conflict, is to enhance its visibility. This increased salience causes members to perceive increased costs in inaction, even if public opinion is not mobilized on one side or the other. The passage of tax reform legislation in the Ninety-ninth Congress presents a vivid example of the impact of increased salience. Tax reform was enacted despite high conflict among interest groups, because its salience through continued media coverage meant that someone would be blamed for its demise, even though polls never showed clear optimism about or support for the measure. Had the salience of tax reform been less in the national press, the outcome might well have been otherwise. As Speaker Thomas P. "Tip" O'Neill said, "I have to have a bill, the Democratic party has to have a bill, and Danny's [House Ways and Means Chairman Dan Rosten-kowski, Democratic representative from Illinois] got to put one together that will sell. If we don't, we'll be clobbered over the head by the president of the United States.[35]

Second, the media also affect *how issues will be understood*. Martin Linsky argues that "The way the press frames an issue is as important as whether or not it is covered at all. If the press characterizes a policy option one way early on in the decision-making process, it is very difficult for officials to turn that image around to their preferred perspective."[36] Savvy members of Congress can shape the debate and help to determine the outcome if they can interest the media not only in a particular area but in their specific proposals.

And third, the media can boost *one's personal influence within the institution* as someone worth paying attention to. Such media visibility may, of course, be helpful for running for higher office. Indeed, such ambition may be the motivation for publicizing an issue—and the legislator's name along with it.[37] But what is often overlooked is that media attention for legislators pushes their policy agenda at the same time. As the press secretary to a prominent House Republican noted, "Promoting the ideas are the same as promoting him. Even a personality column mentions ideas."

Members may attempt to elevate new policy proposals on which they can be the authoritative sources, even though they may not sit on the pertinent committee, as Jack Kemp, the Republican representative from New York, did with the Kemp-Roth supply-side tax cut proposal, or what Representative Edward Markey, a Democrat from Massachusetts, did with the nuclear freeze issue. More typically, members of Congress seek positive reputations among journalists, and these reputations can then be translated into influence within the institution. Such a process can work in two ways: either legislators who have gained renown through the media may be elevated to a position of power in the institution, or those who become official leaders may use that position to win media coverage that enhances their influence.

Two Cases: Les Aspin and Richard Lugar

Representative Les Aspin, a Democrat from Wisconsin, provides the classic case of someone who transformed media visibility into internal clout. From the outset of his House service in 1970, Aspin tirelessly pursued media attention. What set him apart from conventional "show horses" was his interest in what he termed ". . . a good story in something that matters, *The Wall Street Journal, The New York Times,* the *Washington Post.* Not because that carries back home but because it establishes bona fides with the people who it's important to impress, the community you're dealing with."[38] Aspin gained an image of being on top of defense issues through assiduously cultivating the press with quotable comments and information provided well in advance but "embargoed" for later release. Moreover, he was a rarity, an issue-oriented Pentagon critic on the Armed Services Committee, which was mostly filled with pro-defense porkbarrelers. For largely journalistic reasons—his ability to provide good copy and his membership on the Armed Services Committee—Aspin was viewed as an authoritative source. He thus gained considerable salience and respect, and parlayed this image to become chair of the House Armed Services Committee in 1985. Of course, one of Aspin's secrets was that he eschewed unattributed information; asked by an interviewer if he ever leaked stories without his name attached, he quickly responded, "No. There's no benefit in that (chortles). Who needs that? (laughs)."[39]

Senator Richard Lugar, a Republican from Indiana, displays the dynamic in reverse. Lugar had become chair of the Senate Foreign Relations Committee in 1985 almost by accident: the previous chair had been defeated for reelection, the more senior Jesse Helms, a Republican from North Carolina, kept a campaign promise to remain chair of the Senate Committee on Agriculture, Nutrition, and Forestry, and Lugar himself had tried and failed to be chosen majority leader. Lugar would have seemed to have only slight potential for media attention. His personal style was far removed from the image of a mediagenic show horse; one profile noted, "He is not gregarious, he has little sense of humor, his appearance is not striking. His manner seems overly pious and is often smirky."[40] Moreover, prior to 1985, Lugar had spent little time on foreign policy issues, was viewed largely as a lackey for the Reagan administration, and was setting out not to push high-profile issues but to reestablish bipartisan consensus on the committee. Yet a 1987 analysis of Lugar's two years at the helm of Foreign Relations termed him "a national figure . . . the leading Republican voice on Capitol Hill on the most compelling events of the day."[41] Lugar's official place had been enhanced by his skill at building a reputation as a spokesperson in the media. Lugar capitalized on international events, most notably the 1986 Philippine revolution which garnered extraordinary coverage, but his voyage to Manila as head of a team of observers to the election was only one part of a long campaign to raise his stature in Washington. This effort was run by Lugar's press secretary who assiduously cultivated reporters and provided regular on-the-record briefings.[42] By the time the Philippines receded from the front pages, Lugar had been established as a key actor in foreign policy—a reputation he both exploited and enhanced later in 1986 in shaping and shepherding the bill setting sanctions against South Africa.

In short, media strategies can be closely linked with legislative strategies. In and of itself, this is not wholly new. Matthews found ample evidence of senators using the press in the 1950s to communicate with and persuade one's colleagues.[43] Even in the more centralized, "corporate," House of that era, using the media was not unheard of. The pros and cons of such an *outside strategy* were well delineated in Nelson Polsby's account of the contest between Carl Albert, a Democrat from Oklahoma, and Richard Bolling, a Democrat from Missouri, for House majority leader in 1962.[44] Bolling sought to counter Albert's intimate person-to-person style by trying to define the contest not as one within the family but an ideological dispute fought through the media. Bolling's approach was neither doomed to failure nor generally condemned, even in such an internal decision as selecting a leader. Instead, Polsby notes, an *inside strategy* was favored in this case only because the matter was procedural rather than substantive, and because deliberations were protected from outside scrutiny.

But with the power more widely-spread among members, in the 1970s, such conditions rarely hold in either chamber. The outside strategy is thus a credible, perhaps even necessary way to get things done in today's permeable, issue-charged Congress. As Democrat Thomas Downey from New York has phrased it, "Not getting publicity limits your effectiveness . . . I can't think of someone around here who's effective just by being on the inside."[45] The media, far from being an obstacle to lawmaking, could be a complement; members seeking national publicity may not be "show horses" but "work horses" seeking accomplishments in public policy.

DEALING WITH THE NATIONAL MEDIA: HOW MEMBERS COPE

Members of Congress are thus presented with a quandary. Working with and through the national media could help them get things done within the institution. But national media attention is not available on a regular basis to most members of the House or Senate. How can members cope?

Some respond by paying little attention to the national media, or at least devoting few of their resources to pursuing national publicity. House press secretaries, for example, find the national media to be least useful in getting their job done.[46] Moreover, only a minority of House press secretaries interviewed in one study made spontaneous reference to the media's value in the legislative process.[47] Even in Senate offices, customarily assumed to be less parochial, most press operations concentrate all but exclusively on the home state media.[48]

Marketing the Members

To a significant number of legislators, the national media still constitute an important avenue for legislative work, and they must figure out how to woo them and win their ongoing attention. There is no question that the press secretaries will do their best to get as much positive coverage for their members as possible, but first reporters have to be convinced of a member's newsworthiness. What press secretaries do to accomplish that task is a version of marketing a product (in this case, a member of Congress), emphasizing its high points and playing down its drawbacks.

A House press secretary to a three-term conservative southern Democrat presented the marketing metaphor:

> In advertising school, we learned about the unique selling point of a product—the one characteristic that separates your product from the rest. You know, like they say, this one gets your clothes whiter and brighter. I concentrate on the one thing that X has which the [state] delegation doesn't have—what things he can do that will get him exclusive coverage, like a bill coming out of his committee, or if he chaired the hearing on the topic. Things that can be mentioned right away in the lead paragraph or from which we can get a media interview.

Despite the ominous sound of "marketing," we must remember: proper marketing requires an awareness of the audience to get them to buy the product. Press operations must ensure that reporters will be receptive to providing coverage. Press secretaries' work is geared, however, not to make media "hits" so much as to create and maintain a long-term relationship. Isolated incidents of visibility, such as can be obtained from the network news excerpting televised debates, are not highly valued, because they neither boost the member's reputation nor manage the work load. According to the press aide to a freshman midwestern House Democrat, "The ideal situation is to have the press call you, to have them *want* to call you. If I didn't have to write releases enough because *they* called *me*, I'd be doing my job. Sure, it'd be nice if they printed my releases verbatim . . . but it's not my objective to get it printed, but to generate interest."

In short, press operations must stress whatever makes reporters more receptive to future news from and about the member, and that is usually summed up by the word "credibility." A source must be seen to provide a reliable product that can be accepted as newsworthy by reporters' superiors and audiences. Press secretaries concerned about credibility must continually ask themselves why a journalist would want to cover the legislator. For long-term symbiosis to be achieved, the member must be able to claim to be an authoritative source on the particular issue addressed. Without objective, outward signs of that expertise, the members may destroy whatever bases of newsworthiness they already have.

Searching for Credibility

Sometimes, press secretaries realize that those bases are not there. Press aides to freshmen House members indicated there was little point in wooing the national media until the legislators were in a better position to be seen as newsworthy. Press assistants to more senior members concur that credibility could be damaged by seeking press on issues where the member will not be regarded by reporters as authoritative. Certain issues are seen as more appropriate than others to exploit, such as those the members have been grappling with in committee. Chairing a subcommittee, as most majority members do nowadays, is especially useful. Subcommittee chairs are legitimized as authoritative sources on all matters within their jurisdictions. They can hold hearings to give the media a news "peg," one way to convert a continuing story into a breaking news item; and they can use subcommittee staff to boost press operations. But such a post is no guarantee of media coverage. If the chair does not meet the prerequisites of what journalists see as good copy, he or she may end up overshadowed by a more glib or aggressive junior colleague.

Two astute press secretaries to junior House Democrats stated the combinations of skill and placement that are necessary to garner national publicity. First, the press assistant to a three-termer on the House Ways and Means Committee:

> You can get recognition. It's different with legislation on which you can have direct impact. If you're talking about "save the whales" but you're on Government Operations, then there's not much point . . . I haven't been comfortable with making Medicare an issue, but if we get on the Health Subcommittee, we've got legitimacy and we can push the issue. It's surprising, but a lot of people *don't* push so it can happen that aggressive press operations *can* get attention.

The aide to a three-term southern Democrat who had recently been appointed to a subcommittee chair was yet more perceptive:

> You have to have a jump-off point on a consistent basis. If you're not newsworthy every two months or so, no charm or personality can launch you as a spokesman. If you've got the combination of reassuring television presence and a position within the House, you're a really good candidate for it. One without the other is not very helpful. Presence without power doesn't make

you interesting, and power without presence doesn't make you interesting. But the combination makes you a national figure.

Once having established credentials as an authoritative source, the effect can become self-reinforcing. One press aide to a junior California Republican sighed, "It's so much easier when you're seen as plugged in." How "plugged in" one is seen to be, and on what issue, may be a product of media coverage.

Because legislators are generally authoritative only on issues that somehow tie in with their expertise, the national media tend to ask members of Congress only about a limited range of issues, which in turn provides an incentive to specialize. If the legislator can stand out from the crowd on an issue, the press will likely consult him or her when that issue becomes salient in Washington. Members must therefore be careful to choose issues that will be of *continuing* interest to the media. For example Representative Donald Albosta, a Democrat from Michigan, was described by some press aides as someone who got overly involved with a "flash-in-the-pan issue" (Jimmy Carter's purloined debate papers). When that controversy vanished, so did Albosta; there was simply no reason to report about him any more.

Press operations in Congress are not merely concerned with the demands of accessibility and timeliness; they must also anticipate whether the issues chosen for publicity will indeed be deemed newsworthy by reporters. Since the media cannot be interested equally in all issues, aides' preferences have far-reaching effects on the Hill.

COVERING LEGISLATORS: THE LOCAL MEDIA'S RULES APPLIED

Most members of Congress, then, really do not matter much to the national media. And, by and large, the national media does not really matter much to most members. The situation is quite different for the members when dealing with the local press. Local publicity has long been deemed crucial to winning reelection.[49] What's more, the same two rules of newsworthiness that generally work against members' national visibility work much more in their favor back home.

The Authoritative Source at Home

Within Congress, the legislator is merely one out of 435 or one out of 100. Back home, the senator or representative is a key newsmaker, one of a handful of authoritative sources in a position to know about congressional goings-on and how they affect the constituency. Not surprisingly, the local media are the main customers for legislators' products; local reporters include local legislators as part of a regular news beat. A study of House press secretaries estimated that on the average over three-fourths of their time was spent dealing with the district media, even though the press releases sent out were evenly divided between national and local issues.[50] With national news already covered by wire services, a story can be nicely localized by a member's comments. Otherwise, issues that the local media stress can diverge from those preferred by the nationals. As Ben Bagdikian has said, these "diggers and toilers" don't cover the "deep currents of history," but instead write of "dredging obscure creeks in Florida, of federal contracts for nuts and bolts in Connecticut, of slums cleared in Birmingham at central government expense, and the prospects for higher tariffs on Hong Kong shirts."[51] Individual members of Congress are ideally suited to comment on these local issues that are unlikely to be noted by the national media.

Not only are the local media more interested in the individual legislator, but they are more likely to portray him or her in a favorable light for two complementary reasons. First, there is the familiar tendency of hometown media, intentionally or not, to be community boosters, a role that can lead them to defend the powers that be.[52] Members of Congress spend much of their time creating an image at home as "one of you"; the local media may start to believe the image of the hometown kid made good. Second, and more important, the continuing interactions between officeholders and journalists lead to *symbiosis,* which the dictionary defines as "the intimate living together of two dissimilar organisms in a mutually beneficial relationship." An exchange relationship is created; the media receive the copy they require while supplying the politician with the publicity he or she needs. This relationship need not be evenly balanced. In fact, close interconnections between journalist and office holder tend to work to the latter's advantage. Reporters must take care not to alienate crucial sources, who can turn elsewhere for coverage; the media thus report in ways fundamentally like the perspectives of those they cover.

Members of the House receive such favorable publicity back home that incumbents have a valuable advantage against challengers who have trouble persuading the media of their newsworthiness. In daily newspapers, incumbents receive more coverage overall and more positive coverage than challengers, even in hotly contested races.[53] Such local reporting may approach sycophancy in its ardor. One example is an editorial in a small weekly paper in the rural Virginia district of the late Dan Daniel:

> Our first and only contact to date with challenger Frank Cole was over the telephone one morning when he called to threaten a lawsuit against us unless we stopped using Congressman Daniel's weekly newsletter, *Capitol Comments.*
>
> We have used the newsletter for nearly 17 years. It is a service to readers who can glean from it the latest dealings in Washington and our representative's feelings on the issue. Threatening lawsuits does not a voter sway. We were not impressed by such tactics and as is evident in the columns to the right [Capitol Comments], not intimidated either. We urge a resounding vote of confidence for our Congressman on Tuesday, November 4.[54]

More typically, the local media act as a conduit for members' press releases and announcements. Many if not most stories about legislators originate as press releases.[55] Bagdikian documented this when he noted that stories from several small papers in one Wisconsin district all had identical content, all quoting the local representative. Visiting the member's office, he obtained a press release and found, "The papers had run the release word for word as journalistic news. This is hardly a rare phenomenon. Hundreds of press releases . . . are sent to the media by members of Congress, and hundreds are run verbatim or with insignificant changes, most often in medium-sized and small papers, with only rare calls to check facts and ask questions that probe beyond the pleasant propaganda."[56]

Local Television: So Close Yet So Far

There are some flaws in this paradise for legislators. One is that smaller news organizations are more likely to pass along the members' releases as if they were news, but smaller organizations are likely to have smaller circulation. A second, related flaw is that for media with larger circulation, individual members of Congress have considerable competition from colleagues for publicity. Senators from the same state often suffer strained relations from trying to get comparable publicity in the same media outlets. Competition is even more complicated among House members, especially for television coverage. The United States is divided into 211 media markets; each estimates the counties (or portions thereof) that receive their television signals from a particular city. These media markets range in size from New York City with 6.7 million viewing households to Glendive, Montana, with just over five thousand.[57] Although the median population of a media market (approximately 530,000 viewers) is close to that of a House district, they rarely overlap; district lines seldom pay attention to natural geography or social communities. The case of Democratic Representative Leon Panetta of California, whose district is all but coterminous with the Monterey media market, is rare. Instead, most districts are either in a single market with many others in metropolitan areas, or are made up of bits and pieces of different markets in rural locales.[58]

In the ideal world, press secretaries would love to receive television attention. In a survey of House Democratic press assistants, 61 percent agreed with the statement, "If I had to pick one medium to sell a story, I would pick television any day." Yet the competition for television news, caused by the mismatch of media markets and House districts, reduces the value of this ideal considerably. Only about one-third of House members have regular radio or television programs while over one-half write weekly columns. Likewise, campaigns of either incumbent or challenger seldom buy television ads.[59] Press secretaries rate local television as generally less useful in their job than local dailies or weeklies or the tried-and-true press release (see Table

TABLE 4–1   Democratic Press Secretaries'
Evaluations of Media Outlets and
Strategies

Q: "Please rate how valuable each is in getting
your job done (on a scale of 1 to 10 with 1 being
very low and 10 being very high)."

Media (in descending order)	Mean	SD
Local dailies	9.0	1.5
Local weeklies	8.2	2.0
Press releases	8.1	1.8
Newsletters	7.8	2.0
Local television news	7.4	2.6
Targeted mail	6.7	2.7
Radio actualities	5.6	3.3
Recording studio	4.9	2.9
Weekly columns	4.8	3.2
Washington Post	4.7	3.1
Network television news	4.4	3.2
The New York Times	4.3	3.1
Televised floor proceedings	3.8	2.7

$N \geq 120$.

SOURCE: Calculated by the author from Democratic press secretary questionnaire, November–December 1984. Reprinted
from Timothy E. Cook, "Show Horses in House Elections: The
Advantages and Disadvantages of National Media Visibility,"
in *Campaigns in the News*, ed. Jon P. Vermeer (Westport, Conn.:
Greenwood Press, 1987).

4–1). And, the perceived worth of local television is directly linked to the
nature of the media market; the less competition, the more favorably the press
secretary rates local television.[60]

There are other drawbacks to television. First, its format makes it more
selective and thus less likely to present the member's views verbatim. As one
press secretary to a two-term eastern Democrat stated, "TV is the best way to
go but you've got less control . . . [With print] there's a better chance to get
your statements in, whereas the editor in [hometown] in television has more
control over what goes on and what stays out." Second, the electronic media
are cumbersome and time-consuming to use. A press aide to a senior southern Democrat noted, "To do an interview here, it takes thirty to forty minutes
just to get set up and then some more to do it and then he gets seven seconds
of time. Sure seems like lots of trouble for not very much meat." By and large,
the medium deemed most effective in the abstract, then, is not available to
members of the House.

Senators are better able to capture television attention back home, just as they do in Washington. Although media markets frequently cross state lines, television news is accustomed to covering state politicians with regularity, and senators are natural newsmakers. The importance of television to senator's home styles is captured by Richard Fenno's comparison of House members going from bowling alley to coffee shop in search of constituents, while senators rush from one studio (and often one media market) to the next.[61]

The Multiplicity of Local Media

Yet senators do not neglect other forms of communication, as was revealed in 1985 when the Senate disclosed for the first time how much its members spent on mass mailings: almost $11 million from July to September 1985. In fact, one senator (Democrat Alan Cranston from California) spent over $1.6 million sending out 11.5 million pieces of mail.[62] As with their counterparts (and occasional rivals) in the House, the media strategies in the Senate include a variety of approaches.

Most members' press operations in either chamber do not rely exclusively or even principally on any single medium, even one deemed so powerful as television. House press secretaries seem to realize that, despite the popular belief that television is the main source of citizens' news, voters' methods of getting informed are actually haphazard at best.[63] Also, because members pursue cautious, risk-averse strategies, most media operations in Congress try to use as many different means of communication as possible. Different constituents rely on different media; and different media provide different messages. As one House press secretary said, "I think you have to have all three: TV is image, the newspaper is name recognition and the 'continuing to serve' message, radio is the close touch." Another contended, "To get the message totally across, you have to get the message reinforced, [and] get it more widely dispersed."

Members have become talented at getting the message "totally across" by every means imaginable. Many members supplement the printed press release with their electronic counterparts for radio and television. Virtually every House office now sends out its maximum allotment of six newsletters per year sent by government funds to every district domicile, and many Senate offices have followed suit. Most recently, there has been an enormous increase in letters to targeted groups in the district, made possible by widespread computerization. The volume of mail sent out by members of both the House and the Senate has exploded, with estimates that the number of pieces of mail sent from Congress in 1986 topped *one billion*—or over 5,000 pieces sent out by each member every day in the year.[64] This increase is not solely due to responding to increased constituent mail; as Republican Senator Charles Mathias told his colleagues in March 1985, "If we answered every single constituent communication, we would still be talking about 3 or 4 percent of the total [outgoing] mail. Another 4 percent is committee-related.

Ninety-two percent is what we generate on our own. That is the tragedy: it is self-generated."[65]

Such member-controlled communications might be favored for getting out their views exactly as they would like, but their credibility and persuasibility are less than seemingly objective newspaper articles. Both are considered crucial. Members of Congress rarely make either-or choices in media strategies. To the extent that they are using sophisticated methods of public relations, they have grafted them onto tried-and-true methods; members using one media resource are more likely to use others.[66] It may be true that senators and House members alike are more oriented toward television today than before. But it would be fairer to say that they are all initiating and getting out more publicity *of all kinds* than they ever did before.

CONCLUSION: MEDIA EFFECTS IN CONGRESS

Public relations through congressional media operations have become an important preoccupation of members of both the House and the Senate in recent years. But while some have attributed far-reaching effects to PR on the Hill, others are skeptical that the media have changed much in Congress at all.[67] Does media attention provide incumbents with an important new perquisite of office that enables them to accomplish their goals in office? And has the new concern with PR on the Hill transformed how legislators, and consequently the Senate and the House, go about their business?

The media at the local level have worked to reinforce the phenomenon of House victories and Senate defeats in reelections. Local media coverage of House members is provided largely on their own terms. Even the strongest challengers cannot match the quantity or favorability of incumbents' coverage. In news coverage of House elections, issues are secondary to discussion of political and personal characteristics; such coverage reflects the incumbents' own emphasis on personality over issues in their campaign materials.[68] Little wonder, then, that House members win reelection by astronomical figures. On the other hand, Senate elections receive greater, more critical and more issue-oriented coverage; because voters can learn more about both candidates and their stances; senators are more likely to be judged on the issues and to lose their reelection bids.[69]

The national media work in a different way with legislators than their local counterparts. No longer are members of Congress automatic newsmakers; instead, their newsworthiness depends, in large part, on their power within the institution. Although the national media focus on individuals in leadership positions, both formal and informal, other members attempt to woo the media to help accomplish their own goals of formulating public policy and of wielding influence. Indeed, nonleaders are ever alert for possibilities for influence—especially vacuums that occur when leaders shun media attention in favor of behind-the-scenes maneuvering. Thus, an interesting side effect of members' PR on the Hill results: If leaders are to continue to remain key players par excellence, they must begin to use their access to the media systematically and aggressively to set the agenda and frame the alternatives.[70]

In sum, virtually any legislator who is interested in more than just getting reelected would be wise to pay attention to the potential use of the national media. Leaders can no longer shun the press, as did House Speakers Sam Rayburn and John McCormack, or the media's spotlight will select someone else to serve as authoritative source, with the influence that goes along with it. This new job requirement complicates a leader's job. Congressional leadership has traditionally been based on responsibility and fairness toward one's procedural majority; the search for consensus to "keep peace in the family," as the current House leaders express it, takes precedence over pushing particular policies.[71] But searching for consensus may prove to be difficult for those accustomed to individually searching for media opportunities. This dilemma is illustrated by the travails of Les Aspin, who received a vote of no confidence as chair of the House Armed Services Committee in January 1987 only to be narrowly reelected a few weeks later. As Aspin confessed after the second vote, he had not anticipated the demands of being a committee chair after having risen through the ranks as a media whiz; in his words, "There are a lot of things I think I need to do differently in dealing with people. . . . it has to do with the way I deal with my colleagues on a one-to-one basis. A need to be more open, more up front."[72]

Despite these complications, one would expect members of Congress to become increasingly oriented toward the opportunities provided by the media. Seeking media attention is no longer merely an end in itself but now a means to an end, getting something done in an increasingly fragmented political system. Being a "work horse" is no longer distinguishable from being a "show horse."[73] Presidential leadership may now depend on "going public," demanding the skills of campaigning rather than those of one-on-one bargaining.[74] Working through the media has also become a commonly accepted means of lobbying by Washington interest groups.[75] In such an environment, it is logical that members of Congress would try to do the same, that is, use the media to push their particular issues and alternatives. But relying on the media may have unexpected side effects. Such reliance can restrict the choice of issues to those that the media find attractive and can make legislators more dependent on the media's short and shifting attention span.[76]

The growing preoccupation with publicity thus alters how Congress and its members go about their work. Members become political entrepreneurs, but their concern is not so much what sells with the public but what sells with the media. This would not be troubling if we could assume that the media act as a surrogate for the public. Numerous studies, however, have shown that journalists have little knowledge of their mass audience and pay closer attention to the responses of colleagues and superiors.[77] And the media can be biased: The judgments journalists make about the importance and quality of a story push them toward some issues and away from others.

Herbert Gans has convincingly argued that the media partake of a progressive reformist belief system built into these judgments that push reporters toward easily understood problems with "good government" solutions.[78]

Members of Congress in search of media attention have to find such issues, so it is no surprise that three of the major legislative preoccupations of the Ninety-ninth Congress—tax reform, deficit reduction through the Gramm-Rudman-Hollings Act, and drug abuse—were dealt with by broad-stroke legislation with scarce attention either to their details or to their ability to attain the goal that was being sought. Indeed, in all three cases, one might say Congress passed the legislation not because of but in spite of the contents of the bills. In all three cases, the issues rose and sometimes fell with dizzying rapidity; and in all three cases, the legislative process was shaped less by public opinion, which was largely uncommitted, than by the close media surveillance itself. The recurring standards for what makes a good story causes news to be repetitive and formulaic.[79] There are no incentives for members of Congress to pursue complex or innovative responses to problems if they cannot attract media attention. The result is to reinforce the risk-averseness that members exhibit toward reelection and to bring it into the Washington arena.

Marketing themselves can well be a rational strategy on the part of the legislators. After all, it is a time-tested way, especially for House members, to get the message out to one's constituents and to get reelected. It can also help overcome the fragmentation and dispersion of Congress and of the Washington community in order to get something done. But a marketing approach rarely encourages members to act in anything but their own parochial interest; it may discourage innovative and complex responses to problems in favor of familiar, simple story lines that the media appreciates.

Most observers tend to think of members of Congress wooing the media for ego gratification, posturing to get reelected or to get elected to higher office. These "show horse" incentives are undoubtedly present, but one must not overlook the way in which the media can help a member be a "work horse" as well. PR is a new weapon of growing importance in a legislator's arsenal in Washington. Whether or not it is an ideal response to Congress's difficulties in legislating in the collective national interest is another matter.

NOTES

1. Susan Trausch, *It Came from the Swamp: Your Washington Government at Work* (Boston: Houghton Mifflin, 1986), pp. 150–51.
2. See, e.g., Gregg Easterbrook, "What's Wrong with Congress?", *Atlantic*, December 1984, pp. 57–84 at 59; David S. Broder, "Who Took the Fun Out of Congress?" *Washington Post*, National Weekly Edition, February 17, 1986, pp. 9–10.
3. Norman J. Ornstein, "The Open Congress Meets the President," in *Both Ends of the Avenue*, ed. Anthony King (Washington, D.C.: American Enterprise Insti-

tute for Public Policy Research, 1983), pp. 185–211; Austin Ranney, *Channels of Power: The Impact of Television on American Politics* (New York: Basic Books, 1983).

4. Ornstein, "Open Congress," p. 201.

5. Robert O. Blanchard, ed., *Congress and the News Media* (New York: Hastings House, 1974), pp. 8–28, provides excerpts of debates in the House on reporters' access to proceedings in the First and Sixth Congresses. F. B. Marbut's book, *News from the Capital: The Story of Washington Reporting* (Carbondale, Ill.: Southern Illinois University Press, 1971), provides a workable overview of the relations between Congress and the media, particularly in the nineteenth century.

6. Examples are reproduced in James L. Payne, "Show Horses and Work Horses in the U.S. House of Representatives," *Polity* 12 (Spring 1980), pp. 428–29.

7. Of course, not having a designated press aide does not indicate that no one on the staff works with the media. Nevertheless, the designation of press secretary may be a good example of task specialization permitting those both outside and inside the congressional office to concentrate their press efforts more systematically.

8. In a survey of 126 House press secretaries to Democratic members conducted in December 1984, for example, 48 percent listed experience in print, 27 percent cited working in broadcast media, and 32 percent indicated work in public relations. In all, 74 percent of them had worked in at least one of these areas; 41 percent had majored in journalism in college. For further information on this survey, see Timothy E. Cook, "Press Secretaries and Media Strategies in the House of Representatives: Deciding Whom to Pursue," *American Journal of Political Science* 32 (November 1988). Stephen Hess reports that 63 percent of the 92 Senate press secretaries he contacted in 1984 had journalism backgrounds (mostly in print) of three years or more. See Stephen Hess, "A Note on Senate Press Secretaries and Media Strategies," *Brookings Discussion Paper in Government Studies,* no. 9 (Washington, D.C.: Brookings Institution, 1987), p. 6.

9. On the impeachment proceedings, see Gladys Engel Lang and Kurt Lang, *The Battle for Public Opinion: The President, the Press, and the Polls During Watergate* (New York: Columbia University Press, 1983), chapter 7.

10. Michael J. Robinson, "A Twentieth-Century Medium in a Nineteenth-Century Legislature: The Effects of Television on the American Congress," in *Congress in Change,* ed. Norman J. Ornstein (New York: Praeger Publishers, 1975), p. 241.

11. See especially Gaye Tuchman, *Making News: A Study in the Construction of Reality* (New York: Free Press, 1978).

12. See Edie N. Goldenberg, *Making the Papers: The Access of Resource-Poor Groups to the Metropolitan Press* (Lexington, Mass.: D.C. Heath, 1974), and Harvey Molotch and Marilyn Lester, "Accidental News: The Great Oil Spill as Local Occurrence and National Event," *American Journal of Sociology* 81 (Sept. 1975), pp. 235–60.

13. Jarol B. Manheim, "The Honeymoon's Over: The News Conference and the Development of Presidential Style," *Journal of Politics* 41 (February 1979), p. 66, figure 1.

14. This view of reporter as craftsperson is admirably argued in Lee Sigelman, "Reporting the News: An Organizational Analysis," *American Journal of Sociology* 79 (February 1973) pp. 132–51. The Washington press corps' strong sense

of independence from its superiors is documented in Stephen Hess, *The Washington Reporters* (Washington, D.C.: Brookings Institution, 1980), chapter 1.

15. For thoughts on the president's ability to use the media, see especially Samuel Kernell, *Going Public* (Washington, D.C.: CQ Press, 1986).

16. Richard Davis, "News Coverage of American Political Institutions," paper prepared for delivery at the annual meeting of the American Political Science Association, Washington, D.C., August 28–31, 1986; and Norman J. Ornstein and Michael J. Robinson, Where's All the Coverage? The Case of Our Disappearing Congress," *TV Guide*, January 11, 1986, pp. 4–6, 8–10.

17. Still the best description of the White House press corps is Timothy Crouse, *The Boys on the Bus* (New York: Ballantine Books, 1973).

18. "National Media" in this chapter includes those news outlets that are regarded as having a national audience, such as the three major networks, Cable News Network (CNN), National Public Radio, and Cable Satellite Public Affairs Network (C-SPAN), and/or are seen as "papers of record," such as *The New York Times*, the *Washington Post*, *The Wall Street Journal* and the *Christian Science Monitor.*

19. Stephen Hess, *The Ultimate Insiders: U.S. Senators and the National Media* (Washington, D.C.: Brookings Institution, 1986), p. xv.

20. Hess, *Washington Reporters*, p. 49.

21. Quoted in Newton Minow, John Bartlow Martin, and Lee Mitchell, *Presidential Television* (New York: Basic Books, 1970), p. 104.

22. The domination of Senate coverage over House coverage is found in many studies, but it does seem to fluctuate from year to year; on the other hand, senators seem consistently favored over House members. See, e.g., Susan H. Miller, "News Coverage of Congress: The Search for the Ultimate Spokesman," *Journalism Quarterly* 54 (Summer 1977), pp. 459–65 at table 1; Michael J. Robinson and Kevin R. Appel, "Network News Coverage of Congress," *Political Science Quarterly* 94, (Fall 1979), p. 411; Joe Foote and David Weber, "Network Evening News Visibility of Congressmen and Senators," paper presented at the annual meeting of the Association for Education in Journalism, Gainesville, Florida, 1984; Davis, "News Coverage of American Political Institutions," table 3.

23. Miller, "News Coverage of Congress."

24. On the House, see Timothy E. Cook, "House Members as Newsmakers: The Effects of Televising Congress," *Legislative Studies Quarterly* 11 (May 1986), pp. 203–226; on the Senate, see Hess, *Ultimate Insiders.*

25. Unpublished data taken from the Senate Republican Conference's "Network Roundup," as provided by Stephen Hess. On the "Network Roundups," see Hess, *Ultimate Insiders,* pp. 17–18. According to Hess, seventy-seven of the ninety-nine senators serving throughout the period, July 1983 to June 1984, appeared on such shows. Ibid., table B-1.

26. Nelson W. Polsby, "Policy Analysis and Congress," *Public Policy* 18 (Fall 1969), pp. 62–63. See also Michael Foley, *The New Senate: Liberal Influence on a Conservative Institution* (New Haven, Conn.: Yale University Press, 1980).

27. Richard F. Fenno, Jr., "Adjusting to the Senate," in *Congress and Policy Change,* ed. Gerald C. Wright, Jr., Leroy N. Rieselbach, and Lawrence C. Dodd (New York: Agathon Press, 1986), pp. 140–41.

28. Hess, *Ultimate Insiders,* tables 2–1 and 2–2.

29. See Lyn Ragsdale and Timothy E. Cook, "Representatives' Actions and Challengers' Reactions: Limits to Candidate Connections in the House," *American Journal of Political Science* 31 (February 1987), table 1.
30. For details on these interviews, see Timothy E. Cook, "Show Horses in House Elections: The Advantages and Disadvantages of National Media Visibility," in *Campaigns in the News: Mass Media and Congressional Elections*, ed. Jan P. Vermeer (Westport, Conn.: Greenwood Press, 1987), pp. 161–81. Subsequent unattributed quotes are from the author's interviews.
31. Cook, "Show Horses in House Elections," table 5; Robert Dewhirst, "Patterns of Interaction Between Members of the U.S. House of Representatives and Their Home District Media," Ph.D. diss., University of Nebraska, 1983, p. 142. This perception would seem to conflict with the well-known conclusion that national coverage of Congress tends to be more negative than positive; see, e.g., Robinson and Appel, "Network News Coverage of Congress." Recall, however, that much coverage of the institution makes little mention of individuals. See Davis, "News Coverage of American Political Institutions," table 6.
32. Donald R. Matthews, *U.S. Senators and Their World* (Chapel Hill: University of North Carolina Press, 1960), p. 206.
33. John W. Kingdon, *Congressmen's Voting Decisions,* 2nd ed. (New York: Harper & Row, 1981), chapter 7; Michael J. Robinson and Maura Clancey, "King of the Hill," *Washington Journalism Review* 5 (July/August 1983), pp. 46–49.
34. David E. Price, "Policymaking in Congressional Committees: The Impact of 'Environmental' Factors," *American Political Science Review* 72 (June 1978), pp. 548–74.
35. Quoted in Steven V. Roberts, "A Most Important Man on Capitol Hill," *New York Times Magazine* September 22, 1985, p. 48.
36. Martin Linsky, *Impact: How the Press Affects Federal Policymaking* (New York: W.W. Norton, 1986), p. 94.
37. See Cook, "Press Secretaries and Media Strategies," table 4, pp. 10–11.
38. Katharine Winton Evans, "The News Maker: A Capitol Hill Pro Reveals His Secrets," *Washington Journalism Review* 3 (June 1981), pp. 28–33 at p. 32.
39. Ibid., p. 33.
40. Michael Barone and Grant Ujifusa, *Almanac of American Politics, 1986* (Washington D.C.: National Journal, 1985), p. 444.
41. *The New York Times,* May 6, 1987, p. B10.
42. See Paul West, "Competing for Coverage in Congress," *Washington Journalism Review* 8 (June 1986), pp. 37–40 at 40; Susan F. Rasky, "Of Aides and Ink," *The New York Times,* February 27, 1986, p. B10.
43. Matthews, *U.S. Senators,* chapter 9.
44. Nelson W. Polsby, "Two Strategies of Influence: Choosing a Majority Leader, 1962," in *New Perspectives on the House of Representatives,* ed. Robert Peabody and Nelson W. Polsby (Chicago: Rand McNally, 1963), pp. 237–70.
45. Quoted in Burdett A. Loomis, "The 'New Style' Congressional Career and Legislative Policymaking," paper presented at the annual meeting of the American Political Science Association, New Orleans, August 1985.
46. Cook, "Show Horses in House Elections," table 4.
47. Cook, "Marketing the Members," p. 25; fifteen of the forty interviewed mentioned the link of media strategy and legislative strategy.
48. Hess, *Ultimate Insiders,* p. 78.

49. See Charles L. Clapp, *The Congressman: His Work As He Sees It* (New York: Anchor Books, 1964), pp. 438–43.

50. Dewhirst, "Patterns of Interaction," p. 146.

51. Bagdikian is quoted by Robert O. Blanchard in "The Variety of Correspondents," in his *Congress and the News Media*, p. 173.

52. Philip Tichenor, George Donohue, and Clarice Olien, *Community Conflict and the Press* (Beverly Hills, Calif.: Sage Publications, 1980).

53. See Edie N. Goldenberg and Michael W. Traugott, *Campaigning for Congress* (Washington, D.C.: CQ Press, 1984), table 8–5; and Peter Clarke and Susan Evans, *Covering Campaigns: Journalism in Congressional Elections* (Stanford, Calif.: Stanford University Press, 1983).

54. *Farmville (Va.) Herald,* October 29, 1986, ed-op page. My thanks to Betty Dunkum for bringing this editorial to my attention.

55. See Michael J. Robinson's discussion of the press releases of his pseudonymous *Congressman Press* in his "Three Faces of Congressional Media," in *The New Congress,* ed. Thomas Mann and Norman J. Ornstein (Washington, D.C.: American Enterprise Institute for Public Policy Research, 1981), p. 80.

56. Ben H. Bagdikian, "Congress and the Press: Partners in Propaganda," in Blanchard, ed., *Congress and the News Media*, p. 390.

57. These are 1985 figures taken from *Broadcasting/Cablecasting Yearbook, 1986* (Washington, D.C.: Broadcasting Publications, Inc., 1985).

58. James E. Campbell, John R. Alford, and Keith Henry, "Television Markets and Congressional Elections," *Legislative Studies Quarterly* 9 (November 1984), pp. 665–78.

59. Jon R. Bond, "Dimensions of District Attention Over Time," *American Journal of Political Science* 29 (May 1985), p. 337; Goldenberg and Traugott, *Campaigning for Congress,* p. 117.

60. Cook, "Press Secretaries and Media Strategies," tables 1 and 3.

61. Richard F. Fenno, Jr., *The United States Senate: A Bicameral Perspective* (Washington, D.C.: American Enterprise Institute for Public Policy Research, 1982).

62. *Congressional Quarterly Weekly Report,* December 14, 1985, p. 2626.

63. Among others, see Doris A. Graber, *Processing the News* (New York: Longman, 1984) and John Robinson and Mark Levy, *The Main Source: Learning from Television News* (Beverly Hills, Calif.: Sage Publications, 1986).

64. *Congressional Quarterly Weekly Report,* October 19, 1985, p. 2109. For earlier figures, see Stephen E. Frantzich, *Write Your Congressman* (New York: Praeger Publishers, 1986), pp. 34–37.

65. Ibid., *Congressional Quarterly Weekly Report* (October 19, 1985) p. 2109.

66. Bond, "Dimensions of District Attention," p. 342; and Cook, "Press Secretaries and Media Strategies."

67. A key rebuttal to the authors cited at the beginning of this article is Hess, *Ultimate Insiders,* epilogue.

68. Goldenberg and Traugott, *Campaigning for Congress,* tables 8–4 and 8–5.

69. See Lyn Ragsdale, "Do Voters Matter? Democracy in Congressional Elections," in Chapter 2 of this volume.

70. A good overview of House leaders' strategies toward the media is Alan Ehrenhalt, "Media, Power Shifts Dominate O'Neill's House," *Congressional Quarterly Weekly Report,* September 13, 1986, pp. 2131–38.

71. See, e.g., Barbara Sinclair, *Majority Leadership in the U.S. House* (Baltimore, Md.: Johns Hopkins University Press, 1983).

72. *The New York Times,* January 23, 1987, p. A1.

73. Perhaps it never was. The only published article with empirical evidence of such a divergence is Payne, "Show Horses and Work Horses," which is beset by many methodological oversights; I have discussed its failings in detail in Cook, "Show Horses in House Elections," footnote 1.

74. Kernell, *Going Public.*

75. Kay Lehman Schlozman and John T. Tierney, *Organized Interests and American Democracy* (New York: Harper & Row, 1986), pp. 178–84.

76. See G. Ray Funkhouser, "The Issues of the Sixties: An Exploratory Study in the Dynamics of Public Opinion," *Public Opinion Quarterly* 37 (Spring 1973), pp. 62–75.

77. See, e.g., Herbert J. Gans, *Deciding What's News* (New York: Pantheon Books, 1979), chapter 7; and Robert Darnton, "Telling Stories and Making News," *Daedalus* 104 (Spring 1975), pp. 175–93.

78. Gans, *Deciding What's News,* pp. 68–69.

79. This point is made in many places; see, e.g., W. Lance Bennett, *News: The Politics of Illusion* (New York: Longman, 1984).

CHAPTER 5

Individual Outputs: Legislators and Constituency Service

John R. Johannes

Except for the falling snow, everything seemed normal. But when Mrs. Rosehill turned on the heating element of her oven, something popped; the lights went out; the electricity was off. A quick check of the fuse box produced no results. She called the town's only electrician, but there was no answer. The electric company representative said that their serviceman detected no problem in the area, and she could see lights on in her neighbor's house. Frantic, she called several friends, but none could give any better advice than to say that she should call an electrician. She did, again and again, but there was no answer. Finally, in desperation she searched the phone book for some government agency to call; her eyes fell on the number of her congressman. A call to one of his state offices in a nearby city reached a staff assistant. After listening to Mrs. Rosehill's plight, the aide called an electrician and arranged for him to travel the forty miles to the town in which Mrs. Rosehill lived. Within hours the electricity was back on.[1]

Episodes such as this usually do not come to mind when one thinks of what senators and representatives do, and indeed this story is a bit exceptional; but activities geared toward taking care of constituents are more common than one would imagine. Although the glamour and excitement of being a member of Congress focus on the things Congress does when acting as a collection of representatives (hearings, debates, and voting in the House and Senate chambers), much of the day-to-day business of legislative life involves individual activities: offering amendments to bills, adding one's viewpoints to committee reports, meeting visitors, and issuing press releases. Of concern here is yet another individualized activity: the filling of constituents' requests and the resolution of their complaints and problems. Each legislator has become, in Luther Patrick's description:

> An expanded messenger boy, an employment agency, getter-out of the Navy, Army, and Marines, a wardheeler, troubleshooter, law explainer, bill finder, issue translator, resolution interpreter, controversy-oil pourer, glad hand extender, business promoter, veterans affairs adjuster, ex-serviceman's champion, watchdog for the underdog, sympathizer for the upperdog, kisser of

babies, recoverer of lost baggage, soberer of delegates, adjuster for traffic vio-
lations and voters straying into Washington and into the toils of the law,
binder-up of broken hearts, financial wet nurse, a good samaritan, contributor
to good causes—there are so many causes—cornerstone layer, public building
and bridge dedicator, and ship christener.[2]

Constituency service, in its myriad forms, is big business; accordingly, it
is not without controversy. Is it equitable, or do some people receive more
than they deserve? To what extent does an individual member's taking care
of constituents interfere with or contribute to his or her participation in the
legislative and oversight functions of the legislature? What effects are there
on executive agencies? Can favors for constituents be parlayed into votes
every other November? And if so, what impact does that have on the representative function? After a brief discussion of the types of things legislators
do for constituents, and why and how they do them, this chapter examines
the consequences of constituency service—for citizens, for members' political
lives, and for Congress's legislative functions.

WHAT THEY DO AND WHY THEY DO IT

Constituency service is a broad term that includes at least three categories of activities. The first is *federal projects assistance*—work which focuses on
helping state and local government units obtain federal funds for pollution
control, highway construction and renovation, school systems, housing,
demonstration projects, and a variety of other purposes. Federal projects fall
into two categories: *(a)* those written into law, which identifies specific projects or establishes concrete formulae by which administrators make grants to
state and local governments, and *(b)* those over which administrators have
discretion as to where federal funds will go and how much will be spent.

The second category of constituency service includes *constituent requests*
for favors or information. Senators and representatives provide constituents
with American flags that have flown (if for only a few seconds) over the
Capitol, obtain special White House tour tickets, mail government documents
to students writing research papers, and agree to give speeches to local
organizations.

The final group constitutes *casework*, which refers to assisting constituents with problems they are having with the government bureaucracy. Most
of these services concern the federal government. Examples include helping
constituents to file claims for black lung insurance benefits or straightening
out problems with the Social Security Administration, securing and maintaining veterans benefits, supporting applications for small business loans,
obtaining transfers or early discharges for military personnel, appointing
high school seniors to military academies, finding out what happened to a
constituent's tax refund, and assisting citizens and aliens to obtain passports
and visas. No government agency is beyond the reach of a congressional
office. Occasionally, legislators and their staffs become involved with state

and local matters or, less often, purely private activities (such as intervening on behalf of a constituent with an automobile dealer or trying to change the college roommate of someone's daughter). The variety of these particularistic benefits and services is endless. Wherever and whenever people are in need the offices of U.S. senators and representatives are always willing, and usually able, to come to their aid.

According to national public opinion surveys for 1978–84, about 15 percent of American adults at some time have contacted their elected officials in Washington, including roughly 6 percent who wished to express their opinions.[3] Obviously, these categories overlap. Since congressional offices generally do not keep accurate records on all contacts, it is impossible to translate these figures precisely into the number of inquiries and requests received by congressional offices. One survey of House offices in 1982, however, found that representatives reported a weekly average of 354 contacts (including letters and cards) by constituents to express their views on public issues, 91 "cases" (constituents seeking help with their problems), and slightly over 10 requests by local or state governments seeking help on federal projects.[4] Another survey in 1986 found that the total had risen to an average of 1,153, of which slightly over 200 dealt with casework.[5]

If the function of Congress is to make laws and oversee the executive branch, why are legislators so involved in serving constituents' needs? The obvious answer was furnished by a former senator who exclaimed that "No one will survive in Congress without good constituent service; it's that simple." Actually, the matter is not quite so simple, as explained below; but there is no doubt that a desire to curry favor with constituents is a major motive force. A 1977–78 survey found that four-fifths of senators and representatives and 85 percent of their staffs agreed or agreed strongly that "citizens who receive help from their congressmen are likely to vote for them at the next election"; only one in ten members and 3 percent of their aides disagreed.

In part, these legislators are responding to clear-cut citizen expectations that have evolved in recent times. In 1977, the House Commission on Administrative Review asked a sample of over 1,500 Americans what kinds of things were most important for their representatives to do. The most common answer to this open-ended question, given by 37 percent of the respondents, fell into the category described as "works to solve problems in the district, helps the people respond to issues, needs, of our areas." To another question, 70 percent agreed that it was "very important" for legislators to provide "people in their districts with a direct line to the federal government," and another 21 percent saw this as "fairly important."[6] Interestingly, constituents firmly believe that their representatives would be of service if asked. In a series of national opinion surveys, the University of Michigan's Center for Political Studies asked, "If you had a problem that your Representative could do something about, do you think (he/she) would be very helpful, somewhat helpful, or not very helpful to you?" Two-thirds to three-fourths of those responding said their legislators would be "very helpful" or "somewhat helpful." Only one in ten replied "not very helpful."

Members of Congress understand these expectations. A survey of 146 incumbents by the House Commission on Administrative Review asked, "What would you say are the major kinds of jobs, duties, or functions that you feel you are expected to perform?" Four out of five answered in terms of the constituency service role; the number of responses was second only to those citing the legislative function.[7] Beyond meeting the expectations of their constituents (and thus winning favor or at least avoiding anger), legislators engage in constituency service for other reasons. Many are driven by humanitarian motives and the knowledge that most constituents cannot fight the bureaucracy alone: "If congressmen don't do it," said a former senator, "nobody will; there's a lot of people out there who need help." One aide said that his boss "is a populist and has a soft spot in his heart for a schmuck getting screwed."

Antipathy toward the bureaucracy sometimes triggers constituency service activity, while other members see it as a way to inject personal attention into an otherwise impersonal government: it "instills confidence," said a one-time representative. "It has to be done to keep the country's confidence in government. People need that connection. The congressman is the ball bearing that keeps things moving. He's the last link people have with their government." For a handful of legislators, dealing with constituent problems simply makes them feel good. "My greatest satisfaction," proclaimed one representative, "comes from helping others." Still others talk in terms of using constituent complaints to keep an eye on the government bureaucracy, while a few see constituency work as "a link, a fragile bridge, back to the real world." Virtually everyone considers constituency service work as part and parcel of a legislator's job. Thus, no one reason explains the tremendous amount of time and energy devoted to constituents. To quote one staffer, "You can't separate out or isolate any motives; it's a piece of whole cloth."

What is clear is that senators and especially representatives strive mightily to let constituents know that they stand ready and willing to be of assistance. By means of newsletters, mobile offices, town meetings, staff travel throughout the district, statements made at public appearances, radio announcements, matchbook covers, and even billboards, incumbents aggressively advertise their services, and the energy with which they do so seems to have increased greatly during the past twenty years. In 1977, for example, 84 percent of House offices said they solicited constituent casework requests, using an average of 2.5 of the above devices to do so; five years later, 97 percent admitted to "hustling" cases by means of an average of 3.6 of the above techniques.

DEALING WITH CONSTITUENTS

Senators and representatives have little time to devote to constituent affairs, as is readily apparent from Table 5–1. Another survey of thirty-one senators and ninety-eight representatives in 1977 found that the median amount of Capitol Hill time spent dealing with constituents' problems was

TABLE 5–1   Allocation of Representatives' Time

	Average Time	
Location	Hours	Minutes
In the House chamber	2:53	
Committee/subcommittee	1:24	
Hearings		26
Business		09
Markup		42
Other		05
Representative's office	3:19	
With constituents		17
With organized groups		09
With others		20
With personal and committee staff		53
With other members		05
Answering mail and signing letters		46
Preparing legislation and speeches		12
Reading		11
On telephone		26
Other Washington locations	2:02	
With constituents in Capitol		9
At events		33
With leadership		3
With other members		11
With informal groups		8
In party meetings		5
Personal time		28
Other		25
Other activities	1:40	
Total day	11:18	

SOURCE: U.S. Congress, House Commission on Administrative Review, *Administrative Reorganization and Legislative Management*, 95th Cong., 1st sess., 1977. H. Doc. 95–232. Vol. 1, pp. 17–19.

approximately three hours per week, with 24 percent of the representatives and 8 percent of the senators spending over eight hours on these tasks.[8] The median figure for 163 representatives studied in 1982 was four hours. Forty percent spent two hours per week or less, while only 18 percent devoted more than eight hours to assisting needy constituents. When members visit their states and districts, much of their time is taken up addressing or conversing with constituents. Inevitably, during or after such occasions, members and their aides are approached—some would say besieged—by people with favors to ask and complaints to make. Still, the members themselves need not devote much of their own time to the details of these problems because they enjoy ample staff assistance. Each member of the House may employ up to eighteen full-time aides; and Senate staffs, which are determined largely by state population, ranged in 1986 between seventeen (for, now retired, Wisconsin Senator William Proxmire) to sixty-seven (Senator Pete Wilson of California). Especially in the House, many of these aides deal regularly with constituent requests.

The increased congressional workload has led to two developments in staffing. First, constituency service operations have been moved from Washington to state and district offices, where approximately three-fourths of all individual casework and one-third of federal projects work is handled. One of every four staffers now works in a home office, bringing them closer to the constituents who need help and closer to the regional and area offices of the departments and agencies with which the citizens are having problems. To supplement these aides, senators and representatives hire college students as interns in their home offices; in fact, interns may outnumber paid staff two-to-one. Second, especially in Washington but to a growing extent at home, staffs are becoming more specialized. The dominant staffing pattern separates administrative, legislative, and press aides from those specializing in constituency matters. Among the latter group, it is common (especially in the Senate) to assign some staff to assist state and local governments with federal projects applications, others to deal with individual constituent casework, and still others to answer correspondence. In 1982, for example, all but thirteen members of the House had at least one person in the district doing casework, with the average representative having three district staff assistants doing casework on a full-time basis. In Washington, on the other hand, only 60 percent of the offices had someone regularly (not necessarily exclusively) handling casework. In the Senate, where staffs are much larger, specialization is far greater. Their Washington offices might include a half dozen aides who handle constituent problems, with another eight to ten in the home state offices. These project workers and caseworkers themselves are often specialized, with one handling social security and medicare, another military and veterans' problems, and so on.

However many there may be, and however they are organized, the job of these staffers is to answer constituents' questions and to solve their problems as courteously and rapidly as possible, and to encourage the constituents to think that their senators or representatives personally were responsible for whatever favorable result ensued. Of course, when the news is bad, congressional offices usually blame the law or the bureaucracy, often letting executive agencies pass along the negative decisions. For simple matters, such as information on how the member voted, the phone number of the local Social Security Administration office, or requests to supply government documents, responses are almost immediate. For complicated cases, such as renegotiating a constituent's disability claim, reinstating a family in its public housing unit, or straightening out a visa problem with the Immigration and Naturalization Service, matters take time and, often, skill. Calls to the local Veterans' Administration office might have to be rerouted to the regional office and then to Washington, and often a high-level decision may have been made, and must now be overturned, before the staffer can determine how to best correct an original decision. One student intern, working in a Wisconsin senator's home office, reported that he talked with twenty-three different officials in the State Department on one case: "In the end I found myself talking to the same person I started with, and my question was finally answered a week later." Since this young man reported that his office received between fifteen and forty letters a day and that the phone rang on an average of once every two minutes, it is clear that staff members need good doses of patience to go along with tenacity, resourcefulness, and empathy.

Excessive empathy and sympathy, however, can be counterproductive. Many constituency service staff remarked on the danger of getting too involved with constituents: "Sometimes I just bleed for these people who need help," said one. On the other hand, most casework and project work, not to mention the daily handling of the phone lines, is routine, leading to a real danger. "I'm bored out of my skull," complained more than one aide. Whether boredom, burnout, or disgruntlement is at work, turnover among staff is high. The frustration that the Washington office does not always appreciate the work being done for constituents in the home office—indeed, getting problems out of the Washington office is precisely why many legislators locate constituency service activities in their state and district offices—exacts a toll on staff morale and performance.

THE RESULTS: IS JUSTICE SERVED?

Constituency service work presumably has three targets: to help constituents obtain what they need, want, and deserve, and to redress their grievances; to assist legislators in their policymaking and oversight roles and thereby improve the functioning of government; and to win the trust and gratitude of constituents, especially on election day. There is little doubt that congressional intervention with the bureaucracy works. Surveys of 14 members of Congress and 254 of their staff aides in 1977–78 revealed that in an estimated four out of every ten cases of intervention with the bureaucracy on behalf of constituents, some substantive change in favor of the constituents was made in the original agency decision. A 1982 study of 112 staffers put the figure at 31 percent. In both years, the consensus was that if speeding up a decision were included in the definition of "success," the success rate would more than double. Indeed, from the perspective of a constituent who finds bureaucratic red tape trying, the primary virtue of congressional intervention may simply be getting *some* sort of decision and getting it more quickly than he or she otherwise would. No wonder that in survey after survey, 50 percent or more of those interviewed claim to be very satisfied with the efforts their senators and representatives made on their behalf and another 25 percent say they were at least somewhat satisfied.[9]

To say that congressional intervention yields favorable or quicker results is not to imply that government agencies do, can, or are inclined to respond favorably just because some legislator has asked a favor and that, absent his or her intervention, justice would not be done. The process, for the most part, is conducted aboveboard and quite legitimately. When a House or Senate office brings a constituent problem to the attention of an agency, it does so usually in a relatively neutral, businesslike fashion. Seldom are undeserved favors sought, and there is rarely an attempt to dictate the results. Rather, as one caseworker described the process, "We don't ask them to bend or break rules or violate laws, but we do ask them to go back and take another look; and if, under the rules and regs, they can do it, we ask them to reconsider the case."

Success is most likely to come when the congressional staffer is seeking information, documents, or decisions that should have been supplied directly to the constituent at the outset, and such instances constitute a large portion of requests. In complex cases, when an agency has ruled against a constituent, favorable decisions typically occur when the staff person supplies new and relevant information to the agency. Just getting an agency administrator to take a second look at a difficult case may sometimes bring a different decision.

In anonymous 1978 questionnaires and interviews, 200 agency officials replied that virtually never were they asked to break a law on behalf of a constituent; 83 percent said they never were asked to violate an agency rule or regulation. Approximately one out of four, however, said that they had been asked by congressional offices to bend or stretch a rule or make an exception for someone. Interestingly, of 161 bureaucrats responding to the question, only two admitted to having broken a law and three to violating an agency rule or regulation when asked to do so. Fourteen said they had stretched regulations, and another fifteen acknowledged bending the rules. Were these due to congressional pressure? Not according to the respondents. Most said that there were mitigating circumstances, that they were empowered with discretionary authority, or that justice demanded an exception. As one administrator explained, "Usually our problems are interpretations and management discretion. We try to live within the spirit, if not the rigidity, of the law." Only in rare instances did either legislators, their staffs, or agency officials admit that some decisions were made for "political" reasons.

Congressional pressure on behalf of aggrieved constituents at higher levels in the bureaucracy is not unknown, but it is not common. Instances of pressure being successfully applied is more rare. Although 54 percent of agency officials said that decisions made at their levels were overturned at least once by superiors as the result of pressure from Congress, only 6 percent thought that this happened as often as once every ten cases. Even when senators and representatives become personally involved, the substantive results are little different. Only 4 percent of the administrators believed that intervention by members of Congress themselves brought about different results; over 50 percent said that such action would have no effect at all, not even on how fast a case was handled. Said one, "No, just because the congressman calls doesn't mean we can move any faster in reviewing a case than we do when the caseworker calls. It just can't be done." On the other hand, both staffers and agency respondents seemed to believe that additional care and speed would result if the Speaker of the House or the chair of the Appropriations Committee had called.

None of this is to claim that serving constituency requests or working for pork-barrel projects has no undertone of political maneuvering. The relationship between the legislative and executive branches in Washington—and for that matter the nexus between congressional and executive branch offices throughout the country—is fundamentally a political enterprise, with both sides well aware of the consequences. But there is surprisingly little room for maneuvering. For the most part, laws and regulations dictate what can and cannot be done, office routines determine who handles which congressional inquiries and in what fashion, and a strong constituency service ethic pervades both congressional and executive branch offices.

Legislators themselves may be more likely to take a direct interest for VIPs, and their staffs may work a bit quicker, but there seems to be precious little substantive favoritism for key constituents. One House aide thought that "We're probably too squeamish on the ethics of the situation." Another said that her boss might be tempted to finagle a bit for certain constituents but she would not let him. A former chair of a powerful House committee put it this way: "Heck, if some bureaucrat knows the situation and has all the facts, and if he changed a decision just because of a phone call from me, I'd want him fired." Bolstering this sense of ethics is the fear that if pressure were applied for any one constituent's request the word might get out, and that could bring a flood of embarrassing new requests, and, more devastating, negative publicity would result. On the other hand, when a House or Senate aide believes that he or she is correct and that some agency has unjustly rejected a constituent's claim, the staffer feels little compunction in getting the boss (the representative or senator) to take the case to higher administrative levels. Nearly one-half of the staffers surveyed said that they had taken cases as high as a departmental secretary or agency administrator, and over four-fifths asserted they had gone as far as the White House.

Justice can be subverted in a peculiar and almost innocent way. The rule of thumb in most congressional offices is to accept all constituent requests or complaints as having merit. Many cases, however, lack validity. Constituents are not above slanting their stories, telling only part of the truth, and even lying outright. Staffs estimate that about one in five cases lacks any merit whatsoever, either because the constituent is ignorant, because normal channels of bureaucratic redress have not been explored, or because the cases (as well as many of the daily phone calls and letters) are, simply, "crackpot." Legislators have been petitioned to see to it that the college grades of constituents' children are raised. Constituents claiming disability pensions have been found to be perfectly healthy, and on more than one occasion an impassioned plea for justice from an allegedly innocent person serving time in prison has been found to be totally fraudulent. There is little danger that members or their staffs would intentionally force such a case. More worrisome is the possibility that a vigorous request ignorantly forwarded would accidentally or deliberately be granted where none is warranted.

The system works well and does redress grievances, for the most part equitably, but it is not flawless. Congressional intervention actually can slow down the process of administration and adjudication, diverting people's files and causing them to pass through many more hands than they need to, if constituents fail to bring their problems first to the responsible executive branch agencies or, having done so, fail to give them adequate time to resolve difficulties. Bureaucratic resentment against excessively intrusive congressional offices is not unknown, occasionally leading to delays or even "revenge" (for example, by an army sergeant against an enlisted man whose parents or spouse have invoked a legislator's assistance on his behalf). Also, legislators are keenly aware that federal grants and projects allocated to one city or town cannot go to another; the aphorism that a favor done for one in ten petitioners creates one ingrate and nine enemies frequently is true.

CONSTITUENCY SERVICE AND GOVERNING

A standard criticism leveled against constituency service activity is that it interferes with more important work that congressional offices should be doing (e.g., preparing and enacting new laws and keeping watch over the various departments and agencies) and wastes valuable staff resources. As one member said, handling constituent problems is a "misuse of a congressman's time."[10] Such charges have a certain validity. Since in Washington, as in Peoria or Tucson, there are only twenty-four hours in a day, time spent with constituents or handling their requests and problems inevitably is time not spent on other matters.

The first eight activities in Table 5–2 present members' perceptions of how the importance of various legislative activities compares to the time they claim to spend on them. Clearly, there seem to be major discrepancies. Are they due to constituency demands? When the Commission on Administrative Review in 1977 asked these representatives about the "major differences between how you actually spend your time and what you would ideally like to do as a member of Congress," 50 percent cited constituent demands of various sorts as the obstacle.[11] Although real problems exist, the picture may not be quite so bleak.

First, Commission data yielded mixed responses depending on how the question was phrased. Asked about the obstacles which stand in the way of the House doing a better job of performing tasks identified by members as

TABLE 5–2 Comparison of Importance of and Time Spent on Activities of Members of the House of Representatives (percentage of members giving indicated answer)

Activity	How Important Is Activity to Member		How Much Time Does Member Spend on Activity	
	Very Important	Slightly/Not Important	Great Deal of Time	Little/No Time
Work in subcommittee to develop legislation	82%	3%	60%	11%
Study and do research on proposed legislation	73	4	25	30
Work in full committee to develop legislation	71	4	46	17
Debate and vote on legislation on the floor	64	8	30	24
Work in committee or subcommittee on oversight	56	11	16	48
Work informally with other members to build support for legislation	55	6	22	20
Keep track of how agencies administer laws	53	10	9	56
Take time to gain firsthand knowledge of foreign affairs	44	23	16	63
Get back to district to keep in touch with constituents	74	3	67	5
Help people in district who have problems with government	58	14	35	32
Take time to explain to citizens what government is doing	53	10	32	20
Make sure district gets fair share of government money	44	20	24	32
Meet personally with constituents in Washington	35	27	13	44
Send newsletter to district	35	28	10	53
Give speeches to groups in district about legislation	32	26	25	22
Stay in touch with local government officials in district	26	27	16	40

Note: On any given question, up to 5 percent answered "not sure." Those answering "fairly important" or "sometimes" are omitted.
N = 145 or 146.

SOURCE: U.S. Congress, House Commission on Administrative Review, *Final Report*. 95th Cong., 1st sess., 1977. H. Doc. 95–272. Vol. 2, *Survey Materials*, pp. 877–82.

being important, only one in five representatives cited "demands of the district."[12] Second, as the remaining activities stated in Table 5–2 indicate, members think that constituency matters are important and that they do not have enough time to devote to them, either. Third, when members complain about the burdens imposed by their districts, much of what they find tiresome is activity involved in ceremonial functions and stumping for reelection; the approximately twenty-six trips that the average member takes to his or her district each year are not primarily for constituency service (although much service activity is carried out). Fourth, relatively little of the "interference" with their own personal time occurs in Washington; clever members avoid spending much time with visiting constituents (see Table 5–1). Fifth, staffs handle most of the work, both in Washington and back home. As one member pointed out, "There's a difference between what I do and what my staff does."

Although it is true that as much as 40 percent of the entire staff's daily activity must be diverted from legislative and oversight work to casework for constituents, the fact is that Congress created large personal office staffs precisely so both legislative and constituency activities could be handled expeditiously. And most legislative work is handled by committee and subcommittee aides who seldom become enmeshed in constituent affairs. One-fourth of House members and 15 percent of their administrative assistants interviewed by the Commission on Administrative Review thought that the 18-person limit on staffs constituted a problem, but a greater number of administrative assistants thought they were adequately staffed for legislative research activity than believed they needed additional help.[13]

Perhaps time spent with constituents and on their problems is useful; not only does casework keep legislators in touch with the folks back home, but there may be some policy payoffs as well. Given hectic schedules and massive work loads, any feedback senators and representatives receive about public policy is potentially useful. In principle, there may be no better way to learn about how well government programs are working than to listen to constituents complain. As one member said, "If we didn't have cases and projects, we'd have more time for legislation; but we wouldn't know how well the legislation works." A good many members and their staffs try to use constituency service for this purpose. And yet rarely is an opinion poll taken either formally or systematically (fewer than two-fifths of House offices in 1982 reported using computers to track cases) but, rather, aides keep a watchful eye on casework for hints of problems: "It's easy to recognize a pattern," said one staffer. Another volunteered: "Yes, I'm always looking. That's what casework is all about."

When problems or needs are identified from constituent requests or complaints, staff take them to the legislative assistants or, if their office structure allows, to the members themselves. In 30 percent of the offices studied in 1982, for example, staffs reported that the representatives regularly discussed constituent cases with staff members for legislative or oversight purposes, and another 50 percent claimed they did so at least occasionally. Eighteen percent noted that their bosses regularly brought up constituent cases at hearings, meetings, or on the floor of the House, and approximately 50 percent indicated that this occurred occasionally. Fifty percent said that their representatives at least occasionally examined statistical breakdowns of cases to see what patterns were developing. These activities can lead to legislation; for example, a constituent's difficulties in obtaining a liver transplant led to legislation to establish a computerized national network to match organ donors with patients who needed them.[14] In most instances, however, constituency service tends to generate ideas for remedial programs rather than for pathbreaking legislation on new topics. Occasionally, casework has led to hearings at which agency representatives were called on the carpet for poor performance or to committee staff investigations. For example, a student intern recently reported on a constituent who complained that a major credit card company was illegally receiving information on cardholders' bank accounts. The intern contacted the chief counsel of a Senate committee, who moved into action on the case. Finally, some members have decided, or changed, their votes on pending legislation as a result of constituents' entreaties and problems.

To be sure, the utility of constituency service for generating legislative or oversight activities should not be exaggerated. Since so much of what comes to congressional offices from constituents is routine (e.g., inquiries on late social security checks), of little or no genuine consequence (requests for a document or White House tour tickets), or invalid (a false claim for government benefits), the number of opportunities for policy review is limited. Moreover, the path between a constituent problem and a remedial action often is long and tortuous. A staff member discovering a problem in a constituent's letter or phone call must interest his or her superior, who in turn needs to convince the senator or representative to take action; the member must then stimulate interest on the part of an appropriate committee or subcommittee chair or staff; and a decision has to be made to pursue the issue formally. Since not all offices are interested in the policy ramifications of cases, since staffing patterns sometimes make it hard for a caseworker to interest legislative assistants in particular issues raised by cases, and since committees have their own agendas, frequently nothing happens. What is remarkable, then, is that constituency service has any effect on policy, not that its effect is limited. A 1977–78 survey of 350 members and staff found that approximately 70 percent believed casework was very or at least somewhat effective in generating ideas and incentives for legislation or oversight.

There is a downside here as well. More than one observer has pointed out that handling constituent problems on a case-by-case basis not only may waste time, but it may provide an excuse to avoid more systematic and rigorous oversight of bureaucratic activity.[15] This theory may seem plausible, but it implies a zero-sum game that rarely exists. Constituency service is a task handled by members' personal offices; formal oversight is a committee function. Absent the pressure and information about government problems generated by casework, the likelihood that committees and subcommittees would do as much as or more than they now are doing is not certain.

A far more serious complaint comes from some executive branch critics: Congressional intervention disrupts the functioning of the agencies and departments and wastes the bureaucracy's time. In 1978, 216 executive branch officials were asked to respond to the statement that "congressional inquiries on behalf of constituents disrupt the efficient running of the executive agency or office and detract from more important things agency employees should be doing." Surprisingly, only 22 percent of those responding agreed; 63 percent disagreed, as did two-thirds of legislators and their staffs. Asked directly if casework presented a problem, there were two negative replies for every one in the affirmative. Most of the negative comments focused on diversion of manpower and disruption of routines. One relatively high-ranking official explained: "For staff, it is disruptive. Here are staff people who are very busy with stacks of very important things to do; then in comes this 'congressional' that forces them to set all this work aside to deal with something that doesn't seem as important." Two other objections were voiced. First, serious constituency service work may create disrespect for the normal administrative process; citizens may neglect to pursue their complaints through normal channels because they have learned that the only way to "win" is by going to their representatives. Second, congressional intervention damages morale within agencies and undercuts legitimate authority. Nonetheless, administrators by and large took a positive view of the process. Roughly two-thirds of the administrators responded that dealing with congressional inquiries for constituents helped to point out problems and weaknesses in programs and operations, and another 16 percent said that was the case at least occasionally. Only about one-sixth flatly answered in the negative. Most of the negative remarks came from lower-level officials, while higher-ranking administrators took a far more sanguine view, claiming that congressional casework was a "fail-safe" mechanism and often generated the needed "heat" to get the bureaucracy moving to do a better job in the future. As one administrator explained: "When we start getting a series of complaints about the same problem, of course we take a good look at it. And we make sure that the next time the same situation develops, our people handle it the right way." On occasion rules and regulations are rewritten or remedial legislation is proposed.

Constituency service, then, has utility for improving public policy and the delivery of services. As suggested above, however, the process of converting citizen complaints into systematic congressional committee or subcommittee action is long and complicated. Perhaps the greatest roadblock to a more effective use of constituency service for policy purposes is that the primary payoff is not perceived as general policy improvement but rather as helping individual constituents with concrete here-and-now problems. Still, one should not dismiss the policy consequences of this individualized activity out-of-hand just because problems are not always solved or laws and rules not always changed. Constituency service does help to improve government policies and operations; this citizen channel for redress of grievances is part of the overall policymaking picture.

THE ELECTORAL PAYOFF

As mentioned at the outset, participants in the process overwhelmingly believe that constituency service is one of the best ways to build a safe electoral base, at least in the House. Said an aide to Andrew Maguire, a liberal New Jersey Democrat reputed for holding his seat in the seventies by means of voluminous and excellent constituency service, "Help one person and you not only have his vote, but that of his friends, family, and neighbors as well."[16] Most textbooks agree, adopting the view that by successfully "serving" one's constituents, a legislator can foster a sense of gratitude, trust, and loyalty among them. It then becomes easy to ward off strong challengers and pile up votes, which allows the member considerable policy leeway in Washington.[17] Although taking positions on tough issues invariably angers some portion of one's electoral constituency, "pork barreling and casework are pure profit."[18] Considerable evidence exists to support this view. Polls show, for example, that people are more likely to comment favorably on what a member of Congress has done for his or her district than on particular votes he or she has cast. Of citizens responding to a poll in 1977 who had requested some sort of help from their representatives, three-quarters gave them "excellent" or "pretty good" ratings, a finding replicated in virtually every poll taken on the subject. Asked point-blank whether they would vote for their incumbent members of the House more because of what they can do for their communities or more because of their stands on national issues, nearly one-half cited the local benefits compared to one-in-three mentioning issues.[19]

Not satisfied with this evidence, political scientists have sought to subject the "constituency service" hypothesis to rigorous scrutiny, but their efforts have met with mixed results. Several roadblocks stand in the way. The most important concerns the sort of data that should be used. If public opinion surveys are used, one must place faith in the respondents' abilities, on the spot, to deliver coherent responses to what are at times nebulous questions (e.g., "What do you like or dislike about your representative?") or to recall accurately contacts with incumbents ("Have you ever asked your representative for a favor or information?"; "Have you ever received mail from him?"). Statistical analyses are then employed to determine whether, controlling for factors that might affect both people's votes and their propensity to contact their legislators in the first place (ideology, partisanship), those who recalled contacts with or assistance from their representatives actually voted for them. For a variety of reasons, most such tests of the constituency service hypothesis have generated results that are questionable at best and grossly invalid at worst.[20]

Using aggregate data probably is more desirable, but it also is prone to difficulties. The greatest problem is deciding on, and then measuring, what is meant by constituency service. Is it the amount of mail sent to one's district, the number of trips home, the amount of time spent in the constituency,or the number of staff members stationed in district or state offices? Perhaps the volume of casework or the dollar value of federal projects undertaken in the home district is the key. Another difficulty is deciding the period of time during which to measure the supposed effect of constituency service. And there are problems of simultaneous causality. If constituency service activity pays off at the polls, the statistics would show a positive effect on votes. But suppose that comfortable electoral margins discipline members to "work" their constituencies vigorously; if that is the case, safe margins would cause a decrease in constituency service activity. A positive relationship in one direction cancels out a negative one in the other direction, leaving no statistical association between district service and electoral payoff. These problems in principle are not insurmountable, but much work remains to be done.[21] Still, to date no one has produced evidence using aggregate data that constituency service generates votes.

There is no proof, furthermore, that constituency attentiveness has any effect on warding off tough challengers.[22] The growth in the number of safe seats (usually attributed to incumbents' self-protection via constituency service) may have preceded members' adopting aggressive constituency stances. The only scientifically sound conclusion that can be reached after scrutinizing the many studies on this subject is that, despite the theory's inherent plausibility, no one has yet been able to demonstrate its validity. How can this be?

Beyond methodological problems, one must remember that, although almost all constituents who receive favors from or make contact with their representatives are satisfied with the treatment they receive, one-half or more fail to vote. Related to this factor is ingratitude: the "what have you done for me lately?" syndrome. Also, since constituents clearly expect their legislators to perform all sorts of services, they might reason that if incumbent Representative X does a lot of constituency service but is too liberal (or too conservative), and if his challenger, Ms. Y, will be just as helpful but is more in line with their policy preferences, why not vote for her? Indeed, recent research clearly points to a larger degree of ideological and issues-based voting than was previously recognized. Such policy voting, along with (*a*) partisan influences and assessments of party competence, and (*b*) retrospective voting on the basis of the health of the economy and assessments of presidential performance, would overwhelm any effects that might result from favorable impressions created by assiduous constituency service. The same Andrew Maguire whose staff assistant was quoted above on the electoral benefit of service lost his reelection bid in the 1980 election, when ideology, issues, and judgments about President Carter and his handling of the economy played a major role.

It probably is true, moreover, that most of the services delivered by members and their staffs are now so commonplace that few constituents even take note. How many people, for instance, are impressed by receiving a newsletter or printed public opinion survey from their senators? How many today find their representative's presence in their district on weekends particularly noteworthy? How many believe that getting a bit of requested information from a legislator's office is something to be grateful for? Perhaps this take-it-for-granted attitude explains why two political scientists found that when a representative mailed copies of a government-produced booklet on care for newborn infants to new parents, their assessments of him rose noticeably. Such a personalized mailing to new parents—in contrast to the usual congressional junk mail—probably does make a splash. (Interestingly, they also found, in a follow-up poll, that the effects of the mailing diminished rather rapidly.)[23]

Does this mean that senators and representatives should close up all their home offices, fire their constituency service staffs, stop doing favors, and end their biweekly junkets back to their home districts? Not at all. To cease doing what is perceived as a normal part of the job could engender negative feelings. Undoubtedly, the image the congressional member projects (and which is publicized in the constituency) is important; bringing it to ruin would be suicidal. Rather, the question to be asked is whether paying more than the normal and expected amount of attention to constituents pays off. That senators and representatives actively court constituents and solicit their requests and complaints is clear. But should they? Trying to do too much may be as dangerous as not doing enough, since there may be few sins more serious than raising expectations and then dashing them with inept or sloppy service caused by an overload of activities. Doing more than what is expected seems to yield few, if any, benefits.

What would be the consequence if members could buy or at least rent the votes of their constituents by pandering to them? Other things being equal, one would expect a diminution in policy representation. Legislators, thinking they could win reelection or scare off challengers by servicing their constituents, might feel more free to pursue policy interests of their own choosing regardless of constituency views.[24] Such a state of affairs would not signal the end of representative government since most senators and representatives represent their core constituencies fairly well in the course of things. The difference would be that members might feel less pressured into seeking certain committee assignments, might enjoy just a bit more freedom to vote against interests located in their districts, and so on. They could afford to act more like trustees (or to listen more attentively to lobbyists) and less like delegates. But unless representatives are in the business of always voting against the wishes of their constituencies or fear that the folks back home are hopelessly incapable of understanding why they voted as they did, not all that much would change.

CONCLUSION: ON BALANCE, WORTH THE EFFORT

Legislators in Washington, and those in state capitals as well, love to take care of their constituents. At least most of them do. A few members bitterly complain about the time and energy it takes to serve those who elect them, but even they bend every effort to serve. Given an inseparability of incentives and attitudes, it is hard to say what motivates them the most.

The real question remains: Is this individualized activity one that should be carried out, especially in the face of the need for responsible collective operations? The answer depends on how one weighs the various benefits against the costs. Does this form of "re-presenting" constituents to their government have any payoffs? How important is it for citizens, if they really need help in getting some benefit or righting some wrong, to believe that they can turn to their elected representatives? Scholars have not been able to demonstrate that constituency service leads to positive attitudes toward government. Does constituency service then warrant the millions of dollars spent on staff salaries, phone calls, postage, office space, and so on, and does it interfere with the collective tasks of Congress? What about the negative effects on bureaucratic performance? Can the occasional unfair advantage enjoyed by particular members of Congress be justified?

These are judgment calls, with only part of the decision resting on factual evidence. To be frank, political scientists have not been able to answer most of the empirical questions, let alone address the normative ones with certainty. What is clear is that senators and representatives, along with their staffs on the Hill and in the constituencies, are very much in the business of serving constituents' needs and wants. Like those group activities of Congress (legislation, oversight, budgeting, investigations), and like other individual outputs (media appearances, highly personalized questions during hearings, foreign trips), constituency service is one of Congress's products that carries mixed blessings. Critics can and do find serious problems, many of which are real. Governing by means of representative institutions is an imperfect mix of collective and individual arts; when advantages outweigh disadvantages, we probably should count ourselves lucky.

NOTES

1. Except for the name, the story is true. Here and elsewhere below, unattributed references are quotes from the author's interviews with members and staffs of Congress or with executive agency personnel. For elaboration on some of the material in this chapter, see John R. Johannes, *To Serve the People: Congress and Constituency Service* (Lincoln: University of Nebraska Press, 1984).
2. Quoted in Joe L. Evins, *Understanding Congress* (New York: Clarkson N. Potter, Inc., 1963), p. 18.
3. The author is indebted to the Center for Political Studies of the Inter-University Consortium for Political and Social Research at the University of Michigan for

these data, which are taken from their biannual National Election Studies. Neither the original collectors of the data nor the Consortium bear any responsibility for the use of the data here. Data from the Roper Organization reported in *Roper Reports*, 1974–1984, provide essentially the same results.

4. These data are based on responses from 172 House offices for "opinions," 250 for "cases," and 211 for federal "projects." In 1977–78, the House figures for casework were a mean of about 92 and a median of 84. For the Senate, 1982 data (from questionnaires) are very imprecise. The 28 reporting offices showed an average weekly caseload of 175, with a range of between 60 and 475. Note, however, that most large states were not in the sample. For details, see John R. Johannes and John C. McAdams, "Entrepreneur or Agent: Congressmen and the Distribution of Casework, 1977–1982," *Western Political Quarterly* 40 (September 1987), pp. 535–54. Unless otherwise noted, data reported herein are from the author's surveys. See Johannes, *To Serve the People*.

5. Linda L. Fowler and Ronald G. Shaiko, "Voices from the Constituency: A New Attentive Public," paper presented at the annual meeting of the Midwest Political Science Association, Chicago, April 8–11, 1987, table 1.

6. U.S. Congress, House Commission on Administrative Review, *Final Report*, 95th Cong., 1st sess., 1977. H. Doc. 95–272. Vol. 2, *Survey Materials*, pp. 822–24.

7. Ibid., p. 874.

8. A reminder: These data are from the author's surveys. See footnote 5 above.

9. See Johannes, *To Serve the People*, p. 207. Also, on general attitudes toward members, see the 1978 through 1986 NES/CPS surveys.

10. Quote is from the author's interviews. This same point may also be found, for example, in Donald R. Matthews, *U.S. Senators and Their World* (Chapel Hill: University of North Carolina Press, 1960), p. 225; Roger H. Davidson, David M. Kovenock, and Michael K. O'Leary, *Congress in Crisis: Politics and Congressional Reform* (Belmont, Calif.: Wadsworth Publishing, 1966), p. 77; Roger H. Davidson, "Our Two Congresses: Where Have They Been; Where Are They Going," in *Paths to Political Reform*, ed. William T. Crotty (Lexington, Mass.: D. C. Heath, 1980), p. 178; Warren Weaver, Jr., *Both Your Houses: The Truth About Congress* (New York: Praeger Publishers, 1972); Robert Klonoff, "The Congressman as a Mediator Between Citizens and Government Agencies: Problems and Prospects," *Harvard Journal on Legislation* 16 (Summer 1979), pp. 701–34; and Thomas E. Cavanagh, "The Two Arenas of Congress: Electoral and Institutional Incentives for Performance," in *The House at Work*, ed. Joseph Cooper and G. Calvin Mackenzie (Austin: University of Texas Press, 1981), pp. 56–77.

11. House Commission on Administrative Review, *Final Report*, p. 868.

12. Ibid., p. 875.

13. Ibid., pp. 1003, 1043, 1053.

14. Elizabeth Wehr, "National Health Policy Sought for Organ Transplant and Surgery," *Congressional Quarterly Weekly Report*, 42 (February 25, 1984), pp. 453–58. For other examples, see Johannes, *To Serve the People*, pp. 262, note 41, and p. 264, note 50.

15. Morris S. Ogul, *Congress Oversees the Bureaucracy: Studies in Legislative Supervision* (Pittsburgh, Penn.: University of Pittsburgh Press, 1976), p. 168; Walter Gellhorn, *When Americans Complain: Governmental Grievance Procedures* (Cambridge, Mass.: Harvard University Press, 1966), p. 82.

16. Quoted in *Congressional Quarterly Weekly Report,* July 7, 1979, p. 1352.
17. David R. Mayhew, *Congress: The Electoral Connection* (New Haven, Conn.: Yale University Press, 1974); Morris P. Fiorina, *Congress: Keystone of the Washington Establishment* (New Haven, Conn.: Yale University Press, 1977); Richard F. Fenno, Jr., *Home Style: House Members in Their Districts* (Boston: Little, Brown, 1978); Glenn R. Parker, *Homeward Bound: Explaining Changes in Congressional Behavior* (Pittsburgh, Pennsylvania: University of Pittsburgh Press, 1986).
18. Fiorina, *Congress,* p. 45.
19. Among many others, see Glenn R. Parker and Roger H. Davidson, "Why Do Americans Love Their Congressman So Much More Than Their Congress?" *Legislative Studies Quarterly* 4 (February 1979), pp. 53–61; *Public Opinion* 1 (November/December 1978), p. 22; and Parker, "Can Congress Ever Be a Popular Institution?" in Cooper and Mackenzie, eds., *The House at Work,* pp. 31–55. It should be noted that congressional offices see constituency service as a potential electoral tool. In 1982, 40 percent of House offices said they added the names of casework recipients to various "non-political" mailing lists. Although only three of 206 offices admitted to soliciting campaign assistance from service recipients, another 108 indicated that, if a constituent volunteered to help, the office would forward the person's name to the campaign committee. About one-third of the offices routinely publicized successful cases in their newsletters, and 28 percent said they regularly mentioned casework successes at election time. In both cases, another one-fifth said they did so only if constituents volunteered to let their names be used. For the most part, however, offices tend to keep constituency service and electoral activities separate.
20. To review this controversy, see the following from *American Journal of Political Science* 25 (August 1981): Diana Evans Yiannakis, "The Grateful Electorate: Casework and Congressional Elections," pp. 568–80; John R. Johannes and John C. McAdams, "The Congressional Incumbency Effect: Is It Casework, Policy Compatibility, or Something Else?" pp. 512–42; Morris P. Fiorina, "Some Problems in Studying the Effects of Resource Allocation in Congressional Elections," pp. 543–67; John C. McAdams and John R. Johannes, "Does Casework Matter: A Reply to Professor Fiorina," pp. 581–604. See also Gary C. Jacobson, "Incumbents' Advantages in the 1978 U.S. Congressional Elections," *Legislative Studies Quarterly* 6 (May 1981), pp. 183–200; Bruce E. Cain, John A. Ferejohn, and Morris P. Fiorina, "The Constituency Service Basis of the Personal Vote for U.S. Representatives and British Members of Parliament," *American Political Science Review* 18 (March 1984), pp. 110–25; John C. McAdams and John R. Johannes, "The 1980 House Election: Reexamining Some Theories in a Republican Year," *Journal of Politics* 45 (February 1983), pp. 143–62; and McAdams and Johannes, "The Voter in the 1982 House Election," *American Journal of Political Science* 28 (November 1984), pp. 778–781.
21. Johannes and McAdams, "The Congressional Incumbency Effect"; Jon R. Bond, "A Paradox of Representation: Diversity, Competition, Perks, and the Decline of Policy Making in the U.S. House," paper presented at the annual meeting of the American Political Science Association, New York, September 3–6, 1981; Jon R. Bond, "Perks and Competition: The Effects of District Attention Over Time," paper presented at the annual meeting of the Midwest Political Science Association, Chicago, April 17–20, 1985; Richard Born, "Perquisite Employment in the House of Representatives, 1960–1976," *American Politics Quarterly*

10 (July 1982), pp. 347–62; and Paul Feldman and James Jondrow, "Congressional Elections and Local Federal Spending," *American Journal of Political Science* 28 (February 1984): 147–63. For a general discussion of the problems of both survey and aggregate data, as well as an analysis of the 1982 and 1984 elections, see John R. Johannes and John C. McAdams, "Congressmen, Perquisites, and Elections," *Journal of Politics,* 1988 (forthcoming).

22. Jon R. Bond, Cary R. Covington, and Richard Fleisher, "Explaining Challenger Quality in Congressional Elections," *Journal of Politics* 47 (May 1985), pp. 510–29; John C. McAdams and John R. Johannes, "Determinants of Spending by House Challengers," *American Journal of Political Science* 31 (August 1987) pp. 457–83.

23. Albert D. Cover and Bruce S. Brumberg, "Baby Books and Ballots: The Impact of Congressional Mail on Constituent Opinion," *American Political Science Review* 76 (June 1982), pp. 347–59.

24. On this point see Glenn R. Parker's discussion of political leeway in Chapter 3.

PART TWO

The Institutional Congress

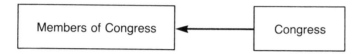

CHAPTER 6

Parties and Coalitions in Congress

Patricia A. Hurley

On January 8, 1987, the House of Representatives considered a bill to amend and reauthorize the Clean Water Act of 1976. One hundred and sixty Republicans joined all 246 Democrats voting for passage of the bill. Only eight Republicans dissented. The House exhibited the same high degree of consensus four weeks later when it passed the bill again over President Reagan's veto. Clearly, there was no partisan disagreement over the desirability of this clean water legislation. Partisan sentiment ran high, however, in the matter of aid to the Nicaraguan Contras. In March 1987 the House considered a six-month moratorium on aid to the Contras. Ninety percent of the Republicans voted against the moratorium, but 84 percent of the majority party Democrats voted for it. The moratorium passed the House by a vote of 230 to 196. And, in June 1987, the House considered whether State Department personnel who handle classified information should be subject to required drug testing. While the measure passed readily enough (307 to 103), a closer look shows that while 95 percent of the House Republicans and 92 percent of the southern Democrats favored a drug-testing program, a majority of non-southern Democrats were against it. The conservative preferences of the Republicans and southern Democrats overrode those of their more liberal non-southern Democratic colleagues on this matter.

These three votes illustrate some of the different kinds of coalitions which form in the United States Congress. The first is a *universalistic* coalition. The policy considered offered something for everyone, so there was little dissent. The second vote pitted one *partisan* coalition against another. The Republicans and Democrats were unified on opposite sides in the matter of temporarily suspending aid to the Contras. Finally, the third vote was an *ideological* one. Those who felt matters of national security took precedence over individual privacy rights voted in favor of drug testing, while those who considered privacy rights paramount voted against the program.

This chapter examines the most common bases on which congressional voting coalitions might be constructed. These include partisanship, particular policy preferences, shared regional concerns, and common ideologies. The focus here is on congressional voting and voting outcomes as group processes. While individual members of Congress make up their own decisions about how to vote, those decisions are shaped, in part, by the groups in which they are members, and thus the concern here is with the collective voting patterns in the House and Senate.

PARTY AS THE BASIS FOR COALITIONS

A principal task of the United States Congress is to propose legislation—to produce new government policies. This seemingly simple task requires that a majority of the House and Senate be in favor of the proposed legislation—in other words, a positive majority is necessary. Negative majorities serve to block legislation and therefore limit the productivity of Congress. Yet, it is always easier to put together a negative majority than a positive one. Members of Congress voting against a piece of legislation need not have a common basis for their dissent, yet a positive majority is more likely to require shared preferences. Thus, proponents of particular bills in the House and Senate must find a common basis of appeal on which to construct a majority. The difficulty of finding such appeals is especially complicated when Congress is considering innovative legislation which departs significantly from the status quo. Many different fears and concerns are raised by innovative legislation, and such legislation provides many bases for opposition.

Leaders generally form positive majorities by appealing to members on the basis of shared party loyalty. If leaders of the majority party could count on the complete support of their rank-and-file members the task of building a sustaining majority would be greatly simplified. But, for a variety of reasons, they cannot. As a consequence, the ability of the majority to assemble a positive coalition depends on two critical factors: its *unity* and its *size*. When combined, these two components represent gross majority party strength. If one is smaller, the other must be larger to compensate. Thus, if the majority party holds 51 percent of the seats in the chamber, party unity must be extraordinarily high to sustain the partisan majority. Conversely, if the majority is large, 75 percent of the seats, for example, a drop in partisan unity is more easily accommodated.

The process of building such a partisan majority is also affected by the behavior of the minority party. Since majority party unity is likely to be less than 100 percent, the minority party, aided by renegade majority members, may be able to assemble a negative majority to block policy initiatives. Here, too, party size and unity are critical. The prospects for the minority party increase with its size and unity. As these two factors become larger, dissenting majority members will find the option of joining the minority in a negative vote increasingly attractive. Yet, if the minority is small and disorganized, a negative victory may be impossible. Thus, the smaller and less cohesive the minority party, the easier it will be for the majority to build a positive coalition in support of legislation. The combined factors of majority and minority size and unity in the House of Representatives have been shown to be important in the passage of innovative legislation in the post–New Deal era. That is, Congresses characterized by large or strong majorities have been able to build coalitions for significant and substantial policy change. Conversely, Congresses with only small or weak majorities have been much less likely to pass such legislation.[1]

In the contemporary House of Representatives, the size of the parties is unlikely to vary drastically from one Congress to the next. The House has become highly professionalized, with many members seeking to make a career of serving in the chamber. Generally speaking, 90 percent or more of House incumbents seek reelection, and less than 10 percent of this group is defeated. There are, of course, exceptions to this pattern. The post-Watergate Democratic landslide of 1974 increased the size of the Democratic House majority from 56 percent to 67 percent. The House elections of 1980 reduced the Democratic majority from 64 percent to 56 percent. More typical are House elections such as those in 1984 and 1986. Following the 1984 election, the Democratic majority dropped three points to 58 percent. After the 1986 election the Democrats held 59 percent of the seats in the House. The practical effect of this circumstance is that size of the party has only a modest influence on the partisan coalition building process. As a consequence, the level of party unity becomes the critical factor determining the ability of the leadership to build a sustaining majority.

The Senate also has become a career-oriented institution. Since World War II, an average of 85 percent of senators have sought reelection. Yet senators have been less successful than House members in obtaining reelection: an average of 40 percent are defeated in any election year. Thus, the size of the parties in the Senate shows greater variance than the size of the parties in the House. Yet, because the Senate is so much smaller than the House, party unity levels are especially critical. It takes only a few senators who wish to bolt their party to turn a majority on paper into a minority in practice. If, for example, the majority party holds fifty-five seats (a 55 percent majority) and five majority party senators choose to vote with a united minority, the working partisan majority is effectively destroyed.

Because party unity is so critical, a closer look at the extent to which party actually determines voting in the House and Senate is warranted.

PARTY VOTING IN THE HOUSE

For party to play a significant role in the process of coalition building, there must be both high *intraparty unity* and high *interparty disagreement*. The importance of party unity has already been discussed. Yet what appears to be party unity by some criteria may, in fact, have no partisan basis whatsoever. If votes are unanimous or nearly so intraparty agreement is very high. If both parties are in agreement, however, no claim for partisanship is warranted. Distinct party coalitions require that the parties disagree. If coalitions are bipartisan, something other than party loyalty drives the majority building process.

Four broad patterns of the effect of partisanship on congressional voting have been identified. First, if intraparty unity and interparty divisiveness are both high, party has a comprehensive influence on voting. Second, if unity remains high but divisiveness is low, the effect of party is segmented. In this case the force of partisanship may be unequal across issue areas, with vote outcomes on some types of policies highly influenced by party, while other factors influence vote outcomes in other policy areas. Third, if divisiveness is high but intraparty unity remains low, party has an impaired effect on the coalition building process. Division of the yeas and nays is based on party generally, but internal party cohesion is weak. Partisan majorities in this case would be narrow (barely above 50 percent). And fourth, both divisiveness and unity could be low, in which case the influence of party on voting must be described as negligible. Internal party squabbling would be high, and coalitions would be largely unstable, varying considerably in composition from one vote to the next.[2]

Keeping in mind these two aspects of party, the extent to which party has structured voting in the House and Senate may be assessed empirically. Separate indicators for each component of party influence must be employed, since no single index adequately measures the two conditions simultaneously.

Divisiveness, or disagreement between parties, is indicated by the *party vote score*. A party vote is one in which a majority of members of one party vote in opposition to a majority of members of the other party. Thus, if 50 percent, plus one, of the Democrats vote yes, and 50 percent, plus one, of the Republicans vote no, the minimum criteria for a party vote would be satisfied. The party vote score is the percentage of roll calls per year, or session, that meet these criteria. The *party unity score* assesses the extent of party agreement and is simply the percentage of members voting together on those roll calls which are party votes. Because unity scores are calculated only for party votes, the artificial inflation of unity by unanimous or near unanimous votes is avoided.

Party voting and party unity in the House of Representatives have declined considerably since the 1890s. Since that time the House has gone through four different periods of internal organization. The movement from each of these periods to the next has been accompanied by a significant drop in the level of party voting. In the earliest era, (1891–1911), partisan divisions characterized over two-thirds of all House roll call votes. In the contemporary period 1969–1988, partisan voting had slipped to an average of only 40 percent. Average party voting and party unity scores for each of these time periods are displayed in Table 6–1.

Internal Institutional Influences on Party Voting

Both internal institutional factors and conditions external to the House have brought about this decline in partisan-based coalitions. Internally, the

TABLE 6–1   Party Voting and Party Unity in the House
of Representatives

Period	Average Party Votes	Average Party Unity	
		Democratic	Republican
1891–1911	68.2%	86.8%	88.5%
1911–1941	56.3	83.0	85.4
1941–1968	49.5	79.8	82.1
1969–1986	40.4	75.9	76.3

Note: Figures averaged by Congress rather than by year.

SOURCE: Figures for 1891–1968 calculated by the author based on data in Joseph Cooper et al., "The Electoral Basis of Party Voting," in *The Impact of the Electoral Process*, ed. Louis S. Maisel and Joseph Cooper (Beverly Hills, Calif: Sage Publications, 1977). Figures for 1969–86 calculated by the author from data in Norman J. Ornstein et al., *Vital Statistics on Congress, 1984* (Washington, D.C.: American Enterprise Institute for Public Policy Research, 1984); *Congressional Quarterly Almanac, 1985;* and *Congressional Quarterly Weekly Report,* November 15, 1986.

first period is one in which the powers of the House leadership, and especially the Speaker, were developed and consolidated. The Republican speaker from Maine, Thomas Reed, and later Joseph Cannon, the Republican speaker from Illinois, employed powerful sanctions—especially control over important committee assignments—to keep the rank-and-file party members in line. Indeed, the influence of "Czar" Cannon is obscured by the averages presented in Table 6–1. In the Fifty-eighth House (elected in 1902), Cannon's first term as Speaker, the percentage of party votes jumped twenty-two points, to 89 percent. In fact, 64 percent of all roll calls in that House pitted 90 percent of the Republicans against 90 percent of the Democrats. Yet Cannon's autocratic techniques for forging party coalitions ultimately led to his downfall. In 1910, a bipartisan coalition of progressive Republicans and Democrats revolted against Speaker Cannon and a substantial change in House procedural rules resulted in a significant loss of power for Cannon and subsequent Speakers. Between the 1890s and 1910, power in the House can be described as highly concentrated, or centralized. Until the revolt against the Speaker, official leaders in the House, particularly the Speaker himself, had extensive power over their partisan colleagues. After the revolt, the House entered a long period of transition (1911–40) and experienced a concomitant drop in the occurrence of partisan voting, although party opposition did increase during the New Deal Congresses of the 1930s.

Power in the House since 1940 may be characterized as dispersed, or decentralized, although it is useful to break this lengthy span of time into two segments. The first period, 1940–68, is one in which seniority was firmly entrenched as the mechanism for determining committee chairs and assignments. Committee chairs were extremely powerful and often at odds with the House leadership. The increased power of the committee chairs represented a net loss of power for the Speaker and his lieutenants, and the level of party voting fell to just under half of all votes.

The post-1968 period is one in which the dispersal of power in the House accelerated. Beginning in the late 1960s a number of informal groups of Congress members emerged within the House, and these groups served as new bases for coalition behavior. The best known of these was the Democratic Study Group, a group of liberal Democratic members who sought common policy objectives. A wide variety of other groups, however, also emerged, including ones based on ethnicity, ideology, or other single-issue concerns. These groups may be seen in part as both a cause and a consequence of the inability of parties to form durable coalitions across issue areas.[3] Moreover, internal House reforms had the perhaps unintended effect of furthering the dispersal of power. In an effort to limit the power of committee chairs, the seniority system was challenged and subcommittees were strengthened. The increase in the power and autonomy of subcommittee chairs, as well as the concomitant rise in the number of subcommittees, further subdivided the finite level of power. Not surprisingly, the average level of party voting in this period fell to 40.4 percent.

But what of party unity? Table 6–1 also displays the average unity figures for the Democratic and Republican parties in the four periods. While unity in both parties has declined, the drop is not as dramatic as that in party voting. (By definition unity cannot be less than 50 percent since it is calculated only on party votes.) Both parties have suffered a decrease of approximately 12 points from the earliest to the latest period. Partisan majorities were certainly more unified in the two earlier periods, but they remain fairly sizable even in the contemporary era, with slightly more than three-fourths of each party voting together on party votes.

One might argue that party voting scores of over 50 percent are high, while those under 50 percent are low. The midpoint of the party unity scale is 75, so scores above this might be considered high, while scores below it are low. By these criteria, the influence of party in the House during the first two time periods can be described as comprehensive, although it was considerably more comprehensive prior to 1911. Since 1940, the effect of party is best characterized as segmented, although the party unity figures for the 1969–86 period are only minimally above the dividing line between the segmented and negligible influence of party. In fact, the average levels of party voting and unity for this period conceal considerable variation in levels of party strength. In some Congresses, the influence of party must be characterized as negligible. For example, in the Ninety-second House (elected in 1970) only 28 percent of all roll call votes were party votes, and the unity level for both the parties was 71. Alternatively, since 1983, party voting in the House has risen considerably, to a high of 61 percent in 1985. Democratic party unity has risen as well, never dropping below 80 since 1983, and reaching a high of 86 in both 1985 and 1986. Republican unity has been somewhat more erratic, reaching a high of 80 in 1983 and 1985, but dropping to 77 and 76 in 1984 and

1986, respectively.[4] (A more detailed analysis of voting patterns in the 1980s is presented later in this chapter.)

External Influences on House Party Voting

Variations in the level of partisan strength in the House *within* time periods cannot be explained by the internal leadership structure. Rather, several external or environmental factors have been shown to influence the extent of party voting and party unity. Party voting levels rise when one or all of several conditions hold. A large influx of first time or freshmen members to the House of Representatives will generally cause the level of party voting to rise. New members, for a variety of reasons, are more likely to vote with the party leadership than are veteran members of the party. First-term members have not yet had the opportunity to develop the policy expertise which aids in independent judgment, yet they are called on to vote on many highly technical matters. The absence of independent information heightens the salience of the party cue for these new members. Moreover, these freshmen reap no benefits from a seniority system at this point in their careers. To some extent good committee assignments may depend on being a good party member, so there is an incentive to vote the party position. Nor have new members yet developed as fine an instinct for constituency opinion as veteran members, and they are probably more likely than their senior counterparts to see as their constituency only the members of their own party in the district, rather than the district at large. Thus, there is less temptation or necessity to vote against party to represent the constituency. When first-term Democrats and Republicans vote with their respective party leadership, they raise the level of partisan conflict in the chamber.

The relationship of the House majority to the president also has an effect on the extent of party voting. If the president and the House majority are of the same political party, prospects for increased party voting are improved. Conversely, if control of the government is divided, with the presidency controlled by one party and the House by the opposition, party voting often declines as the president and his legislative liaison seek to build bipartisan coalitions.

Finally, the extent of conflict or ideological opposition between the two parties affects greatly the rate of party voting in the House. If the parties are strongly opposed on solutions to major problems of the day this disagreement carries over into Congress. If ideological differences between the two parties are low and interparty differences on issues are minimal, interparty differences on roll call votes will be low as well. Recent research has shown that the extent of ideological opposition between the parties has a greater effect on party voting than either the rate of membership turnover or the partisanship of the president.

External factors also have an influence on internal party cohesion, although the effects are not the same for the two parties. For the Republican party, both the percentage of new members and the partisanship of the president affect intraparty agreement. The more freshmen Republicans, the more unified the party. If the president is a Republican, the House Republicans will be more unified. Partisan conflict does not appear to influence Republican party unity. Alternatively, the extent of partisan conflict has major consequences for the unity of the Democratic party. Partisanship of the president plays a role as well, but an influx of new members does not affect Democratic party unity. The extent of regional polarization within the Democratic party also affects the level of internal party agreement. Since the late 1930s, the Democratic party has been split into two factions, with southern and border Democrats considerably more conservative than the remainder of the party. As the size of the southern and border component approaches that of the non-southern component, party cohesion declines.[5]

Two important features of these external factors should be emphasized. First, they are electorally based phenomena. If there are large numbers of new members in the House, it is because the voters put them there. If control of the government is divided, it is because voters split their tickets. If the size of the southern and border faction of the congressional Democratic party declines, it is because southern constituencies sent Republicans to Washington. Thus, the roots of partisan coalitions in the House must be traced back to the electorate. Second, numerous scholars have documented the declining importance of party for the individual voter. A large portion of the public professes no preference for one party over the other, and thus tickets are often split. House incumbents, regardless of party, have the advantage over challengers and are able to build power bases independent of party organizations. These trends reached their peak in the 1970s, and it should come as no surprise that the influence of partisanship on voting in the House reached its nadir during that time.

PARTY VOTING IN THE SENATE

In theory, the same internal and external influences that condition party voting in the House might also be expected to influence the Senate. Differing internal patterns of power distribution should give rise to different patterns of partisan division in roll call voting, and variations in levels of party strength within periods should be accounted for by external influences on Senate voting behavior.

Past research has suggested three patterns of power distribution within the Senate: *centralization*, *decentralization*, and *individualism*.[6] When power is centralized it is concentrated in the hands of the party leadership. Committee chairs, while powerful, essentially owe their allegiance to their party leadership. Individual senators are also allegiant to this leadership. Party voting should be highest in periods of centralization. During periods of decentralization, power is divided between leaders and committee chairs who have their own power bases. Individual senators are allegiant to their committees rather than the party. Party voting should drop when power is decentralized. In periods of individualism, the individual senator's power is greatly increased, either in his or her own right, or as the chair of a subcommittee. Power is thus drawn away from both standing committee chairs and party leaders, and party voting levels should be lowest. Research on the period from 1869 to 1969 suggests that the power of the Senate party leadership has not declined in a linear fashion as it has in the House. Rather, between 1869 and 1937, the power distribution fluctuated in the following manner:[7]

1869–1885	Individualism
1885–1905	Centralization
1905–1911	Decentralization
1911–1917	Centralization
1917–1933	Individualism
1933–1937	Centralization
1937–1955	Decentralization
1955–1961	Decentralization/Individualism
1961–1969	Individualism

Between the New Deal period and 1969, then, power in the Senate declined in a linear fashion, similar to that described for the House. Analysis of the contemporary Senate suggests that individualism intensified during the 1970s.[8] Data on party voting in the Senate are available only since 1933, and data on party unity only since 1955. These data allow at least a partial assessment of the impact of the twentieth century dissolution of power in the Senate.

As expected, the level of party voting dropped in each period between 1933 and 1969, from a high of 62 percent to a low of just under 40 percent. Contrary to expectation, party voting rose slightly in the 1970–86 period. Since 1955 the level of party voting in the Senate has remained quite low and differences between the three periods of power distribution since 1955 are minimal. The unity figures for both parties are virtually constant, although the small declines that do occur are in the expected direction. It appears that once power in the Senate moves away from decentralization the influence of party decays rapidly, but further subdivisions of power do not speed the process. Average party voting and party unity scores for the Senate are displayed in Table 6–2.

Several factors suggest that the influence of the power structure in the Senate on partisan voting may not be as strong as the averages in Table 6–2 imply. First, between 1933 and 1969 there is considerable annual variation around the mean. For example, party voting in the Senate was 70 percent in 1933 and 1934, but fell to 54 percent and 51 percent in 1935 and 1936, respectively. An examination of the trends in the index of party likeness (a similar statistic) between 1856 and 1978 implies only a modest correlation between

TABLE 6–2   Party Voting and Party Unity in the Senate

Period	Average Party Votes	Average Party Unity	
		Democratic	Republican
1933–1937	62.4%	n.a.	n.a.
1938–1954	56.3	n.a.	n.a.
1955–1961	44.3	78.6%	78.5%
1962–1969	39.8	75.0	76.3
1970–1986	43.5	74.9	75.3

n.a. = Not available.

SOURCE: Figures for 1933–54 calculated by the author from data in Mack C. Shelley II, *The Permanent Majority* (Tuscaloosa, Ala.: University of Alabama Press, 1983). Figures for 1955–86 calculated by the author from data in Ornstein et al., *Vital Statistics on Congress, 1984–85; Congressional Quarterly Almanac, 1985;* and *Congressional Quarterly Weekly Report,* November 15, 1986.

the pattern of power distribution and the level of party conflict.[9] Party conflict rose and fell in rough correspondence to the changes in power distribution in the Senate, but several periods exhibit patterns contrary to expectation. The return to centralization in 1933, for example, was accompanied by a modest increase in party conflict, but the average level of conflict was lower than that which prevailed during the decentralized period from 1905 to 1911. In general, party strength in the Senate was stronger in the latter part of the nineteenth century than it has been in the twentieth century, even when leadership power has been centralized.

Do external factors affect party voting in the Senate as they do in the House? The answer is yes, but the effects are different than those in the House. Between 1933 and 1972 (the only years for which a complete set of data is available) both the percentage of freshmen Senators and the partisanship of the president influenced party voting. Alternatively, in direct contrast to the House, external party conflict had virtually no effect on the rate of party voting in the Senate. This is probably best explained by the Constitutional insulation of the Senate from the presidential election cycle. With only one-third of the members facing the electorate in a given year, the direct effects of external factors are muted.

This assessment of the effects of external factors is based on a multiple regression analysis, the details of which are displayed in Table 6–3.[10] The column labeled "Raw B" gives an indication of the magnitude of the effects of each external factor (or independent variable) on Senate party voting (the dependent variable). For example, every increase of one percentage point in the number of freshmen Senators should cause party voting to rise 1.63 percentage points. Thus, if the percentage of freshmen Senators increased by 5 percent, say, from 15 to 20 percent, party voting should rise by 8.15 percentage points. Similarly, when the presidency and the Senate are controlled

TABLE 6–3   Regression Results: The Effects of Party
Conflict, Percent Freshmen, and Presidential
Partisanship on Senate Party Voting, 1933–1972

Independent	Raw B	Standard Error	Beta
Party conflict	0.10	0.08	.16*
Percent freshmen	1.63	0.36	.56†
Presidential partisanship	13.03	3.27	.51†
Constant	17.17	6.16	

R square = .51.

* Not statistically significant.
† Statistically significant at the .001 level.

SOURCE: Calculated by the author.

by the same party, party voting should be about 13 percentage points higher than when the two institutions are controlled by opposite parties. Notice, however, that a one unit rise in the party conflict index produces only a fractional increase in party voting: one-tenth of 1 percent.

The column labeled "Beta" indicates the relative importance of these three external factors in determining Senate party voting. Both the percentage of freshmen and presidential partisanship have roughly equal weights (.56 and .51), which are much larger than the weight for party conflict (.16). Finally, the R-square statistic shows that these three external factors account for slightly more than one-half of the changes in Senate party voting levels between 1933 and 1972. Thus, other factors not included in this regression are important, too, and would account for changes in party voting unexplained here. Yet the external influences are clearly important.

ALTERNATIVES TO PARTY AS THE BASES FOR COALITIONS

Despite the recent upswing in party voting, the parties have weakened during the twentieth century as determinants of voting behavior in Congress. Yet during this time, positive majorities have formed to enact policy, and negative majorities have formed to block policy. This leads logically to the question of what alternatives to party serve as the basis for voting alliances. Scholars have identified three such alternatives: issues, region, and ideology. Yet the reader should be aware that these possible roots of voting alliances are not mutually exclusive. What appears to be a regional alliance, north versus south, for example, may also be an ideological alliance of liberals versus conservatives. Regional alliances of midwesterners versus others may in fact reflect shared positions on agricultural policy. Thus it is difficult to determine the true basis of such coalitions. Nonetheless, some basic patterns and persistent groupings have been identified.

Issue-Based Voting Alliances

When party structures congressional voting behavior, specific policy proposals in a wide variety of issue areas are perceived by members as highly interrelated. A roll call vote can be placed on a single, underlying continuum or dimension with its end points defined as party positions. In other words, members of the same party will vote together, in opposition to the other party, across a whole range of dissimilar policy issues. Yet the possibility exists that congressional voting is multidimensional and that different voting alliances will form in different issue areas. The voting alliances will be stable and predictable within a single issue area, but the composition of voting alliances varies from one issue area to the next. For example, suppose House members Brown and Jones always vote in favor of civil rights extensions, while members Smith and Watson always vote against such legislation. Suppose, however, that when the policy under consideration is assistance to farmers, the vote pattern shifts: Jones and Smith are always in favor of, and Brown and Watson against, aid to farmers. Assume that Brown and Jones are Democrats and that Smith and Watson are Republicans. The civil rights voting pattern is highly partisan, while the farmers' assistance pattern is completely unrelated to partisanship.

Aage Clausen has identified five basic policy dimensions which define congressional voting: civil liberties, international involvement, agricultural assistance, social welfare, and government management of the economy.[11] Clausen's examination of roll call voting for 1953–64 revealed that these dimensions existed in both the House and the Senate and were stable and continuous over this period. The influence of party, however, was unequal across policy areas. Party was an excellent predictor of voting divisions on roll calls concerning government management of the economy. Party was somewhat less successful in explaining voting on agricultural assistance and social welfare roll calls. In other words, partisan differences characterized voting on agricultural assistance and social welfare matters, but intraparty unity levels were lower than for government management. Party was not a good predictor of voting alliances on international involvement or civil liberties roll calls. Rather, presidential influence explained bipartisan coalitions on international involvement while regional, constituency related factors explained voting alliances on civil liberties.

The utility of focusing on policy dimensions over a much longer span of time has been demonstrated by Barbara Sinclair.[12] Her analysis indicates that the government management and agricultural assistance dimensions existed in the House of Representatives as early as 1925. The social welfare dimension appeared with the Great Depression and the New Deal. Voting on government management was partisan prior to the New Deal, agricultural assistance became related to partisanship during the 1930s, and social welfare voting was partisan from its inception. The civil liberties and international involvement dimensions emerged later. International involvement appeared when Congress began to respond to the crisis in Europe in the late 1930s, and voting here was not highly partisan.

The early civil liberties voting patterns are especially interesting. This dimension was really two: black civil rights and subversive activities roll calls. Both northern Democrats and Republicans voted in favor of civil rights for blacks, in contrast to the southern Democrats. The north-south split within the Democratic party held on subversive activities, but was not as strong. On these roll calls, however, the Republicans voted more often with the southern Democrats.[13]

Analysis of these dimensions over a fifty year period provided evidence for both change and stability in House voting alignments. The Eisenhower period (1953–60) was marked by considerable stability.[14] At other times, the composition of these policy-based groupings altered substantially as a result of membership turnover, but also as a result of changed voting behavior on the part of returning incumbents.

A notable feature of this changed behavior was the development of a regional character in the voting alignments of both parties on particular policy dimensions. Between 1939 and 1952 the north-south regional split within the Democratic party intensified and affected voting on both government management and social welfare roll calls. Republicans representing districts in the Northeast also developed distinctive voting patterns. These Republicans were much more supportive of social welfare initiatives than were Republicans from other parts of the country. During the 1960s, the behavior of the members from these two regions became even more distinctive. Southern Democratic voting became more conservative and northeastern Republicans became more liberal. Thus, regional characteristics eroded the influence of party even in those policy dimensions where partisan influence had been strongest. During the 1970s, the regional character of intraparty voting patterns began to abate, although it did not disappear altogether.[15]

What is it precisely about geographic regions which influences congressional voting behavior? There is nothing about being a southerner or a northeasterner per se that causes a member of Congress to vote a particular way. Rather, members of Congress from a particular region represent constituencies which are fairly similar in demographic composition. Moreover, while there is variation in political culture in the entire United States, political culture within regions has traditionally been relatively homogeneous. Thus, region is actually a surrogate for constituency.[16] Regionally based policy coalitions are policy coalitions built on constituency interests which cut across party lines. This also suggests that as diversity increases within a region, members of Congress from that region may vote together less frequently as they each respond to separate, dissimilar constituencies. This should be particularly true for southern members, whose region has undergone considerable social and economic change in the past two decades. This speculation is consistent, as well, with the observation that the north-south Democratic split muted somewhat in the 1970s.

One should also raise certain caveats about the policy dimension approach to understanding congressional coalitions. If party determines voting across dimensional lines, then the distinctiveness of individual policy areas is less important. The consistent finding that party is a good predictor of voting divisions on government management of the economy, social welfare, and agricultural assistance suggests that focusing on them as separate dimensions may be of limited utility. To be sure, the influence of party on voting in these three areas has declined between the 1930s and the late 1970s, and this decline is *commensurate* with the general drop in party voting documented above.[17] Nonetheless, no other factor has emerged which predicts voting splits *consistently* better than party. This inability to predict voting behavior within policy areas arises as a consequence of the instability of coalitions within dimensions in the late 1970s.[18] Fragmentation of coalitions within policy areas also suggests that this approach to understanding congressional voting alliances may be less fruitful than it once was.

The Conservative Coalition

One of the most durable alternatives to party as the basis for a coalition has been the *Conservative Coalition,* or the informal voting alliance between a majority of Republicans and southern Democrats in opposition to a majority of northern Democrats. Despite the nomenclature, a number of scholars have pointed out that the Conservative Coalition is not a coalition at all. It has traditionally had no formal leaders, no articulated strategy for developing internal unity, and no formal meetings. Deliberate collusion between Republicans and "boll weevil" (southern conservative) Democrats has taken place, however, in the 1980s.

The Conservative Coalition has appeared as a voting bloc in every Congress since it first formed in the 1930s and it is based on specific policy issues, ideology, and for the Democrats, region. The impetus for the original appearance was the shared opposition of Republicans and southern Democrats to the increased activity of the government in the economy during the New Deal. Between 1933 and 1980 the Conservative Coalition appeared most frequently on roll call votes in this issue area, but it also formed on roll calls dealing with international matters, social welfare, and civil liberties.[19]

The coalition has been dominated by Republican issue concerns.[20] As such, it functioned most frequently as a negative or blocking coalition between the 1930s and 1980. Despite the election of three Republican presidents in this period (Eisenhower, Nixon, and Ford) the domestic political agenda was dominated by Democratic party initiatives. Many of these initiatives, especially in the areas of government management of the economy, social welfare, and civil rights, were ideologically unpalatable to Republicans and southern Democrats. Thus the Conservative Coalition frequently, and often successfully, sought to block these policy efforts.

Following the 1980 election, the coalition was transformed from a negative to a positive one. The election of Ronald Reagan and the capture of the Senate by the Republicans shifted control of the political agenda to the Republicans. Further, the activity of the coalition in the House was indispensable to the success of the Reagan policy efforts during the Ninety-seventh Congress (1981–82), since the Democrats still controlled the chamber. Coalition activity increased somewhat in 1981, but more important the success rate, or the percentage of votes won by the Conservative Coalition, in both the House and the Senate jumped dramatically in 1981 and remained high in 1982. The coalition remained successful in the Republican controlled Senate, but appearances and successes have declined in the House since 1983. This accords neatly with observations based on earlier periods where coalition appearances were positively related to the size of the Republican party in the chamber.[21] The Republicans retained control of the Senate through 1986 and thus the coalition remained successful. In the House, the number of Republicans lessened following the 1982 midterm elections and Conservative Coalition activity subsided as well.

The activity of the Conservative Coalition has often served to depress the level of party voting. The coalition has been characterized as the "permanent majority" based on the fact that the number of Republicans plus the number of southern Democrats has almost always equaled more than one-half of the membership of both chambers. Thus the "permanent majority" is a bipartisan one. Yet one must consider the effects of increased party competition in the South on this bipartisan majority.

The South has long been an aberration in American politics—solidly Democratic, but solidly conservative. In the last twenty years, however, two-party competition has been gradually increasing in the South. In the Eighty-ninth Congress (1965–66) only 15 percent of the southern seats were held by Republicans. By the Ninety-fifth Congress (1977–78), approximately 25 percent of the southern seats were held by Republicans. By the Ninety-ninth Congress (1985–86) well over one-third of the southerners in the House and Senate were Republicans. Moreover, a number of the remaining southern Democrats are not particularly conservative. While they are "members" of the coalition by definition, they are more likely to vote with their northern Democratic colleagues. The southern Democrats are the least cohesive of the three groups relevant to the coalition, and recently their roll call behavior has become less distinctive relative to that of northern Democrats.[22] The practical effects of these trends is that the bipartisan nature of the coalition is eroding. Southern Democrats are a smaller and smaller part of the coalition. If electoral competition continues to increase in the South, the prospects are that the bipartisan Conservative Coalition will give way to a more natural coalition based on party. Again, the roots of coalition behavior in the House and Senate are to be found in electorally related phenomena.

Ideologically Motivated Voting Alliances

One final possibility for House and Senate voting coalitions must be discussed explicitly, although it is implicit in the discussion of the Conservative Coalition. This is the possibility that congressional voting is in fact unidimensional, and the underlying continuum is a left-right one. In other words, liberals, regardless of party, vote together in opposition to conservatives, who may also be members of either party. Moreover, these ideological groupings are consistent from one policy area to the next. If a member is a conservative on government management of the economy, he or she is also a conservative on social welfare, agricultural assistance, and so on.

Several scholars have presented findings which suggest that voting in both the House and the Senate on all issues is motivated by the ideological preferences (liberal or conservative) of the members. Research based on interview data as well as roll call votes in 1971, 1972, and 1975 suggests that this is a reasonable way to think about congressional voting alliances.[23] An examination of the Senate between 1957 and 1976 demonstrates that over this period there has been movement away from multiple, issue specific coalitions toward a single alliance for all issues based on ideology alone.[24]

One must be aware that ideological coalitions are different than partisan coalitions only when the parties are divided internally on an ideological basis. If one finds liberals and conservatives within each party, then the left-right dimension crosscuts the Democratic-Republican dimension. In this case, ideological voting will serve to depress the level of party voting as liberal Democrats vote together with liberal Republicans against conservative Democrats and conservative Republicans. If party and ideology are logically connected, however, ideological coalitions and partisan coalitions are synonymous. In other words, liberal Democrats (the entire party) vote together against conservative Republicans (the entire party). Thus, an important concern is with the extent to which party and ideology are logically interrelated.

Several scholars have argued that, on balance, there are clear ideological divisions between Democrats and Republicans, and that ideological opposition between the two parties has increased in recent years. William Shaffer writes that "for the nation as a whole, and for the six regions defined in this study, the two parties differed substantially on the fundamental issues" between 1965 and 1976.[25] These differences may be the product of members responding to the more ideologically extreme members of their party or constituency.[26]

Nearly every study that finds evidence of a single ideological continuum in Congress makes at least some use, and in some cases exclusive use, of interest group ratings of members of the House and Senate. The possibility exists that interest groups select only highly ideological votes when constructing their rankings, and thus the left-right ordering of congressional coalitions is over estimated. Even if this is true it would not explain the high correlation between party and ideology which some analysts have found. Moreover, each year the House and Senate take a huge number of recorded votes. Treating all votes equally, as general assessments of party voting levels do, includes roll calls on minor matters with those that are extremely consequential. It may be that basing analysis on only votes designated as important by various rating organizations is a viable way to discover the critical determinants of congressional voting. Party or ideology may have great influence when Congress is considering salient issues, but much less so for more mundane concerns.

A CLOSER LOOK AT CONGRESSIONAL VOTING IN THE 1980s

Earlier in this chapter it was observed that party voting had risen considerably in the House of Representatives beginning in 1983. Party voting also rose in the Senate in 1985 and 1986. Why, after years of decline in the House, and years of hovering in the mid-40 percent range in the Senate, did party voting show a sudden and dramatic increase? Since the internal leadership structure did not change in either chamber, the cause of this increase must be sought in external phenomena.

One might have expected the 1980 election to have a major effect on partisan voting in Congress, especially in the Senate. Following the 1980 election, eighteen freshmen Senators were seated, and majority status shifted to the Republicans, giving control of the presidency and the Senate to the same party. While the Democrats retained control of the House, the Republicans won an unusually large number of seats from the Democrats. Moreover, the parties as organizational entities were certainly polarized in 1980, and this ideological opposition should have served to raise the level of partisan conflict in the House.

Why then was a rise in party voting not observable in 1981? The answer seems to be in how members themselves read the 1980 election results. In 1981, especially, President Reagan had firm control of the policy agenda. Democrats in Congress, as well as their Republican colleagues, behaved as if the election results were a mandate for Reagan's policies. That is, members of Congress from both parties voted in favor of legislation advanced by the Reagan administration. By 1982, Reagan's control of the agenda began to slip, and the 1982 House elections, in which twenty-six seats reverted to the Democrats, signaled the end of any mandate Reagan may have had from the voters.[27] It was immediately after the 1982 elections that party voting rose in the House as Democrats voted against administration initiatives and raised their own policy alternatives. The effects of the 1982 election in the Senate lagged those in the House, but recall that staggered elections can depress electoral effects on Senate voting.

This interpretation of the general contours of party voting in the 1980s is quite consistent with the thesis that elections affect congressional voting. Precisely because the 1980 election was interpreted as a policy mandate, party voting did not rise. A number of congressional Democrats, especially in the House, voted with the Republicans in favor of Reagan's efforts in 1981 and 1982. This kept the level of partisanship low. When Democratic members of Congress ceased to behave as if 1980 were a mandate, party voting rose and Reagan's success with Congress declined.

The effects of the 1982 election on congressional voting are even more apparent if analysis is restricted to roll calls designated as important by the various organizations that rate congressional voting. Since 1981, the weekly publication *National Journal* has compiled a list of roll calls designated as important by ideological groups, as well as those interested in business and labor, foreign policy and defense, environmentalism and consumer protection, and civil liberties, moral, and religious issues. Those votes designated as key by the *Congressional Quarterly* are also included in the tally.[28] The number of important votes per chamber per year between 1981 and 1985 ranged from thirty-nine to fifty, with an average of forty-seven.

If analysis of congressional roll call voting in the 1980s is restricted to these important votes, the rate of party voting is quite high, even in 1981 and 1982. Nonetheless, the percentage of party votes jumps sharply in the House and the Senate beginning in 1983. One might infer from this that even Senate Democrats responded to the outcome of the 1982 House elections. Democratic party unity in the House also increased following the 1982 elections. The rates of party voting and party unity for these important votes are presented in Table 6–4.

The votes may be further subdivided into roll calls on economic matters, foreign and defense policy, and social issues. Both parties exhibited the highest unity levels on economic matters, although House Republicans were equally unified on foreign policy. In the House, party voting was highest on economic matters, while in the Senate the most partisan issue was foreign policy. The parties, and especially the Senate Republicans, have been the least united internally on social issues in the 1980s. Yet the differences between issue areas should not obscure the main point: partisanship in all three areas was important, especially after 1983.

It is perhaps ironic that this return to partisanship resulted from the building of negative Democratic majorities in the House. As of this writing, the Democrats have regained control of the Senate, and the odds are even if not better that they will regain the presidency in 1988. It remains to be seen if, under those circumstances, the level of party voting will remain high, and whether the Democrats will be capable of building positive majorities.

TABLE 6–4   Party Voting and Party Unity on Selected
Votes in the House and Senate in the 1980s

| Year | Party Votes | Average Party Unity | |
		Democratic	Republican
House			
1981	74.4%	70.2%	81.1%
1982	76.0	70.4	76.3
1983	92.8	79.7	84.8
1984	85.1	75.4	81.9
1985	91.5	76.5	83.4
Senate			
1981	75.6	69.6	79.5
1982	71.4	76.7	76.6
1983	80.5	76.3	76.8
1984	84.8	74.6	81.9
1985	84.0	77.9	81.8

SOURCE: Calculated by the author on the basis of those votes identified as important by the *National Journal*. See Note 28 at the end of the chapter.

CONCLUSION: PARTIES, COALITIONS, AND REPRESENTATION

Members of the House and Senate are elected as individuals, but in Congress they function as members of groups. The most salient group is certainly the party, but members may find themselves pulled away from party and into alliances based on particular policy issues or ideological concerns. Thus one finds a variety of voting coalitions in Congress.

These voting coalitions in Congress are the product of a number of factors. The internal leadership structure of the institution, in particular, has a major effect on the appearance of partisan coalitions. Yet a persistent theme of this chapter has been that floor voting is shaped, as well, by external, environmental factors. The partisanship of the president, the number of freshmen members and the extent of ideological opposition between the parties all influence the building of partisan coalitions. The size of the Republican party in each chamber, which is the product of election outcomes, also has an influence on the extent of Conservative Coalition activity. Attention to constituency concerns sometimes produces deviations from partisan voting in particular policy areas.

These external phenomena do not directly produce the coalitions that appear on roll call votes. Rather, they combine to produce a particular set of conditions which might be called *the floor situation*. The floor situation is the relative size and unity of the two parties, as well as their respective regional and ideological composition. The floor situation, in turn, determines the kind of coalitions that can be built. Nonetheless, the importance of these external factors cannot be overemphasized. Because House and Senate voting respond to changing external circumstances, Congress functions, as intended, as a representative institution.

NOTES

1. For a more complete discussion, see Patricia A. Hurley, "Assessing the Potential for Significant Legislative Output in the U.S. House of Representatives," *Western Political Quarterly* 32 (March 1979), pp. 45–58; and Patricia A. Hurley, "Predicting Policy Change in the House: A Longitudinal Analysis," *British Journal of Political Science* 12 (July 1982), pp. 375–84.
2. For a more complete exposition of these patterns, see Joseph Cooper, David W. Brady, and Patricia A. Hurley, "The Electoral Basis of Party Voting: Patterns and Trends in the U.S. House of Representatives, 1887–1969," in *The Impact of the Electoral Process*, ed. Louis S. Maisel and Joseph Cooper (Beverly Hills, Calif.: Sage Publications, 1977).
3. On the proliferation of informal groups, see Susan Webb Hammond, Daniel P. Mulholland, and Arthur G. Stevens, Jr., "The Institutionalization of Interests in Congress: An Organizational Perspective on Informal Groups," paper presented at the annual meeting of the Southwestern Social Science Association, Dallas, Texas, 1981. On the effects of informal groups see David W. Brady, Joseph Cooper, and Patricia A. Hurley, "The Decline of Party in the U.S. House of Representatives, 1887–1968," *Legislative Studies Quarterly* 4 (August 1979), pp. 381–407.
4. These figures have been corrected to remove the effects of absences.
5. For a more detailed statistical analysis of these factors, see Brady, Cooper, and Hurley, "Decline of Party."
6. Randall B. Ripley, *Power in the Senate* (New York: St. Martin's Press, 1969), pp. 6–13.
7. Ibid., p. 15.
8. Norman J. Ornstein, "The Open Congress Meets the President," in *Both Ends of the Avenue*, ed. Anthony King (Washington, D.C.: American Enterprise Institute for Public Policy Research, 1983) pp. 185–211.
9. Jerome M. Clubb, William H. Flanigan, and Nancy H. Zingale, *Partisan Realignment: Voters, Parties, and Government in American History* (Beverly Hills, Calif.: Sage Publications, 1980), pp. 235–39.
10. Party conflict is measured by the index of critical capitalism in Benjamin Ginsberg, "Critical Elections and the Substance of Party Conflict, 1844–1968," *Midwest Journal of Political Science* 16 (November 1972), pp. 603–625. The Ginsberg index is not available for presidential election years after 1971. Presidential party is a dummy variable with a value of one when the president and the Senate majority are of the same party. The adjusted R-square for the regression model is .47. The Durbin-Watson statistic is 2.17, indicating no serial correlation. Interested readers should note that these results are different from those

presented by Samuel C. Patterson and Gregory Caldeira, "Party Voting in Congress," paper delivered at the annual meeting of the Midwest Political Science Association, Chicago, April 8–11, 1987. Their analysis covers a different time span and uses twelve independent variables to predict party voting in the Senate.

11. Aage R. Clausen, *How Congressmen Decide: A Policy Focus* (New York: St. Martin's Press, 1973).

12. Barbara Sinclair, *Congressional Realignment, 1925–1978* (Austin: University of Texas Press, 1982).

13. Ibid., pp. 40–41.

14. Note that this period substantially overlaps the Congresses studied by Clausen in *How Congressmen Decide.*

15. Sinclair, *Congressional Realignment,* chapters 4, 6, and 7. See also Barbara Sinclair, "Coping with Uncertainty: Building Coalitions in the House and Senate," in *The New Congress,* ed. Thomas E. Mann and Norman J. Ornstein (Washington, D.C.: American Enterprise Institute, 1981), pp. 178–220.

16. Sinclair, *Congressional Realignment,* pp. 15–16.

17. Melissa P. Collie and David W. Brady, "The Decline of Partisan Voting Coalitions in the House of Representatives," in *Congress Reconsidered,* 3rd, ed. Lawrence C. Dodd and Bruce I. Oppenheimer (Washington D.C.: CQ Press, 1985), pp. 272–87. See also Sinclair, *Congressional Realignment,* and Sinclair, "Coping with Uncertainty."

18. Melissa P. Collie, "Party Voting and Policy Content Perspectives of Alignments in the Post-New Deal House of Representatives," Ph.D. diss., Rice University, 1984. See also Sinclair, "Coping with Uncertainty."

19. Mack C. Shelley II, *The Permanent Majority: The Conservative Coalition in the United States Congress* (University of Alabama Press, 1983), pp. 41–64. See also David W. Brady and Charles S. Bullock III, "Is There a Conservative Coalition in the House?" *Journal of Politics* 42 (May 1980), pp. 549–52.

20. Shelley, *Permanent Majority,* p. 145.

21. Ibid., pp. 144–46.

22. On the former point, see ibid., pp. 146–49; on the latter, see Charles S. Bullock III, "Congressional Roll Call Voting in a Two Party South," *Social Science Quarterly* 66 (December 1985), pp. 789–804, for evidence on the House; and William R. Shaffer, "Ideological Trends Among Southern U.S. Democratic Senators: Race, Generation, and Political Climate," *American Politics Quarterly* 15 (July 1987), pp. 299–324, for evidence on the Senate.

23. Jerrold E. Schneider, *Ideological Coalitions in Congress* (Westport, Conn.: Greenwood Press, 1979).

24. Steven S. Smith, "The Consistency and Ideological Structure of U.S. Senate Voting Alignments, 1957–1976." *American Journal of Political Science* 25 (November 1981), pp. 780–95.

25. William R. Shaffer, *Party and Ideology in the United States Congress* (Washington, D.C.: University Press of America, 1980), p. 329.

26. Keith T. Poole and Howard Rosenthal, "The Polarization of American Politics," *Journal of Politics* 46 (November 1984), pp. 1061–79.

27. Barbara Sinclair, "Agenda Control and Policy Success: Ronald Reagan and the 97th House," *Legislative Studies Quarterly* 10 (August 1985), pp. 291–314. See

also Patricia A. Hurley, "Electoral Change and Policy Consequences: Representation in the 97th Congress," *American Politics Quarterly* 12 (April 1984), pp. 177–94.

28. Richard E. Cohen, "Rating Congress: A Guide to Separating the Liberals from the Conservatives," *National Journal,* May 8, 1982; William Schneider, "Party Unity on Tax, Spending Issues: Less in House, More in Senate in 1982," *National Journal,* May 7, 1983; William Schneider, "Democrats, Republicans Move Further Apart on Most Issues in 1983 Session," *National Journal,* May 12, 1984; William Schneider, "Politics of the '80s Widens the Gap Between the Two Parties in Congress," *National Journal,* June 1, 1985; William Schneider, "A Year of Continuity," *National Journal,* May 17, 1986.

CHAPTER 7

Leadership Strategies in the Modern Congress

Barbara Sinclair

An extremely popular president sees his veto of the South African Sanctions Bill easily overridden. Although foreign policy is universally conceded to be an area of special presidential responsibility, even the president's fellow partisans in the Congress desert him; more than half in each house vote to override, thus supplanting the foreign policy judgment of the leader of their party with their own.[1]

The leaders of the majority party in the House beg and plead with their members to support the party's budget resolution and thus prevent the gutting of programs the Democratic party has long supported. Despite all their efforts, they are unable to amass enough votes and the minority party passes its budget resolution with the help of majority party defectors.[2]

Accustomed to a different governmental system, citizens of other countries find such instances mystifying. A legislature that makes policy, especially foreign policy, independent of the executive, rank-and-file legislators who desert their party leaders inside and outside the chamber with impunity are phenomena not possible under the more common systems of government. In fact, the United States Congress is uniquely powerful for a modern legislature. Unlike the British Parliament, for example, Congress plays a significant role in policy formulation independent of the executive. Yet, because the political parties are weak, numerical majorities do not automatically translate into policy majorities. In Congress, majorities must be constructed.

Despite their weakness, parties have usually provided the basis upon which majorities are built. Consequently congressional party leaders, especially leaders of the majority party in a chamber, are expected to play a central role in coalition building. In fact, the attentive public—including the press—judges the party leadership largely upon its coalition-building success.

Satisfying the expectations of followers and of other significant actors is central to successful leadership. To meet those expectations, the congressional majority party leadership must perform two principal functions. First, the leadership is charged with *building winning coalitions* on major legislation

135

and thereby satisfying the legislative output expectations of its membership and of significant actors outside the chamber, particularly interest groups allied with the party and the president if he is a fellow partisan. Second, the leadership must *keep peace in the family.* Both parties are heterogeneous; the often conflicting policy and power goals of members pose constant threats to party coherence. Generalized dissatisfaction among members with the institution and their role within it can also endanger party harmony. "Keeping peace in the family" (also referred to as "party maintenance") dictates that leaders help members satisfy their expectations about their individual roles in the chamber; it requires leaders to mitigate intraparty conflicts and foster cooperative patterns of behavior among party members.

This chapter describes how current House and Senate party leaders perform these functions and analyzes the factors that affect the strategies used and the chances of success.

THE INSTITUTIONAL AND POLITICAL ENVIRONMENT

Scholars increasingly agree that congressional leadership is best understood from a contextual perspective.[3] The context or environment shapes and constrains leadership styles and strategies. During the strong Speakership era of 1890–1910, the Speaker of the House assigned all members to committees, he chose committee chairs and, through his control over the Rules Committee which he chaired, he largely determined what legislation would get to the floor. With these great resources, the Speaker could directly and significantly affect whether a member attained a position of power in the chamber, whether the policies a member espoused became law, and, to the extent power or policy success had an impact, whether a member's chances for reelection were good or bad. Furthermore, because parties were strong during this period, a member's probability of reelection was heavily dependent upon the success of his party in government. Such an environment made possible party leadership that was highly centralized, command-oriented, and nonpermissive.

In the aftermath of the revolt against Speaker Cannon in 1910, House Speakers were stripped of their great powers. The parties were weakened and, increasingly during the twentieth century, members of Congress are elected on their own: they build their own organizations, they raise their own money and, to a considerable extent, they manage to cultivate their constituencies to insulate themselves from national tides. Consequently, party leaders cannot influence whether members attain their reelection, power or policy goals to the extent that the pre-1910 party leadership could. To be sure, current leaders do have resources that can be employed to influence their members, but, for most members, most of the time, what the leadership can do for them or to them is not critical for their goal attainment. Current leaders must rely upon persuasion-based strategies; they do not possess the resources necessary to command.

Institutional Change and Its Impact

In terms of the functions they are expected to perform and their limited resources for doing so, the party leaders of the 1980s face a situation not very different from that faced by all majority party leaderships since early in the century. What has changed is the institutional context. In the 1970s both House and Senate underwent major internal changes that significantly altered the distribution of influence, and, consequently, made new leadership strategies necessary.

In the 1950's, influence in Congress was distributed in a decentralized but highly unequal fashion. Decision making was committee-centered and, within committees, the chairs and other senior leaders dominated. Both the distribution of resources and norms militated against junior members playing an active legislative role. Because seniority was the sole criterion for appointment to chairmanships, party leaders had no real control over committee chairs. They were forced to bargain with the chairs and their resources for doing so were scanty.

The 1970's saw a constellation of House rules changes aimed at curbing the power of committee chairs.[4] As a result, the discretion of full committee chairs has been severely limited. Their power to run their committees has been strictly curtailed and, because they are dependent upon the Democratic caucus for their positions, they must be responsive to the wishes of the party majority. Subcommittees have gained very considerable autonomy. Subcommittee chairs are no longer beholden to the full committee chair for their position, their workload, or their resources. The rules changes, in addition, encouraged participation by rank-and-file members, participation made more feasible by the increase in such members' staff resources.

The Senate has also changed. In the contemporary Senate, influence is much more equally distributed and members are accorded very wide latitude. The typical senator no longer specializes; he becomes involved in a broad range of issues, including ones that do not fall into the jurisdiction of his committees. Generous staff resources and the demise of the specialization norm make such participation possible. He is active not only in the committee room but also on the Senate floor, in offering amendments and, not infrequently, in filibustering. The typical 1980s senator is much less restrained than his 1950s or 1960s counterpart was in exploiting the great powers the Senate rules confer upon the individual.[5]

Both House and Senate are more internally democratic and afford rank-and-file members greater opportunities to participate in the policy process since the 1970s. The so-called *sunshine rules,* which opened to the public committee markups, in which bills are drafted, and conference committee meetings, in which differences between the chambers are worked out—have made the congressional decision-making process more open and more accessible to a variety of outside influences. The late 1960s and the 1970s saw an explosion in the number and diversity of interest groups active in Washington. Most of those groups focus their attention on Congress where the public character of decision making gives groups without strong ties to influential insiders a better chance to have an impact on decisions.

These changes have made the environment in which the party leaders operate less predictable. The number of significant actors is larger; there is more going on and in a larger number of arenas. According to a top leader, "The democratization of the House has proceeded so far that all kinds of things can come percolating up from below, and that can cause problems for the leadership." To be sure, committee chairs are less formidable competitors for power than they were in the pre-reform period; by the same token, they are less valuable as allies. With the dispersion of influence has come the need to deal with the much larger number of significant participants and the uncertainty over whether one has indentified them all. As (then) Majority Leader James Wright, a Democrat from Texas, explained:

> The leadership's task must have been infinitely less complicated in the days of Mr. Rayburn and Mr. McCormack. In Mr. Rayburn's day, about all a majority leader or Speaker needed to do in order to get his program adopted was to deal effectively with perhaps 12 very senior committee chairmen. They, in turn, could be expected to influence their committees and the subcommittee chairmen whom they, in those days, appointed . . . . Well, now that situation is quite considerably different. There are, I think, 153 subcommittees. The full committee chairmen are not inviolable in their own precincts. They are not the great powers that they once were . . . . [Therefore] we have to deal with a great many more people than was the case in Mr. Rayburn's day or Mr. Mc-Cormack's day.[6]

The high level of subcommittee activity and the decrease in the full committee chairs' control over subcommittees presents a major information problem for the majority party leadership. Keeping track of what is going on is more difficult because more is going on and in a larger number of arenas.

The floor of both chambers has become a more important and less predictable decision-making arena. A longtime observer contends that:

> There is more of a tendency now, if a committee has difficulty reaching a consensus, to throw it onto the floor and have it resolved by floor amendments. There are some committees that just sort of throw up their hands and say "Let the members decide." Lots of controversial amendments are brought to the floor that used to be decided in committee. Perhaps committees found it easier to reach a consensus when you didn't have as much public participation in the process. Also, perhaps the issues are more complex.

Since neither junior status nor party affiliation nor lack of expertise bars members from offering amendments, amendments can come from anywhere; it is impossible to anticipate all the amendments which may be offered. The large number of amendments offered to many major bills strains the leadership's resources and increases the probability of the committee majority and the leadership getting "ambushed" on the floor.

Some of the rules changes of the 1970s, however, augmented the resources of the House party leadership. The power to make committee assignments was taken from the Democrats on the House Ways and Means Committee and given to the Steering and Policy Committee, which the Speaker chairs (and to which he appoints a number of members). Rules Committee nominations were made solely the prerogative of the Speaker. The Speaker has been granted increased power over the referral of bills; in those cases in which a bill is referred to more than one committee—an increasingly common occurrence—he can set time limits on the committees for reporting the bill out. The Senate party leadership, in contrast, did not gain significant new resources in the 1970s.

The challenge the House leadership faces is that of using its augmented but still limited resources effectively to build coalitions and to keep peace in the family within an environment characterized by high participation and thus considerable uncertainty. The environment within which Senate leaders work is even less predictable; individual senators have considerably more power to influence the legislative process on a variety of issues than House members do; legislative battles of consequence attract large numbers of participants which, when combined with the looseness of Senate floor rules, make their likely course highly unpredictable. Senate leaders thus face the same tasks as House leaders but they are armed with fewer resources and must operate in an even more uncertain environment.

The Impact of the Political Context

The partisan and ideological balance within the chambers constitutes a second set of context variables that influence leadership strategies and the leadership's chances of successful coalition building. The larger the size of the party's majority and the more ideologically homogeneous its members on the key issues of the day, the easier is the leadership's task in building winning coalitions. Democrats have controlled the House in every Congress since 1955 but the size of their majority has varied. A close party balance through most of the 1950s was replaced after 1958 with Democratic predominance; from 1959 through 1980, Democrats held on the average 61.6 percent of the House seats. During the 1980s, Democratic majorities have been somewhat smaller; the 1981–82 Congress saw the narrowest margin when Democrats held 243 seats and Republicans 192. From 1955 through 1980, Democrats also controlled the Senate with the size of their majority generally paralleling that in the House. In the 1980 elections, however, Republicans won twelve Senate seats to take a majority (53 to 47). Republicans held a narrow majority until 1987 when Democrats regained control.

Majority leaders in the 1980s have had to contend with narrower majorities than their predecessors in the 1960s and 1970s and the problem has been especially acute for Senate leaders. But even the substantial Democratic majorities of the 1960s and 1970s seldom translated into automatic policy majorities. Then and now leaders must forge majorities from an ideologically heterogeneous membership split particularly but by no means exclusively along north-south lines.

Although not as heterogeneous as the Democratic party, Republicans when in the majority in the Senate have also found the maintenance of high cohesion problematical. Ideological differences between purists of the far right such as Jesse Helms and more pragmatic members have strained party harmony. In other instances, constituency interests have led senators to oppose their leadership as when many farm state Republicans joined Democrats in supporting more generous farm aid than the leadership or the administration wanted.

Partisan control of the presidency influences what congressional party leaders are expected to do and their chances of success. If the president's party controls a chamber, the majority party leaders are expected to build winning coalitions on the president's legislative priorities. They do not and are not expected to serve blindly and exclusively as the president's lieutenants; they represent their members' views and interests to the president; they may occasionally refuse to support the president; but most of the time, they work closely with the president in attempting to pass his program which is what their members and interest groups allied with the party expect them to do. The president is, after all, the leader of his party.

For the majority party leadership, having a president of their own party in the White House is a mixed blessing; they are expected to pass his programs, but if they cannot because of a narrow majority or an ideologically split membership, their reputation may suffer. Some of the president's policies may split the party membership, straining intraparty harmony. The Reagan administration's agriculture policies were vigorously opposed by many farm state Republicans who feared the unpopular policies' impact on their chances of reelection. In 1985, President Reagan's abandonment of the Senate's proposed budget, which froze social security cost-of-living increases, demoralized Senate Republicans who believed they had made politically perilous but responsible decisions only to have the White House pull the rug out from under them. On balance, however, control of the White House is of great advantage for the majority party leadership because the president brings major resources to coalition-building efforts. The prestige of his office, his potential ability to rally public opinion, and his ability to extend a variety of favors make the president a formidable persuader.

A majority party leadership that faces a president of the other party can cooperate with the president to pass compromise policies, simply try to defeat the president's program, or try to pass its own program. Of course, the actual strategy pursued will be a mixture of these three pure strategies, varying from issue to issue and over time. A majority party leadership under *divided control,* Congress by one party (or both) and the presidency by the other party, often faces the problem of a lack of consensus among its own members and among allied interest groups as to its best strategy. Some will urge cooperation, believing that what can be gained by compromise will be more than can be gained by confrontation and that the political cost of opposing the policies of a popular president are too high. Others will contend that even if confrontation does not result in the enactment of desired policies, it will pay off politically by positioning party members favorably on a salient issue and, perhaps, by making the president veto a popular bill. A majority party leadership under divided control thus faces conflicting expectations. And, of course, if the leadership decides not to cooperate with the president, the resources of the presidency will be used against it. Divided control greatly complicates the tasks of the majority party leadership and reduces its chances of success.

HOUSE LEADERSHIP RESOURCES

The Speaker, the majority leader, and the majority whip are the core of the majority party leadership in the House of Representatives. The Speaker as an officer of the House is formally elected by its full membership but is actually selected by and is the leader of the majority party in the House. The majority leader and the whip are party officials and both are elected by the Democratic caucus, the organization of all House Democrats. In 1987, when Jim Wright, who had been majority leader, became Speaker, Thomas S. Foley of Washington moved up from whip to majority leader, and Tony Coelho of California became the first elected whip.

The Speaker is the presiding officer of the House; as such, he recognizes members who wish to speak and decides points of order. He refers bills to committee. He appoints the members of select committees, of conference committees, of some commissions, and the chairs of the Committee of the Whole. The majority leader schedules legislation for floor consideration; he is the chief party spokesman on the House floor. The whip oversees the whip system which is charged with collecting and disseminating information. Conducting *whip polls,* which determine how members stand on important legislation, is the whip system's single most important function. As discussed later in this chapter, these duties provide resources useful in coalition building and party maintenance. The Speaker's influence on the interpretation of House rules, for example, can be used within the limits of fairness to his party's advantage.

The need to perform the traditional leadership functions within the context of an environment characterized by wide participation and high uncertainty dictated new leadership styles and strategies in the 1970s. Democrat Sam Rayburn of Texas, the most highly regarded Speaker of the pre-reform era, used a highly personalized leadership style. He made little use of formal leadership structures; an informal network of colleagues served as his primary source of information. In coalition building, he relied on personal negotiation with a few key actors. Norms of apprenticeship and deference to senior members contributed to keeping peace in the family. So too, Rayburn believed, did his highly informal and personalized style by providing as few forums as possible for antagonistic elements in the party to confront each other directly. In addition, Rayburn was heavily engaged in doing favors for members, again on a very personal and informal basis.

Changes in the House have made the Rayburn strategy obsolete. Given the highly unpredictable environment—weak party discipline, openness, and external pressures—more formal and more systematic ways of gathering information have become necessary. Given the increase in the number of significant actors, a strategy based upon personal negotiation with a few key actors is obviously untenable.

The Extended Leadership Circle

The core leadership group is far too small to carry out alone all the tasks necessary for successful coalition building and party maintenance in the post-reform House. The core leaders depend on an extended leadership circle consisting of the whip system, the Steering and Policy Committee, and the Rules Committee for help.

The whip system carries on an extensive information collection and dissemination effort and is centrally involved in persuasion. Under the direction of the majority whip, the whip system of the One-hundredth Congress consists of a chief deputy whip (currently David E. Bonior of Michigan), ten deputy whips, twenty-one zone whips, and forty-eight at-large whips. Each of the zone whips is elected by the Democratic members from a geographical zone; the deputy and at-large whips are appointed by the leadership.

All the whips are involved in conveying information to and from the leadership. As a regional whip explained:

> I see the job as providing a liaison between the Democratic leadership and the members. This is a difficult thing in an organization as big as the House of Representatives. We need to have sort of a mechanism for keeping everybody up to date, providing two-way communications. The whip organization meets once a week, every Thursday morning, and we go over the schedule for the next week and discuss any matters that seem to be important from a party standpoint, and especially anything that the Speaker wants to get to the members or that the individual members want to bring up, any problems; it's sort of a problem clearinghouse.

As this whip implies, the weekly whip meetings are an important information source for the leaders. They hear rumors and member gripes. Because the regional whips collectively are representative of the diversity of the party, discussions at whip meetings can provide an early warning of trouble. In addition, the meetings serve a safety valve function by allowing the expression of rank-and-file complaints directly to the leadership. The leaders also find the meetings useful for conveying information to their membership. A number of the zone whips write up a summary of the major points covered in the meeting and send it, along with a copy of the tentative schedule, to all members in their zone. Particularly critical information spreads quickly even without such a formal procedure.

The addition of appointed whips to the traditional zone whips has made a division of labor possible. Because they are chosen by members of their regions, the elected whips are not necessarily supportive of the party position; consequently, they are simply expected to conduct the initial count of members' voting intentions on major legislation. Most of the appointed whips act as an arm of the leadership in persuasion efforts.

The Steering and Policy Committee serves as the House Democrats' committee on committees. The Speaker chairs the committee and appoints a number of its members while other top leaders—committee chairs and formal party leaders—serve ex officio on the committee. Consequently, the party leadership has considerable influence over the assignment of Democrats to committees, influence that can be used to do favors by helping members get coveted assignments or to shape committees so they will be friendly to the leadership's views. The leaders do not, however, control the assignment process. Over one-third of the committee's members are regionally elected and charged with representing the interests of their zone members. Voting is by secret ballot.

The composition of the Steering and Policy Committee includes the core leaders, the chairs of the four most important committees, the regionally elected members, and a group chosen by the Speaker both for their skills and their representativeness. Because of its broad representation, the committee makes an excellent sounding board for the discussion of policy and serves as a forum for the exchange of information and the working out of intraparty disagreements. When the committee endorses legislation, as it sometimes does, it places the imprimatur of the party on that legislation. Occasionally the Steering and Policy Committee has been involved in policy formulation, a role Speaker Wright intends to expand.

The majority party leadership's control over the floor schedule is its most important resource. The power to decide whether a measure reaches the floor, when it reaches the floor, and under what ground rules gives the leadership its greatest leverage in the legislative process. Although floor scheduling is a central leadership task, the party leaders control scheduling only so long as the Rules Committee acts as an arm of the leadership. It is the Rules Committee that decides on procedural rules, for example, those that allow legislation to be taken up out of order, or that establish debate time. In this way the Rules Committee can decide which amendments will be allowed.

Rules changes in the 1970s that gave the Speaker the right to nominate Democratic members of the Rules Committee subject only to ratification by the Democratic caucus produced a committee that is an arm of the leadership; the committee almost invariably grants rules on the legislation the leadership wants to consider and grants them when the leadership wants them. Bruce

Oppenheimer has observed that some members also play a "field commander" role for the leadership. He quotes a senior Rules Committee Democrat:

> It's sort of like people on the Rules Committee treating themselves as if they were responsible field commanders reporting to the chief in Paris. Intelligence comes from us to the leadership. Our responsibility is to inform, advise, and execute.[7]

Particularly important to the leadership's position is the Rules Committee's increasing use of complex rules to structure floor debate. By adroitly structuring the choices members face on the floor, complex rules can increase the likelihood that the leadership's position will prevail (see Chapter 9).

Complex rules are powerful tools but, since a majority of the House must approve a rule, their construction is a task calling for a high degree of political astuteness. On important and highly controversial bills, the leadership and Rules Committee Democrats will discuss the type of rule to be granted. Conflicts are rare, but when they arise, the leadership prevails. In sum, Rules Committee Democrats may have lost their independence of the Speaker, but, in return, those who are interested have become part of the leadership.

LEADERSHIP STRATEGIES

Successful leadership always requires satisfying the expectations of followers. For leaders who do not control entry into the organization and who are directly dependent on their followers for their leadership position, developing strategies consonant with member expectations is certainly a prerequisite to success.

Members of the post-reform House expect to pursue their goals of reelection, influence, and policy with little restraint. They expect to participate broadly in the legislative process and to engage freely in other reelection-directed activities. Party maintenance requires that leaders facilitate rather than hinder members' high level of activity and broad participation; it dictates that they do so for all their members, not just for those whose participation is likely to be helpful to them. Yet extensive participation results in an unpredictable legislative process, which makes coalition building more difficult.

In their attempts to cope with these problems, the current leaders have developed a three-pronged strategy: they are heavily engaged in *providing services* to members; they make use of their formal powers and influence to *structure choice* situations; and they attempt to *promote the involvement* of as many Democrats as possible in the coalition building process.

Providing Services

A senior O'Neill aide said of the Speakership, "This is a service organization."[8] Providing services to members absorbs a great deal of the leaders' time and that of their aides. Because the leaders have more influence with other significant actors than rank-and-file members, they receive numerous requests for help. The Speaker explained:

> [The Speaker] does have the power to be able to pick up the telephone and call people. And oftentimes they have problems from their area and they need aid and assistance, either legislativewise or administrativewise. We're happy to try to open the door for them, having been in the town for so many years and knowing so many people. We do know where a lot of bodies are and we do know how to advise people.[9]

The leaders' official functions and their influence within the chamber can be used to do favors for members. A member may ask the Speaker to intercede with a committee that has eliminated a project of importance to his district; another may ask the majority leader to schedule a pet bill at a particularly advantageous time. The leaders are asked for help in getting desirable committee assignments. Members also make a large number and wide variety of minor requests to the leaders; for example, an important constituent may want to meet the Speaker and perhaps have his picture taken with him.

The leaders also do a great deal of speaking, generally at fund-raisers, on behalf of Democratic members in their districts. Such a visit is a relatively important favor which the leadership can bestow on a member; the appearance of one of the top leaders is likely to raise the status of the member among his politically attentive constituents and, because the leaders are good draws, the member is likely to raise more money.

In addition to doing favors for individual members, the leadership is heavily engaged in providing services to the membership collectively. The whip's office has become a major disseminator of information to the membership. A *whip packet* containing the projected floor schedule for the week and, when available, copies of scheduled bills and committee reports is sent to all Democratic members over the weekend. A *whip advisory*—a single-sheet summary of the content and legislative history of and amendments expected to a measure scheduled for floor action—is prepared for every scheduled bill, resolution, and conference report and is sent to all Democratic members prior to floor consideration.

By providing services to members collectively and individually, the leaders help them play the role they desire in the chamber and facilitate their goal achievement. Thus, the services the leadership provides contribute to party maintenance and to producing a favorable climate for coalition building.

For the leaders, these activities have another payoff as well. In the process of doing favors for members, the leaders pick up information vital to the successful performance of both their primary functions. Spending some time in a member's district, for example, provides the leadership with information which can be very useful when it comes to persuasion. As a leadership aide explained, these trips provide a feel for the member's political situation.

> If a guy tells [the Speaker], "I can't go with you on this one. It will hurt me in the district," [the Speaker] can say, "Aw come on, they love you back home. You can do anything you want to," or he knows the guy does face a tough reelection fight and shouldn't be pushed.

Although doing favors for individual members has long been a leadership strategy, the post-reform leadership is much more involved in providing services to its membership collectively than its predecessors were. Because of new rules and norms, almost any member can cause problems for the leadership. Rank-and-file satisfaction or dissatisfaction is more important than it was in the pre-reform House.

Structuring Choice

By using their formal powers and their influence, leaders can often structure the choices members face in such a way as to be advantageous to the leadership's position. Such structuring is not a new leadership strategy, but the reforms of the 1970s have augmented leadership resources for doing so effectively. The Panama Canal Treaty implementation legislation of 1979 exemplifies the usefulness of the new multiple-referral rules; using those rules, the Speaker referred that legislation to four committees. By so doing, the Speaker brought into the process committees friendly to the administration position to counter the basically hostile Merchant Marine Committee and, by using a reporting deadline, he forced the Merchant Marine Committee to report the bill out in timely fashion. Both the Panama bill and synthetic fuels legislation, also passed in 1979, illustrate the significance of control over the floor schedule. Such control allowed the leadership to postpone the Panama legislation until the votes to pass it were in hand. Consideration of synthetic fuels legislation was moved up so that a possible opposition tactic of attempting to delay a vote until after the recess would stand little chance of success. The Speaker's control of the Rules Committee is an immensely important resource because it makes possible the use of carefully constructed rules to structure floor choices. The 1980 reconciliation bill was considered under a *closed rule*, meaning no amendments were allowed; thus the choice members faced was whether to vote for or against savings; if amendments had been allowed, the choices would have been whether to vote for or against cutting a number of popular programs.

Structuring choices is a means of coercing members collectively. The strategy is limited by the requirement of overt or tacit member approval. When the strategy is skillfully used, members will acquiesce because what they gain is greater than what they lose by having their choices constrained. If, for example, members' policy goals dictate a pro-leadership vote but their reelection needs a contrary vote, structuring the choice situation so that the key roll call occurs on a procedural motion may allow members to vote their policy preferences. Members may, for instance, be willing to vote for a rule barring amendments requiring a balanced budget or prohibiting school busing, even though, were the amendments offered, they would feel constrained to vote for them.

The tools the leadership possesses for structuring the choice situation are not sufficiently powerful and flexible to create an ideal choice situation for most legislation. Usually creative use of the tools will increase the probability of, but not ensure, success. Furthermore, the use of the tools is subject to member approval. During the battle over President Reagan's 1981 budget cuts, the Democratic leadership proposed a rule that would have forced its opponents to vote on each of the major cuts in popular programs separately rather than voting on the whole package at once as Reagan wanted. Both sides believed that were members forced to vote on Reagan's proposed cuts individually, as the rule specified, they would not pass. The leadership could not, however, muster sufficient votes to pass the rule.

From the leadership's point of view, the need for member acquiescence is both a disadvantage and an advantage. On the one hand, that need for acquiescence limits the use of the strategy of constraining choice; on the other hand, coercion to which one has consented tends not to be perceived as unreasonable. Because of the uncertain environment, leaders do not always know what their members will consider acceptable. Misjudgment may lead to a legislative defeat; members may, for example, vote down a rule. But for the leadership, losing almost any particular legislative battle is preferable to creating serious dissatisfaction among the membership. Few legislative battles are worth winning at the price of a severe reduction in the probability of future coalition-building success.

The Strategy of Inclusion

The attempt to involve as many Democrats as possible in the coalition-building process is the third element of the current leadership's strategy. As rule and norm changes dispersed influence more widely in the chamber, more extensive vote mobilization efforts became necessary. The high rate of activity in a multitude of arenas also made more formalized information gathering essential. In response, the leadership expanded and uses formal leadership structures. The greatly expanded whip system conducts large numbers of whip polls and is centrally involved in the persuasion effort and in the dissemination of information to the membership. The Steering and Policy Committee is involved in coalition building, formally by virtue of its role of endorsing legislation and informally by providing a forum for working out intraparty disputes. The Rules Committee has lost its independence of the Speaker but, in recompense, committee Democrats who so desire have become members of the leadership.

The leadership also involves other members in specific coalition-building efforts. On certain bills that are highly important to the party, the Speaker appoints a *task force* and charges the members with passing the legislation. Membership will include Democrats from the committee of origin and also others who are simply interested in the legislation for policy or reelection reasons. Often when no task force is appointed, such interested members are nevertheless included in the coalition-building effort in an informal way.

The 1984 battle over MX production illustrates the character of such efforts. During 1983 and early 1984, opposition among Democrats to the MX missile program had been growing. Nevertheless, in mid-May, a leadership-supported proposal to block production of the MX was narrowly defeated in favor of a compromise proposal sponsored by Les Aspin, a Democrat from Wisconsin, and supported by the Reagan administration.[10] Determined to win the next engagement which would come in only a few weeks, the leadership appointed a task force to coordinate the persuasion effort. Richard A. Gephardt, a deputy whip, directed the joint efforts of long-time MX foes and of experienced leadership tacticians. Among those involved were Democrats who had established themselves as leading MX opponents such as Nicholas Mavroules of Massachusetts, a junior member of the Armed Services Committee, and Thomas J. Downey of New York; members with skill and experience at coalition building such as Gephardt himself and Tony Coelho, Chair of the Democratic Congressional Campaign Committee; Charles E. Bennett of Florida, a sympathetic senior member of the Armed Services Committee; and certain other members, like Mike Synar, a three-termer from Oklahoma who serves on no defense-related committee but who was simply interested in the issue and willing to work. To dramatize the leadership's commitment to the effort, Majority Leader Jim Wright closed debate for the MX opponents. On a 199 to 197 vote, the majority leadership won and thereby handed Reagan a significant policy defeat.[11]

The campaign to pass the first budget resolution in 1983 featured a leadership attempt to involve the entire Democratic membership. After two years of failing to pass the Democratic budget resolution, the leadership was determined to prevail. Before the Budget Committee drafted its resolution, all Democrats were sent a questionnaire that simulated the tough choices the Budget Committee majority would have to make. The Speaker pressured members to fill it out and over 200 did so. The results provided the Budget Committee majority with some guidance about sentiments within the party and gave rank-and-file Democrats some influence on the Budget Committee's resolution. Members' perception that they had had some influence and their increased understanding of the difficult trade-offs involved in writing a budget made leadership appeals for floor support more effective and the resolution passed handily.

The current leaders' use of task forces and of less formal ad hoc groups to work on specific legislation and their use of the expanded whip system, the Steering and Policy Committee, and the Rules Committee are all elements of the strategy of inclusion. Leaders' regular interactions with members of the extended leadership circle provide information vital to successful coalition building in the unpredictable post-reform House. By enlisting a large number and broad variety of Democrats in leadership efforts, the leaders get the help they so badly need. The large number involved makes one-on-one persuasion with a large proportion of the membership possible. The broad variety ensures that the group as a whole will have ties to all sections of the party. The strategy of inclusion thus contributes to coalition-building success.

The leaders believe that the strategy of inclusion also contributes to party maintenance. In the post-reform House, rules allow and norms dictate high rank-and-file participation. Involvement in the extended leadership circle and in specific coalition-building efforts gives a large number of members the opportunity to participate actively, but in a way that helps rather than hurts the leadership.

LEADERSHIP IN THE INDIVIDUALIST SENATE

The Senate Majority leader, as the title implies, is the leader of and is chosen by the members of the majority party in the Senate. During the past decade three different men have held the position. Robert Byrd of West Virginia served as majority leader from 1977 through 1980. When Republicans took control of the chamber in 1981, Howard Baker of Tennessee, who had been minority leader, became majority leader. In 1985, after Baker's voluntary retirement from the Senate, he was succeeded by Robert Dole of Kansas. In the 1986 elections, Democrats regained a majority in the Senate and Byrd, who had served as minority leader during the period of Republican control, resumed the position of majority leader for a final Congress before announcing that he would step down as Democratic majority leader.

Leadership Resources and Constraints

The resources the Senate majority leader commands are far less potent than those of the Speaker of the House. He is not the chamber's presiding officer and, in any case, the presiding officer of the Senate has much less discretion than his House counterpart does. The only important resource the Senate rules give the majority leader to aid him in his core tasks of scheduling legislation and floor leadership is the right to be recognized first when a number of senators are seeking recognition on the Senate floor.

Not only do institutional rules give the majority party leadership few special resources, but they bestow great powers on rank-and-file senators. In most cases, any senator can offer an unlimited number of amendments to a piece of legislation on the Senate floor and those amendments need not even be germane. A senator may hold the Senate floor indefinitely unless *cloture,* a procedure which limits debate and requires the extraordinary majority of sixty votes, is invoked. Senators are much more willing than they used to be to fully exploit the powers inherent in the rules; consequently, the job of the Senate majority leader has become even more difficult.

Since a single senator can disrupt the work of the Senate, a partisan minority of any size could bring legislative activity to a standstill. The Senate majority leader must confer with the minority leader on an almost continuous basis. In the House with its more constraining rules, floor scheduling is largely a majority leadership function; in the Senate, the majority leader schedules in close consultation with the minority leader.

Structuring the choice situation members face so as to advantage the party position, a frequently used House leadership strategy, is less available to the Senate majority leadership. The party leaders' control over the floor agenda is tenuous. By offering non-germane amendments on the floor, individual senators can force action on issues committee and party leaders would prefer to avoid. Strong opposition from Majority Leader Howard Baker, Finance Committee Chair Robert Dole, and President Reagan was not sufficient to keep junior Republican Bob Kasten of Wisconsin from getting his proposal to repeal interest-withholding on the floor in 1983.[12] Conversely, by filibustering or by threatening to do so, rank-and-file senators can delay or block action on legislation the party leadership wants considered. Late in 1986, opponents mounted a filibuster to prevent consideration of product liability reform legislation. The Senate successfully invoked cloture (Rule XXII of the Senate) on the motion to consider the bill. Democratic Senator Ernest ("Fritz") Hollings from South Carolina, the lead opponent, then threatened to filibuster the bill itself, and Majority Leader Robert Dole pulled the legislation from the floor. It was too near the end of the session to spend large amounts of floor time on discretionary legislation.[13] Senators have recently used extended debate to force the majority leader to schedule a measure. In February 1985, farm state Democrats blocked the confirmation vote on Edwin Meese to be attorney general and all other Senate business. Their purpose was to force action on a totally unrelated issue—aid to farmers. To end the filibuster, newly elected Majority Leader Dole had to promise the filibusterers prompt floor action on emergency farm credit legislation the Reagan Administration opposed.[14]

Because of senators' capacity and willingness to disrupt leadership plans, scheduling has become an increasingly difficult exercise in accommodating all interested parties. Senators expect the leadership to schedule around their own personal schedules. Reporter Alan Ehrenhalt tells a story that illustrates the problems leaders face in scheduling when everyone must be accommodated. In 1980, then-Majority Leader Byrd was on the Senate floor trying to find a time the following Monday for a vote on the budget resolution. "One senator after another announced that a particular time would be inconvenient. Byrd was reduced to writing all the preferences on a long yellow legal pad, a process that made him look more like a man sending out for sandwiches than the leader of a deliberative body."[15] As William Hildenbrand, a veteran Senate staffer explains, "Everyone who wants to be accommodated is accommodated. If someone doesn't want a vote on Monday, there's no vote on Monday. The leadership just coordinates the individual requests."[16]

The Senate majority leader thus has much less capacity to structure the choice situation than the House leadership. The majority leader does have more influence over the timing of floor consideration than anyone else in the chamber and this can be used to strategic advantage. He is centrally involved in the negotiating of unanimous consent agreements which are often employed to set the ground rules for the consideration of legislation on the Senate floor. If he is skillful, he can gain some advantage for his position, but such agreements, as their name implies, require unanimous consent. The right of first recognition can sometimes be used strategically; Senate rules specify that no more than *second degree amendments,* amendments to previously offered amendments, are allowable; by using his priority in gaining recognition to offer amendments, the majority leader can sometimes make opponents' amendments out of order and thereby block them.

Leadership Strategies

The inclusion of a large number and broad variety of members in coalition-building efforts is less a strategy than a necessity in the Senate. If a senator and his staff are skillful, it is difficult for anyone to prevent him from participating in making decisions on almost any issue before the Senate. The majority leader must work with the significant players and, given the powers and resources of individual senators, they will often have as much to say about the terms of the cooperative effort as the majority leader. Nevertheless, inclusion does have payoffs for the party leadership. As Mississippi Republican Thad Cochran said, "Dole involves more people in decisions. He gets them on the inside, working to put a package together. Then they have a stake in the process. He keeps widening the circle."[17]

Because the Senate membership is so much smaller than that of the House, party committees and other formal structures are less important instruments of coalition building. In neither party is the whip system of much importance, although Alan Cranston, the Democratic whip from California, is renowned as an expert vote counter. The Democratic Policy Committee, which the party leader chairs, primarily provides him with highly useful staff resources. The Republican leader does not even chair his party's Policy Committee. From the leader's perspective, the committee's weekly lunches for all Republican senators are its most useful function; they provide a forum for the exchange of information. The lunch is "a temperature-taking session," a staff aide explained. "It's very useful from the point of view of getting a sense of where sentiment lies . . . . A leader who has his antenna tuned will find these meetings very helpful for his understanding of what the membership wants."

If structuring the choice situation and inclusion are less efficacious leadership strategies in the Senate than in the House, providing services and doing favors are even more important. Like their House counterparts, Senate leaders direct an extensive information dissemination system. In making their legislative scheduling decisions, leaders attempt to accommodate the membership as a collectivity. For example, recent leaders have seldom scheduled votes for Mondays or Fridays, thus enabling senators to be away from

Washington for the long weekend. General member satisfaction with Dole's leadership was attributed, in part, to his providing this service.[18] Because most senators have a full schedule away from Washington arranged long ahead of time for weekends and recesses, the leader's threat to keep the Senate in session provides him with a significant resource, one that Dole used frequently. In August 1986, just before the scheduled recess, Dole managed to negotiate a unanimous consent agreement providing for a vote on Contra aid even though the pro-Contra forces did not have enough votes to invoke cloture. Almost certainly it was his willingness to jeopardize the recess that made the anti-Contra forces willing to accept the agreement.[19]

Senate leaders also perform a myriad of favors for individual members. As we saw earlier, senators expect to be accommodated in scheduling; they often expect the leaders to hold a vote open beyond the regulation 15 minutes so they can be recorded. The leader is at the center of an extensive information network; he can often provide a senator with timely information gleaned from other senators, the administration, or interest groups. He can use his right to first recognition to let a senator offer a particularly attractive amendment. During the 1985 battle over the budget resolution, for example, Dole made sure that a popular amendment on social security bore the names of two junior Republicans up for reelection in 1986, not that of a Democrat. The leader may be able to use his influence to expedite a senator's pet legislation or to aid a senator in dealings with the administration. He can make campaign appearances for a fellow senator and help him raise campaign funds.

By assiduously using the limited resources he possesses to do favors for members, the majority leader creates a favorable climate for coalition building. The favors he can do are not negligible and members generally are grateful. Yet what the Senate majority leader can do to or for his members is seldom decisive for the attainment of their goals; for example, his impact on their reelection is marginal at best. Consequently, the Senate majority leader must rely upon persuasion; he certainly cannot command. Furthermore, lacking the powers to structure the choice situation that the House Speaker has, he is even more dependent than the House leadership on a favorable political context for success.

CONCLUSION: LEADERSHIP IN THE LATE 1980s AND BEYOND

In the late 1980s and beyond, leadership success will continue to depend most heavily on the political context—on the size and ideological homogeneity of the party membership and on whether control of Congress and the presidency is divided.

But, whatever the variations in the political context, a significant development in leadership style can be anticipated. The late 1980s and early 1990s are likely to see a continued evolution in the leadership's use of the media as a major element of strategy. Traditionally congressional party leaders have been inside players; they have attained and retained their positions because of their skills at one-on-one persuasion, their knowledge of the rules and customs of the chamber, and their ability and willingness to do favors for their fellow members. Increasingly, however, members expect their leaders also to be adept at using the media to promote the party's image and its policy positions.

This change in expectations was well under way when Ronald Reagan became president, but the Reagan presidency has accelerated the change. Congressional Democrats saw Reagan make extremely skillful use of the media in pursuing a course that threatened their policy, reelection, and power goals. Commenting on the 1981 budget resolution vote that the Democratic leadership lost after the administration's media campaign had deluged members with mounds of constituency mail, a participant in the leadership's persuasion effort said; "You can't take a guy like [a southerner from a marginal district] and say, 'I'll give you such and such a public works project in your district; therefore, vote for my budget resolution,' because that won't work for _____ in this situation. You have to go to the people and get the people with you and then it will become possible for a guy like _____ to vote with you and then he'll be happy to do it." The majority leadership under Tip O'Neill of Massachusetts did respond; it became more aware of the need for a media strategy and more sophisticated in orchestrating media campaigns. "Sometimes to pass a bill," House Majority Leader Tom Foley has said, "you have to change the attitude of the country."[20] Before major votes, an effort is made to sell the party position through a variety of means: the Speaker's press conference, the appearance by party or committee leaders on TV interview programs such as "Meet the Press" and the "MacNeil/Lehrer NewsHour," the placement of op-ed articles in newspapers, and arranging floor speeches by Democrats with an eye to their usefulness on the nightly network news.

In the coming years, congressional leaders are likely to combine newer media-based strategies with older insider strategies more frequently. Doing so is a necessary adjustment to the changing context of American politics and again illustrates the extent to which leadership styles and strategies are shaped by the political and institutional context. Leaders are expected to build winning coalitions and to keep peace in the family; the strategies most likely to produce success change as the environment changes.

NOTES

1. *Congressional Quarterly Weekly Report,* October 4, 1986, pp. 2338–42.
2. Barbara Sinclair, *Majority Leadership in the U.S. House* (Baltimore, Md.: Johns Hopkins University Press, 1983), pp. 190–93.
3. See Joseph Cooper and David W. Brady, "Institutional Context and Leadership Style: The House from Cannon to Rayburn" and Charles O. Jones, "House

Leadership in an Age of Reform," in *Understanding Congressional Leadership*, ed. Frank H. Mackaman (Washington: CQ Press, 1981).

4. See Sinclair, *Majority Leadership*, pp. 3–6.
5. Barbara Sinclair, "Senate Styles and Senate Decision Making, 1955–1980," *Journal of Politics* 48 (November 1986), pp. 877–908.
6. Quoted in Christopher J. Deering and Steven S. Smith, "Majority Party Leadership and the New House Subcommittee System," paper presented at "Understanding Congressional Leadership: The State of the Art," conference sponsored by the Dirksen Center and the Sam Rayburn Library, Washington, D.C., June 1980. Unattributed quotations are from interviews conducted by the author.
7. Bruce I. Oppenheimer, "The Rules Committee: New Arm of Leadership in a Decentralized House," in *Congress Reconsidered*, ed. Lawrence C. Dodd and Bruce I. Oppenheimer (New York: Praeger Publishers, 1977), p. 4.
8. *National Journal*, June 18, 1977, p. 941.
9. Ibid., p. 942.
10. *Congressional Quarterly Weekly Report*, May 19, 1984, pp. 1155–60.
11. *Congressional Quarterly Weekly Report*, June 2, 1984, pp. 1291–93.
12. *Congressional Quarterly Weekly Report*, March 12, March 19, April 29, 1983.
13. *Congressional Quarterly Weekly Report*, September 27, 1986, p. 2316.
14. *Congressional Quarterly Weekly Report*, February 23, 1985, pp. 335–38, March 2, 1985, pp. 371–74.
15. Alan Ehrenhalt, "In the Senate of the '80s, Team Spirit Has Given Way to the Rule of Individuals," *Congressional Quarterly Weekly Report*, September 4, 1982, p. 2182.
16. Ibid.
17. *Congressional Quarterly Weekly Report*, June 29, 1985, p. 1270.
18. Christopher J. Deering, "Leadership in the Slow Lane," *PS* (Winter 1986), p. 41.
19. *Congressional Quarterly Weekly Report*, August 16, 1986, pp. 1878–79.
20. *Congressional Quarterly Weekly Report*, September 23, 1986, p. 2134.

CHAPTER 8

Influence in Congressional Committees: Participation, Manipulation, and Anticipation

C. Lawrence Evans

In 1984, the Senate Judiciary Committee debated legislation aimed at easing restrictions on the sale of rifles and handguns. Deliberations were deadlocked for a full six months while liberal Democrats led by Edward M. Kennedy from Massachusetts sought to derail the initiative, and proponents led by Republican Orrin Hatch from Utah tried to bring the matter to a vote. This stalemate ended very abruptly in the middle of a committee meeting in May 1984 when Democrat Joseph R. Biden from Delaware proposed an amendment that resulted in the bill being reported to the floor by unanimous vote. A key aide to committee Republicans described the scene:

> Senator Biden came out of the clear blue sky and said something like: "Now wait a minute, you're saying you want this, and you want that, but if I understand it you're really not that far apart, are you?" He was just explaining things in a different way and all of a sudden everybody's heads were going up and down and I thought to myself, this is it.[1]

Thus, who *participates* in committee deliberations, and the form of the participation, is central to understanding the politics of congressional committees.

In July 1964, the Senate Commerce Committee was trying to confirm a nominee as head of the Community Relations Service, a program of major importance to the civil rights movement. On this day, the committee needed the attendance of just one more member to establish the quorum necessary to act. Strom Thurmond from South Carolina, a committee member opposed to the nomination, was standing outside the door to the hearing room.[2] Another member of the committee, Democrat Ralph Yarborough from Texas attempted to nudge Thurmond into the room so that the committee could vote, and what followed made headlines. As described on the front page of *The New York Times*,

> Within minutes of their encounter, the 200-pound Texan and the 170-pound South Carolinian, both with their coats off, were rolling and thrashing across the marble floor to the startled dismay of an audience of secretaries and clerks.[3]

The melee ended when the committee chair emerged and told them to stop. Although this is a relatively extreme example, it points to the general importance of procedural tactics and *manipulation of the process* for understanding the politics of congressional committees.

In fall 1985, the Senate Judiciary Committee considered two proposed constitutional amendments to allow prayer in public schools. The first called for vocal prayer and was supported by the Reagan administration, while the second would have allowed only silent prayer. Although a majority of members were on record as supporting the stronger measure, vocal prayer, the committee decided to focus instead on the provision calling for silent prayer because they believed it stood a better chance of passage in the full Senate. Thus, perceptions of the mood of the full chamber can influence decisions made in committee because committee members often *anticipate* what will be successful on the floor.

These examples illustrate three mechanisms through which members of Congress typically influence legislation in committee: active participation, manipulation of the process, and the anticipation of reactions. This chapter examines how members of Congress influence legislation in committee by a combination of these three mechanisms. Of course, it is important not to oversimplify a complex process, and influence in Congress is nothing if not complex. But the categorization adopted here is a useful device; it reflects some important features of committee decision making and is consistent with the way participants view the process.

OF TIME AND INFLUENCE

Until the mid-1960s, congressional politics was often described as committee government. In both chambers, most members focused on the work of their own committees while deferring to the committee of jurisdiction on other topics. Within a committee, adherence to the seniority rule meant that influence tended to be concentrated in the hands of the chair, the ranking minority member, and a few other senior members. Indeed, it was possible for a single member of Congress like Democrat Howard W. "Judge" Smith from Virginia, the chair of the House Rules Committee, to bottle up items supported by a majority of his party. The legislative landscape has changed markedly since the heyday of Judge Smith, and members of Congress now draft, introduce, and amend legislation in an institution where the opportunity to participate in legislative work is widely shared.

Congress changed because its membership changed. During the 1960s there was an influx of new members, most of whom had little at stake in the old system. In the Senate, the norms of specialization and apprenticeship have atrophied. Nowadays, most senators are issue-oriented generalists and freshmen senators are encouraged to participate. In the House, a series of committee reforms culminating in the *Subcommittee Bill of Rights* curbed the prerogatives of committee chairs and institutionalized the role of subcommittees. The result is a dispersion of legislative influence that parallels the more informal changes that occurred in the Senate.

What is the role of committees in the post-reform Congress? Congressional committees are certainly less autonomous in that proposals are now more likely to face amendment on the floor; nevertheless, committees continue to be the primary arenas for policymaking in Congress. Most of the crucial early decisions about a bill are made in committee, and committee staffs continue to be the most valuable source of expertise on Capitol Hill. Although floor amendments have increased in frequency, most committee proposals emerge from the floor unscathed. As an aide to the Senate Committee on Environment and Public Works stated,

> We don't lose on the floor very often. The committee is ready to debate this stuff and knows more about it than anybody else. You know how the floor works. You've got half a dozen senators there. Somebody will get to a senator, somebody from the state or somebody who gave him a bunch of PAC [political action committee] money, and he'll agree to carry their water and get up and extol the virtues of some amendment for fifteen minutes to an empty chamber. Then people file in and vote with the committee. . . . If it's so damn crazy that the floor is going to ram it back down your throat, odds are you aren't going to get it out of committee.

These remarks suggest the continued relevance of Woodrow Wilson's adage, "Congress in session is Congress on public exhibition, whilst Congress in its committee-rooms is Congress at work."[4] Perhaps not on budget politics or major foreign policy issues, but for the vast majority of initiatives considered on Capitol Hill, policymaking remains committee-centered.

The decline in barriers to participation in Congress has not resulted in patterns of widespread influence on individual pieces of legislation. Senators and representatives work under constraints that force them to focus on those activities that best further their goals. Richard Fenno has argued that members of Congress tend to be motivated in their behavior by some combination of three goals: the desire for reelection, good public policy, and influence within the chamber.[5] These goals are pursued subject to environmental constraints inherent to the decision-making context in which the legislator is acting.

Fenno conceptualizes the environment in terms of individuals and groups: other legislators, clientele groups, the executive branch, and the two political parties. But perhaps the most striking constraints on legislators are time and an overabundance of opportunities to pursue their goals.[6] Although there has been a proliferation of staff and other office perquisites, members of Congress still operate under binding resource constraints that force them to make choices about whether and to what extent they will become involved in legislation.[7] Staff time used to develop the political and technical expertise necessary to exert influence on one issue reduces the resources that can be allocated to constituency service or other legislation and legislators themselves face trade-offs when allocating their time between Washington and the folks back home.

Most observers agree that time has become increasingly scarce on Capitol Hill. In large part this is due to the enormous growth in federal spending since the 1960s and an accompanying increase in the workload of Congress. The number of bills passed in each Congress has declined slightly, but those becoming law in recent years tend to be longer and more complex; the concomitant increase in demand for casework and other forms of constituency service also contributes to the frantic pace on Capitol Hill.[8] Indeed, establishing a quorum to proceed with committee business can take twenty to thirty minutes, and the amount of floor time available for debate and amendment, particularly toward the end of a session, has been greatly reduced.[9]

Participants in the process speak readily about the pervasive impact of time constraints. As one Senate aide assigned to Judiciary Committee issues said,

> My senator is always on the run. They all seem to be. That's why it takes Thurmond twenty minutes to get a quorum. Certain senators don't participate and the views of three or four tend to dominate. There would be a lot of improvement if the senators even spent ten minutes, just ten minutes, with their staff before markup covering the agenda and what issues are going to be brought up. A lot of them walk in cold and just slip open the book.

The diminished barriers to exerting legislative influence engendered through reform and increased staff resources thus do not necessarily lead to patterns of broad participation and dispersed influence. Within an environment structured by the scarcity of time, legislators have to focus to be influential since exerting influence on one bill may preclude involvement in another. Legislators choose from a menu of issues and become active in those that maximize benefits in terms of goal achievement and minimize cost in terms of opportunities forgone. As a result, members of Congress continue to focus on the issues before their own committees, and even within a committee participation is necessarily selective.

The remainder of this chapter examines the three mechanisms through which members of Congress typically influence committee legislation: active participation, manipulation of the process, and anticipation of reactions. Influence through active participation occurs when a representative helps draft the initial version of a bill or successfully amends it during a subcommittee or full committee meeting. Influence through manipulating the process occurs when a representative accelerates a bill's progress through the process or employs dilatory tactics to slow it down. Influence through anticipated reactions occurs when the managers of a bill anticipate problems from another member and incorporate the preferences of that member into their bill in committee to "grease the skids" and facilitate passage. In this third mechanism, the managers of the legislation are not exerting influence; rather, influence is being exerted by the member whose views they are incorporating into the bill.

INFLUENCE THROUGH ACTIVE PARTICIPATION

Most influence is exerted through participation in constructing the initial draft of a bill or by successfully amending the draft during markups—subcommittee or full committee at which final bill language is discussed and agreed upon.[10] For example, Joe Biden clearly influenced the shape of the gun bill mentioned in the opening paragraph of this chapter by proposing an amendment that led to consensus. The consequence of influence through active participation is some alteration in the substance of the bill itself, or in the language of the accompanying report. A staffer for the Senate Committee on Labor and Human Resources noted the importance of active participation:

> This is a put up or shut up game. . . . The whole system operates on a speak now or forever hold your peace basis, because the next chance you get is on the floor of the Senate. You can speak there too, but in terms of credibility, if a senator is on the committee and he has not participated and he goes down to the floor, what's he going to say? "Hey, my colleagues put one over on me"? First of all, it would be the height of political stupidity. That's basically admitting you or your staff didn't do your job. If you have participated and your view was not adopted, then you have a perfect opportunity to go down on the floor and raise a ruckus.

The drafting stage is particularly crucial. Here the contours of debate are usually set, the range of alternatives is formulated, and the process of accommodation begins. The draft is almost always constructed at the staff level, not by committee members themselves. The proportion of actual drafting done by legislators and their staffs varies from bill to bill, by committee, and across chambers of Congress. On some pieces of legislation, all of the language is provided by individuals not on the committee, by executive agencies or interest groups, for example. On others, the entire draft is the product of internal congressional efforts. But the typical pattern falls somewhere between these two extremes, with the draft being a mix of group and agency proposals, language from similar bills introduced in previous Congresses, and the views of interested committee members. Most often, modification of the draft in markup and on the floor is incremental. Nonetheless, even when significant amendment occurs the primary point of reference is the draft legislation—or *vehicle* as it is sometimes called.

In the Senate, influence on the shape of the draft brought into subcommittee or full committee markup tends to be concentrated among the four formal leaders on a bill: the full committee chair and ranking minority member and the relevant subcommittee chair and ranking minority member. Staffers on the Environment and Public Works Committee regularly refer to these senators as "my big four" and markup vehicles on that committee are almost always the product of staffers working for some combination of the formal leaders on a bill. The senators in full committee leadership posts, of course, are the same across bills, but those holding subcommittee leadership positions vary depending on the subcommittee of jurisdiction.

The role of committee leaders in drafting legislation is revealed in the data provided in Table 8–1. Sixty-two bills from four Senate committees were divided into two categories: bills falling within the jurisdiction of a subcommittee and bills that were clearly full committee issues. While almost all legislation in the House is eventually referred to a subcommittee, Senate committees typically reserve areas of the committee jurisdiction for full committee consideration alone. Issues held at full committee tend to be salient to many committee members, or of particular interest to the chair. For example, the full committee on Labor and Human Resources retains control over health issues due to widespread interest among committee members, but also because the current chair, Senator Edward M. Kennedy, is a national leader in the area. Occasionally, a chair will hold an issue at full committee to avoid a subcommittee chair with different views: When Strom Thurmond, at this juncture a Republican, became chair of the Judiciary Committee in 1981, he chose not to recreate the Subcommittee on Antitrust, it is alleged, because the subcommittee chair would have been liberal Republican Charles McC. Mathias, Jr., from Maryland.

Participation in drafting the markup vehicle in the Senate is clearly selective and concentrated in the hands of those in formal leadership positions and their staffs. For each committee, the average number (per bill) of formal leaders (committee chair, ranking minority member, subcommittee chair, subcommittee ranking minority member) influencing committee drafts is provided in Table 8–1, as well as the average number for nonleaders. On all four committees, it is clear that the typical markup vehicle is primarily the product

TABLE 8–1   Committee Leader and Nonleader Participation in Drafting, Selected Senate Committees, Ninety-ninth Congress

Subcommittee bills	Leaders	Nonleaders	Number of Bills
Subcommittee bills			
Commerce	1.60*	0.20†	15
Environment and Public Works	2.50	0.50	8
Judiciary	1.93	0.60	15
Labor	2.00	0.78	9
Full committee bills			
Commerce	1.00	0.00	1
Environment and Public Works	1.50	1.00	2
Judiciary	0.33	0.33	3
Labor	1.56	0.78	9

*Average number of leaders (full committee chair, ranking minority member, ranking subcommittee chair, subcommittee ranking minority member) participating in drafting the markup vehicle per bill.
†Average number of nonleaders participating in drafting the markup vehicle per bill.

SOURCE: Interviews with Senate staff.

of committee members in leadership posts. The strength of those in leadership positions can be appreciated by noting that only four committee members from a total membership of fifteen to seventeen senators are in formal leadership positions on any given bill falling in the jurisdiction of a subcommittee. Data for issues kept at the full committee level are also provided in Table 8–1 except, of course, formal leadership at that level consists of only the full committee chair and ranking minority member. Although the number of bills is relatively small, influence over markup vehicles is exerted primarily by the chair and ranking minority member on all of the committees except the Judiciary committee.

In House committees, patterns of influence on the draft are similar to those found in the Senate, but full committee chairs and ranking minority members play a less prominent role, and rank-and-file members of the subcommittee of jurisdiction are more likely to have an effect.[11] In large part this is because in the House, the agenda and staff prerogatives associated with Senate chairs have been transferred from full committee leaders to subcommittee leaders. Whereas Senate chairs often take the lead in drafting markup vehicles, House chairs tend to defer to the relevant subcommittee leaders or focus their attention on specific titles of a bill. Representatives also have fewer subcommittee assignments than senators and can devote more time to each assignment, increasing the likelihood that rank-and-file subcommittee members will affect markup drafts in the House.

A subcommittee staff director on the House Committee on Banking, Finance, and Urban Affairs described the role of the full committee chair, Fernand St Germain, a Democrat from Rhode Island:

> The chairman devotes most of his time to his own subcommittee, which is the most important one anyway, so the committee is compartmentalized in that sense. The committee staff follow up on the subcommittees and the chairman can be very actively involved even before the hearing, but that's rare. Mostly, it's the members of the subcommittee, organized and led by _____[the subcommittee chair].

John D. Dingell, Democratic chair of the Energy and Commerce Committee, is often desribed as the most powerful chair in the House, but his influence over Energy and Commerce Committee bills is constrained by activist subcommittees. Indeed, as a subcommittee chair during the 1970s, Dingell led a coalition that stripped West Virginia Democrat Harley O. Staggers, the full committee chair, of everything from his control over subcommittee agendas to his power to allocate parking spaces.[12] As one aide said,

> John inherited the boundaries he helped create. The business of restoring the traditional structure of a committee is not easy. Once you've let the quicksilver out of the thermometer, you'll never get it all back in.[13]

Although the markup vehicle usually sets the tone for committee deliberations, subcommittee members can offer amendments during subcommittee markups, and all committee members can offer amendments in full committee markup. The opportunity to offer amendments in markup is particularly important to committee members not included in negotiations over the draft. How widespread is influence through the amendment process in congressional committees? The source of amendments passed during subcommittee and full committee markup for the legislation and committees of Table 8–1 is displayed in Table 8–2. The data denote the average number (per bill) of committee members who successfully participated in the amendment process in subcommittee or full committee. Legislation is again divided into subcommittee and full committee issues. And, the data illustrate that successfully amending legislation in subcommittee or full committee markup is also selective. With the exception of the Committee on Environment and Public Works, the average number on nonleaders successfully amending the markup vehicle never exceeds one per bill.[14] Of course, on salient and complex pieces of legislation, participation in the amendment process can broaden considerably. For example, during the Environment and Public Works Committee's 1985 reauthorization of Superfund (the toxic-waste cleanup program), over one-half of the committee introduced amendments that were incorporated into the bill. But this level of amendment activity is rare. Formal markups are an important opportunity to modify committee proposals, but the incidence of amendment is low on most bills.

More amendments are incorporated into committee bills during markups in the House than in the Senate.[15] In part, this is because House committees are larger in size, but also because there are more restrictions on offering amendments on the House floor than on the floor of the Senate. Senators

TABLE 8–2   Sources of Amendments in Committee, Selected Senate Committees, Ninety-ninth Congress

Subcommittee bills	Leaders	Nonleaders
Subcommittee bills		
Commerce	0.27*	0.47†
Environment and Public Works	0.75	1.38
Judiciary	1.00	0.67
Labor and Human Resources	0.89	0.44
Full Committee bills		
Commerce	0.00	0.00
Environment and Public Works	1.00	4.00
Judiciary	0.67	0.33
Labor and Human Resources	0.11	0.56

*Average number of leaders successfully amending per bill.
†Average number of nonleaders successfully amending per bill.

SOURCE: Records of the committees on Commerce, Environment and Public Works, Judiciary, and Labor and Human Resources.

desiring to modify a committee bill often withhold their amendments until the floor, where their proposals may get a more sympathetic hearing. Amendments offered and passed during House markups originate disproportionately with members of the subcommittee of jurisdiction. Indeed, one study of three House committees found that members of the subcommittees are responsible for between 67.5 and 85.0 percent of amendments passed in full committee markup.[16]

Thus, influence through active participation (drafting and amending legislation) is in general not widely dispersed among committee members in either chamber. In Senate committees, influence through active participation is focused on the formal leaders on a bill: the committee chair and ranking minority member, and the subcommittee chair and ranking minority member.[17] Senate subcommittees are important because the subcommittee chair and ranking minority member are important. In the House, full committee chairs tend to be less influential than Senate chairs, but rank-and-file subcommittee members in the House tend to be more active both in shaping the draft and in participating in the amendment process than rank-and-file subcommittee members in the Senate.

MANIPULATION OF THE PROCESS

The second mechanism of policymaking influence in congressional committees is manipulation of the process through which a bill is constructed. This form of influence differs from the first in that it need not affect the actual content of the bill. In the contemporary Congress, however, the content of a bill may be irrelevant if it is reported too late in a session to allow floor consideration. Delaying or speeding up committee consideration is an important component of legislative influence in congressional committees. Committee chairs can accelerate action on legislation to maximize the time available for floor consideration and facilitate final passage. One tactic available to Senate chairs is to simply hold legislation at the full committee level and remove the subcommittee layer of the process.

Although legislation can be put on a fast track, the nature of congressional rules ensures that many procedural strategies can be dilatory. Points of obstruction are built into the rules and practices of congressional committees in both chambers. Committee chairs, for example, have formal control over full committee agendas and can delay consideration of bills they oppose. The committee can be bypassed, but prospects for success on the floor are much higher when a bill is reported by the committee of jurisdiction. Similarly, if a majority of committee members strongly support a bill, a chair cannot keep it off the committee agenda indefinitely, but the costs of bypassing a chair can be prohibitive. As one staffer noted, "There are a million little ways that a chairman can get you back."

Congressional committees cannot take formal action on legislation in the absence of a quorum, usually a simple majority of the committee to report a bill. Thus, one delay tactic available to rank-and-file committee members is simply to leave the committee room, or not show up in the first place. This was the logic underlying Strom Thurmond's bout with Ralph Yarborough. Senators can also filibuster in committee, as well as on the floor. When Republicans organized the chamber from 1981 to 1987, Democrat Howard M. Metzenbaum from Ohio often used the tactics of extended debate to delay conservative bills he adamantly opposed. Metzenbaum filibusters were particularly common on the Judiciary Committee, where conservative Republicans attempted to pursue the social agenda of the New Right. Another committee liberal, Edward Kennedy, also took a lead in delay tactics. As one Republican staffer for the Judiciary Committee said,

> Kennedy and Metzenbaum are partners in crime. On the big bills they won't let us vote. There's a lot of talk and amendments that everybody knows will never pass. It's obstructionism. . . . But what the hell: Senator Thurmond did the same things when Kennedy was chairman and the Republicans were in the minority. That's the way this game is played.

Procedures exist to invoke cloture and cut off discussion, but in Senate committees, as well as on the Senate floor, strong norms against curtailing deliberation increase the effectiveness of extended debate.

While the incidence of influence through active participation is similar across committees and between chambers, use of the committee process differs widely. Three committee characteristics shape the way committee members use the process: The degree of conflict over an issue, the location of the conflict, and the strategic posture adopted by the chair.[18] These three characteristics generate four patterns, each with different consequences for use of the committee process: (1) consensus committees, (2) facilitating committees, (3) free-for-alls, and (4) suppressed conflict.

Consensus Committees

Certain congressional committees have jurisdiction over legislation that usually generates little controversy, and what conflict that does arise can be negotiated away. These, *consensus committees* jurisdictions are typically constituency-oriented and of moderate to low salience to most legislators. On committees oriented toward bipartisan and consensual decision making, use of the process for dilatory purposes, or to put legislation on a fast track, is rare. Legislation is processed in as orderly a fashion as possible, and usually passes on the floor by unanimous consent or under suspension of the rules.

An example of a panel in this category is the Senate Commerce Committee. The Commerce Committee's jurisdiction over consumer protection and regulatory issues generated significant controversy during the 1960s and 1970s, but these policy areas have become less salient in recent years. Indeed, the committee's active agenda is now dominated by a plethora of reauthorizations which are usually handled quietly and without controversy. The committee's jurisdiction is reflected in the ideological complexion of its membership. Senators select the Commerce Committee primarily to further the economic interests of constituent groups, and the Commerce Committee is now dominated by relatively liberal Republicans and conservative Democrats. Because the issues are rife with consensus there is little to be gained from manipulating the process, and legislative influence is primarily exerted through other modes.

In general, committees in this category have jurisdictions that attract members for constituency purposes, and the committees will produce bills of interest to only a narrow spectrum of legislators. Except for its jurisdiction over environmental issues, the House Committee on Interior and Insular Affairs fits this category well.[19] House Interior's active agenda includes public lands and water resources policy and is of particular interest to westerners. Central to decision making on this committee is the orderly processing of projects.[20] Within this environment there is little manipulation of the committee process and, in many ways, decision making in House Interior resembles the Senate Commerce Committee.

Facilitating Committees

Another pattern arises when consensus can be achieved among committee members, but conflict which may exist off the committee increases the difficulty of success on the floor. These *facilitating committees* tend to draw members interested in the committee for constituency purposes, but they have jurisdiction over issues of more salience than those typically dealt with by House Interior or Senate Commerce. In other words, their agendas contain issues of disproportionate interest to particular constituency groups, but also touch on questions of broad national policy. Committee members are from the districts or states with the most to gain or lose from the policy area, and are able to forge consensus in committee. But the wider scope of interest leads to conflict in the parent chamber. Within this environment there exist incentives for committee leaders to accelerate committee deliberations and move legislation to the floor as quickly as possible, maximizing the time available to iron out differences in the chamber. Backers of the legislation seek to facilitate committee action.

The Senate Committee on Environment and Public Works falls in this category. Its membership is dominated by ideological moderates with a strong commitment to maintaining the major environmental programs in the committee's jurisdiction: programs which include Superfund, the Clean Water Act, and the Clean Air Act. Industry groups are represented by western senators on the committee, but environmentalists tend to have the upper hand. The committee also has jurisdiction over the traditional pork-barrel issues of water resource development and highway construction. Although water projects and highway funds are targeted toward particular geographic areas, these programs are usually aggregated into huge "omnibus" packages with very high expenditure levels. Due to general demands to hold down spending in Congress, the pork-barrel side of the committee's agenda has also provoked conflict on the floor in recent years. Indeed, before the Water Resources Development Act of 1986, no new water projects had been funded for over half a decade.

The strategic response of committee members has been to mark up bills early in the session and keep important legislation on a fast track. For example, Republican Senator Robert T. Stafford from Vermont used the process in guiding through the Superfund reauthorization in 1985. The bill was highly technical and, in addition to consideration by the Environment and Public Works Committee, sequential referral to both the Finance and Judiciary committees was necessary. To maximize the time available for House and conference committee action, Stafford introduced the bill on January 3, 1985, held markup sessions the following month, reported the legislation out of committee on the first of March, and pushed the bill through the full Senate by September 26. Thus, the entire second session was available for House and conference committee consideration, and subsequent events revealed that the time on the floor was necessary.

Free-for-Alls

The third, *free-for-all,* pattern occurs when conflict is present and the chair has a working majority. When committee deliberations generate conflict, the role of the committee process depends heavily on the strategic posture of the full committee chair. If the chair assumes the offensive, there will be a tendency for much of the battle to be fought in terms of procedure. Opposing committee members will often attempt to slow the process down and impede committee action. In response, the chair will attempt to counteract dilatory strategies by pushing the process along. Both sides will concentrate on procedural tactics and committee deliberations can become free-for-alls. Congressional committees falling in this category have jurisdictions with highly partisan and nationally salient issues, and draw members interested in developing their version of good public policy. The policy preferences of members have usually congealed before the committee process begins, and the fate of legislation in committee is more a question of time and timing than negotiation and compromise.

The politics of the Senate Judiciary Committee during the period of Republican control from 1981 to 1987 fits this description well. Strom Thurmond was chair and usually had a working majority of eight staunchly conservative Republicans and two moderately conservative Democrats. In addition to jurisdiction over criminal law, antitrust, and intellectual property, the committee has jurisdiction over most of the social agenda of the New Right, including abortion, school prayer, and busing. Liberal Democrats lacked the votes to defeat conservative bills in committee, and adopted a strategy of trying to slow things down. Thurmond's response was to attempt to move the process forward. Thurmond, who once spoke on the floor for twenty-five hours without rest, was constantly urging liberal Democrats not to obstruct and to let the committee vote. Indeed, in 1986 he bypassed his own committee and brought to the floor Republican legislation that was being blocked in committee. If decision making on a committee is conflictual and the full committee chair adopts an offensive posture, both opponents and proponents will make extensive use of the process, with the chair trying to move things forward and opponents trying to slow things down.

Free-for-alls are less common in the House than they are in the Senate, primarily because Senate rules provide all senators with significant procedural powers. In contrast, House rules are more restrictive and, as a result, influence over the process in the House is primarily exerted by committee chairs through their power over committee agendas. There are exceptions, of course. Republican members of the House Committee on Education and Labor occasionally seek to thwart liberal initiatives by breaking quorum, and Republicans on the Energy and Commerce Committee walked out of that committee's organizational meeting in 1985 in protest over subcommittee allotments. But these tactics are relatively rare in the House, where procedural strategies are usually concentrated in the hands of committee leaders.

Suppressed Conflict

The fourth pattern, *suppressed conflict,* arises when conflict is present and the chair is on the defensive. In the presence of significant and entrenched conflict in committee, not all chairs adopt an offensive posture. The utility of that leadership style depends on the policy preferences of the chair relative to other committee members, as well as the individuals and groups that comprise the committee's environment. If the chair is opposed to the legislative proposals being pushed by other committee members, interest groups, the administration, or executive agencies, the most strategic response may be to restrict the size of the committee's agenda to block consideration of those measures. The conflict inherent to the jurisdiction remains, but it is suppressed down to the agenda-setting level. When full committee leaders assume a defensive posture, the committee's active agenda tends to shrink and members lose interest in the committee.

An example of a panel characterized by suppressed conflict is the Senate Committee on Labor and Human Resources during the chairmanship of Republican Orrin Hatch from 1981 to 1987. Although Republicans had a numerical majority of nine to seven, two of the Republicans were relatively liberal on issues in the committee's jurisdiction, and Hatch faced a wall of liberal Democrats. Hatch was successful in restricting the committee's agenda to issues where he had the votes. As an aide to Edward M. Kennedy, the ranking minority member, expressed it,

Hatch really doesn't want to do more than the required reauthorizations. He's got a few little bills that he gets excited about, but they're more of a symbolic nature. He doesn't have the votes. If you're a chairman, you don't want to meet if you're going to keep losing votes and you can't control the bills.

As a result, the ideological cleavages which characterized the committee were suppressed down to the hearing stage. Hatch resisted authorizing a number of hearings requested by the minority, which led to intense partisan infighting, with Kennedy seeking to expand the committee's agenda and Hatch using his procedural powers to contract it.

Until his retirement in 1988, Democrat Peter W. Rodino, Jr. of New Jersey adopted a defensive posture as chair of the House Judiciary Committee. Unlike Hatch, Rodino had a solid ideological majority in committee: Rodino was a liberal Democrat and the House Judiciary Committee had long been a bastion of liberalism. But as the committee's environment became more conservatively oriented during the 1980s, outside groups, the administration, and other members of the House have exerted strong pressure on the committee to consider controversial items important to conservatives. Rodino's response has been to use his control over the agenda to block those bills, a tactic which has earned him a reputation as "a premier legislative undertaker."[21] On occasion, the strategy has backfired. In 1985, when the Senate passed legislation to relax the 1968 Gun Control Act, Rodino characterized the bill as "dead on arrival" in the House. To keep Rodino from bottling up the measure, conservatives initiated procedures to bypass the Judiciary Committee. When it became clear that these efforts were succeeding, Rodino quickly moved an alternative measure. But he had obviously lost control over the process on the issue and the bill which finally passed the House diverged sharply from his preferences. In general, though, Rodino's use of the chair's agenda prerogatives has been effective in suppressing conflict and blocking conservative initiatives.

In summary, use of the process varies across committees depending on the level of conflict generated by committee issues, the location of the conflict, and the strategic posture of the full committee chair. In the absence of conflict, procedural tactics are rare. If conflict arises in the chamber as a whole, but consensus exists in committee, there will be a tendency for committee leaders to accelerate legislation to maximize the time available for consideration on the floor. If conflict arises in committee, as well as on the floor, the strategic posture of the chair shapes use of the process. When the chair is on the offensive, committee politics will tend to degenerate into procedural warfare, with one side attempting to bring bills to a vote and the other employing various tactics of delay. When the chair is on the defensive, he or she will tend to restrict the scope of the committee's active agenda. In general, influence over the committee process is more prevalent in the Senate than it is in the House because individual senators have important procedural prerogatives that are not widely available to individual representatives.

INFLUENCE THROUGH ANTICIPATED REACTIONS

The strategy of anticipated reactions occurs when proponents of a bill anticipate potential problems in committee or on the floor and adjust the content of their bill to dampen opposition. The legislator exerting influence need not take action. Instead, the potential behavior of the committee member is anticipated by a bill's managers and the member's preferences are incorporated to preempt reaction.[22] Influence through anticipated reactions was particularly prevalent during the Senate Environment and Public Works Committee's consideration of a bill in 1985 to reauthorize the Clean Water Act. Throughout the process, debate focused on a politically popular sewage treatment grant program that would channel $2.4 billion per year to local governments. Committee staffers began work on producing a formula for allocating the money with a 1984 Environmental Protection Agency (EPA) study of each state's needs, but the EPA formula would have had difficulties making it through committee. Indeed, one senator not on the committee, Republican Senator John C. Danforth from Missouri, suggested during floor debate that "a majority of members of the Environment and Public Works Committee are not benefited by the Environmental Protection Agency's need survey, so they had to doctor the figures."[23]

Staff associated with a core group of just four committee members drafted an alternative formula for the committee, but it was clear that they anticipated the reactions of the members and shaped the formula to ease passage. As one staff member said,

> We knew we could not put together a formula that would screw a majority of the committee; that's political suicide. There's lots of ways you can use the needs survey as input data to an allotment formula . . . but we had to consider the political criteria. It had to improve the position of at least a majority of members on the committee or it wasn't going to get out of committee.

Indeed, Texas, the state of the committee's ranking minority member at that time, Senator Lloyd Bentsen, would have received more money under the EPA formula, but his staff had been active in devising the committee alternative because it was more in line with political reality. Thus, senators outside the core group influenced the choice of an allotment formula, but the mode of influence was through anticipated reactions, rather than active participation.

The potential reactions of legislators not on the committee of jurisdiction can also shape decision making in committee. Congressional committees are not islands of decision. For a bill to move forward in the process, it must pass on the floor. There may exist incentives for committee leaders to exercise foresight and strategically adjust the contents of legislation in committee to minimize conflict during succeeding stages. Arkansas' Wilbur Mills, Democratic chair of the House Ways and Means Committee, was extremely successful in committee and on the floor, in part because of his uncanny ability to anticipate the preferences of other legislators and incorporate them into his legislation.[24] Proponents of a measure may anticipate the reactions of members off the committee, as well as other committee members.

Of course, the managers of a bill in committee do not always anticipate the reactions of other legislators. One observer described the actions of the House Committee on Science and Technology in reauthorizing NASA:

> The Committee can report a bill out unanimously and that has no meaning on the floor of the House. Members just say, "Oh, it's that committee again." They have no feel for the reality of the House. It's just bad politics.

Thus, the decision of legislators at one point in the process to anticipate the reactions of other stages to their bill is a strategic decision that varies from context to context.

The discussion that follows examines use of the strategy of anticipated reactions in light of the decision made by committee members about whether or not to anticipate potential problems on the floor and adjust the bill to ease passage. But the same arguments can be applied to other stages in the process, such as anticipation of the reactions of other committee members. The political profitability of the strategy of anticipated reactions is shaped by seven factors: (1) the presence or absence of conflict on the floor; (2) how representative the committee is of the parent chamber; (3) the presence or absence of overlapping jurisdictions; (4) the degree to which differences are negotiable; (5) the clarity of the opposition; (6) the expenditure level; and (7) the point in the session when a bill is reported.

Conflict.   The decision to anticipate reactions depends on the decision-making context in which committee members are operating. An important aspect of context is the presence or absence of conflict on the floor. If no conflict exists, there are no incentives to change the bill. On the routine reauthorizations that constitute a large part of the typical committee's workload, the absence of controversy precludes the need to adjust a bill prior to floor consideration. In the absence of some degree of conflict, the need to anticipate reactions is irrelevant to committee decision making.

Representativeness.   The potential for conflict increases the more the committee is unrepresentative of the parent chamber. House members from oil-producing states have traditionally been overrepresented on the Ways and Means Committee. If Ways and Means reported legislation that reflected the true preferences of committee members, their legislation would be heavily amended on the floor. As a result, committee leaders often adjust their bills in committee to minimize opposition on the floor.[25] Both unrepresentativeness and conflict are necessary conditions for anticipated reactions to be politically profitable. If an issue is controversial, but the committee is representative of the floor, it follows that conflict will also arise in committee. Many of the issues considered by the Senate's Labor and Judiciary committees are in this category. If a bill's opponents are represented on the committee, managers of the legislation will tend to concentrate on getting the bill out of committee and worry about the floor after committee action has been completed.

Overlapping Jurisdictions.   Jurisdictional overlaps tend to buttress incentives to employ the strategy of anticipated reactions. Congressional committees are highly territorial when it comes to matters of jurisdiction. Republican representative Tom Tauke of Iowa described chairman John Dingell's attitude about the jurisdiction of the House Energy and Commerce Committee:

> John Dingell feels about his committee much as Lyndon Johnson felt about his ranch. Johnson didn't want to own the whole world, he just wanted to own all the land surrounding his ranch. Dingell doesn't want his committee to have the whole world, just all of the areas surrounding its jurisdiction.[26]

Even relatively noncontroversial issues can become politically charged if one committee perceives that another is moving in on its jurisdiction. The presence of a jurisdictional overlap raises the prospect that opposition to a committee's bill will emerge from senators off the committee due to disagreements over turf. When jurisdiction over an issue is shared, it is often advantageous to coordinate action with the other committee before the bill is brought to the floor.

Negotiable Differences.   The strategy of anticipated reactions is difficult in the absence of negotiable differences. Some committees regularly deal with issues that allow only a limited number of outcomes. A limited array of alternatives makes compromise difficult because there is less middle ground. It is not feasible to shape a school busing proposal in committee to buy off floor opposition. Indeed, many of the bills in the jurisdictions of the Labor and Judiciary committees have that characteristic, but "take it or leave it" legislation can emerge on the agenda of most congressional committees. During the Senate Commerce Committee's 1985 consideration of legislation setting terms for the sale of Conrail substantial floor trouble was expected, but no significant attempts were made to alter the bill in committee and dampen opposition on the floor. As one staffer involved in the bill said,

> We tried to persuade senators to support the bill but there were very few changes. It was more a question of arguing the merits. Either you're for the bill or you're against it and there's not much you can do to the bill itself that's going to change that.

The array of politically meaningful alternatives on that issue was narrow and the intensity of the opposition was insensitive to incremental adjustments to the bill.

Clarity of the Opposition.   If floor opposition is diffuse and preferences are not congealed around concrete alternatives to provisions in the committee bill, committee leaders may lack the information necessary to adjust the legislation to preclude opposition. On particularly technical and complex pieces of legislation, floor opposition may be imminent but opponents might lack the information necessary to have concrete demands until after the committee has deliberated. In addition, opponents not on the committee may hold their cards close and strategically withhold information about their views to leverage a better deal from the committee. Both of these tactics will decrease the information available to committee members about floor opposition, increasing the likelihood of compromise when the bill is brought to the floor.

Expenditure Levels.   Another contextual factor influencing the value of anticipated reactions is the expenditure level. The most prominent constraints on most programs are fiscal, and the more money a bill involves, the greater the probability that opposition will emerge on the floor. Constraints on funding levels are set by the relevant Appropriations subcommittee subject to an overall limit set by the Budget Committee. What this division of labor obscures, though, is the significant informational and logistic problems of coordinating the authorizing and spending functions. Authorizing committees and Appropriations subcommittees typically do their work simultaneously. But authorizing committees need information from the appropriators about the availability of funds, and Appropriations' subcommittees set expenditure limits using information from the authorizing committees about programmatic needs. The result is a reciprocal uncertainty as authorizing panels and Appropriations' subcommittees simultaneously attempt to anticipate each other's reactions. The greater the sum of money involved, the higher the stakes. Proponents of bills with high price tags will be particularly likely to anticipate the floor.

Point in the Session.   The point in a session when a bill is to be considered on the floor can be an important contextual influence on the utility of anticipated reactions. Time on the floor increases in scarcity toward the end of a session and immediately before recesses. Party leaders in both chambers, but particularly in the Senate, are less likely to schedule a bill if large quantities of floor time are required. In the Senate, opponents of a bill often signal their displeasure by placing a *hold* on it; in reality, a hold is no more than a threatened filibuster, and its only force is the willingness of the opponent to stand up on the Senate floor and start talking. But toward the end of a session, holds take on added weight. A deluge of holds functions as a signal to the majority leader that a bill will require substantial floor time, and the probability of it being scheduled falls accordingly. Thus, the closer to the end of a session, the more crucial it is to work out problems in advance of the floor.

In general, Senate committees are more likely to employ the strategy of anticipated reactions than their House counterparts. The differential is due in large part to the greater procedural powers of individual senators on the floor, which increase the value of ironing out conflict with even a small number of senators. Although the need may exist to adjust a bill prior to floor consideration, House rules make obstruction on the floor by a minority of legislators much less effective than it is in the Senate. As a result, it is easier for committee leaders in the House to secure floor time in the presence of significant opposition. The sheer size of the House also plays a role. "Greasing the skids" for floor consideration may require anticipating the reactions of over 400 individuals. Although committee members can simplify their environment by thinking about opinion on the floor in terms of coalitions, rather than individuals, the size of the membership increases the costs of gathering the information necessary for committee members to employ the strategy of anticipated reactions. In the Senate, the number of potential floor opponents to committee bills is smaller, and gathering the information necessary to iron out potential conflict prior to presentation on the floor is less time consuming.

CONCLUSION: PARTICIPATION, MANIPULATION, AND ANTICIPATION

To understand the sources of influence in committee, it is necessary to examine how influence is exerted. In generalizing about the relative influence of full committee chairs, subcommittee chairs, and other individuals or groups in committee, observers usually focus on active participation: who drafts the vehicle and who modifies the bill during the amendment process. In both chambers, active participation tends to be concentrated in predictable ways, but generalizations about the selective nature of influence in committee need qualification. Committee members can influence bills through manipulation of the process, particularly in the Senate. And in both chambers, the legislators managing a bill often have an incentive to be sensitive to the mood of the committee and the chamber. Indeed, the high success rates of most committees on the floor mask the extent to which floor success is purchased through anticipating problems in the chamber and adjusting legislation to decrease opposition. All three mechanisms of influence shape committee decision making.

The focus of this chapter has been on the behavior of individual legislators and their staffs, but it is clear that the institutional arrangements of Congress go a long way toward explaining the way representatives and senators influence legislation in committee. In the Senate, for example, formal leaders are more likely to participate in drafting the bills brought into markup because committee rules grant them disproportionate control over the staff resources necessary to participate effectively. Similarly, acceleration and delay are integral components of committee politics because of the multitude of points of obstruction built into standing rules and informal practices of both chambers. Finally, the most striking institutional characteristic of Congress is that decision making is sequential. Committees have first crack at a bill, but their recommendations are not binding once a measure reaches the floor. It is the sequential nature of congressional decision making that provides incentives for committee members to anticipate the floor and shape their bills to facilitate favorable action by the chamber as a whole. Individual representatives and senators determine the content and timing of committee bills, but the mechanisms through which legislative influence is exerted are conditioned by the broader institutional context of Congress.

NOTES

Author's note: Larry Bartels, Richard Fenno, and Richard Hall provided many useful comments on earlier drafts. Arguments in this chapter are adopted from C. Lawrence Evans, "Influence in Senate Committees," manuscript, 1987.

1. All unattributed quotations are from interviews conducted by the author with congressional staff. All of the individuals interviewed were promised anonymity, and all but a few of the interviews were taperecorded and then transcribed.
2. Later in 1964, Thurmond left the Democratic party and became a Republican.
3. Cabell Phillips, "Two Senators Resort to Wrestling Over Collins Post," *The New York Times,* July 10, 1964, pp. L1, 10.
4. Woodrow Wilson. *Congressional Government* (New York: Mentor Books, 1954), p. 79.
5. Richard F. Fenno, Jr., *Congressmen in Committees* (Boston: Little, Brown, 1973).
6. Thomas J. O'Donnell, "Controlling Legislative Time," in *The House at Work,* ed. Joseph Cooper and G. Calvin Mackenzie (Austin: University of Texas Press, 1981).
7. Harrison W. Fox, Jr., and Susan Webb Hammond, *Congressional Staffs: The Invisible Force in American Lawmaking* (New York: Free Press, 1977).
8. On complexity see Allen Schick, "Complex Policy Making in the United States Senate." In U.S. Senate, Commission on the Operation of the Senate, *Policy Analysis on Major Issues,* 94th Cong. 2nd sess., 1977. Committee Print. pp. 4–7.
9. Bruce I. Oppenheimer, "Changing Time Constraints on Congress," in *Congress Reconsidered,* 3rd ed., ed. Lawrence C. Dodd and Bruce I. Oppenheimer (Washington, D.C.: CQ Press, 1985), pp. 393–413.
10. For a systematic study of participation in the House Education and Labor Committee, see Richard L. Hall, "Participation and Purpose in Committee Decision Making," *American Political Science Review* 81 (March 1987), pp. 105–128. The conceptualization and operationalization of committee participation in this chapter is drawn from that article. Following Hall's lead, I analyze participation in committee by focusing on a sample of bills and interviewing the staff persons most knowledgeable about each one.
11. Ibid.

12. David Maraniss, "Powerful Energy Panel Turns on Big John's Axis," *Washington Post*, May 15, 1983, p. Al.

13. Ibid, p. A15.

14. The data of Table 8–2 denote the average number of leaders and nonleaders successfully amending a bill. Of course, on some of the bills, individual committee members passed more than one amendment, but this behavior is not captured in the table. Rather, my goal is to show that, on average, the number of committee members successfully participating in the amendment process is very small.

15. Richard L. Hall and C. Lawrence Evans, "The Role of the Subcommittee in Committee Decision Making: An Exploration," paper presented at the annual meeting of the American Political Science Association, New Orleans, August 1985.

16. Ibid.

17. Randall Ripley has made similar arguments about power in Senate committees during the 1960s. See Randall B. Ripley, *Power in the Senate* (New York: St. Martin's Press, 1969). Given the well-documented changes in the Senate over the past two decades, it is interesting to note how similar the results of this section are to his observations. For a different view, see Steven S. Smith, "New Patterns of Decision Making in Congress," in *The New Direction in American Politics*, ed. John E. Chubb and Paul E. Peterson (Washington D.C.: Brookings Institution, 1985).

18. David Price has emphasized the importance of environmental conflict and salience in shaping committee politics. See David E. Price, *Policymaking in Congressional Committees: The Impact of Environmental Factors* (Tucson: University of Arizona Press, 1979).

19. Steven S. Smith and Christopher J. Deering, *Committees in Congress* (Washington, D.C.: CQ Press, 1984), p. 107.

20. Richard F. Fenno, Jr., *Congressmen in Committees* (Boston: Little, Brown, 1973) pp. 97–101.

21. Nadine Cohodas, "Peter Rodino Turns Judiciary into a Legislative Graveyard," *Congressional Quarterly Weekly Report*, May 12, 1984, p. 1097.

22. This third mechanism of policymaking influence often occurs across the various stages that comprise congressional policymaking. For example, subcommittee members may anticipate problems with key members of the full committee, perhaps the chair, and adjust their bill to mitigate dissent during the full committee markup. In the absence of a formal subcommittee markup, those senators or staff involved in shaping the draft to be considered by the full committee may employ a similar strategy.

23. *Congressional Record.* 99th Cong., 1st sess., June 13, 1985, p. S8111.

24. John F. Manley, *The Politics of Finance: The House Committee on Ways and Means* (Boston: Little, Brown, 1970).

25. Ibid.

26. Maraniss, "Powerful Energy Panel," p. A15.

CHAPTER 9

Legislative Procedures and Congressional Policymaking: A Bicameral Perspective

Walter J. Oleszek

"The aggregate power of the Senate is almost precisely equal to the aggregate power of the House," said former Democratic Representative and now Senator Albert Gore, Jr., from Tennessee (who ran for the Senate in November 1984 after serving four terms in the House) "but in one body you have one-hundredth of that power and in the other you have one-435th."[1] Gore's statement highlights why so many House members seek election to the Senate and why the reverse is so rare. Representative Claude Pepper, a Democrat from Florida, is the only member of the One-hundredth Congress to have served previously in the Senate. By contrast, 39 senators in the One-hundredth Congress are former House members.

Individual power is only one feature that distinguishes the two bodies. Size, term of office, constituency, media coverage, and prestige are other factors that make the Senate more politically attractive and visible to office-seekers and voters alike. Another significant bicameral difference undergirds much of this chapter's focus: each chamber has its own unique lawmaking process. This process influences how the House and Senate debate and decide issues.

The larger and more clamorous House needs and adheres to rather well-defined rules and precedents to accomplish its congressional workload. The many bulky volumes of House precedents—rulings of the Speaker that constitute the chamber's "common law"—stand in sharp contrast to the single and smaller Senate volume. It has been said that the Senate has only two rules: unanimous consent and exhaustion. It operates more informally and unpredictably than the larger House. These differences mean that the policymaking context of each body is both unique and subject to dissimilar strategies for passing laws. Illinois Democratic Senator Paul Simon, a former House member, pointed out that in the House "no single member can tie the body in knots; in the Senate, any member can."[2] House procedures, in short, emphasize the mobilization of voting blocs to make policy; deference to individual prerogatives is the hallmark of senatorial decision making. The procedural environment in which senators and representatives operate shapes their policymaking behavior and opportunities.

To be sure, the Founding Fathers, as Alexander Hamilton put it, deliberately employed "dissimilar modes" of constituting the House and Senate to "permanently nourish different propensities and inclinations."[3] In an oft-quoted anecdote, Thomas Jefferson asked George Washington why he supported a two-chamber Congress. "Why did you pour that coffee into your saucer?" asked Washington of Jefferson. "To cool it," responded Jefferson. "Even so," remarked Washington, "we pour legislation into the senatorial saucer to cool it." (Because of the popular election of senators, the House can reverse the process by acting as guardian against hasty Senate action.)

That the House and Senate are unlike does not mean that each is immune to the "propensities and inclinations" of the other. In fact, both chambers during recent years have converged in some important respects. Contemporary senators imitate House members, for example, by constantly running for reelection (despite their longer terms) and stressing constituent services. House members emulate senators by relying more heavily on staff aides. Given contemporary workload changes, such as greater issue complexity and inter-connectedness, many of today's representatives are less able to become policy specialists to the same degree the their predecessors did.

Bicameral differences and similarities serve as the orienting themes of this study. To highlight dissimilarities, a significant practice unique to each chamber will be examined. For the House, it is the innovative role of the Rules Committee in establishing the conditions, including debate limitations, for considering policy choices on the floor. For the Senate, it is the senators' right of extended debate. "Probably the one characteristic that most distinguishes this body from any other parliamentary body in the world," said former Florida Senator Lawton Chiles, "is the right of extended debate."[4]

Unlike the Senate, nearly every second of House floor debate is regulated by some rule, practice or precedent, restrictions made necessary as membership increased. The irony is that the larger House is more manageable than the smaller Senate, because the Rules Committee crafts procedures to limit debates and floor amendments on major legislation. By comparison, every senator possesses the right of unlimited debate and wide freedom to amend legislation on the floor. One result: bills take longer to complete in the Senate than in the House. Frustration with senatorial procedures prompted one senator to declare, "What we need is something like the Rules Committee."[5]

Bicameral similarity will be explored by discussing the notion of "separate, sequential action by the two chambers."[6] Although this situation frequently prevails, each body also attempts to influence the other; members of both chambers directly or indirectly influence each other's decision. This chapter's review of bicameral differences and similarities will illustrate the general tendencies associated with each house.

THE HOUSE RULES COMMITTEE AND FLOOR DECISION MAKING

When representatives introduce bills, the bills are referred to one or more committees to follow a three-stage policymaking process: hearings, markups, and report. There is no guarantee that measures will be acted on by committees or that reported bills will be considered by the whole House, (there are, however, instances when bills became law without ever having been reviewed by committees).

The actual route bills take to reach the floor is variable and shaped in part by the nature of the policy proposal itself. Minor measures reported from committee enjoy an almost automatic right to the floor during specified days of the month. These bills are assigned to the *Consent Calendar* and can be called from it on the first and third Mondays of the month; they are given *privileged* status by House rules. Semicontroversial measures often follow another route to the floor: the *suspension* pathway. Every Monday and Tuesday the Speaker may recognize any representative to suspend House rules and pass a specific measure ("Mr Speaker, I move to suspend the rules and pass H.R. 1234"). Suspension requires a two-thirds majority, permits no floor amendments, and limits debate to forty minutes. Clearly, neither of these expedited procedures is suitable for taking up major and controversial legislation, such as immigration rules or tax reform.

Enter the strategic role of the House Rules Committee. This panel may grant privileged status to any measure by writing a rule (i.e., a simple resolution) which, if adopted by majority vote of the House, establishes a tailor-made procedure for debating and amending the legislation.[7] The panel's crucial discretionary power therefore lies in determining whether and in what manner measures will be subject to amendment on the floor.

The Rules Committee is an agent of the majority leadership. This connection was formalized in 1858 when the Speaker became a member of the panel, and later its chair. In 1910, the House revolted against the arbitrary rule of Speaker Joseph Cannon, and removed him from the committee. The panel then operated as an independent power, extracting substantive concessions in bills in exchange for rules. It blocked measures it opposed and advanced those it favored. One well-known Rules Chairman, Democrat Howard W. Smith from Virginia, who directed the committee from 1955 to 1967, even refused to call committee meetings to consider civil rights measures. On one occasion Smith used the excuse that he had to tend to a burning barn on his Virginia farm. Upon hearing this, Speaker Sam Rayburn, exclaimed: "I knew Howard Smith would do almost anything to block a civil rights bill, but I never knew he would resort to arson."[8]

By the time President John F. Kennedy took office in 1961, frustration had mounted against the Rules Committee. A majority of representatives joined Speaker Rayburn to weaken Smith's grip on the panel by expanding its membership. During the next decade, the committee came under even greater majority party control. In 1973, the Democratic Caucus (consisting of all Democratic members) limited the authority of the Rules Committee and in 1975 the caucus authorized the Speaker to appoint, subject to party approval, all of the panel's majority members, including the chair. Today, the committee functions as an arm of the majority leadership.

New "Rules" for the House

With activism and visibility highlighting floor decision making, it is no longer sufficient to describe rules issued by the Rules Committee as *open* (all germane amendments are in order), *closed* (floor amendments are not in order), or *modified* (some parts of the bill are open to amendment and some are not).[9] Rules Committee members now fashion rules that impose greater predictability in an environment grown more unpredictable. As Missouri Democrat Richard Bolling, one of the most creative Rules chairs ever, said:

> What the Rules Committee finds it has to do is to come up with all kinds of ingenious . . . procedures to keep the whole [floor decision making] process going in a fashion that allows the members of the House the right to deal with major elements of the conflicts before them.[10]

Recent examples of these ingenious procedures are *structured, self-executing*, and *king-of-the-hill* rules. All three variations, which may overlap one another, are designed to achieve policy, political, and parliamentary objectives.

Structured Rules.   These limit the number of floor amendments, establish a specific order in which those amendments are to be offered, identify the member who may offer each amendment, and typically prohibit any change in the amendments made in order. The thrust of these rules is to restrict members' general right to offer floor amendments, often resulting in the ire of minority party members. Although most rules permit an open floor amendment process, as Table 9–1 indicates, measures that dominate the atten-

TABLE 9–1   Open and Restrictive Rules, Ninety-fifth through Ninety-ninth Congresses

	Open Rules		Restrictive Rules		
Congress	*Number*	*Percent*	*Number*	*Percent*	*Total*
Ninety-fifth (1977–78)	213	88	28	12	241
Ninety-sixth (1979–80)	161	81	37	19	198
Ninety-seventh (1981–82)	90	80	22	20	112
Ninety-eighth (1983–84)	105	72	40	28	145
Ninety-ninth (1985–86)	65	64	36	36	101

SOURCE: *Congressional Record*, April 23, 1987, p. H2144.

tion of the nation and the House are frequently subject to restrictive floor procedures.

Despite the restrictions, structured rules can expand the range of policy options put before the membership. Issues that are not eligible under normal parliamentary procedures (they are "out of order") can be made in order. The Rules Committee can make in order nongermane amendments, legislation stuck in committee, or even measures that have never been introduced. During debate on a controversial rule relating to legislation on Central America, Republican Leader Robert H. Michel from Illinois engaged in this exchange with the Speaker:

Mr. Michel:

Might I inquire as to who introduced that measure you just made reference to? [House Joint Resolution 601.]

The Speaker:

The Chair will state that it was made in order by the rule.

Mr. Michel:

With no author?

The Speaker:

It does not have to have an author. It was made in order by the rule.

Mr. Michel:

Well, that is something unique around here. They are now falling from the sky.[11]

Whether restrictive, expansive, or both, a fundamental thrust of structured rules is to define the sequence in which specific amendments are to be voted upon. Sometimes the purpose is to benefit the committee that reported the legislation; sometimes it grants non-committee members an opportunity to revamp the reporting committee's priorities. Nevertheless, there is little question that the ability of the Rules Committee to determine the sequence of action can influence the ultimate outcome. And with a disproportionate number of majority party members—9 Democrats to 4 Republicans in the One-hundredth Congress—the majority leadership is assured of having rules granted that maximize its opportunities to achieve predetermined goals.

An example will illustrate the power of the Rules Committee to determine votes on amendments. In 1982, the Democratic leadership reluctantly brought to the floor a constitutional balanced budget proposal. (The Republican-controlled Senate had already passed such a proposal and their decision put "political heat" on the House for comparable action.) The Speaker's hand was forced when 218 members signed a discharge petition to bring the measure to the House floor. Speaker Tip O'Neill "decided to force the issue. Rather than let [President] Reagan brand [Democrats] as obstructionists, and wary of letting [Republicans] control" the time allotted to floor debate under the discharge process, the Speaker directed the Rules Committee to fashion a rule that favored Democratic control.[12]

The rule made only two amendments in order "which shall be considered only in the following order and which shall not be subject to amendment."[13] One amendment was the Democratic alternative which required the president to submit a balanced budget to the Congress. Under the rule, it was voted on first. The second amendment was Republican-sponsored, and required Congress *and* the president to ensure a balanced budget. (In the end, the Republican sponsor chose not to offer the amendment because it reflected the same objectives as the underlying legislation: a proposed constitutional amendment.)

The order of voting was critical, however. With the November elections only a month away, many Democrats wanted the opportunity to vote for a balanced budget proposition to fend off criticisms that they were fiscally irresponsible. "I do not dispute that there is political advantage to be gained by seeking this [constitutional] amendment," said Speaker O'Neill, "and that political costs may be suffered by opposing it."[14] The rule minimized those electoral costs. Many Democrats voted for their party's alternative, which was overwhelmingly rejected (77 to 347), and then voted against the constitutional amendment proposal. They provided the margin to defeat the balanced budget amendment, for it fell 46 votes short of the necessary two-thirds required for passage. This sequence of action produced two results favored by the majority leadership: protection for electorally vulnerable Democrats and rejection of an unwanted proposition.

Self-Executing Rules.   These stipulate a two-for-one procedure: adoption of the rule simultaneously enacts another measure, amendment, or both. The House, in short, is deemed to have passed a separate proposition when it adopts the rule. Traditionally used to expedite consideration of Senate amendments to House-passed legislation, self-executing rules now appear in more complex guises. An example will illustrate the point.

In 1986, House and Senate conferees struggled to reach agreement on an omnibus drug bill. The House's drug bill included a death penalty provision for certain drug-related murders; the Senate rejected this controversial feature of the legislation. Both chambers engaged in a battle of "legislative chicken" over the death penalty. House supporters vowed that the drug bill would never reach the president's desk unless it contained the death penalty feature. A bipartisan group of senators, opposed to the death penalty, threatened to stall the measure through a filibuster. Pressured by imminent elections and strong public interest in the drug problem, House and Senate negotiators agreed to an unusual procedure that accommodated both chambers. The House, in one vote on a rule, agreed to pass two proposals: the onmibus drug bill without the death penalty provision and a companion measure that authorized the death penalty. As one representative explained during debate on the rule:

> In adopting the rule, we will adopt the drug conference report and in addition will adopt a separate resolution that will contain the death penalty language

that this House has supported in the past, and both of those will be sent out as a package to the [Senate] upon the adoption of this rule.[15]

The Senate could take up one or both measures. It ignored the resolution and passed the drug conference report, thus obviating the filibuster threat. On this occasion, the self-executing rule served to facilitate bicameral accord on controversial legislation.

King-of-the-Hill Rules.   These rules are completely new to Capitol Hill. "As far as I know," said Rules Chairman Bolling during a May 1982 debate on a rule governing consideration of the concurrent budget resolution, "this procedure is unique."[16] The rule is unusual in a parliamentary sense for two major reasons. First, it permits the House to vote on an array of major policy alternatives—so-called substitutes that are the equal of new bills—in seriatim fashion. Significantly, no matter the outcome—yea or nay—on any of the substitutes, the king-of-the-hill rule typically stipulates that the vote on the last substitute is the only one that counts for purposes of accepting or rejecting a national policy.

Second, the king-of-the-hill rule waives scores of procedures and precedents. For example, parliamentary principles state that once part of a bill is amended, it is not in order to vote on that part unless another amendment, broader in scope, changes the part plus a "bigger bite" of the legislation. The massive substitutes made in order by the king-of-the-hill rule amend literally everything in the pending legislation. Technically, nothing is left to be changed and the amending process automatically terminates under traditional House procedures. Traditional procedures, however, are not followed when this type of rule is utilized, because political and policy objectives are of overriding concern.

When this type of rule was used in May 1982 on the concurrent budget resolution—Congress's spending blueprint for domestic and defense programs—one of its fundamental objectives was to allow major House factions a fair opportunity to achieve their fiscal purposes. Democrats and Republicans alike supported the rule, because it represented, said Republican Whip Trent Lott from Mississippi, the "best effort of the leadership on both sides of the aisle to fashion a fair and equitable approach to this extremely complex issue."[17] The complexity stemmed in part from bipartisan predictions that no budget blueprint could pass the House because of wide disagreement over expenditures for defense and domestic programs.

The king-of-the-hill rule presented the House with seven consecutive fiscal choices. However, three major substitutes were to be presented simultaneously following disposition of the other four plans. The king-of-the-hill rule stated:

If more than one of [the major substitutes] made in order by this [king-of-the-hill procedure] has been adopted, only the last such [substitute] which has been adopted shall be considered as having been finally adopted and reported back to the House.[18]

The House voted first on the GOP leadership plan, then on the moderate plan by Democratic Representative Les Aspin of Wisconsin, and finally on the Budget Committee plan prepared by Democratic Chairman Jim Jones from Oklahoma. For the GOP plan to win, the minority party had to pass its plan and defeat the Aspin and Jones substitutes.

This complicated procedure reflected a political gamble on the part of the joint leadership. With such a wide range of budgetary choices available to the members, the expectation was that at least one plan would eventually survive the parliamentary gauntlet. The procedure provided political cover to legislators who could cast votes on seven budgetary plans and explain their actions to constituents in any manner they chose. In the end, not one of the alternative budgets received a majority. Still, the value of the king-of-the-hill procedure is evident to the Rules Committee, which employs it on a wide range of issues (e.g., the Anti-Apartheid Act of 1985 and the Supplemental Appropriations Act of 1987).

In sum, the contemporary House operates more openly than at any time in recent history. Broad participation is a central character of the contemporary House. Unfortunately, this characteristic also makes it difficult for the House to act; there are so many bases to touch that the majority leadership must emphasize integration over fragmentation. Such innovative rules are a powerful new tool for this purpose.

UNLIMITED DEBATE IN THE SENATE

Because the Senate emphasizes individualism and minority rights (one senator, a group, or the minority party), "going from the House to the Senate is like going from prison to freedom," declared Floyd M. Riddick, parliamentarian emeritus of the Senate.[19] The right of extended debate best highlights Riddick's observation; extended debate is the Senate's most prominent and famous feature. Simply by talking at length—the so-called *filibuster*—senators can delay or stop legislative action and perhaps win favored policy modifications in exchange for ending their talkathon.

Until 1917 the Senate had no way to terminate filibusters. In that year the Senate adopted a cloture rule (Rule XXII) in response to President Woodrow Wilson's outrage at having a "little group of willful men" filibuster to death his proposal to arm merchant ships against enemy submarine attacks. (The cloture rule requires sixteen senators to sign a petition that permits a motion to be made imposing debate limitations—currently thirty hours—on a pending matter.) Even the threat to talk at length—an aspect of the "silent filibuster" that will be discussed below in the context of "holds"—is a potent parliamentary weapon. Sometimes the Senate majority leader, who has the main responsibility for scheduling the chamber's business, may decide not to take up controversial substantive measures unless their advocates have garnered in advance the sixty votes now required to invoke cloture.

Rule XXII underscores two important characteristics of the Senate: it is an antimajoritarian institution and its practice of unlimited debate grants inordinate power to every senator. A simple majority is sufficient to pass major and controversial legislation in the House. In the Senate, sixty votes might be needed—sometimes more than once—to move legislation to final passage.

To expedite floor action, the Senate regularly employs *unanimous consent agreements.* They prescribe debate limitations in an institution noted for unlimited debate. Such agreements, for example, may stipulate that every amendment to a bill can be debated for only one hour and any other debatable motion for only twenty minutes. Usually worked out in behind-the-scenes discussions among party leaders and their staff aids and other senators, unanimous consent agreements are the Senate's version of a "rule" from the Rules Committee.

Because the Senate lacks the debate-limiting procedures of the House, majority and minority leaders must be sensitive to the personal legislative needs and policy concerns of individual senators. Otherwise, any member can say the two magic words—"I object"—and bring the Senate to an impasse. Without unanimous consent, also called time-limitation agreements, the Senate must resort to its Standing Rules of the Senate. They are cumbersome to employ and permit extended debate.

Filibuster Changes

Long a powerful device to stymie action, the filibuster has undergone significant changes in the modern Senate. During the 1950s and 1960s, it was largely associated with southern Democratic opposition to civil rights measures and related attempts by the opposition to make it easier to invoke Rule XXII. Filibusters were infrequent at least in part because they required great physical stamina as senators debated around-the-clock. Senator Strom Thurmond holds the individual record by talking for more than 24 hours against the 1957 civil rights bill.

In today's Senate, the filibuster is employed routinely by senators of every ideological stripe. Democratic Senator Tom Eagleton of Missouri, who voluntarily retired from the Senate in 1986, observed that "We've had many more filibusters in the 17 years I have served in the Senate than in the 120 years before I got here."[20] Filibusters do not occur simply on issues of great national importance and visibility but on a wide range of less momentous topics. Moreover, there is a new style of filibuster that relies less on talking than on exploitation of Senate rules to frustrate action on measures (for ex-

ample, appealing the presiding officer's parliamentary rulings and demanding roll call votes).

Concomitantly, there has been an increase in the use of Rule XXII. "The
Senate has cloturitis," declared Republican Dan Quayle from Indiana.[21] Just
the threat of a filibuster prompts senators to file cloture petitions on the
legislation even before it reaches the floor. From sparing use of cloture (it was
invoked only four times from 1917 until 1962), the 1970s and 1980s have
witnessed routine use of the cloture procedure. Where one cloture vote per
measure was once the norm, the modern Senate reached a record seven
cloture votes on one measure during the 1980s.

Cloture is also used for purposes other than ending debate. The Senate,
unlike the House, has no general *germaneness* rule, but the requirement of
"relevancy" for amendments can be required if the Senate invokes cloture.
Republican Senator Gordon J. Humphrey from New Hampshire, for example,
offered a non-germane amendment (repealing a legislative pay hike) to a
homeless aid measure. "This can very well be a killer amendment," declared
Majority Leader Robert C. Byrd.[22] To prevent a vote on Humphrey's amendment, Senator Byrd filed a cloture petition. (If cloture is invoked, all amendments must then be germane to the pending legislation.) The Senate invoked
cloture by a 68 to 29 vote. "Under the precedents of the Senate," declared the
presiding officer in ruling Humphrey's amendment out of order, "once cloture
is invoked, the Chair is required to rule out of order each non-germane
amendment that is pending and subsequently called up."[23]

The surge in filibusters and cloture attempts stems from a variety of
factors. One is the influx of many new senators who prefer to push their own
agendas even if the Senate's institutional activities grind to a halt. There are
occasions, noted Republican Mark O. Hatfield, a senator from Oregon, when
senators are "determined to follow [their] own perspective even to the per-
version, the distortion, and the destruction of the [legislative] process."[24]
Senate rules permit—even encourage—this behavior, for they provide aggressive senators with an arsenal of devices to advance their objectives.

In 1975, the Senate amended Rule XXII to make it easier to invoke cloture. The amendment permitted cloture on substantive matters by a three-
fifths vote of the entire membership rather than the two-thirds previously
required. Ironically, the 1975 change that eased the requirements for cloture
produced an innovative dilatory tactic. Senator James Allen, a Democrat from
Alabama, developed the *post-cloture filibuster*—calling up scores of amendments, requiring each to be read in full, and demanding roll call votes on
each—to frustrate final action on legislation. Thus, the real filibuster began
after cloture was achieved. The Senate twice (1979 and 1986) amended Rule
XXII to deal with this tactic, but the potential for post-cloture filibusters is
still available to any senator.

Another reason for the wider use of filibusters is their enhanced potency
in an institution that is workload-packed and deadline-driven. There is insuf-

ficient time to accommodate the manifold claims on the Senate's agenda. In such an environment, senators who even indicate their intention to debate at length exercise significant policy leverage, especially near the end of any congressional session.

Gone, too, are internal incentives ("to get along, go along, " for instance) that fostered deference to seniority and party leaders, such as to Majority Leader (1955–60) Lyndon Baines Johnson. Johnson exercised tight control over floor proceedings, including use of the filibuster.

> While Johnson went to great lengths to avoid filibusters, once they had begun . . . he tended to regard filibusters as a personal challenge to his stewardship. Instead of making an end run around the combatants . . . , he often preferred to break the filibuster by keeping the Senate in session for long hours, even around the clock, and forcing the minority ultimately to give up in exhaustion.[25]

By contrast, contemporary party leaders are likely to accommodate filibustering senators who have meetings to attend back home. "The Senate has simply recessed," noted a journalist, "taken weekends off and gone on to other business until the would-be filibusterers returned to the Capitol."[26]

Scheduling the Senate's business, in brief, is fraught with uncertainty and unpredictability. Party leaders constantly face the struggle of reconciling institutional objectives and individual needs. "Senators are always coming to me and saying, 'I've got to go here, I've go to go there,' " said Democratic Leader Byrd. "It's become impossible to schedule the work of the Senate."[27] The leader's scheduling problems are compounded by the "hold"—another type of silent filibuster—that has seen a resurgence and which can prevent floor action on measures or matters.

"Holds"

Holds are an informal custom unique to the Senate. They permit any number of senators—individually or in clusters—to stop (sometimes permanently, sometimes temporarily) floor consideration of legislation or nominations simply by making requests of their party leaders not to take up such matters. For example, a Senate committee might report a measure by a 17 to 1 vote. The bill could even be slated for floor debate. And yet a single dissenting senator can put a hold on the legislation and halt action on the measure. To be sure, party leaders can move ahead with the bill anyway, but then they face the daunting prospect of overcoming the probable filibuster. Unlike filibusters, which are ostensibly education and occur in full view of everyone, holds require no public utterance and occur in shrouded circumstances.

Relatively little is known about holds even among the cognoscenti of Washington, D.C. There is no public record of who places holds, how it is done (often by letter to the party leader), how many holds are placed on any bill, or how long they will be honored by the leadership. Most holds, noted

Democratic Leader Byrd, are used so senators "might be assured that they will be informed or contacted so they can be present when the matter is called up, or have an opportunity to offer an amendment."[28] Yet secret holds can stymie action without anyone—press, constituents, interest groups, executive officials, or even other senators—knowing who is preventing consideration of a particular issue. "There is a hold on S. 1407," declared Democratic Senator James Exon from Nebraska, and "this Senator cannot even find out which Senator or the staff of which Senator has placed a hold on that bill."[29]

Holds are a potent blocking device because they are linked to the Senate's tradition of extended debate and unanimous consent agreements. Party leaders understand that to ignore holds can precipitate both objections to unanimous consent requests and filibusters. "As many as six senators had 'holds' on the [bridge repair] bill," wrote a journalist, "thereby blocking the unanimous consent that would be needed before the Senate could even consider it."[30] Holds are a more prominent feature of today's Senate because assertive senators recognize the political and policy potential that are inherent in the concept. Holds "have come into a form of reverence which was never to be, " declared Republican Whip Alan K. Simpson from Wyoming.[31] Periodically, party leaders assert that senators cannot put indefinite or anonymous holds on matters. As Majority Leader Howard Baker noted during the closing days of the Ninety-seventh Congress:

> Senators are aware, of course, that holds on both calendars, the calendar of general orders and the calendar of executive business, are matters of courtesy by the leadership on both sides of the aisle and are not part of the standing rules of the Senate. Therefore, members should be on notice that in these closing hours of this session, as indeed was the case last year and I believe the year before, holds will become distinctly perishable.[32]

Information on the implementation or effectiveness of these pronouncements is, at this juncture, spotty and scant. For example, despite Baker's claim that holds become perishable during the closing days of a legislative session, this is also the period when Senators are strategically positioned to employ the hold. Senator Howard M. Metzenbaum, often employs holds during the Senate's waning days to block action on matters he opposes. Republican Senator Ted Stevens of Alaska became so angry on one occasion that he addressed the Senate on the consequences of legislative holds and vigorously stated his objections to Metzenbaum's "choke hold" on measures beneficial to numerous states. "Every bill this senator has a hold on, " responded Senator Metzenbaum, "is a giveaway to a special interest."[33]

Yet it is precisely on special purpose legislation that holds can be most effective. "Must" legislation, such as continuing resolutions that fund the government, cannot be killed by holds. Where a hold really works, observed Republican Senator William L. Armstrong from Colorado, "is on a bill where nobody cares except two or three Senators."[34] If these few senators can resolve their differences, then the hold will fall by the wayside.

Holds encourage bargaining not only among senators but between the Senate and the executive branch. Senator Jesse Helms from North Carolina, frequently places holds on diplomatic nominations to extract concessions from the State Department. Another senator blocked the confirmation of an undersecretary of the Commerce Department for three weeks because he wanted the "Commerce Department to award a $1 million grant for a marina development project in his home state."[35] The Reagan White House asked Senator Hatfield to place a hold on a measure that would limit the perquisites afforded former presidents.[36] Lobby organizations, too, can ask sympathetic senators to place holds on legislation.

Holds can also be placed on House-passed legislation. Senator Humphrey employed the hold—"on all House-passed bills in the Senate to find a vehicle for his amendment repealing the raise"—on the previously mentioned pay raise issue.[37] Unfortunately for Humphrey, the strategy was unsuccessful because he chose a House-passed bill (aid to the homeless) that had large bipartisan support and his amendment was defeated on a procedural vote. Still, Senator Humphrey can try again and attempt to compel the House to act on his proposal.

The House has nothing comparable to holds or extended debate. Nor does the Senate have anything like a Rules Committee or a general germaneness provision. Such procedural differences often mask the wide range of interactions that occur between the House and Senate. Bicameralism, after all, is a fundamental factor in shaping legislative activity and member behavior. The effectiveness of the legislative branch even hinges in part on whether House-Senate interactions resemble intramural warfare or cooperation. This two-way relationship, which affects each chamber's performance, politics, and policies, is explored next.

THE HOUSE IN THE SENATE AND VICE VERSA

While books and journals are replete with studies of legislative-executive relations, there are precious few studies of the other pair of governmental branches: the House and the Senate. Beyond a few studies of conference committees, House-Senate relations are seldom subject to intensive or extensive analysis. The situation is something like the old story of tourists visiting the House and the Senate and then asking a Capitol police officer: "Where's the Congress?"

Granted the complexity of "the Congress," at least one aspect of it involves the way each chamber affects or is affected by the other body. To give some "feel and flavor" to bicameralism, this section sketches some House-Senate interactions along three overlapping dimensions: institutional, partisan, and policy. Neither chamber, in short, operates in isolation from the other despite periodic admonitions to that effect from senators and representatives.

Institutional Interactions

Cooperation and conflict are broad and ever-present features of the bicameral context. Yet in several traditional areas customary patterns of bicameral activity are undergoing significant change. Financial interactions and public visibility are two examples. During the 1980s, for instance, the GOP-controlled Senate's imprint on appropriation, budget, and tax measures often surpassed that of the Democratically controlled House. The GOP Senate even grasped the initiative in 1981 and 1982 in launching major tax bills despite the Constitution's requirement that the House must originate revenue-raising measures. As one 1981 account noted of the Senate's change from reactive to an active tax role:

> Usually the Senate waits for the House to originate major tax bills, but [the House tax-writing] Ways and Means [Committee], with Democrats in charge, has been moving more slowly than the Reagan administration wants. But Reagan has called upon Congress to send him a tax bill by August, and yesterday's start in the Republican-run [Senate] Finance Committee was an effort to pressure the Democrats to comply.[38]

The Senate technically complied with the Constitution, because it took a minor House-passed revenue measure, struck everything after the *enacting clause* (the opening phrase of every House and Senate bill), and then substituted its own tax plan. In 1982, an election year, the Democratically controlled House did not want its "footprints" or "fingerprints" on any measure calling for tax increases. It preferred to let the GOP Senate initiate the legislation.

In consideration of concurrent budget resolutions, some scholars believe that under the terms of the Budget and Impoundment Control Act of 1974 the Senate is advantaged over the House.[39] Not only can the Senate initiate its own resolution as well as the accompanying *reconciliation* process (requiring committees to raise revenue or cut expenditures to meet the aggregate tax and spending levels prescribed in the budget resolution), but membership on the Senate Budget Committee is permanent, unlike the limited-service (or rotational) system used by the House Budget Committee. Senators, therefore, are the beneficiaries in this arena of the *specialization* advantage usually associated with House members. (The larger House enables its members, who serve on a smaller number of committees and subcommittees than senators— on average, six assignments per representative compared to twelve for senators—to concentrate in fewer subject areas and thus master the legislative details important to sustaining the House's position during *conference committees*—special, temporary panels of senators and representatives created to iron out differences between House and Senate bills— with the Senate.)

Public visibility is another area where interchamber changes are occurring. In 1979, the House permitted gavel-to-gavel coverage of its floor proceedings over C-SPAN. Soon thereafter an intense Senate effort got underway to imitate the House. First Republican Leader Baker and then Democratic

Leader Byrd took on the issue until in mid-1986, TV coverage was finally achieved. A telling argument for television was made over and over again. As Senator Baker phrased it:

> My point is that the House of Representatives will become the dominant congressional branch of government of the United States, simply because the public has access to their proceedings, if we do not provide similar access here.[40]

The House's increased public visibility (still less than for the Senate) has several consequences. Like senators, House members can use the floor to attract attention to their ideas, appeal to national constituencies, and even launch presidential campaigns. While the Senate remains a superior launching pad for presidential aspirants, C-SPAN permits representatives to become more nationally known, which may strengthen their chances of contesting seriously for the White House. In the judgment of Democratic Representative Morris Udall, a 1976 presidential aspirant:

> I used to complain that the day you come to the Senate, you're presumed to be a presidential candidate if you're under 65, not under indictment, and not living in sin . . . while better quality and real experience coming out of the House will not be looked at. I think that's changing.[41]

Other factors are involved in the improved but still up-hill presidential prospects for House members. "There is no . . . one and only route to the presidency," said 1988 presidential candidate Jack Kemp, the Republican representative from New York, "so why not from the House?"[42]

Partisan Interactions

The first half of the 1980s was unique in contemporary bicameral politics. Republicans took control of the Senate in 1981 for the first time in twenty-six years, producing a situation that last occurred nearly fifty years ago: split party control of Congress. President Reagan's first term programmatic successes largely occurred because the GOP-controlled Senate promoted the agenda of the White House and put "political heat" on the Democratically controlled House to act on administration requests. Alternatively, the Senate blocked Democratically passed measures that the White House opposed. In effect, the GOP Senate served as the political and policy "broker" (or "referee," on occasion) between the Republican President and Democratic House.[43]

During the six-year period of split party control (1981–87), bicameral discussion often involved the two majority parties rather than the members of the same party. With "governing" responsibility lodged in House Democrats and Senate Republicans, the Leaders of these parties consulted regularly on a wide range of topics.

> House Democratic and Senate Republican leaders have developed a closer relationship with each other than with their party colleagues in the other

chamber, leaving some feeling of isolation among House Republicans and Senate Democrats.[44]

The 1980s period of split party control had a variety of other effects on each house. One consequence was an increase in the complexity of bicameral maneuverings. Recounted a House GOP committee aide:

> Because we have a Republican Senate, [the Democratic committee majority] has come to recognize the value of getting the minority on board. . . . If they tick off the Republicans totally, what we will usually do . . . is get to the Senate people and say "we need to kill this bill." That unspoken threat—the realization that the Republicans control the Senate and the White House—has been very important. . . . During the Carter administration, you found that [committee Democrats] were much less willing to accommodate Republican concerns.[45]

Even internal partisan struggles within one house can be influenced by the other body. When House Democrats voted to oust moderate Les Aspin as chair of the Armed Services Committee for the One-hundredth Congress, this initial party decision set in motion a four-way struggle for that position. Although temporarily deposed, Aspin still remained in contention against three announced Democratic challengers from Armed Services: Charles E. Bennett (from Florida), Nicholas Mavroules (from Massachusetts), and the presumed front-runner, Marvin Leath (from Texas). Aspin eventually won back the Armed Services chairmanship by defeating the challengers. A factor that affected the votes of some House Democrats when Aspin went head-to-head against Leath was the chairmanship of the Senate Armed Services Committee:

> The prospect of Leath's heading up the House Armed Services Committee, while the Senate Armed Services Committee is headed up by conservative Senator Sam Nunn (D) of Georgia, leaves many Democrats wondering whether the views of liberal Democrats will get short shrift when it is time for the two chambers to bargain over the size and shape of the defense program.[46]

It is worth noting that when Aspin successfully ousted Melvin Price as chair of Armed Services in January 1985, one of the factors in Aspin's favor was concern among many House Democrats that Price's frail health and age had led to Armed Services being overpowered by its counterpart in the Senate.[47]

The tumultuous Democratic battle over Armed Services also affected the internal Senate GOP struggle over who would be the ranking minority member on the Foreign Relations Committee during the One-hundredth Congress. Republican Senator Richard G. Lugar, who chaired Foreign Relations during the previous Congress, wanted to remain as ranking party member. Senator Helms, who had seniority over Lugar on Foreign Relations, claimed the ranking spot for the One-hundredth Congress. In the previous Congress, Helms headed the Agriculture Committee because of promises made during his 1984 reelection campaign. He preferred Foreign Relations, however.

Helms emerged the winner over Lugar in the Republican Conference—the organization of all Senate Republicans. Several GOP Senators were influenced, noted GOP Whip Simpson, by the fight over Aspin in the House Democratic Caucus. Simpson said these senators were worried about "recurring 'popularity contests' and possible threats to their own futures in the Senate committee hierarchy if the seniority system were breached."[48]

Everything from cooperation to conflict characterizes bicameral partisan relations. Speaker Jim Wright and Senate Majority Leader Byrd, leaders of the One-hundredth Congress, pledged to work cooperatively and emulate, to the extent feasible, the close ties that existed between Speaker Sam Rayburn and Senate Majority Leader Johnson during the Eisenhower years. Scholars and journalists who advocate close bicameral ties stress these benefits:

> [T]he development of more coherent and cohesive policies by Congress, the reduction of internal friction and internecine clashes, the removal of some unnecessary delays, duplication, and strains in the legislative process, the strengthening of Congress vis-à-vis the President, the promotion of cooperation and consensus between the legislative and executive branches, the enhancement of party responsibility and accountability, and a greater credibility for Congress in the eyes of the public.[49]

The achievement of these purported virtues is no easy task, because there are so many uncontrollable factors (politics, ideology, or traditional jealousies, for example) that invite bicameral controversy.

Policy Interactions

House-Senate policy interactions are too extensive to catalog in detail. There are many instances, for example, where one chamber will try to pass a bill by a large margin in the hope that this will build momentum for its consideration by the other body. Senators may fend off non-germane floor amendments by arguing that they will be unacceptable to the House. Representatives will argue that certain issues should be dropped, because they will provoke a filibuster by senatorial opponents. Or Senators will filibuster measures to provide time for their House allies to plan strategy for dealing with the legislation when it arrives in their chamber. One chamber will pass a bill in the expectation that the other will kill it. Or one house will wait for the other to act first on certain matters. Senators lobby House colleagues just as representatives try to sway senators.

Congressional policymaking, in short, is an interconnected enterprise. Not only does the Constitution mandate the connection, but deliberate bicameral decisions produce this result as well. For example, senators and representatives understand that major controversial issues are likely to reach the conference committee stage. (In a Congress noted for the wide diffusion of power, conference committees perform an important integrative role.)

In the expectation that measures will reach conference, senators and representatives employ common strategies at each major lawmaking juncture: introduction, committee hearings and markup, and floor consideration. House and Senate members regularly introduce "companion" legislation. These bills, which are identical twins, are introduced at or about the same time in each house to expedite bicameral progress on the legislation. This strategy was used by Senator Simpson and Democratic Representative Romano L. Mazzoli from Kentucky in their struggle of several years to pass comprehensive immigration reform legislation.

> They were to introduce the same bill, at the same time, to each of their respective chambers. They knew their bills would change as they proceeded through the House and Senate, but they hoped that by introducing one bill they could focus the debate on basic concepts and more easily reconcile differences emerging in a conference of the two Houses should the bills pass.[50]

Hearings and markups are integral parts of committee decision making. Hearings serve a variety of purposes, such as building a public record, gathering information, or investigating public problems. Bicameralism can be accentuated through the use of joint hearings, as in the case of the House and Senate panels that investigated the Iran-Contra affair. Also, House (Senate) committees will invite senators (representatives) to testify and then encourage them to support the legislation in the Senate (House) and later in conference.

Markups occur sometime after the hearings—if they take place at all. It is at markup sessions that committee members shape the final contents of the measure sent to the House or Senate floor. The vehicle used for markup purposes has implications for conference committee deliberations. When the House passed the landmark Tax Reform Act of 1986, the chair of the Senate Finance Committee, Bob Packwood, had several options: he could use the House-passed bill, a Senate proposal, the administration's plan, the tax code itself, or a staff-prepared document.

The Finance Committee started from scratch rather than with the House bill when it began to revise the tax laws. Thus, the eventual House-Senate conference was required to settle many details.[51] It is worth noting that Democratic Senator Bill Bradley from New Jersey often called the "father" of tax overhaul, played a crucial lawmaking role throughout, including during markups of the House Ways and Means Committee. For example, he gave Ways and Means Democrats a "pep talk" on the eve of their markup sessions and argued that tax reform is a natural Democratic issue.[52]

On the floor, senators and representatives engage in a variety of activities to strengthen their hand in conference committees. A common ploy is to accept numerous amendments on the floor, which can be used as trading material in conference. Senator Russell Long who voluntarily retired after 38 years in the Senate, called this practice "corn shucking."

> He would sit quietly while the Senate passed dozens of amendments. Then, in conference with the House, he would throw the amendments away, like the

husk on an ear of corn, until he reached the legislative kernels he wanted to retain.[53]

In short, to compare and contrast the House and Senate along these different dimensions is no easy task. Both bodies are flexible and adaptable entities that change over time and in their relations with each other. Each chamber, too, has its own lawmaking procedures that present obstacles and opportunities for policymaking. On the one hand, bicameralism can lead to the defeat or delay of legislation. On the other hand, review of ideas by two chambers can produce better legislation or prevent unwise policies from becoming law.

CONCLUSION: THE IMPORTANCE OF BICAMERALISM

The House and Senate are paradoxically, separate yet interlocked institutions. The Framers, as Madison pointed out, wanted the House and Senate to be "as little connected with each other as the nature of their common functions and their common dependence on the society will admit."[54] Certainly each chamber's distinct set of procedures underscores their unconnectedness. Where the House can limit both debate and the number of floor amendments, the Senate can do neither except by unanimous consent or cloture.

Despite such differences, the House and Senate are linked in policymaking by more than constitutional dictate. Actions by one chamber trigger reactions by the other. One house can thwart the will of the other. Or frustrated members of one chamber can try to accomplish their goals in the other.

Senators and representatives have multiple avenues for pursuing their policy and political objectives. The existence of two separate policymaking arenas on Capitol Hill is another manifestation of this. Nonetheless, many accounts of legislative activity overlook bicameralism as a force in influencing member behavior and policy outcomes. The House and Senate are independent institutions, but that independence does not mean that each chamber's members act in isolation from one another. Their linkages are as varied as they are complex.

In sum, the separation between the chambers is something like the separation between Congress and the White House. "To study one branch of government in isolation from the other is usually an exercise in make-believe," remarked Louis Fisher.[55] This theme applies to the House and Senate as well.

NOTES

1. *The New York Times,* May 9, 1984, P. B14. Senator Gore ran for the Senate in November 1984 after serving four terms in the House.
2. Paul Simon, "Trying on the Senate for Size," *Chicago Magazine,* November 1985, p. 150.

3. Alexander Hamilton, *The Federalist,* no. 60, ed. Clinton Rossiter (New York: Mentor, 1961), pp. 367–68.
4. *Congressional Record,* October 22, 1985, p. S13775.
5. Alan Ehrenhalt, "Special Report: The Individualist Senate," *Congressional Quarterly Weekly Report,* September 4, 1982, p. 2182.
6. Richard F. Fenno, Jr., *The United States Senate: A Bicameral Perspective* (Washington, D.C.: American Enterprise Institute for Public Policy Research, 1982), p. 5.
7. For additional procedural details, see Walter J. Oleszek, *Congressional Procedures and the Policy Process,* 2nd ed. (Washington, D.C.: CQ Press, 1984). For example, the debating and amending of major bills regularly occurs in the Committee of the Whole. The "rule" authorizes the Speaker to resolve the House into the Committee of the Whole, which is simply the House in another form. Its purpose is to expedite action on the legislation. For example, a quorum in the House is 218 members; in the Committee of the Whole, it is 100 members.
8. Alfred Steinberg, *Sam Rayburn* (New York: Hawthorn Books, 1975), p. 313.
9. The Rules Committee may also waive specific House rules so bills or floor amendments are not subject to points of order that could prevent the legislation from being taken up or cause measures to be yanked from the floor because they violate formal procedural requirements. Waivers appear in open, closed, or modified rules.
10. *Congressional Record,* February 9, 1982, p. H263. For a helpful analysis of the wider use of complex rules see Stanley Bach, "The Structure of Choice in the House of Representatives: The Impact of Special Rules," *Harvard Journal on Legislation,* 18 (Summer 1981), pp. 555–602.
11. *Congressional Record,* April 16, 1986, p. H1849.
12. *Congressional Quarterly Almanac, 1982* (Washington, D.C.: Congressional Quarterly, Inc., 1983), p. 394.
13. *Congressional Record,* April 16, 1986, p. H8256.
14. Ibid., p. H8335.
15. *Congressional Record,* October 17, 1986., p. H10777.
16. *Congressional Record,* May 21, 1982, p. H2519.
17. Ibid., p. H2524.
18. Ibid., p. H2519.
19. Robert Conot, "Anonymous in the House of the U.S. Power," *Los Angeles Times,* part V, p. 6.
20. *Congressional Record,* November 23, 1985, p. S16476.
21. *Congressional Record,* September 28, 1984, p. S12271.
22. *Congressional Record,* April 8, 1987, p. S4825.
23. Ibid, p. S4944.
24. *Congressional Record,* September 27, 1984, p. S12137.
25. *Congressional Record,* March 3, 1986, p. S1915.
26. *The New York Times,* October 4, 1984, p. B6.
27. *The New York Times,* November 19, 1986, p. A24.
28. *Congressional Record,* February 24, 1986, p. S1512.
29. *Congressional Record,* October 5, 1984, p. S13779.
30. *Washington Post,* December 10, 1980, p. C6.
31. *Congressional Record,* December 5, 1985,p. S16916.
32. *Congressional Record,* December 6, 1982, p. S13901.

33. See *Congressional Record,* October 1, 1982, pp. S13408–13410, and *Washington Post,* October 1, 1982, p. A3.

34. *Congressional Record,* February 24, 1986, p. S1511.

35. *Washington Post,* April 25, 1986, p. B9.

36. *Congressional Record,* July 25, 1984, p. S9129.

37. Jaqueline Calmes, "Pay Hike for Members of Congress Takes Effect," *Congressional Quarterly Weekly Report,* February 7, 1987, p. 220.

38. *Washington Post,* June 19, 1981, p. A5.

39. See John W. Ellwood, "Inter-Chamber Relations in the U.S. Congress and the Congressional Budget Process," paper prepared for the Conference on the Congressional Budget Process, Carl Albert Center for the Study of Legislative Affairs, University of Oklahoma, February 12–13, 1982.

40. *Congressional Record,* April 14, 1982, p. S3476.

41. Janet Hook, "House to White House: How Tough a Trail?" *Congressional Quarterly Weekly Report,* May 10, 1986, p. 1026.

42. Ibid. Nonetheless, Kemp and the only other serious House candidate, Richard A. Gephardt, a Democrat from Missouri, were quickly eliminated from the presidential race.

43. Roger H. Davidson and Walter J. Oleszek, "Changing the Guard in the United States Senate," *Legislative Studies Quarterly* 9 (November 1984), pp. 635–63.

44. Richard E. Cohen, "A Congress Divided," *National Journal,* January 18, 1986, p. 131.

45. Quoted in Richard L. Hall, "Participation in Committees: An Exploration," paper presented at the annual meeting of the American Political Science Association, Washington, D.C., August 30–September 4, 1984, p. 21.

46. *Christian Science Monitor,* January 20, 1987, p. 4.

47. Representative Price died April 22, 1988, while still holding office.

48. *Washington Post,* January 21, 1987, p. A1. The Simpson reference is from John Felton, "In Victory for Seniority System, Helms Wrests Post From Lugar," *Congressional Quarterly Report,* January 24, 1987, p. 144.

49. Walter Kravitz, "Relations Between the Senate and House of Representatives: The Party Leaderships," in *Policymaking Role of Leadership in the Senate: A Compilation of Papers Prepared for the Commision on the Operation of the Senate* (Washington, D.C.: Government Printing Office 1976), p. 123.

50. Harris N. Miller, "The Right Thing To Do: A History of Simpson-Mazzoli," *Journal of Contemporary Studies* 7 (Fall 1984), P. 68.

51. *U.S. News & World Report,* March 3, 1986, p. 51.

52. *The Wall Street Journal,* June 4, 1986, p. 24.

53. *The New York Times,* January 27, 1986, p. A19.

54. James Madison, in *The Federalist,* no. 51 (New York: Mentor 1961) p. 322.

55. Louis Fisher, *The Politics of Shared Power: Congress and the Executive,* 2nd ed. (Washington, D.C.: CQ Press, 1987), p. ix.

CHAPTER 10

Congress and Organized Interests

John T. Tierney
Kay Lehman Schlozman

Capitol Hill seems to be swarming with lobbyists these days. The hallways outside the hearing rooms of House and Senate committees often are packed with special pleaders, haranguing lawmakers on behalf of a remarkable range of interests. One could populate a minor city with the more than 10,000 Washington professionals who spend their days—and many of their evenings—attempting to influence governmental policy decisions. And the organizations they represent include all kinds: corporations, trade associations, labor unions, professional societies, social welfare and civil rights organizations, single issue cause groups, and so on.

A common conception about the role of interest groups in American politics is that they are battering rams, attempting to bludgeon reluctant policymakers into making concessions. But this view of organized interest influence is inadequate. It ignores the extent to which the paths connecting interest groups to Congress and the executive branch bear two-way traffic. That is, relationships between representatives or organized interests and public officials in both the legislative and executive branches are reciprocal and mutually beneficial. Obviously, government officials are in a position to supply desired concessions to organized interests. But the organized interests command much that is valued by policymakers as well—especially information and political support, but also campaign contributions, lucrative speaking fees, and other attractive inducements.

A second, less obvious way in which the relationship between the government and interest groups is reciprocal is that the latter not only *affect* policy outcomes, they are *affected by* the government and by the larger political system. Organized interests reflect the constitutional, institutional, legal, and electoral systems in which they are embedded. These aspects of the political environment impinge on pressure politics in terms of how many and what kind of interest organizations emerge, the techniques they use, the strategies they adopt, and the extent of their influence. In the legislative context, for example, it is clear that institutional changes in Congress in the 1970s contributed to the explosion of organized interest activity and that the enactment in 1971 of the Federal Election Campaign Act and the subsequent rulings of the Federal Election Commission led to dramatic increases in the number of political action committees and, thus, to a major alteration in the role of organized interests in financing congressional election campaigns.

These pathways of mutual influence and exchange that link organized interests with Congress are precisely what arouse public concerns, inspire enterprising investigative reporters, and incite ground swells of reformist fervor. These days, if one were to pay attention only to what the national newsweeklies, the network news programs, and the other media have to say about pressure politics one's whole understanding of this part of American politics might easily be clouded by a loose mixture of truths and half-truths. There are four impressions that seem particularly prominent and thus worth exploring here. First, the media have been correct in suggesting that there has been explosive growth over the past two decades in the numbers of interest groups active in Washington and in the scale of their political operations. Less accurate is the second popular notion: that with this growth in interest group activity, the interests of the general public and of previously underrepresented interests (the poor, consumers, whales, baby seals, etc.) have achieved organized representation equal to that of the business interests that for so long dominated interest group politics. Third, and still more misleading, is the idea that pressure group politics is a realm only of dirty politics, a realm in which lobbyists induce cooperation or consent from members of Congress by plying them with what has been called "the three Bs—booze, bribes, and broads." Finally, popular accounts of American politics seem to foster the belief that organized interests somehow dictate legislative outcomes—that Congress is merely some kind of institutional anemometer registering the force of prevailing interest group winds. As the balance of this chapter argues, the realities of organized interest politics are more complex and less viscerally satisfying than these popular impressions, but not necessarily more reassuring.

INCREASES IN INTEREST GROUP ACTIVITY

Journalists and politicians often note (and just as frequently lament) recent increases in interest group activity, all but declaring this the age of the "imperial pressure group." And the apparent ubiquity of interest groups and lobbyists in Washington is not just a figment of politicians' imaginations. There has indeed been tremendous growth over the past two decades both in the numbers of interest groups active in Washington and in the scale of their political operations. Charting this growth, one finds that of the 2,800 organizations that had lobbying offices in the capital as of 1982, 40 percent have been founded since 1960, and 25 percent since 1970.[1] Some of these relatively young organizations are groups representing the disadvantaged and broad publics such as consumers or taxpayers.[2] Others are organizations or associations representing new interests that have emerged in recent years as the result of the growth of new technologies, new industries, new professions, or new ways of producing or providing goods and services—organizations such as the National Cable Television Association, the National Computer Graphics Association, the American Academy of Physician Assistants, and the U.S. Hang Gliding Association. In addition to these newborn organizations, many previously apolitical organizations—in particular, corporations—have recently gotten involved in politics.

Not only are there more lobbying organizations on the Washington scene, but these organizations are more active in the 1980s than they were in the past. A survey of 175 lobbying organizations in Washington in the early 1980s found that the explosion in interest group activity has taken place across all kinds of interest group techniques—direct lobbying of officials, testifying at hearings, helping to plan legislative strategy, making financial contributions to electoral campaigns, mounting grassroots lobbying efforts, filing lawsuits or otherwise engaging in litigation, and so on. Table 10–1 shows the percentage or organizations in our sample that use each of twenty-seven different techniques of influence. Table 10–2 shows the percentage of organizations reporting that they are using particular techniques more now than in the past. And even though these lobbying organizations report that their activities have increased across all of the government's institutional arenas (Congress, the White House, executive agencies, and the courts), Congress is clearly their primary institutional target, as Table 10–3 indicates.

The centrality of Congress in American national policymaking and its traditional openness to interest group importuning clearly account for the legislature's status as the institutional focal point of lobbying organizations in Washington. But over the past fifteen years there have been a number of changes on Capitol Hill that have rendered Congress even more accessible and open to organized interests while at the same time recasting the institutional character of Congress, making it more individualistic and unpredictable—and thus harder for organized interests to deal with—than it had been in the past. These changes have altered the environment of legislative lobbying, opening up some new avenues for potential influence but also multiplying the number of persons on Capitol Hill who may have a say on policy matters and thus leaving interest groups that are intent on influencing legislative outcomes with little choice but to escalate the range and volume of their political activities.

In the House of Representatives, in particular, the weakening of committee chairs and the decentralization of power to subcommittee heads and to rank-and-file legislators has complicated the work of lobbyists who must now cultivate a broader range of contacts to keep tabs on activities across a much more diffused legislative landscape. There are more subcommittees with overlapping jurisdictions. Single committees and subcommittees no longer exercise the complete control over legislation as they once did. With the growing tendency to refer bills to multiple committees, and with the general relaxation of legislative norms that once inhibited floor challenges to commit-

TABLE 10–1   Percentage of Organizations Using Each of Techniques of Exercising Influence

1. Testifying at hearings.	99%
2. Contacting government officials directly to present your point of view.	98
3. Engaging in informal contacts with officials—at conventions, over lunch, and so on.	95
4. Presenting research results or technical information.	92
5. Sending letters to members of your organization to inform them about your activities.	92
6. Entering into coalitions with other organizations.	90
7. Attempting to shape the implementation of policies.	89
8. Talking with people from the press and the media.	86
9. Consulting with government officials to plan legislative strategy.	85
10. Helping to draft legislation.	85
11. Inspiring letter writing or telegram campaigns.	84
12. Shaping the government's agenda by raising new issues and calling attention to previously ignored problems.	84
13. Mounting grass roots lobbying efforts.	80
14. Having influential constituents contact their congressional representative's office.	80
15. Helping draft regulations, rules, or guidelines.	78
16. Serving on advisory commissions and boards.	76
17. Alerting congressional representatives to the effects of a bill on their districts.	75
18. Filing suit or otherwise engaging in litigation.	72
19. Making financial contributions to electoral campaigns.	58
20. Doing favors for officials who need assistance.	56
21. Attempting to influence appointments to public office.	53
22. Publicizing candidates' voting records.	44
23. Engaging in direct-mail fund raising for your organization.	44
24. Running advertisements in the media about your position on issues.	31
25. Contributing work or personnel to electoral campaigns.	24
26. Making public endorsements of candidates for office.	22
27. Engaging in protests or demonstrations.	20

SOURCE: Kay Lehman Schlozman and John T. Tierney, *Organized Interests and American Democracy* (New York: Harper & Row, 1986), p. 150.

tee decisions, threats to a group's legislative interests may come from anywhere in the chamber and at many more points over a bill's progression through the legislative labyrinth.

The expansion and professionalization of congressional staff also have complicated the work of organized interests by multiplying the number of people with whom lobbyists need to establish contacts. Staff members can

TABLE 10–2 Percentage of Organizations Using Each of Techniques More Than in Past

1. Talking with people from the press and media.	68%
2. Entering into coalitions with other organizations.	68
3. Contacting government officials directly to present your point of view.	67
4. Testifying at hearings.	66
5. Sending letters to members of your organization to inform them about your activities.	65
6. Presenting research results or technical information.	63
7. Mounting grass roots lobbying efforts.	59
8. Inspiring letter writing or telegram campaigns.	58
9. Engaging in informal contacts with officials—at conventions, over lunch, and so on.	57
10. Attempting to shape the implementation of policies.	56
11. Helping to draft legislation.	54
12. Shaping the government's agenda by raising new issues.	54
13. Consulting with government officials to plan legislative strategy.	54
14. Having influential constituents contact their congressional representative's office.	52
15. Making financial contributions to electoral campaigns.	49
16. Alerting congressional representatives to the effects of a bill on their district.	45
17. Helping to draft regulations, rules, or guidelines.	44
18. Filing suit or otherwise engaging in litigation.	38
19. Serving on advisory commissions and boards.	32
20. Engaging in direct-mail fund raising for your organization.	31
21. Attempting to influence appointments to public office.	23
22. Doing favors for officials who need assistance.	21
23. Running advertisements in the media about your position on issues.	19
24. Publicizing candidates' voting records.	19
25. Contributing work or personnel to electoral campaigns.	18
26. Making public endorsements of candidates for office.	14
27. Engaging in protests or demonstrations.	9

SOURCE: Kay Lehman Schlozman and John T. Tierney, *Organized Interests and American Democracy* (New York: Harper & Row, 1986), p. 155.

provide valued access to the legislators and are increasingly seen as a policy-making force in their own right.[3] Another change on Capitol Hill increasing lobbyists' workload is the so-called *sunshine rules* adopted by both chambers in the 1970s that liberalized access to conference committee sessions and markup sessions. Lobbyists serious about watching out for their organizations' interests can scarcely afford to be absent at such crucial stages of the legislative process.

TABLE 10–3   Institutional Targets of Organization Activity

A. Recognizing that the focus of your activity may change from issue to issue or even over the life span of a single issue, in general, how important is [each institution] as a focus of your organization's activity—very important, somewhat important, or not too important?

	Very Important	Somewhat Important	Not Too Important		
Congress	89%	8%	2%	=	99%
White House	55	32	12	=	99
Executive agencies	65	28	6	=	99
Courts	22	27	51	=	100

B. Percent responding "very important"

	Corporations	Trade Associations	Unions	Citizens' Groups
Congress	94%	91%	95%	92%
White House	67	59	37	40
Executive agencies	68	82	58	40
Courts	18	21	28	28

SOURCE: Kay Lehman Schlozman and John T. Tierney, *Organized Interests and American Democracy* (New York: Harper & Row, 1986), p. 272.

The accelerated turnover in congressional membership also has meant more work for many organized interests. The average tenure of legislators in the House and Senate increased throughout the twentieth century until the 1970s, when it began to decline as more and more representatives began to leave Congress voluntarily and more and more senators were defeated by challengers. Lobbyists say that the diminished institutional memory that accompanies this increase in turnover has forced them to intensify their efforts: they have to spend more time patiently informing programmatically ignorant new legislators and staff members about the purposes, operations, and benefits of cherished programs.

The dramatic alteration in recent years in the congressional budget process is still another development that has had implications for the activity and prospects of organized interests. As used by the Reagan administration in 1981, the revised process gave the White House a vehicle to package a wide array of highly controversial changes in a single reconciliation bill. With one floor vote, the House adopted complex and far-reaching legislation that prevailed over more moderate program changes that had been sent to the floor by its authorizing committees. The administration's job was made easier by the high turnover among legislators and by the breakdown both of party discipline and the sanctity of the seniority system. The White House won the support of legislators not committed to particular programs or even a partic-ular party.[4] This experience taught lobbyists that they henceforth would have to focus more of their attention on the difficult task of trying to affect out-comes on the floor of each legislative chamber rather than just in committees, as was previously the case.

All these developments, taken collectively, spell both more opportunities for influence and more work for lobbyists: more policymakers with whom they must consult and to whom they must present their case; more legislative freshmen and issue amateurs requiring education; more meetings to attend; more hearings at which to testify and present technical information and policy rationales; more campaigns demanding contributions. These develop-ments help explain why there has been such a dramatic increase in recent years in the political activity of interest groups. It is not merely that there are more lobbyists or that they are more ravenous than they used to be or less relenting in pursuit of their objectives. Rather, part of the explanation rests with these important institutional changes.

CONTINUED IMBALANCES IN REPRESENTATION

Although the vast increase in the *number* of organized interests involved in Washington politics constitutes a substantial change, there is little new or different about the *kinds* of interests that predominate in the Washington lobbying community. Describing the Washington pressure community of the 1950s, E. E. Schattschneider observed not only that some interests were ex-cluded altogether but also that some kinds of interests—those of the less advantaged and of diffuse publics—are systematically less likely to achieve vigorous representation.[5] In the past twenty years, however, precisely these sorts of interests have found representation through organizations such as Common Cause, Friends of the Earth, the Food Research and Action Center, and the Mexican-American Legal Defense and Education Fund. But despite the large wave of organizational births that brought these and other such groups into existence, of the the nearly 7,000 organizations that have their own lobbying operation or representation by lobbyists-for-hire, less than 5 percent represent those in society with few resources. (And that figure is beefed up, in fact, by making the dubious assumption that all unions, civil rights groups, minority organizations, social welfare groups, poor people's organizations, and groups representing the elderly, the handicapped and women represent political have-nots.) Only 4 percent of all groups represent broad "public interests," where individuals have no selective interest at stake in a controversy. These would include consumer, environmental and civic groups, and single-issue cause groups.[6]

By contrast, a full 70 percent of all the interests that have some form of Washington representation are business interests, especially trade associa-tions and corporations. Trade associations are the most numerous of all or-ganizations having Washington offices; there are well over one thousand trade association offices in the capital. They vary enormously in size and political weight.

On the one hand are Goliaths like the National Association of Home Builders with over 100,000 members and a budget of well over $10 million; on the other are Lilliputians like the Bow Tie Manufacturers Association with fewer than ten member-companies and a budget under $10,000. But size is not necessarily a determinant of political clout. For example, the Fertilizer Institute, representing a small assortment of chemical firms and agricultural companies is effective because it has rather narrow interests, focuses on them, and pursues them relentlessly. The huge American Bankers Association, by contrast, suffers diminished influence because its many members' irreconcilable positions on key issues muddle the association's lobbying efforts.[7] Whatever their success in influencing policy decisions, trade associations maintain Washington lobbying operations to keep from being taken unaware by political or governmental developments and to protect their members' interests as best they can when government is making new policy that might affect them.

Much the same political calculus also accounts for the extraordinary increase in recent years in the political involvement of individual corporations and the increasing legitimacy accorded their activity. More than 3,000 corporations have some kind of Washington representation, and well over five hundred—ranging from giants like Exxon to small companies like Hershey Foods—have their own offices. Given how deeply the government's tentacles penetrate into the economy, it is not surprising that corporations find that they must attend to what is happening in Washington.

The growing presence of corporations in Washington is part of a larger trend having to do with the new prominence of nonmembership organizations in the Washington interest community.[8] That is, usually when one thinks of interest groups, voluntary membership groups come to mind. But nearly one-half of all the organizations now having representation in Washington politics are not membership groups at all, but are "institutional interests" of various sorts—corporations, public interest law firms, large hospitals and universities, radio and television stations, and think tanks.

One can see this development clearly by examining an individual policy area, such as health care. It used to be that the constellation of health interest groups could be identified by the lights of the original "medical-industrial complex," membership organizations such as the American Medical Association, the American Hospital Association, the American Association of Medical Colleges, and the Pharmaceutical Manufacturers of America. But in the past two decades the "corporate transformation of American medicine" has produced an extraordinary number of new health insurance companies, prepaid health plans, chains of hospitals and walk-in clinics, home care companies, medical equipment manufacturers and hospital suppliers, and other corporations. Many of these individual organizations and firms have established Washington lobbying operations of their own.

This development is important not because these institutional interests are terribly distinctive in their political comportment (they are not), but because when institutions such as hospitals, insurance companies, or medical equipment manufacturers establish their own lobbying offices in Washington they usually achieve multiple representation in the political process. These institutions tend already to be represented by the associations of which they are members (such as the Federation of American Hospitals or the Health Industry Manufacturers Association), thus adding considerably to the volume of their political input.

In sum, while there has been a noticeable increase in the number of organizations representing the interest of consumers, the poor, and the others traditionally unrepresented in the lobbying process, there has been a parallel increase, of far greater proportions, in the number of organizations representing corporate and other business interests. Moreover, there are important differences between the kinds and levels of politically useful resources that are available to most of the business interests and those available to interests representing broader interests. One of the most obvious differences is with respect to financial resources. Consumer groups, for example, typically have very small operating budgets that pale by comparison with the resources that big corporations and trade associations devote to their Washington lobbying operations. Moreover, the marginal costs of engaging in political activity are relatively low for the well-established business organizations, inasmuch as they already have an organizational apparatus with staff and other resources that can be expanded for, or diverted toward, political tasks. The consumer groups, however, are constantly engaged in organizational maintenance activities such as raising money and recruiting members—all of which swallow time and resources that are then unavailable for application toward political influence.

Of course, all of this does not mean that business interests always win in American politics (surely they do not). Nor does it mean that the interests of broad publics such as consumers or the indigent are consistently ignored. After all, now there are at least a handful of organizations in Washington trying to protect such interests. More important, we know that at various times and under various circumstances, various governmental institutions and political actors have adopted the causes of the less advantaged and of broad publics. Sometimes, especially in periods of social ferment and unusual party polarization, Congress takes on this role. Sometimes it is the president who carries the banner. In the recent past, activist federal judges as well as policy entrepreneurs in both the legislative and executive branches have acted as advocates of such interests.

Still, contrary to what media commentaries all too often suggest (that interest group politics is now dominated by citizen groups pressing their claims on issues such as abortion, gun control, nuclear power, minority rights, and environmental protection), the overwhelming majority of organizations active in Washington represent business interests. As the balance of the chapter suggests, understanding that composition of the Washington lobbying community is important because of what it suggests about the unlikelihood that Congress will hear equally from all sides in a political conflict.

INFLUENCING LEGISLATORS

One of the legacies of nineteenth-century lobbyists like Samual Ward—who regaled politicians at nightly banquets of ham boiled in champagne and paid off the gambling losses of debt-ridden legislators—is the stereotype of the fat-cat lobbyists living opulently and spending lavishly, wallowing in ill-gotten and ill-spent lucre as they work to subvert the common good.[9]

The stereotype is reinforced these days by the way the media typically portray interest groups and their lobbying activities—as somehow illegitimate, sordid, and sleazy. The stock figure political cartoonists still use to represent lobbyists is the corpulent man whose suit pockets are overflowing with cash and whose visage betrays a sinister or lowly intent. The newspapers and television networks, ever eager for a story that combines celebrity with scandal, lavishly trail stories that link lobbyists to officials in sweetheart deals, conflicts of interest, cash bribes, malfeasance in high places—in short, corruption.

While all too many of these stories turn out to be based on fact, organized interests actually have so many avenues for exercising influence in legitimate ways that, Abscams to the contrary, outright illegal activity is quite rare. There are, after all, many things organized interests can do well within the boundaries of the law to make legislators obliged to them. Most controversial in this regard are the furnishing of campaign contributions through political action committees (PACs) and the offer of honoraria, cushy vacations, and other valued inducements. Two other means of influencing legislators also merit special mention—providing them with badly needed substantive information, and exerting grassroots pressure on them.

PAC Contributions and Other Inducements

Political action committees are nonparty organizations, set up in accordance with federal law, to collect money and funnel it into the campaign coffers of candidates for Congress. Most PACs are established as the campaign-giving arm of another organization—a corporation, a union, a professional association, or the like. Contributions from the PAC are ordinarily construed as still another instrument through which the parent organization can realize its political goals. Nevertheless, some PACs—for example, the National Committee for an Effective Congress (which supports liberals) and the National Pro-Life Political Action Committee (which supports opponents of abortion)—are not affiliated with another organization but, rather, are founded solely to make collective efforts on behalf of candidates they deem deserving.

Whether or not the emergence of PACs is, as some have maintained, the most significant development in American politics of the past fifteen years, there is no question that, by any measure, the increase in PAC activity has been of stunning proportions. From the end of 1974 to the end of June 1986, the number of PACs registered with the Federal Elections Commission jumped more than six-fold, from just over 600 to more than 4,000. In dollar terms, aggregate PAC contributions to federal campaigns skyrocketed over the same period from $12.5 million to well over $132 million. While overall campaign spending has soared as well, the increase in PAC contributions has outstripped the increase in campaign expenditures: in 1972 PAC contributions accounted for 13.7 percent of the spending in House and Senate races; in 1986 the figure was 28 percent. (House candidates got $87.2 million from PACs in 1986, 34 percent of their funds. Senate candidates in 1986 received $45 million from PACs, 21 percent of their total receipts.)[10]

Political scientists and other observers are by no means like-minded about what policy influence having a PAC confers on an organized interest. Some see PAC contributions as constituting a form of "institutionalized bribery" in which the quid pro quo is a policy favor, a purchased vote in Congress.[11] Most legislators and lobbyists insist—and the data from one recent study also suggest—that what is being "purchased" is not policy influence but access, the opportunity to be heard.[12] But such a distinction appears to make little sense in practice, since the latter is so crucial to achieving the former. While it is important to distinguish access from influence in the abstract, access, in practice, begets influence. And unequal access begets unequal influence.

If what PAC contributions buy is not policy influence but access, then even relatively small sums of money (which is what most PAC donations are) may have an impact when there is no PAC money coming from opposing interests. This point is especially important because, contrary to the popular assessment that "every group in the world has now got a PAC," the proliferation of PACs has not yielded full mobilization of all interests, much less equal representation. Of the nearly 3,000 PACs existing in 1980, business accounted for the dominant share, while the disadvantaged, especially the poor and racial minorities, were hardly represented at all.[13] In the words of Senator Robert Dole, a Republican from Kansas, "There aren't any Poor PACs or Food Stamp PACs or Nutrition PACs or Medicare PACs."[14] In addition, the interests of certain diffuse publics, especially environmentalists and consumers, figure only marginally in the PAC picture.

Campaign contributions are by no means the only controversial inducements that organized interests can offer members of Congress and their aides. Although the arts of influence have changed considerably from the days when lobbyists routinely plied legislators with wine, women, and song, contemporary organized interests surely engage in "social" lobbying, nurturing relationships with government officials by providing them with relaxation and entertainment: cocktail parties, three-martini lunches, lavish dinners, tickets to the theater or to sporting events, or trips off the Florida coast for deep-sea fishing expeditions. An increasingly common and controversial way of funneling cash or its equivalent to legislators is to provide them with a handsome honorarium (and, often, a free minivacation) for delivering a speech before a group holding its convention in some attractive resort.[15]

These other inducements raise the same concerns about unequal resources begetting unequal access begetting unequal influence. After all, not all organizations have the wherewithal to engage in the more expensive forms of social lobbying. For example, in 1981, just before the House Appropriations Committee held its markup sessions on the Defense Department spending bill, the vice president for government affairs at Hughes Helicopters, Inc. (the prime contractor on a controversial attack helicopter that had run substantially over the original cost estimates) learned that two committee members wanted to go elk hunting. He arranged for them to take a three-day hunting trip in Montana and found a speaking engagement for one of them in order to pay the costs of the trip.[16] Presumably, the lobbyists for a smaller, less affluent organization like the Coalition for a New Foreign and Military Policy—a group committed to reducing federal military spending in favor of spending on "human needs"—would be hard-pressed to make such arrangements.

But lest organized interests be unfairly portrayed as single-mindedly devoted to harnessing legislators and subjugating the public interest to special interests through the pressure of seductive PAC contributions and other blandishments, two important qualifications bear note here. First, it is not as if politicians are reluctant virgins helpless at the approach of ardent lobbyists. In the case of campaign contributions, for example, there is ample evidence that the candidates are just as eager to receive as PACs are to give. PACs are quite simply besieged with requests for money from candidates who shamelessly try to dun them for contributions.[17]

Second, PAC contributions and other inducements constitute only part of the larger picture of interest group lobbying activity in Washington. Most lobbyists insist—and most observers would support their contention—that the whole enterprise of interest representation has become both more professional and more heavily issue-based over the past fifteen years. As the chief lobbyist for an international airline said, "The lobbying process has become more complex and requires more sophistication. The old boy network has broken down. Now a lobbyist has to be much more knowledgeable and articulate about the issues." Thus, among the lobbyist's most commonly used and most important tools of persuasion is information.

Substantive Information

Participants on both sides of the lobbyist-legislator nexus argue that the principal reason for information's growing importance is that legislators are in desperate need of it, in part because issues have increased in technicality.

Members of Congress and their staffers are confronted every day with a staggering number of complex issues about which they are expected to make informed judgments. In the face of these complexities, public officials need all the help they can get in trying to determine the consequences of their assorted decisions—who will be affected, in what ways, to what extent, and with what reaction.[18]

When policy issues involve highly complex economic or technical problems, informational input from lobbying organizations is likely to be especially important. Consider, for example, policies governing the generation of electricity by nuclear power—controversial because of the complicated, risky, and uncertain scientific and technological processes involved. Policy decisions relating to the timing and direction of nuclear energy development depend on technical information concerning the health and safety effects of the nuclear fuel cycle, the reliability and cost of different technologies, and the availability of various alternate energy resources. Because scientists and antinuclear groups also provide policymakers with information on these subjects, the nuclear power industry—represented by organizations such as the Atomic Industrial Forum (AIF)—lacks a complete information monopoly. However, the AIF's input is important. Politicians have to rely on the industry not only to provide them with the answers to technical questions but also to inform them of the assumptions embedded in those answers and their implications for policy choices. In other words, the difficulty from the perspective of legislators is that because interest groups naturally tend to present information in a way that serves their own cause, the distinction between efforts to inform and efforts to persuade becomes quite fuzzy.

But lobbyists insist that they know better than to present deliberately distorted information or to provide bad advice. They argue that the information they present must be accurate and reliable because they would lose legislators' confidence if they were found to be misrepresenting the facts. They say that when presenting information for legislators to use in their deliberations, organizations avoid outright misrepresentation but do attempt to place the facts in a favorable light.

For their part, legislators and their staff aides understand that the information provided by organized interests is tendentious—that, especially when the information is supplied to buttress a particular point of view, the process of gathering and presenting information entails selection and thus inevitably introduces bias. One congressional staffer explained:

> We know we're getting biased information from everybody. But in just about every case we can pretty well figure out what the direction of that bias is and what effect it's likely to have on the data. We look for areas of agreement and assume that stuff is valid. On the things where disagreement exists, you keep going to other sources to try to finally elucidate the common ground and the area of dispute. Then, in that area, we use our judgment.[19]

This highlights the importance of the point made above about equality of representation. Since the interests of broad publics and those having few political resources remain underrepresented in the Washington lobbying community, policymakers presumably do not always have information from multiple sources to sift and evaluate. A legislator who hears from only one side, or who hears much more from one side than the other, is likely to be persuaded by the arguments and information to which he or she is exposed. In short, the argument that the provision of information has replaced the provision of the three B's as the staple of Washington lobbying activity is not necessarily reassuring, since it would seem to place a special burden on congressional policymakers to sift the wheat from the chaff and to be sensitive to the potential absence of, or deficiencies in, countervailing information and advocacy.

Another kind of information that organized interests work hard to furnish elected officials is political intelligence—information about which groups and individuals are lined up in support of and in opposition to various proposals, which of them are powerful, how much they care. In particular, legislators want to know how the enactment of a given bill will affect their constituents and how they feel about it. And because most members of Congress these days suffer from heightened feelings of electoral vulnerability, they are especially sensitive to the expressed preferences and particularistic needs of their constituents.[20] Interest groups know that when politicians try to assess the public's preferences, what often matters to them is not an amorphous perception of the views of the general public but, rather, the understanding that there is a narrower group of citizens who care intensely about a policy matter and are likely to act on their views.

This explains why, for example, the National Rifle Association (NRA) managed in 1986 to secure House approval of a bill weakening federal regulations governing the sale of firearms, even though the public at large heavily favors stricter gun control measures. Elected officials know that members of such groups as the NRA and Gun Owners of America are attentive to their decision on this issue and are likely to back up their preferences at the voting booth, whereas this is not the most important issue to the larger, less attentive general public. In short, an organization's ability to convince policymakers that an attentive public is concerned about an issue and ready to hold them accountable for their decisions may be critical in determining policy outcomes.

Grassroots Lobbying

Naturally, organized interests have devised various ways of commanding legislators' attention by mobilizing attentive constituents—that is, by mounting "grassroots" pressure. Two forms of grassroots lobbying are especially common and conspicuous. The first involves organizing networks of grassroots activists who can be relied on to contact policymakers in response to an organizational "action alert." Organizations of all types—from the NRA to Common Cause, from the Chamber of Commerce to the National Organization for Women—have developed elaborate systems for producing a flow of "spontaneous" communications from concerned citizens to their legislators.

When Congress was considering increasing milk price supports in 1980, legislators heard from thousands of worried managers of fast-food restaurants: the industry's trade association had put out an issue action alert. When a House committee in 1982 was deliberating on a bill to deregulate the American Telephone and Telegraph Company (AT&T), legislators heard protests from thousands of telephone company managers and employees: not only had AT&T put out an issue alert, but so had the Communications Workers of America, 90 percent of whose members at the time were AT&T employees.

Another form of grassroots lobbying is to try to create the semblance of a popular movement in support of the organization's cause. (Sometimes groups manage this task so well that they actually *do* create a popular movement, not merely the semblance of one.) To achieve this objective, interest groups sometimes rely on provocative advertisements or direct-mail appeals to inspire deluges of cards, letters, telegrams, and telephone calls to Capitol Hill.

One of the more dramatic examples of such a campaign in recent years occurred in 1977 when the Food and Drug Administration (FDA) proposed to ban saccharin, the artificial sweetener, after having reviewed the final results of a study by the Canadian government showing that laboratory rats fed high dosages of the substance suffered an alarming incidence of cancerous bladder tumors. The leading role in opposition to the ban was assumed early and vigorously by the Calorie Control Council (CCC), an organization representing the interests of diet food and soft drink producers, which were seriously threatened by the proposal because of the absence at the time of any other FDA-approved artificial sweetener. Determined to fight the FDA's proposed ban, the CCC hired some of the nation's largest advertising and public relations firms and launched a huge advertising campaign in major newspapers ridiculing the FDA and the scientific tests that led to the proposed ban. The ad's text evoked the image of mad scientists feeding the poor rats amounts of saccharin equivalent to what a human would ingest only by drinking 1,250 cans of diet soda every day. The ad ended by urging readers to participate in an experiment of their own: "It's called an experiment in democracy, and it works like this: WRITE OR CALL YOUR CONGRESSMAN TODAY AND LET HIM KNOW HOW YOU FEEL ABOUT A BAN ON SACCHARIN."[21]

The ad was a stroke of political genius. It invoked the symbol of Big Government arbitrarily meddling with consumers' right of choice and appealed to consumers' loyalties to products they not only enjoyed but presumed to have health benefits. But perhaps the best indicator of the ad's genius is that it achieved its intended effect. In the following weeks, mail from irate citizens poured into congressional offices and into the offices of the Food and Drug Administration. In response to the flood of letters, virtually all of them opposed to the ban, Congress eventually passed legislation postponing the ban and merely requiring warning labels about the ill effects of ingesting saccharin.

A more recent example of the successful generation of high-volume constituency pressure involved an effort by bankers to repeal a provision in the 1982 tax bill that would have required commercial banks and savings and loan associations to withhold 10 percent of the interest and dividends paid to depositors. The main objective of the provision had been to capture income that taxpayers failed to report. To the bankers, however, the provision meant administrative headaches. In order to exert pressure on behalf of the repeal of the provision, the American Bankers Association and the U.S. League of Savings Institutions (with the assistance of one of the nation's leading advertising firms) undertook a multimillion dollar, multifaceted public relations campaign.[22]

The bankers had a ready-made constituency and a ready-made communications channel—the millions of customers with whom they are in touch regularly by mail. By including an appeal for action with the monthly statement, the bankers were able to reach a large number of interested citizens directly. Some Senate offices reported receiving from 150,000 to 300,000 letters, mailgrams, and postcards on this issue, and Congress ultimately voted to repeal the provision.[23]

Just because these campaigns succeeded in flooding government mailboxes, one cannot conclude that the grassroots lobbying effort was alone responsible for the ultimate resolution of the controversy. After all, the conventional wisdom about high-volume mail campaigns has generally held that communications inspired by organizations typically betray their origins and that elected officials ignore or discount constituent communications bearing the scent of having been orchestrated from some lobbying office in Washington.

But reflecting the current wisdom that legislators feel electorally vulnerable these days, many lobbyists believe that if the mail arrives in sufficient *quantity* in congressional offices, it will be heeded no matter how orchestrated they seem. As Bill Murphy, a prominent lobbyist (and son of a former congressman) says:

> Members of Congress have to care about this mail, even if it's mail that is almost identically worded. Labor unions do this sort of thing a lot. The congressman has to care that *somebody* out there in his district has enough power to get hundreds of people to sit down and write a postcard or a letter—because if the guy can get them to do *that,* he might be able to influence them in other ways. So, a member has no choice but to pay attention. It's suicide if he doesn't.[24]

Talking with a reporter a few years ago, Richard Conlan, former staff director of the House Democratic Study Group, echoed those comments, saying:

> The conventional wisdom you'll hear is that a few thoughtful letters have more impact than 100 names on a petition. That's generally true. But a lot of these

new members [of Congress] are like cats on a hot tin roof and they start dancing all over. They can't take any pressure at all—including contrived pressure.[25]

THE AGE OF IMPERIAL PRESSURE GROUPS?

Despite the formidable strategies and tactics employed by organized interests legislators are not the hand maidens of lobbyists and, contrary to some popular beliefs, the Congress is not simply some kind of anemometer spinning to the force of prevailing interest group winds. But even the more detached and objective scholarly community long has held to an only slightly more benign variant of this theme, regarding the ties that link legislators and lobbyists as close and mutually beneficial. That is, for the better part of a quarter century, scholars who have studied the relationship between Congress and interest groups have been guided by (some might say "shackled") the concept of policy *subgovernments.* The fundamental proposition of the subgovernment model is that routine policymaking within individual substantive policy areas (especially distributive programs with low visibility) is dominated by relatively narrow, circumscribed, and autonomous sets of actors that operate virtually without interference by the president or the majority of legislators. The form of subgovernment most commonly invoked by analysts is the *iron triangle* or *triple alliance*—a subgovernment consisting of an agency or bureau within the executive branch, a committee within Congress, and an organized interest group—all united by their concern with a given policy area and all motivated by a consensual desire to maintain a mutually supportive and beneficial arrangement in which policies are formulated in ways that meet the needs of all partners to the triad. Iron triangles have been said to prevail at one time or another in many policy areas characterized by the distribution of benefits, for example, weapons procurement, veterans' benefits, agricultural subsidies, merchant shipping, and water resources.

Political analysis of these sorts of "distributive" policies suggests that when the benefits of a policy or program are concentrated on an identifiable interest in society (sugar farmers, inland waterways operators, veterans, etc.) but the costs are to be borne by everybody—or at least by a substantial portion of society—the lobbying activity surrounding the issue is likely to be imbalanced. Organizations representing the beneficiaries will be vigorous in their support of the proposal, but since the costs are distributed at a low per capita rate over a large number of people (through price increases or generally higher taxes), the public has little incentive to organize in opposition. Such policies tend to produce symbiotic relationships between the legislators who authorize and appropriate money for these programs, the agency officials who administer them, and the beneficiaries or "clients," who work hard to maintain and expand their benefits. To the extent that these programs encounter any organized opposition at all, it is likely to come from politically disadvantaged consumer and taxpayer groups.[26]

The political logic here is hard to dispute, but in fact the cozy relationships among legislators, bureaucrats, and lobbyists that promote and sustain these programs are beset on all sides by changes in the institutions, processes, and larger political environment. One can point to many diverse factors that appear to be contributing to the decline of the iron triangle as an autonomous force in public policymaking: the rise of large numbers of new citizens' groups and advocacy organizations, new patterns of investigative reporting and the enlarged role of the media in national politics, the greater policymaking role of the federal courts, and the increasing aggressiveness of presidents intent on controlling the bureaucracy.

The changing character of Congress also is making it more difficult for distributive policymaking to persist in its old form. With the increases in size and professionalism of congressional staffs and the devolution of power from committee to subcommittee chairs and rank-and-file legislators, Congress has become a highly individualistic (even atomistic) institution in which nervous and unstable coalitions are subject to wild changes in composition and direction when political trends shift. As Steven Smith has noted, the decentralization of power in Congress has meant that "The scope of conflict changes continually, usually expanding, as legislation passes from one stage to the next. Deals and accommodations devised at one stage cannot be adhered to later because negotiations must be reopened at each stage."[27]

The decentralized Congress is also one in which policy entrepreneurialism abounds. Legislators, especially senators, are more likely to be policy generalists than specialists. And with the help of their larger and more expert staffs, these legislators pursue many different hobby horses on their own, developing new legislative initiatives, offering more floor amendments to the bills of others, offering more amendments to bills from committees other than their own, and intervening in the processes of administrative policymaking as well.

For these and many other reasons, observers of Washington politics are having a harder and harder time sticking to the view that organized interests are able to dictate public policy benefits for themselves by virtue of their position in cozy, triangulated relationships with policymakers.[28] Most policy areas now are characterized not by such "mutual self-help arrangements," but by complex webs of policy activists from both inside and outside the government who are linked by their common commitment and expertise with respect to a particular issue area. These activists "policy watchers" are drawn not just from a few interest groups but from every conceivable quarter: the Office of Management and Budget (OMB) and the White House Office of Policy Development, presidential study commissions and task forces, congressional committee staffs and congressional staff agencies, think tanks, universities, the staffs of trade journals and journals of opinion, law firms and consulting firms, foundations, and the general citizenry. The participants in these larger "issue networks" are much more likely to share policy expertise than policy preferences or political stakes.[29]

While all this is true, there are certain circumstances under which the involvement of organized interests is still likely to have policy consequences, even in this more chaotic and fluid political environment. Consider one last example that helps make the point. In the early 1980s, the Federal Trade Commission proposed a new rule requiring that used car dealers inform potential buyers of the known defects of cars offered for sale. The National Automobile Dealers Association, whose members would have to bear the cost of such a measure, swung into action and blocked the adoption of such a rule. The auto dealers won their objectives, one of which was to block the proposed rule rather than to get a new one adopted. This is a distinct advantage because the fragmented nature of the American political system means that there are multiple arenas for the exertion of political pressure and thus many opportunities for throwing up roadblocks to unwanted action. In other words, the system has a built-in bias in favor of the policy status quo. An interest that is trying to stymie some measure it finds threatening is in a stronger position than those pressing for its adoption.

To take advantage of the system's bias, interest groups try to locate their policy battles in whatever governmental arena seems most likely to yield a favorable outcome. In this case, when the FTC proposed its used car rule, the unhappy auto dealers, unable to block the measure there, turned for relief to Congress—an institutional arena where, unlike the bureaucracy, officials have to pay special attention to the exigencies of constituency pressure.

The hand of the auto dealers in this conflict also was strengthened by the fact that they were able to concentrate their substantial political resources on this fight, while their opponents, consumers' groups, were simultaneously fighting political skirmishes on many different fronts. In addition, while this was an issue of high visibility and importance to used car dealers and thus aroused vigorous political activity on their part, it was not an issue about which members of the public were intensely aware or concerned.

CONCLUSION: A SPECIAL BURDEN ON LEGISLATORS

Observers of American democracy long have been concerned about the consequences of unrestrained interest group activity for the way we are governed and for the public good. Two hundred years ago, James Madison feared tyranny of the majority as the pernicious consequence of factional politics, arguing that the ordinary operations of democratic procedure would lead to the trampling of minority preferences. On the contrary, it seems that the politics of organized pressure builds into the American system a minoritarian tendency to counterbalance the more majoritarian proclivities of other parts of the political process, such as elections and social movements. In general, organized interest politics tends to facilitate the articulation of demands by the narrowly interested and well organized. By and large, the collectivities thus benefited are well heeled; business, in particular, finds pressure politics a useful mechanism for pursuing political goals. Larger aggregates—especially society's less advantaged and those seeking nondivisible public goods, such as safer consumer products or lower taxes—fare rather less well through interest group politics.

Moreover, the explosion over the past two decades in the number of organized interests, and in the amount of activity in which they engage, seems to have introduced a potentially dysfunctional particularism into national politics. If policymakers in Congress are forced to find an appropriate balance between deference to the exigencies of the short run and the consideration of consequences for the long run, between acquiescence to the clearly expressed wishes of narrow groups that care intensely and respect for the frequently unexpressed needs of larger publics, the balance may have shifted too far in the direction of the near-term and the narrow.

One obvious way to overcome these potentially unhealthy consequences for democracy would be to quiet the din. On the laundry list of proposed reforms are many—for example, prohibiting legislators from accepting honoraria for speeches given to pressure groups—that would still be consistent with First Amendment guarantees. But other reforms, such as limiting more severely the lobbying activities of former members of Congress, must be introduced with care, lest, as Madison warned, the cure be more pernicious than the disease. Even to urge greater self-restraint on the part of clamorous interest groups is to place the burden on the wrong shoulders. The right to petition government collectively is so constitutionally protected that it is the obligation of those who presume to govern to watch out for the general public.

In an era when an expanded Washington pressure community speaks so loudly and so cacophonously, members of Congress bear a special—and perhaps untenable—responsibility. This is not to suggest that they rely solely on their own judgment and ignore public preferences in making public policy. Rather, their responses to the public should be informed by an understanding that the expressions of opinion transmitted by organized interests are selective and that such communications over represent the views of narrow, intense publics at the expense of broad, diffuse ones and the views of the affluent at the expense of the less advantaged. Similarly, their policy deliberations should reflect their awareness that the inducements, information, and expressions of preference on which they rely emanate more readily from some interests than from others.

There is a saying, sometimes attributed to German Chancellor Bismarck, that "a statesman is a politician who thinks about his grandchildren." At a time when the enlarged and more contentious nature of organized interest activity renders their presence especially vital, there may not be a sufficient supply of statesmen on Capitol Hill.

NOTES

Authors' note: This article is a product of our collaboration on *Organized Interests and American Democracy* (New York: Harper & Row, 1986), from which the bulk of this chapter is extracted and in which can be found more evidence and elaboration on the arguments advanced here.

1. Kay Lehman Schlozman and John T. Tierney, *Organized Interests and American Democracy* (New York: Harper & Row, 1986), pp. 74–82.
2. This development has received considerable attention from both journalists and scholars. See, for example, "Single Issue Politics," *Newsweek,* November 6, 1978, pp. 48–60; and John Herbers, "Grass Roots Groups Go National," *New York Times Magazine,* September 4, 1983, pp. 22ff. Among the academic observers who have noted this trend are Andrew MacFarland, *Public Interest Lobbies* (Washington, D.C.: American Enterprise Institute for Public Policy Research, 1976); Jeffrey M. Berry, *Lobbying for the People* (Princeton, N.J.: Princeton University Press, 1977); David Vogel, "The Public-Interest Movement and the American Reform Tradition," *Political Science Quarterly* 95 (Winter 1980–81), pp. 607–627; Jack L. Walker, "The Origins and Maintenance of Interest Groups in America," *American Political Science Review,* 77 (June 1983), pp. 394–96; and Jack L. Walker, "The Mobilization of Political Interests," paper presented at the Annual Meeting of the American Political Science Association, Chicago, September 1983, pp. 15–18.
3. See Harrison W. Fox, Jr. and Susan Webb Hammond, *Congressional Staffs: the Invisible Force in American Lawmaking* (New York: Free Press, 1977); Michael Malbin, *Unelected Representatives: Congressional Staff and the Future of Representative Government* (New York: Basic Books, 1980).
4. On the Reagan administration's revolutionary use of the reconciliation process, see Howard E. Shuman, *Politics and the Budget: The Struggle Between the President and Congress,* 2nd ed. (Englewood Cliffs, N.J.: Prentice-Hall, 1988), chapter 9.
5. E. E. Schattschneider, *The Semisovereign People: A Realist's View of Democracy in America* (New York: Holt, Rinehart & Winston, 1960), chapter 2..
6. Schlozman and Tierney, *Organized Interests,* pp. 63–82.
7. See Burt Solomon, "Measuring Clout," *National Journal,* July 4, 1987, pp. 1706–11.
8. Ibid., p. 49. On this point, also see Robert H. Salisbury, "Interest Representation: The Dominance of Institutions," *American Political Science Review* 78 (March 1984), pp. 64–76; and Robert H. Salisbury, "Interest Groups: Toward a New Understanding," in *Interest Group Politics,* ed Allen C. Cigler and Burdett A. Loomis (Washington, D.C.: Congressional Quarterly Press, 1983), pp. 354–67.
9. Karl Schriftgiesser, *The Lobbyists* (Boston: Little, Brown, 1951), p. 14.
10. Jeremy Gaunt, "Hill Campaign Spending Hits All-Time High," *Congressional Quarterly Weekly Report,* May 16, 1987, pp. 991–93.
11. This is an issue that divides observers sharply. For one view, see Elizabeth Drew, *Politics and Money* (New York: Macmillan 1983). For the opposite view, see Robert Samuelson, "The Campaign Reform Failure," *New Republic,* September 5, 1983, pp. 28-36, and Herbert Alexander, *The Case for PACs* (Washington, D.C.: Public Affairs Council, 1983). For a general review of the arguments and evidence on both sides, see Schlozman and Tierney, *Organized Interests,* chapter 10.
12. See Laura I. Langbein, "Money and Access: Some Empirical Evidence," *Journal of Politics,* 48 (November 1986); pp. 1052–62.
13. Schlozman and Tierney, *Organized Interests,* pp. 247–52.

14. Quoted in "Money Talks, Congress Listens," *Boston Globe*, December 12, 1982, p. A24.

15. On the current popularity of honoraria, see Burt Solomon, "Bite-Sized Favors," *National Journal*, October 11, 1986, pp. 2418–22; and Thomas B. Edsall, "Serving One's Country Is a Great Honorarium," *Washington Post*, June 29, 1987, p. 11.

16. Walter Pincus, "Helicopter Maintenance on the Hill," *Washington Post*, March 14, 1982, pp. A1–2.

17. For more on the pressure to contribute, see Schlozman and Tierney, *Organized Interests*, pp. 242–46, and Burt Solomon, "When Fat Cats Cry," *National Journal*, February 21, 1987, pp. 418–22.

18. See Richard A. Smith, "Advocacy, Interpretation, and Influence in the U.S. Congress," *American Political Science Review* 78 (March 1984); pp. 44–63.

19. Quoted in Susan E. Fallows, "Technical Staffing for Congress: The Myth of Expertise" (Ph.D. diss., Cornell University, 1980), pp. 103–104.

20. On this theme see, for example, Morris Fiorina, *Congress—Keystone of the Washington Establishment* (New Haven, Conn.: Yale University Press, 1977); John A. Ferejohn, *Pork Barrel Politics* (Stanford, Calif.: Stanford University Press, 1974); David R. Mayhew, *Congress: The Electoral Connection* (New Haven, Conn.: Yale University Press, 1974); and Richard F. Fenno, Jr., *Home Style: House Members in Their Districts* (Boston: Little, Brown, 1978).

21. See the ad in *Washington Post*, March 13, 1977, pp. 18-19.

22. On the banking lobby's fight to repeal the withholding provision, see Bill Keller, "Lowest Common Denominator Lobbying: Why the Banks Fought Withholding," *Washington Monthly*, May 1983, pp. 32–39. See, also, Paul Gardner and Ronn Kirkwood, "The Ability to Say 'No': An Analysis of Executive and Legislative Behavior in the Interest Withholding and Social Security Reform Debates," paper presented at the annual meeting of the Midwest Political Science Association, Chicago, April, 1984.

23. Again, See Keller, "Lowest Common Denominator."

24. Author's interview with William T. Murphy, 1981.

25. Bill Keller, "Special-Interest Lobbyists Cultivate the 'Grassroots' to Influence Capitol Hill," *Congressional Quarterly Weekly Report*, September 12, 1981, p. 1740.

26. The analysis in this paragraph is derived from the approach of James Q. Wilson, presented by him in varying forms and with varying degrees of elaboration in the following: James Q. Wilson, *Political Organizations* (New York: Basic Books, 1973), chapter 15; James Q. Wilson "The Politics of Regulation," in *Social Responsibility and the Business Predicament*, ed. James W. McKie (Washington, D.C.: Brookings Institution, 1974), pp. 135–68; "The Politics of Regulation," in *The Politics of Regulation*, ed. James Q. Wilson, (New York: Basic Books, 1980); and James Q. Wilson, *American Government: Institutions and Policies*, 3rd ed. (Lexington, Mass.: D.C. Heath, 1986), especially chapter 14.

27. Steven S. Smith, "New Patterns of Decision making in Congress," in *The New Direction in American Politics* ed. John E. Chubb and Paul E. Peterson (Washington, D.C.: Brookings Institution, 1985), p. 221.

28. For example, Thomas L. Gais, Mark A. Peterson, and Jack L. Walker conclude that iron triangles no longer govern policymaking—if they ever did. See "Interest Groups, Iron Triangles, and Representative Institutions in American National Government," *British Journal of Political Science* 14 (1984); pp. 161–85. For case studies that illustrate the diminished ability of once

dominant interests to dictate continued benefits to themselves, see T. R. Reid, *Congressional Odyssey* (San Francisco: W. H. Freeman, 1980); and Martha Derthick and Paul J. Quirk, *The Politics of Deregulation* (Washington, D.C.: Brookings Institution, 1985).

29. On the concept of "issue networks," see Hugh Heclo, "Issue Networks and the Executive Establishment," in *The New American Political System*, ed. Anthony King (Washington, D.C.: American Enterprise Institute for Public Policy Research, 1978), pp. 87–124.

CHAPTER 11

Congressional Policymaking: Cloakroom Politics and Policy

Carl E. Van Horn

In 1987, Congress overrode President Reagan's veto and enacted the Clean Water Act, a bill loaded with projects for more than 400 congressional districts and every state in the nation. James Weaver, a maverick Democratic representative from Oregon, tried in vain to eliminate questionable projects. He proposed cutting Oregon's Elk Creek Dam, a project deemed costly and unnecessary by the Army Corps of Engineers and the General Accounting Office. But Republican Representative Robert Smith, also from Oregon, objected: "We should deal with this project as the member representing the area desires."[1] The Elk Creek Dam survived!

Former Speaker of the House Thomas "Tip" O'Neill was fond of saying "all politics is local." In much the same way, congressional policymaking has a distinctive local flavor. National policy concerns are handled by politicians who filter the world through the lenses of their home turf—the districts and states that send them to the Capitol. The overarching concern about the local impact of policy choices engenders *cloakroom politics.*

Cloakroom politics is the process through which members of Congress make sure that public policy serves their interests. It affects the way Congress organizes itself and tackles policy problems; it produces certain common legislative policy problems; it produces certain common legislative policy outputs; and it even has important consequences for the success of governmental policy. It is a visible, democratic, and at times chaotic method for making laws. It ensures that Congress is the most *responsive* political institution *and* in some ways the least *responsible* one too.

THE SCOPE AND NATURE OF CLOAKROOM POLITICS

The scope of cloakroom politics is incredibly broad. It includes economic affairs, environmental protection, defense and foreign policy, health, education, and welfare issues, law enforcement, and government operations. Every year members of Congress cast votes on hundreds of public laws and resolutions. Countless issues receive some attention from committees, subcommittees, and individual members. Cloakroom politics occurs on three distinct levels: the individual member, the subcommittee and committee, and the institution. Issues follow different paths to each level, but the underlying concerns of individual members are always present.

When *members of Congress* stand for reelection every two or six years, they must account, however loosely, for their action or inaction on important matters of the day. Voters and the journalists (who shape evaluations of legislators) ask, "What have you done for us lately?" Despite the fact that more than 90 percent of the representatives who seek reelection win their contests, most run scared even in districts that appear safe for the incumbents. Indeed, it is because they work so hard at reelection that makes the seats safe.[2]

The policy concerns of representatives and senators are strongly influenced by the concerns of citizens and organizations from their districts and states. Dealing with constituency problems consumes the time of members and their personal staffs. Senators and representatives use their influence to speed up grants for sewer projects, obtain tax breaks for a steel mill, or fight for more student financial aid. Collectively, the constituent interests play a strong role in shaping the policy activity of Congress.

The policy activity of *committees and subcommittees* are at the core of congressional lawmaking. Committee chairs exercise a great deal of power. They control the committee's resources and direct its policy focus. Nonetheless, they are responsive to concerns expressed by people from their political base, the executive branch, organizations and industries affected by their policy domain, the leadership of the institution, and the mass media.

Interest groups influence committee and subcommittee behavior because they often supply the milk and honey of politics: money and grateful voters. Running for a U.S. Senate seat now costs millions of dollars. The quest for campaign funds compels legislators to curry favor with potential contributors. To some extent, then, the interests of campaign contributors become the interests of officeholders.

Organizations with money have many means to convince subcommittees and committees to cater to their concerns: they hire lobbyists to monitor legislation, pay to meet with members and staff, and pay legislators to speak at group meetings. For example, dozens of lobbyists contributed $5,000 to Oregon Senator Robert O. Packwood's reelection fund for the privilege of having breakfast with the Senate Finance Committee Chair once a week.[3] A large Virginia coal company flew more than a dozen members of Congress concerned with mining legislation in a private jet and paid them $2,000 each for attending a discussion of energy issues and visiting a coal mine.[4] If you cannot deliver money or votes, you may have a tough time getting attention to your concerns.

Issues that dominate the attention of the entire *Congress* usually arise from the president, legislative leadership, broad societal concerns or some combination of the three. But even on policy issues where the president or the leaders take a strong lead, the final policy output will reflect the parochial concerns of dozens of legislators. Take the issue of antidrug legislation, for example. At the urging of House and Senate leadership, Congress appropriated nearly $2 billion toward new programs in late 1986. House and Senate members saw antidrug laws as an issue with strong electoral appeal and moved the bill swiftly through both chambers. Despite the absence of reliable statistics showing increases in drug use, opinion polls revealed increasing public anxiety about drug abuse among young people: Two well-known athletes, a college basketball star and a professional football player, had died of cocaine overdoses. *The New York Times* reported: "Antidrug bills that have lingered in committees for months or years are now passing out [of committee] in minutes. . . . Cost doesn't seem to be an object now.[5]

Another issue that dominated the attention of Congress was tax reform. Why would a landmark tax law pass in 1986 and not in 1980 or some other year? An answer can be found by sketching the basic features of the political landscape at that time. Public opinion polls revealed displeasure with the tax system's complexity and favoritism, and a popular Republican president advocated tax reform. Democrats, who were the majority in the House of Representatives, were loath to bear the blame for blocking reform because their 1984 presidential nominee, Walter Mondale, had promised a tax increase and was defeated in all but one state; and, seeking desperately to retain their control of the U.S. Senate, Republicans felt they needed a tax bill to be successful in the 1986 elections.

Painting tax reform politics in such broad brush strokes conceals the inside ballgame of cloakroom politics. To get a bill through, committee chairs, legislative leaders, and the president are obliged to satisfy the parochial demands of legislators and interest groups. In late 1985, defections by House Republicans gravely threatened tax reform. As noted in the following excerpt from the *Washington Post*, the bill's fortunes were reversed by doling out valuable favors:

> President Reagan may have wanted to talk taxes when he invited Republican Steven Gunderson to the Oval Office last week, but the young Republican from Wisconsin wanted to talk cows. . . . By the time the session was over, both men had what they wanted: Gunderson knew Reagan would sign the farm bill sought by his rural district; Reagan knew that Gunderson would vote for the tax-overhaul legislation in the House. . . . Says Gunderson, "I think that's a sensible way for adults to do business." and that's the way business was done up and down the Republican and Democratic aisles of the House.[6]

Similar politics mold hundreds of less prominent laws. As you shift your gaze from the big picture—the White House, unemployment, public opinion—you discover that cloakroom politics are characterized by fragmented power, bargaining and compromise, and legislative and presidential leadership.

Policymaking in Congress is *fragmented*. No one controls or commands the Congress. Each member elected to the House of Representatives represents roughly one-half million people; Senators cast a single vote whether they are from California or Rhode Island; House and Senate *elected* leaders retain their positions only as long as the members support them. Unlike bureaucracies where there is a chain of command—a hierarchy of authority— Congress is a collection of independent contractors. It often seems that there are 535 "leaders" on Capitol Hill and no "followers."

Committees and subcommittees are the heart and soul of congressional policymaking. Writing about Congress one hundred years ago, president and political scientist Woodrow Wilson referred to congressional committees as "little legislatures."[7] What Wilson observed then is no less true today. Committees are powerful vehicles for policy deliberation and action. In fact, Congress's ability to shape policies is vastly expanded by the division of labor and development of expertise made possible by the committee and subcommittee system.

Congress is divided into hundreds of little legislatures. In 1988, the House of Representatives had 23 major legislative committes and roughly 130 subcommittees; the Senate had 17 committees and more than 100 subcommittees. Since subcommittees are chaired by members of the majority party, at least half of the Democrats in the House chaired a subcommmittee. Each majority party Senator chaired at least one subcommittee and many chaired two.[8]

In fact, power is so widely dispersed on Capitol Hill that the media and the public have trouble keeping track of the star players. Even such powerful groups as the House Ways and Means Committee (which handles tax matters, social security, trade policy, and health programs, among others) are practically invisible to the public. Most committees and subcommittees are more obscure. Few people beyond the Beltway (the superhighway that encircles Washington, D.C.) know that the House Appropriations Subcommittee on Labor, Health and Human Services, and Education appropriates more than one-third of the entire federal budget.

Many important policy decisions are made within this subcommittee-centered power structure and escape notice by the general public. This system of fragmented power satisfies legislators because organizations affected by the subcommittee contribute to the member's campaign. Interest groups and executive branch officials are pleased because they gain access and attention to their concerns. If tobacco companies want to weaken government regulations about smoking, the Subcommittee on Tobacco and Peanuts, whose members hail from tobacco-producing states, afford them an opportunity to press their case. When the fishing industry is upset about environmental regulations, the Subcommittee on Fisheries, whose members are from coastal areas, will try to help out.

Subcommittees also create powerful organizations for promoting new policies. The chair and subcommittee chairs of the House Energy and Commerce Committee, for example, have used their platforms to launch investigations and formulate sweeping changes in health policy, environmental protection, and telecommunications. According to Chair John Dingell, a Michigan Democrat, the jurisdiction of the committee is "anything that walks and anything that thinks about walking."[9]

The formulation of the legislation designed to remove asbestos from the public schools provides a fine example of subcommittee-based entrepreneurship. The bill's principal sponsor was Democratic Representative James J. Florio, chair of the Subcommittee on Commerce, Transportation and Tourism. A policy activist, Representative Florio uses his subcommittee to advance laws in diverse policy areas. Notice that the words "schools" and "health" do not appear in the title of the subcommittee. But representative Florio, who would like to become New Jersey's governor, captured this issue because the Chair of the House Education and Labor Committee, Democrat Augustus F. Hawkins from California, did not seize it for his committee.

As they often do, politics and public policy intertwine in this episode. The new asbestos law serves diverse audiences. Curbing asbestos hazards pleases worried parents and teachers. School board members are relieved because new funding will be available. The asbestos industry is grateful because limits are placed on their liability for health effects. The Environmental Protection Agency is happy that federal policy was clarified on an important health hazard. Legislative victories can be translated into future electoral rewards and in the meantime they enhance the reputation of Representative Florio and increase the flow of contributions from political action committees (PACs).

Because power is widely dispersed, *bargaining and compromise* are central features of cloakroom politics. Fragmentation enhances the power of members and subcommittee and committee leaders, but it makes reaching consensus more difficult. A few determined individuals can stall the process. Congress may fail to make progress on important policy issues for months or even years. At times the process moves at a snail's pace; yet, when agreement is reached and the deals are struck, Congress can move with blinding speed.[10]

A majority in Congress must support a bill repeatedly before it reaches the president's desk for signature: majorities must be obtained in subcommittees, committees, and in the entire House and Senate. If there are disagreements between House and Senate (and there usually are), a temporary conference committee is appointed to iron out the differences and then seek yet another majority in each chamber.

Although members often take cues from party leaders and the president, majorities assembled to pass one law may not stick together for the next battle. As new issues arise, majority votes at each stage of the legislative process must be reassembled—one vote at a time. Putting coalitions together is painstaking work and often resembles Monty Hall's "Let's Make a Deal." David Stockman, former budget director for President Reagan, calls the task of pulling coalitions together in Congress the "politics of giving."

An actual majority for any specific bill had to be reconstructed from scratch every time. It had to be cobbled out of the patchwork of raw, parochial deals that set of a political billiard game of counterreactions and corresponding demands. The last 10 or 20 percent of the votes needed for a majority in both houses had to be bought, period.[11]

If presidents prefer *wholesale* politics—good ideas—legislators prefer *retail* politics—rewards for their districts. A House leadership aide put it simply; "No matter how members ask the question it always comes down to one issue: How will it affect me?"[12] Crafting laws requires many different types of agreements. Deals between members may involve one agreeing to vote aye on a bill today with the understanding that another day the favor will be returned. Or, the legislation may include a higher appropriation, lower taxes, or favorable treatment for any industry in the member's district as the price for a positive vote.

Some observers regard the horse-trading, compromise, and vote swapping that characterize Congress as distinctly unsavory. To these critics, German Chancellor Bismark was correct when he remarked: "Politics is like sausage. Neither should be viewed in the making." Yet, the nature of representative democratic institutions makes it unlikely (and even undesirable) for them to behave otherwise. In order to fashion laws in an open democratic institution, a broad consensus must be achieved and sustained. "Good" policy provides benefits (or at least does not harm) the people and interests represented by members of Congress.

This underlying dynamic helps explain why Congress often procrastinates until the last possible moment before making decisions. Just before adjournment or an election, Congress may rush through hundreds of bills. Why does Congress act like professional football teams during their two-minute drill—quickly and effectively moving the ball down the field for a touchdown when before they seemed unable to move the ball two feet? Why can't Congress move with the same determination the rest of the year as it does when a deadline is upon them? Action is often postponed primarily because everyone waits until the end to get the best deal. The fact that decisions on major legislative initiatives, tax and spending bills may not be made until the eleventh hour encourages everyone to withhold commitments.

Members of Congress also delay action in the hope that unfavorable political conditions will improve. Perhaps public opinion opposing a controversial policy will change; maybe the president will take a different position; perhaps the next election will bring more like-minded individuals to Congress. Without deadlines, Congress would often be unable to make decisions. The end of a fiscal year, the expiration of a law's authorization, an impending election, and adjournment force Congress to act, whether they are "ready" or not.

Fragmented power and the importance of compromise increase the need for *leadership* to put things together. Legislative leaders help set priorities for the institution and assemble coalitions to get bills passed.[13] Leaders derive their power from the members, however, and must defer to their wishes in order to maintain continued support. Leadership preferences on policy matters usually flow from the positions adopted by party members or by the White House, rather than from their independent views. Majority and minority leaders are more influential on procedural matters—when a bill is considered or how an issue is framed for a vote—than on the substance of legislation.[14]

Probably the most important "legislative leader" in Washington, D.C., is the president who not only sets congressional agendas, but also formulates policies and pushes them through to final adoption. Presidents possess considerable political powers that are unavailable to members of Congress. Chief among these powers is the ability to be heard above the clamor of voices. As Democratic Representative David R. Obey from Wisconsin stated, "The President has the only megaphone in Washington, D.C."[15] Presidents attract media and public attention and can exert pressure on legislators to go along with their wishes. Thus, the president at times can mobilize forces that make it difficult for Congress to engage in cloakroom politics as usual.

CLOAKROOM POLICIES

The characteristics of cloakroom politics profoundly influence the public policies produced by Congress and its committees. When there is a conflict between the legislator's desire and need to serve constituent concerns and the need for more long-term, carefully crafted solutions, Congress leans strongly in the direction of serving the immediate and parochial desires of the voters who put them and keep them in office. The mixture of legislators' needs, fragmented power, compromise, and leadership produce a variety of public policy responses, but all are designed to maximize the control and interests of individual members.

Symbolic Policies

Symbol often triumphs over substance in congressional policymaking. A lot of legislative activity involves talk, not action. Hearings are held, bills introduced, speeches delivered, but no legislation passes. Significant policy change is harder to achieve because Congress must authorize government agencies to regulate public and private behavior, spend money, and raise taxes. Making the wrong move can cost members their seats in Congress.

Sometimes primarily symbolic laws are passed in order to reassure politically aroused groups.[16] Without offering tangible benefits, the legislature addresses the concerns of aggrieved parties with policy pronouncements that presumably mollify them. The less sophisticated and organized the group, the more likely they will receive and accept symbolic responses. Disadvantaged groups such as the unemployed and the poor do not have sufficient political clout to hold elected officials accountable.[17]

Congress often adopts policies that are long on goals but short on the means for carrying them out. The gulf between rhetoric and reality is frequently exposed by the difference between authorizing language and appropriations bills. Authorizations set out the objectives and strategies for ameliorating a problem; appropriations bills supply money for programs and benefits to people. An example of a policy with lofty goals but insufficient cash is the Housing and Community Development Act. Its avowed goals are to create "viable urban communities by providing decent housing and a suitable living environment for persons of low and moderate income."[18] Congress's $3 billion annual appropriation since 1974 may seem generous, but it falls short of reaching the law's ambitious objectives. In fact, during the mid-1980s more public housing units were destroyed than built.[19]

Incremental Change

Protracted policymaking and fragmented power often yield *incremental* policy changes: Problems are typically addressed in small, manageable steps rather than major new departures. The forces militating against fundamental change are very powerful. Agendas are crowded with proposals; only a few receive serious attention. Members of Congress have abundant opporunities to veto or water down proposals. Policy issues are rarely considered comprehensively. Congress slices up broad policy domains into many smaller questions so that a larger number of members serving on committees and subcommittees can participate.

Fear of the unknown also inhibits rapid and radical change. Members of Congress are risk-averse. They usually would prefer to tinker with solutions, through trial and error, rather than to embrace innovative approaches entailing risk and the potential of disastrous consequences. Moreover, lawmakers want to avoid controversy and conflict. It is often prudent to seek only modest changes in current policy. Opposition from others is less likely when changes from the status quo are minor and do not threaten vested interests.

Budgetary policymaking is a prime example of incrementalism at work. Congress usually makes minor adjustments from year to year. Major departures, such as the substantial increases in defense spending during the 1980s, are rare and only possible with strong presidential leadership. This year's budget typically equals last year's budget, plus or minus a small percentage.[20] Battles occur over what seem like inches of territory to the outside observer. Will spending increase by 2 or 3 percent? Will formulas governing grants-in-aid programs benefit cities with less than 25,000 residents? The competition is fierce, but the public rarely understands what, if anything, is at stake. To insiders, these battles are important because they are often the principal policy issues before the Congress.

Distributive Policies

Legislators want to deliver benefits to people, businesses, and communities in their districts. The desire to parcel out particularized benefits or so-called pork-barrel projects produces what are called distributive policies.[21] Members prefer the politics of giving and claiming credit to budget cutting and finger pointing. For instance, to justify expanding the naval fleet in the 1980s, the Secretary of the Navy announced a policy of "strategic dispersal." Rather than locating navy ships in the few ports where they have been berthed for decades, he proposed several new port facilities around the nation. This action would create thousands of new jobs in the chosen cities. But critics, including former naval officers, charged: "It's a blatant attempt to curry political favor. It can't be justified in strategic terms, except for the strategic politics."[22]

Organized interests benefit from this system of handing out government largess. The economically disadvantaged and unorganized usually lose when their interests conflict with the organized. For example, President Reagan convinced Congress to drop public jobs programs for long-term unemployed and poor people, but Congress refused to terminate the Economic Development Administration (EDA)—a program characterized by Reagan budget director David Stockman as a "boondoggle" and "demonstrably useless." The difference: EDA distributes low-interest loans and other assistance to businesses and construction companies in 80 percent of the country. Public service jobholders did not have political action committees; the construction industry did.[23]

Gridlock

When Congress deals with extremely controversial policies, the policy process often gets stuck in a gridlock of opposing viewpoints and power. David Price observed: "Congress is often difficult to mobilize, particularly on high-conflict issues of broad scope."[24] Congress has gridlocked over civil rights policy, aid to education, and other issues in the past, but the situation seemed to be worse in the 1980s. According to Allen Schick, "Congress now has difficulty legislating because the role demanded of it by economic conditions is not congruent with the type of legislation encouraged by its organizations and behavior."[25]

Congress's handling of the acid rain problem is illustrative. More than a decade ago, scientists warned that the buildup of sulphur dioxide and other substances in the atmosphere (caused primarily by the burning of coal) was damaging trees, crops, and drinking water. Yet, no significant laws were enacted because members of Congress from the regions whose industries created the pollution were unable to agree with those from the areas of acid rainfall. The pollution continues as the debate drags on.

The federal budget deficit is another typical gridlock. From 1981 to 1985 Congress ceaselessly debated deficit reduction strategies without taking strong action. By 1985, the budget deficit had swollen to $200 billion. The deficit deadlock stemmed not so much from disagreements over whether the problem was serious, but rather over which course of action to pursue. Most Democrats favored tax increases and lower defense spending; most Republicans preferred no tax increases and less domestic spending. But meaningful deficit reduction will require one or more painful policy actions: hiking taxes or slashing popular programs.

While Congress groped for a solution, the deficit problem worsened and the available options became fewer and more painful. Reluctant to adopt sufficient program cuts and tax increases, the president and Congress decided to borrow huge sums of money. By the end of 1985, the public debt had risen above $1.8 trillion—more than double what it was at the beginning of 1981. This spectacular growth in the nation's debt brought about an even more spectacular growth in interest payments to service the debt—from $53 billion in 1980 to approximately $130 billion in 1985.[26] The gridlock was eventually released by adopting the Gramm-Rudman-Hollings (GRH) deficit reduction plan—named after its sponsors, senators from Texas, New Hampshire, and South Carolina, respectively. GRH mandated reductions in federal spending that promised a balanced budget by fiscal year 1991. Whether that target is reached or not, GRH provided the short-term political relief demanded by members.

Innovation

Occasionally, public policy changes radically. Landmark laws may increase or decrease government involvement—such as providing health insurance for the elderly—or substantially enhance or lower resources devoted to a problem. The Social Security Act of 1935, which guaranteed government support for senior citizens, and the Civil Rights Act of 1964 which forbade discrimination against minorities, and tax and spending cuts enacted in 1981 represent fundamental innovations in public policy.

From time to time, conditions fostering innovation may arise. According to political scientist Charles Jones, significant policy shifts may occur when a well-organized and vocal public unites and demands government action and/or when policymakers achieve a temporary consensus around unprecedented proposals.[27] Strong political leadership, often from the president, can be a powerful agent of policy innovation. The Civil Rights Act of 1964 was championed vigorously by President Lyndon Johnson. Major changes in the tax system and federal spending priorities were achieved with effective leadership from President Reagan.

Congressional committees usually follow the president's lead in making policy innovations, but there are exceptions. Senator Edmund Muskie from

Maine, Democratic chair of the Public Works Committee, since renamed Environment and Public Works, galvanized the environmental movement in promoting the Clean Air Act of 1970 and other environmental laws. As chair of the Judiciary Committee's Subcommittee on Immigration and Refugee Policy, Wyoming Senator Alan Simpson led the fight to reform the nation's immigration laws in the late 1980s.

Events, political conditions, and the state of the economy must also be considered. When federal budget deficits are high, as they are in the 1980s, opportunities for greater federal spending are severely restricted, but other innovations became more likely, including deregulation and increased privatization of public services. Conversely, when federal revenues exceeded projected expenditures in the mid-1960s, President Johnson declared "War on Poverty" and delivered both "guns"—for the war in Vietnam—and "butter"—domestic spending programs.

Delegation

Broad, vague, and sometimes contradictory laws are a direct by-product of the need to reconcile competing claims and preferences and to fashion major support in subcommittees, committees, and the floor of the House and Senate. The task of translating aspirations into programs and services is delegated to government administrators, other levels of government, courts, private businesses, and citizens. Indeed, the more controversial the policy, the more likely that legislators will ask others to make the tough choices.[28] When the legislators delegate hard decisions to others, they often garner political rewards and soften the wrath of aggrieved parties elsewhere. Delegating authority to others gives legislators leeway to blame federal agencies or other governments for failing to fulfill legislative intent and to take credit for correcting faults through constituent casework.[29]

The most common form of policy delegation occurs when Congress defines a problem in legislation and then mandates federal agencies to do something about it. Congress often imposes difficult "policy" decisions on individuals and businesses and on states and local governments. Affirmative action hiring policies are carried out by private organizations which decide whether to follow the letter and spirit of the law or ignore it. Responsibility for enforcing immigration laws rests with private employers who must verify an individual's citizenship or permit to work in the United States, and failure to do so can result in a substantial fine. Congress may require states to upgrade the education of young children, reform their welfare systems, enhance air and water quality, and improve highway safety. Funds to support new programs and agency staff are often supplied, but the goals of the policy typically exceed the supply of funds.

THE CONSEQUENCES OF CLOAKROOM POLITICS

The practice of cloakroom politics influences not only policy outputs but also policy outcomes. Even when Congress delegates authority, it usually establishes some ground rules for who gets what, when, and how from the government. Congress and its committees are often the final arbiters of how much government spends on important societal goals, and from whom money will be raised to pay for those commitments.

Congress is a policymaking institution, not an administrative agency. To legislate is to set a goal, define a problem, raise an issue. Lawmaking is in the beginning of the long process of delivering public goods, services, and regulations. Making law does not guarantee positive outcomes: There is often a wide gap between policy intent and the actual results achieved in society.

Members of Congress are held accountable for policy *positions*, not for policy *results*. Indeed, if members were responsible for the impacts of public policies, they might enjoy considerably less electoral success. Elected representatives are typically more capable of *discussing* policy problems than they are in crafting solutions or overseeing their implementation and impact. This is understandable given their objective (reelection), the style of legislative politics (compromise), and the difficulty of reaching agreement on controversial issues.

Implementing Policies

Laws are seldom written with the potential problems of implementation in mind. For Congress it is difficult enough to reconcile competing interests in order to pass legislation; Congress leaves it to administrative agencies to figure out how to put the laws into effect. Actually, legislative goals that are excessive and may not be met are often regarded as an effective means of achieving change. Thus, for example, the authors of the Clean Air Act of 1970 are proud of their achievement, even though it quickly became obvious that the law's air quality standards would not be met.[30] They reasoned that setting high standards would stimulate the auto industry to work harder at lowering pollution and it probably did.

Nevertheless, a disregard for potential implementation difficulties can reduce the likelihood of achieving positive results and ultimately erode respect for government. Public laws are sometimes endorsed before committees and subcommittees carefully define the problems the laws are supposed to address. Subcommittee-based policy activists who perceive a need for government programs may not be sure how to translate their aspirations into workable policy. Before they know the solutions to problems like drug abuse, they will seize opportunities to advance innovative policies when they arise.

A classic illustration of this common theme may be found in the youth employment initiatives passed during the early months of the Carter administration. The Youth Employment Demonstration Project Act (YEDPA) of 1977 embodied a collection of legislative intentions that were extremely hard to carry out in practice. In less than four months, President Carter convinced Congress to authorize $1 billion for new programs, and YEDPA became a grab bag of new and old programs. Unable to choose among the dozens of approaches advanced by several House and Senate subcommittees, Congress essentially decided to experiment with all of them.

Within three years most of the YEDPA programs vanished from the scene. Federal, state, and local administrators were unable to successfully implement so many new initiatives simultaneously. There was simply too much money, too many programs, too many objectives. Worthwhile programs were mounted, but it was hard to sort these out from the ensuing mess and chaos. Positive results were probably doomed from the start by haphazard lawmaking. By 1981, Congress and a new president were no longer enamored of youth employment experiments, especially those without successful performance records.

Who Benefits?

Members of Congress and committee leaders tend to be concerned about the distribution of program benefits. Generally, they assume that programs or policies will have the desired impact if they are only implemented properly. This view, however, may be highly inaccurate. A member of the House Education and Labor Committee may believe that spending more money on education is an end in itself, but the ultimate impact of education programs is difficult to gauge (and may not materialize) until long after the legislator has left office. Legislators' perspectives on policy implementation not only influence lawmaking, but also have consequences for the distribution of benefits in society.

Government benefits come in many different forms: tax breaks for companies; grants to fund social service programs or to build bridges; income-support payments for the unemployed, poor, and retired; regulations that protect domestic industries from foreign competition; and so on. Underlying all tax and expenditure decisions, regulations, and policies is the question of who benefits and who does not.

Congressional policy often favors the haves over the have-nots, the organized over the unorganized, and the middle-class over the under-class.[31] Those with money and resources have an advantage because they can use the leverage afforded by campaign contributions and lobbyists to press their point of view. Unemployed people and the poor cannot support lawyers to prowl the halls of Congress, let alone fund reelection campaigns.

Even when programs originally intend to serve the disadvantaged, Congress often expands them to help the better-off segments of society too. Take the Economic Development Administration (EDA) grants program, for example. As originally conceived in 1965, EDA was supposed to help chronically depressed regions, such as Appalachia, but by the 1980s, aid formulas had been revised to include virtually the entire country. Social security and senior citizen health care programs, originally intended to care for needy individuals without alternative means of support, now pay benefits to even those older Americans who are quite well off.

In fact, most programs that benefit low- and moderate-income Americans contain substantial benefits for others, too. Government-subsidized health care programs, such as medicare for the aged and medicaid for the poor, supply physicians with a substantial amount of their income; training programs for disadvantaged youth benefit several large corporations that run the facilities for the government; nutrition programs for low-income citizens support large agricultural industries and food stores; grants for low-income college students benefit the institutions of higher education that rely on the student's government checks to pay their bills.

Indeed, when government programs try to exclusively serve the poor they generally do not last very long. During the 1970s, federal lawmakers doled out billions of dollars to state and local governments to create jobs for the unemployed. Many of those hired were recently laid-off, essentially middle-class workers. Stories about well-heeled and well-connected federally funded jobholders abounded. In an effort to serve the truly needy, Congress sent an unambiguous message to local officials: Hire only the long-term unemployed and poor. Two years later, practically everyone in the program was truly needy, but achieving the law's new objectives was purchased at a high cost. When President Reagan proposed eliminating the program in 1981, elected officials stood by and watched the program die.

Effective lawmaking depends upon finding the delicate balance of benefits that holds the majority together until passage. This is particularly difficult when the legislative struggle pits one advantaged group against another as it often does: the middle-class against industry; manufacturers against service providers; the public against the chemical, insurance and banking industries. It is considerably harder to find the right balance when everyone participating is able to make a strong case and to exact a price for "wrong" decisions.

CONCLUSION: THE LOGIC OF CLOAKROOM POLITICS

From the standpoint of some observers, congressional policymaking appears to be a crude enterprise. When elected representatives attempt to cope with difficult problems, like cleaning up the environment or providing for the nation's defense, they often approve politically appealing but poorly designed policies. Congress even has trouble stopping the delivery of programs that no longer make sense. Congress is "production oriented" even when its products cannot be defended! Thus, questionable water projects continue despite high deficits, and Congress continues to address complex and far-reaching problems like poverty and the environment with piecemeal, fragmented, and incremental solutions when long-term, integrated approaches would be appropriate and helpful. Members of Congress do not typically concern themselves with problems of program implementation unless bureaucrats run into difficulty and people start complaining.

But from the perspective of most members of Congress, cloakroom politics works rather well. By serving up short-term fixes that satisfy constituents, current political problems are solved and others are avoided. Cloakroom politics satisfies legislators because it serves their need to participate in the policy process and to deliver products for supporters and voters.

NOTES

Author's note: This chapter is derived from an earlier version of a chapter that appears in Carl E. Van Horn, Donald C. Baumer, and William T. Gormley, *Politics and Public Policy* (Washington, D.C.: CQ Press, 1988). It is used with their permission.

1. Cass Peterson, "Despite Gramm-Rudman Diet, the House Still Likes Its Pork," *Washington Post,* National Weekly Edition, November 25, 1987, p. 13.
2. Thomas Mann, *Unsafe at Any Margin* (Washington, D.C.: American Enterprise Institute for Public Policy Research, 1978).
3. *Washington Post,* National Weekly Edition, February 16, 1987, p. 12.
4. *Washington Post,* National Weekly Edition, October 6, 1986, p. 13.
5. "Competing for the Last Word on Drug Abuse," *The New York Times,* August 7, 1986, p. 10.
6. "Deals are Struck, Hands Are Held—And the Tax Bill Sneaks By," *Washington Post,* National Weekly Edition, December 10, 1985, p. 10.
7. Woodrow Wilson, *Congressional Government* (Boston: Houghton–Mifflin, 1885).
8. U.S. Congress, *Congressional Directory, 1985-1986* (Washington, D.C.: Government Printing Office).
9. Personal Interview, November 19, 1984.
10. John F. Hoadley, "Easy Riders: Gramm-Rudman-Hollings and the Legislative Fast Track," *PS* 19 (Winter 1986), pp. 30–36.
11. David Stockman, *The Triumph of Politics* (New York: Harper & Row, 1986), pp. 250–51.
12. Personal Interview, December 10, 1984.
13. "Legislative leaders" in this sense are individuals elected by their respective party memberships. In Congress, the leadership included the Speaker of the House, the majority and minority leaders, assistant leaders (sometimes called party whips), and the party caucus officers in the House and Senate.
14. Barbara Sinclair, *Majority Party Leadership in the U.S. House* (Baltimore, Md.: Johns Hopkins University Press, 1983) and Randall B. Ripley, *Majority Party Leadership in Congress* (Boston: Little, Brown, 1969)
15. Personal interview, May 29, 1985.
16. Murray Edelman, *The Symbolic Uses of Politics* (Urbana: University of Illinois Press, 1964).
17. Randall B. Ripley and Grace A. Franklin, *Congress, the Bureaucracy, and Public Policy,* 3rd ed.. (Homewood, Ill.: Dorsey Press, 1984).
18. Carl E. Van Horn, *Policy Implementation in the Federal System* (Lexington, Mass.: D.C. Heath, 1979), p. 106.

19. John Herbers, "Outlook for Sheltering the Poor Growing Ever Bleaker," *The New York Times,* March 8, 1987, p. 1.
20. Aaron Wildavsky, *The Politics of the Budgetary Process,* 3rd ed. (Boston: Little, Brown, 1979).
21. David R. Mayhew, *Congress: The Electoral Connection* (New Haven, Conn.: Yale University Press, 1974); Theodore Lowi, *The End of Liberalism,* 2nd ed. (New York: W.W. Norton, 1979).
22. Michael Weisskopf, "A Ship in Every Port, A Vote in Every Committee," *Washington Post,* National Weekly Edition, September 16, 1985, p. 13.
23. Stockman, *Triumph,* p. 209.
24. David E. Price, "Congressional Committees in the Policy Process," in *Congress Reconsidered,* 3rd ed. Lawrence C. Dodd and Bruce I. Oppenheimer, (Washington, D.C.: C.Q Press, 1985), pp. 211–22.
25. "The Distributive Congress," in *Making Economic Policy in Congress,* ed. Allen Schick (Washington, D.C.: American Enterprice Institute for Public Policy Research, 1983), p. 258.
26. U.S. Congress Joint Economic Committee, *Annual Report on the Economy,* 99th Cong., 1st Sess., May 15, 1985, pp. 47–49.
27. Charles O. Jones, "Speculative Augmentation in Federal Air Pollution Policymaking," *Journal of Politics* 36, no. 2 (May 1974), pp. 438–64.
28. Lowi, *Liberalism.*
29. Morris P. Fiorina, *Congress: Keystone of the Washington Establishment* (New Haven, Conn.: Yale University Press, 1977).
30. Charles O. Jones, *Clean Air: The Policies and Politics of Pollution Control* (Pittsburgh, Penn.: University of Pittsburgh Press, 1975).
31. Ripley and Franklin, *Congress, the Bureaucracy, and Public Policy.*

PART THREE

Congress in the Political System

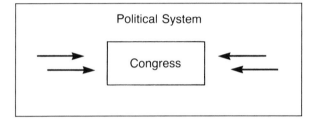

CHAPTER 12

The Focusing Skill and Presidential Influence in Congress

Paul C. Light

It has become fashionable of late to bemoan the lack of presidential and congressional cooperation in solving our nation's economic and social problems. Why, some ask in this bicentennial decade, can't these two great institutions get along? The answer, of course, is that the Founding Fathers never intended the two to exist in harmony. Instead, they created what Richard Neustadt once called separate institutions sharing power.

The competition between Congress and the presidency is rarely more intense than in setting the national policy agenda. Members of Congress have become much more assertive in recent years, and are more than willing to challenge the president for legislative supremacy. Thus, even though Ronald Reagan won impressive legislative victories in 1981, his social agenda never had a hearing.

Looking back over the Reagan, Carter, Ford, and Nixon years, some would argue that presidential leadership does not matter much in Congress. Members of Congress do not like to admit they can be swayed by presidential favors—whether a weekend at Camp David or a few million dollars in pork-barrel benefits for the folks back home. As one member of Congress said in 1982, "Ronald Reagan is a great guy, a real charmer. He's got a great sense of humor, always has an anecdote for the occasion. But I'd never vote for his program on that basis. I'd no more vote for his legislation because he's a nice guy than I'd walk over hot coals for a handful of jellybeans."

For those who enjoy the Washington intrigue, the message is hardly comforting. According to the best political science research, no matter how much we like to think last-minute presidential telephone calls make a difference, the data do not agree. After examining thousands of congressional roll call votes, for example, George Edwards argues that "Presidential legislative skills do not seem to affect support for presidential policies, despite what conventional wisdom leads us to expect." Stories of backdoor influence and smoke-filled rooms may still sell newspapers, but that is not the stuff of which presidential influence is made. "When we rigorously and systematically evaluate the evidence," Edwards reports, "we reach different conclusions."[1] According to the data, all that really matters is public approval, pure and simple.

Edwards is not the first to question the impact of presidential skills. Not a few presidents themselves have scratched their heads in wonderment after losing a close roll call in the wake of a massive lobbying campaign. As President Lyndon Johnson once said of his fellow politicians, "You can tell a man to go to hell, but you can't make him go." The phrase seemed "particularly apt," he later wrote in his memoirs, "when I found myself in a struggle with the House or Senate. I would start to speak out . . . and remember that no matter how many times I told the Congress to do something, I could never force it to act."[2]

So what is a president to do? Disband the congressional relations office and timidly await congressional action? Obviously not. Presidents know better. Public approval does not drive the congressional process in some great vacuum. It gets "spent" as presidents set their agendas. Indeed, the president's ability to link abstract public support to specific legislative initiatives may be the most important skill of all.

That is what arm-twisting, horse-trading, and the rest of the president's *focusing tactics* are all about. These focusing skills help Congress concentrate attention on the president's priorities. Focusing ensures the most effective deployment of political and organizational resources. A strong focusing skill can make a weak president much more effective, spelling the margin for victory or sustaining vetoes. A weak focusing skill can render a strong president much less successful, spelling the difference between a presidency of stalemate like Jimmy Carter's or a presidency of great legislative success like Lyndon Johnson's.

As this chapter suggests, the president's ability to focus congressional attention is particularly important for passing *nonincremental policy*—more specifically, the highly visible, large-scale proposals at the very top of the White House agenda. By their very nature, these programs are more controversial than the less visible, smaller-scale proposals that occupy so much congressional and presidential energy. Because the legislative price tag for nonincremental policy is high, and because the obstacles to passage are varied and great, these proposals demand the utmost in presidential focusing skills. If Congress is not constantly reminded of the president's top concerns, legislative attention will drift elsewhere, leaving even the most popular president with little legislative success.

SOME INITIAL ASSUMPTIONS

This chapter is guided by several very simple assumptions about Congress and the presidency. First, I assume that Congress pays at least some attention to what presidents say and how they say it. Members of Congress watch television and read the papers. If a president launches a major legislative initiative, but never talks about it, Congress will get the message and move onto other business. If, however, the president launches a bill and talks about it incessantly, Congress will take note of the president's interest. Given a choice between acting on the first bill or the second, all other things being equal, Congress will move on the one the president cares about, particularly if the president is publicly popular and has a reasonable number of seats in his own party in Congress.

Second, I also assume that Congress pays attention to whether the president shows any real, tangible interest. If the president is all talk and no action, all posturing and no bargaining, Congress will move onto other business. Congress often looks for ways to establish a pecking order among bills, taking note of what the president says first, second, third, and so on up to a point. Congress will also take note of just when in the legislative calendar a president chooses to act. If the president fails to give Congress timely notice of legislative priorities, Congress will act on its own. Congress waits for no one.

Finally, I assume that Congress can tell the difference between presidential requests. All presidential programs are not created equal—some initiatives are more controversial, expensive, complicated, and so forth, than others. Congress knows that medicare reform is more important than highway beautification, that the Strategic Defense Initiative ("Star Wars") is more expensive than drug abuse education. After all, Congress is a thinking—albeit highly political—institution. It limits presidential influence in some policy areas and creates success in others. Even so, congressional scrutiny is more likely in nonincremental than incremental policy, more specifically, in large-scale rather than small-scale policy, spending rather than nonspending policy, and in new rather than old policy. I assume that each presidential program has a reasonably clear cost, and that some kinds of programs are more expensive than others.

For example, the cost of getting a president's bill through Congress is clearly higher than sustaining a veto: the first requires a majority vote in both chambers, the second requires a one-third-plus-one minority in but one. Moreover, whereas presidents must win repeatedly to pass a bill—in subcommittees, full committees, the Rules Committee in the House, on the floors of both chambers, in a conference committee, and back again on both floors—they must only win once on a veto.

Presidents and their staffs certainly act as if Congress knows how much programs cost politically. They talk of legislative cost and ways of "buying" congressional support. They think about legislative strategy and trading options. They calculate congressional-support and count votes. Assuming that every presidential proposal has a price tag, the types of programs a given president can afford will vary with the chief executive's *political capital*—public approval outside Washington and party seats inside Congress. With only minority support in both the public and Congress, the kinds of proposals Nixon and Ford could "purchase" were very limited compared to Reagan.

Whereas Nixon had been elected in 1968 with a bare plurality in a three-party race, and Ford had been the first appointed president in American history, Reagan was swept into office with a Republican Senate and strong public support. He even had an ideological majority in the House composed of "boll weevil" southern conservative Democrats and a mass of intensely loyal Republicans.

WHY NONINCREMENTAL PROGRAMS COST SO MUCH

There are several reasons why nonincremental policy requests cost more than routine presidential proposals. According to Paul Schulman, "Nonincremental, indivisible policy pursuits are beset by organization thresholds or 'critical mass' points closely associated with their initiation and subsequent development. These policies must rely for their success upon factors which come into play only at high levels of political and resource commitment."[3] In order to secure passage of a nonincremental proposal, a president needs to do much more than merely adjust an old program. Nonincremental programs require a leap of national commitment: there was no way President Johnson could establish a medicare program by simply refining some already successful program; it was too new, too different from the past.

The manned space program is another example. When Kennedy announced his intention to land a man on the moon by the end of the 1960s, the United States had not even launched a man into orbit around the earth, let alone created the kind of rocketry and vehicles to send three astronauts to the moon and bring them home safely. As Schulman writes, "Nonincremental policies must expand greatly if they are to expand at all. Only then can they overcome the inertia, external resistance, or internal start-up problems which act as barriers to policy expansion."[4] Commenting on the need for imagination, Schulman notes that,

> No barrier is more essential for nonincremental policy to breach and overcome permanently than the penchant for thinking small. Overcoming this trait is a major necessity in developing the imagination and receptivity closely associated with organizational innovation. In addition, thinking small is also a detriment to the planning and jurisdictional extensions upon which nonincremental policy depends.[5]

In many respects, of course, this is what presidential policy leadership is all about: Thinking big.

Perhaps the best way to understand the amount of effort involved in drafting and passing nonincremental policy is to consider a more precise definition of the term. According to Schulman, nonincremental policies are "distinguished by their demand for comprehensive rather than incremental decisions, synoptic rather than piecemeal outlooks and vision. These policies are characterized by an indivisibility in the political commitment and resources they require for success. . . . This class of nonincremental, indivisible policies is perhaps small but is nonetheless significant. It consists of large-scale government undertakings commanding major shares of the public budget.[6] In the manned space program, for example, Kennedy could hardly settle for a program that would get a man to the moon, but not back. The Apollo program required total political commitment.

Beyond the fact that such programs are "indivisible," nonincremental policies involve three other characteristics. First, nonincremental programs often involve *federal spending*. In an era of $200 billion budget deficits, Congress finds it harder to pass programs which increase the deficit. Indeed, current congressional rules place a premium on the search for *revenue neutral* programs—a contemporary phrase meaning cheap or cost-free. Clearly, Congress and the president have become more sophisticated in how they craft spending programs. Spending can involve more routine direct grants, as well as revenue forgone through tax cuts, tax expenditures, and tax loopholes, plus a host of direct loans and loan guarantees now totaling almost $1 trillion in federal liabilities. Budget cuts can be nonincremental, too. It just depends on how big. Reagan's 1981 budget and tax cuts were among the boldest nonincremental proposals in modern history, primarily because they involved wholesale changes in what had been status quo.

Second, nonincremental programs involve *large-scale initiatives*. The key question, according to John Campbell, is whether the proposal is large or small. "At the extreme," Campbell writes, large-scale decisions "have a large fiscal impact and they significantly alter the relationships among social groups or between state and society. Accordingly, they are controversial and receive considerable publicity; participation is relatively broad (interest groups, political parties or subgroups, chief executive, perhaps several agencies), and the outcome in some sense will represent the political balance of power for the society as a whole." In contrast, "Small new decisions do not have as broad an impact and probably will receive little publicity; participation is often confined within a 'subgovernment' of officials, interest groups, representatives, and the few politicians directly and routinely concerned with a specific policy area; outcomes often depend on the balance of power or views within the subgovernment."[7]

The large/small question is best seen as a continuum. Surely Kennedy thought his proposal for expanded oceanographic research was important, but he could not have considered it as significant as medicare. Similarly, Johnson must have thought a land conservation fund was in the public's interest, but in no way as significant as federal aid to education or civil rights. Reagan must have seen cuts in the Small Business Administration as a valued national goal, but not in the same league as tax cuts. In these and countless other cases, the presidents recognized the difference between the size of the respective proposals. And so did Congress.

Third, nonincremental programs generally involve *new departures in national policy*. New programs alter the prevailing structure of policy in a given area; they involve either major expansions or contractions of the federal role, and frequently create new constituencies. In contrast, proposals dealing with old programs evoke old coalitions and support. The key is the nature of the status quo at the beginning of a president's term.

Reagan's 1981 domestic agenda, for example, was "new" in every sense of the term. It involved a dramatic reversal in the focus of federal spending, and certainly created a host of new constituencies, when it ·changed the established distribution of federal benefits. In one sense, the agenda was "de-distributive"—asking for sacrifice across the domestic spending board, even including social security and medicare cuts for the elderly. In another sense, it was "re-distributive"—taking from the poor in welfare and medicaid cuts, and giving to the rich in tax cuts. In contrast, Reagan's defense program was anything but new. It continued a buildup started under Jimmy Carter in 1979. Both presidents apparently recognized the need for a renewed emphasis on weapons development and modernization.

Clearly, thinking big involves higher political costs. At the front end of the policy process, nonincremental proposals demand a very high investment of presidential time and energy. Consider Nixon's proposal for sweeping welfare reform as an example. According to Martin Anderson, a White House staff aide at the time, and later to become Reagan's top domestic policy advisor, "The bright, clear notions some of us had developed during the [1968] campaign about how a president and staff would make national policy soon tarnished and blurred. We have naively assumed that we would simply review whatever issue was a problem, identify the major areas of difficulty, consult leading experts,and with their help craft a solution." As Anderson soon discovered, welfare reform "required many years before those involved felt any degree of confidence in what they were doing. The domestic side of the federal government had gotten so big that it was literally impossible to grasp it, intellectually, in its entirety."[8]

At the back of the process, nonincremental proposals involve more congressional and public scrutiny. And the greater the scrutiny and conflict, the greater the resources needed to win final passage. Further, nonincremental proposals tend to attract more participants. In a legislative process which produces very few final decisions, a presidential proposal takes on more "freight," or unrelated business. Because Congress passes less than one out of six proposals introduced, members take advantage of the opportunities for decisions that arise, whether nonincremental or not. Few major programs can be drafted without the cooperation of a variety of agencies and actors, all of whom must be persuaded on the merits of the nonincremental goal.

BUILDING A BETTER BOX SCORE

Presidential influence in Congress depends on a number of factors, not the least of which is Congress's own agenda, what Jeff Fishel calls "volume."[9] Carter, for example, had the bad luck to enter office at the tail end of one of the busiest periods in modern legislative history. Over 15,000 bills and joint resolutions were introduced in 1977–79, down from a high of 22,000 in 1967–69, but substantial nonetheless.

Unfortunately for Carter, the number of bills may have dropped, but the average length of the bills had more than doubled. Moreover, the number of presidential/executive department messages to Congress had grown from 2,600 in Kennedy's first year to just under 5,200 in Carter's. And the number of draft bills cleared through the president's review process jumped 60 percent—from 355 to 552—over the same period.[10]

Reagan, of course, had the good luck to follow Carter just two years later. Only 8,000 bills and joint resolutions were introduced in Reagan's first two years, the lowest activity level in over forty years. Though the average length of the bills had inched up slightly, the number of presidential bills and messages were on their way down. Part of the slowdown was Reagan's own doing. Unlike Carter, who sent a stream of separate proposals to Congress, Reagan packaged his legislative requests into several omnibus bills, most notably the budget and tax cuts. Moreover, unlike Carter, who presented his program as an ad hoc collection of unrelated ideas, Reagan wrapped his agenda in a mantle of ideological consistency. Finally, unlike Carter, who steadfastly refused to tell Congress what was most important, Reagan let it be known that the budget and tax cuts were his top, and ultimately only, priorities. Whatever Reagan said publicly, Congress knew he would not fight the social agenda on school prayer and abortion.

The question is, what makes the difference—political capital or focusing skills, economic luck or presidential lobbying? The only way to answer is to look at the record, comparing presidents across a variety of independent factors. And that means developing a new box score of success. Such a box score must focus only on the president's agenda, excluding the rest of the executive branch and legislative agenda. Among the 15,000 bills handled in the House during Carter's first two years, only 29 involved top presidential priorities! If we want to know why 17 passed and 12 failed, it makes no sense to track the other 14,971 proposals. Luckily, presidents care a great deal about keeping lists of their programs. The Office of Management and Budget (OMB) keeps one such list in its legislative clearance division, ensuring that nothing leaves for Capitol Hill unless the president and/or the White House staff says "go."

Once OMB gives clearance to a bill, it gives Congress a sense of the president's interest by assigning one of three labels to the request. If a bill is part of the president's own program, it is stamped "in accord." If a bill is not part of the president's agenda, but is still a good fit with the overall philosophy, it is labeled "consistent with." If a bill is not quite bad enough to be rejected or is so routine that OMB does not care, it is marked "no objection." If a bill is clearly out of touch with the president's outlook, it isn't stamped at all—it's tossed out. Clearly, the president's priorities can be found somewhere in the first list—the bills cleared in accord. Still, even the "in accord" list includes some department and agency bills. Thus, the president's agenda must be "scrubbed" even further to remove any non-presidential proposals. Perhaps the easiest way to get down to the top priorities is to use the president's State of the Union message as a screen. Although the address sometimes includes a laundry list of requests, it is viewed within the Washington policymaking community as a key, if not the key vehicle for announcing what the president truly wants. "Cabinet members, White House aides, and others are quite aware of the significance of getting material included in the State of the Union message," John Kessel writes. "Favorable mention of a policy gives visibility to it and confers presidential backing to the enterprise at one and the same time. Since there are obvious limits to the number of policies that can be thus favored, very real contests take place over control of this scarce resource."[11] If a proposal is not mentioned in at least one State of the Union message during the term, it is unlikely that the president is very interested.

Thus, we can create a new box score by simply combing both lists at the same time, taking only those proposals that are stamped "in accord" by OMB and mentioned in the State of the Union message, and then checking whether they passed in Congress. The key question is, what constitutes success? After all, presidents rarely get exactly what they ask for. Congress amends, presidents compromise. Luckily, most bills are relatively easy to decide, but where the choice is difficult the standard rule is to give the president the benefit of the doubt.

Unfortunately, because access to the OMB records has been highly restricted since 1981, the box score can only cover the Kennedy–Carter era. Over that period, 266 items meet this double test; during the same time, over 170,000 bills were introduced in Congress. Little wonder presidents need a bit of focusing skill. They must find a way to tell Congress what comes first.

If past experience is any guide presidents can expect to win on roughly half their proposals (see Table 12–1). Even so, Kennedy, Johnson, Nixon, Ford, and Carter had very different success rates. Johnson leads the five with a 59 percent success rate; Kennedy follows in second with 53 percent; Carter is in third with 49 percent; and Nixon and Ford trail with 35 and 31 percent, respectively. Furthermore, because Democrats held majorities in both houses of Congress during the period, it is no surprise that they have a higher success rate (55 percent) than their Republican colleagues (36 percent). (The Watergate scandal did not help Nixon and Ford, either.)

Even when presidents have a reasonably high congressional support score, as Table 12–1 also shows, they may be unable to win on their own requests. Noting that the other box scores in Table 12–1 measure general success across all votes on which the president takes a position, it may well be that presidential influence in Congress is multidimensional. Some presidents might be more successful lobbying someone else's agenda than their own.

Finally, it is important to note that success rates only tell part of the story. The point is not to have a high success rate per se (for example, Nixon could have achieved a 100 percent rate if he had only asked for one bill); the point is to establish a legislative record. Whereas Johnson's 59 percent success rate

TABLE 12–1   Presidential Box Scores, 1961–1980

Year		Agenda Box Score			Congressional Quarterly Box Score	Congressional Quarterly Support Score
		Requested	Passed	Percent		
1961		25	15	60%	48%	81%
1962	Kennedy	16	7	44	44	85
1963		6	3	50	27	87
1964	Johnson (1st term)	6	3	50	58	88
1965		34	28	82	69	93
1966	Johnson	24	14	58	56	79
1967	(2nd term)	19	8	42	48	79
1968		14	4	29	56	75
1969		17	7	41	32	74
1970	Nixon	12	3	25	46	77
1971	(1st term)	8	2	25	20	75
1972		3	1	33	44	66
1973	Nixon	20	8	40	31	51
1974	(2nd term)	5	2	40	34	60
1975	Ford	10	3	30	29	61
1976		6	2	33	—	54
1977		21	14	67	—	75
1978	Carter	8	3	38	—	78
1979		8	2	25	—	77
1980		4	1	25	—	75

Note: The new box score is compared to two previous measures. The first, the "presidential box score" only runs to 1975. It had so many problems that its creator, *Congressional Quarterly, Inc.*, finally gave it up in 1975, rendering it of no use in understanding any president elected after Ford. The second measure, the "presidential support score," was also created by *Congressional Quarterly, Inc.*, but is maintained to the present. It is a fine measure indeed of how presidents do when they take a stand on congressional votes, but does not tell us much about how presidents do on their own requests.

SOURCE: Paul C. Light, "Passing Nonincremental Policy: Presidential Influence in Congress, Kennedy to Carter," *Congress & the Presidency* 9 (Winter 1981–82), p. 67.

reflects a huge legislative accomplishment—57 victories out of 97 requests—Kennedy's only slightly lower 53 percent rate involves a relatively modest achievement—24 victories out of 47 requests.

How Nonincremental Programs Get Passed

A president's legislative reputation depends on nonincremental success, on whether Congress passes the big ticket proposals. Great Societies, New Frontiers, and Reagan Revolutions are not made from incremental adjustments. Among the 266 proposals, only 127 can be classified as spending proposals, 131 can be defined as large-scale, and 163 can be separated as new. Clearly, within the tens of thousands of congressional bills, only a small fraction—roughly one in one hundred—belong to the president's non-incremental program. And, as Table 12–2 suggests, presidents can expect to win on half of their top requests, with Democrats clearly ahead of the Republicans.

More surprisingly, Nixon and Ford did reasonably well on nonspend-ing, small-scale, and old requests. It was only when they dared to tread on spending, large-scale, and new ground that Congress said no. On modifica-tions of old programs, for example, Nixon and Ford stayed almost even with their Democratic colleagues. When they turned to new ideas, they did only half as well. The same pattern shows for small-scale versus large-scale requests.

The reason is simple: Congress can tell the difference between presidents and their proposals. Congress was more than willing to give Nixon and Ford an occasional success on more trivial requests, but not on major issues. After all is said and done, presidential influence in Congress depends on politics. A Democratic majority has little reason to help a Republican president, and vice versa. In the shifting tide of the separation of powers, a resurgent Con-gress has little interest in helping expansive chief executives. Indeed, there are at least three reasons why some presidents do better in Congress: (1) they have more political capital; (2) they have greater economic and institutional good fortune; and/or (3) they have better focusing skills. Each will be ad-dressed below.

TABLE 12–2   Relationship between Policy Content and Congressional Passage, Kennedy to Carter

	Percent Passage		
Variable	All Presidents	Democrats	Republicans
Program means			
Non-spending	47%	52%	39%
Spending	52	58	25
Program size			
Small	49	54	42
Large	50	57	23
Program newness			
Modification of old program	54	56	53
New program	46	55	24

Note: N = 266 for all presidents; N = 185 for Democrats; N = 81 for Republicans

source: Paul C. Light, "Passing Nonincremental Policy: Presidential Influence in Congress, Kennedy to Carter," *Congress & the Presidency* 9 (Winter 1981–82), p. 68.

Political Capital

Presidents clearly suffer when they must work with congressional majorities from another party. Though party discipline may have declined over the past two decades, parties still determine who chairs the key committees and who controls the legislative calendar. According to George Edwards, party seats in Congress and public popularity are the sine qua non of presidential influence. In somewhat of an understatement given his analysis of congressional support scores, Edwards writes that members of the president's party in Congress "tend to give him more support than members of the opposition party. While much of this support is due to shared policy preferences, on some issues the pull of party affiliation provides the president with additional support."[12] For Edwards, public approval is the key resource. Since presidents cannot do much to increase their majorities once in office (when vacancies arise through death or resignation, state governors appoint Senate seats, and special elections fill empty House seats) Edwards advises that "a president interested in increasing his congressional support should not overlook the influence potential of his popularity. In other words, he should attempt to influence members of Congress indirectly by strengthening his support among the American people . . . members of Congress do respond to public opinion."[13]

The Johnson and Ford administrations are two cases in point. In explaining Johnson's phenomenal political success in 1965, Joseph Cooper and Gary Bombardier suggest that "whatever skills Johnson displayed, the critical element in his success was primarily a large reservoir of sympathetic fellow partisans on which to draw." When Cooper and Bombardier compare Kennedy's problems in 1963 to Johnson's success only two years later, they conclude that

> the degree of party cohesion among House Democrats on issues on which the president took a stand did not increase significantly from the Eighty-seventh to the Eighty-ninth Congress. Nor, as we might expect, did the degree of presidential support. We may therefore conclude that increased partisan support is not the critical variable for explaining the higher degree of success that Johnson enjoyed.

The conclusion is obvious: If Johnson did not win because of more support from the same members, he must have won because of roughly the same support from still more Democratic members. Indeed, as Cooper and Bombardier write, "Johnson, by maintaining the same level of support as Kennedy, could win victories denied to Kennedy because he was drawing on a larger population of fellow partisans, a population in which the northern Democrats alone could come very close to furnishing all the votes needed for a majority."[14]

The situation with Ford was just the opposite. Starting his abbreviated term in 1974 with his dramatic pardon of Nixon, the president who had appointed him, Ford's public support plummeted. According to the Gallup Organization, Ford's approval rating fell 30 points between August 19 and December 12, the fastest decline ever recorded by Gallup. By the end of his three-month "honeymoon," Ford had vetoed 27 bills. And when the mid-term congressional results were counted, Ford had lost 34 seats in an already thin and divided Republican House minority. As a former minority leader, Ford was certainly well liked on Capitol Hill. Nevertheless, he could only count on 144 Republicans in the House, the lowest level of support of a sitting president in this century. It is hard to imagine a lower legislative "bank account"—little public support, a dwindling minority in Congress, and a public still fascinated by the Watergate scandal. It should come as no surprise that Johnson succeeded with roughly 60 percent of his nonincremental proposals, while Ford could barely cross 20 percent.

Broadly defined, political capital rests upon party seats, public approval, and the president's initial electoral margin. All three have an apparent impact on the president's nonincremental success, as Table 12–3 shows. Public approval is measured by the Gallup Opinion Index at the time when a specific proposal is sent to Congress by OMB; party seats are the combined number of what Cooper and Bombardier call "fellow partisans" in the president's party in the House and Senate; vote margin is the popular vote percentage that the president received in the most recent presidential election.

TABLE 12–3 Policy Content and Congressional Passage by Presidential Resources, Kennedy to Carter

	Percent Passage		
Variable	Spending Programs	Large Programs	New Programs
Vote margin			
Below 50 percent	45%	37%	36%
50 to 60 percent	47	50	50
Above 60 percent	59	61	53
Party seats in Congress			
Below 50 percent	25	28	24
50 to 65 percent	49	48	47
Above 65 percent	70	67	67
Public approval			
Below 50 percent	35	30	38
50 to 60 percent	26	29	24
Above 60 percent	65	61	56

Note: N = 163 for new programs; N = 131 for large programs; N = 127 for spending programs.

SOURCE: Paul C. Light, "Passing Nonincremental Policy: Presidential Influence in Congress, Kennedy to Carter," *Congress & the Presidency* 9 (Winter 1981–82), p. 73.

The data clearly attest to the role of political resources in shaping legislative influence. It is clear why Nixon and Ford did so poorly. Nixon's first election was by the slimmest of pluralities; his second election was tainted by Watergate and falling public approval; Ford was never elected at all; and both faced huge Democratic majorities in Congress. A president's nonincremental influence starts with the presidential vote margin and party seats in Congress, and is further strengthened by public approval.

Economic and Institutional Climate

If political capital shapes the broad possibilities for presidential influence, the economic climate conditions congressional support for specific nonincremental policies. During the 1950s, for example, inflation averaged only 2 percent per year. It crept up slowly in the 1960s, but quadrupled in the mid- to late-1970s. Whereas wages adjusted for inflation moved up 27 percent during the 1950s and 18 percent during the 1960s, they actually fell 2 percent during the 1970s. To the extent Congress pays attention to those kinds of statistics—and there is no doubt that it does—perhaps it punishes the president in charge. And to the extent Congress becomes more cautious about federal spending and the role of deficits in poor economic performance, perhaps it restricts presidential action on nonincremental proposals.

Clearly, the 1970s raised the stakes of presidential policymaking. Whereas money seemed no object in the 1950s and 1960s, Congress may have grown increasingly concerned about federal dollars, especially for huge nonincremental initiatives. In protecting highly popular programs like social security and medicare from the budget ax, Congress may have become less willing to consider new initiatives like welfare reform.

One way to measure the impact of economic climate on presidential success is to look at specific performance. As Table 12–4 shows, neither the budget deficit nor the unemployment rate seems to have much of an impact on a president's nonincremental success. That said, inflation appears to matter a great deal. When inflation is running hot, Congress is less than half as likely to pass spending programs, and, according to Table 12–4, not at all willing to pass large-scale initiatives. Reagan's 1981 budget cuts would seem to be an exception until we realize that the legislation involved *reverse spending*, wholesale cuts in the face of double-digit inflation in the wake of the Carter administration.

There is no doubt that Nixon, Ford, and Carter faced a more intense battle for federal funds than either Kennedy or Johnson. Some of the pressure came from the steady drop in spending flexibility that followed implementation of Johnson's Great Society. As clients discovered the new federal programs, spending moved inexorably up. Some of the press came from the fact that Congress put the federal government on automatic pilot, indexing an increasing number of programs to rise with inflation. Unfortunately for the federal budget deficit, Congress found no reason to index revenues to rise as

TABLE 12–4   Policy Content and Congressional Passage by the Economic Climate, Kennedy to Carter

	Percent Passage		
Variable	Spending Programs	Large Programs	New Programs
Federal budget deficit			
Below $10 billion	54%	51%	51%
$10 billion to $30 billion	43	41	29
Above $30 billion	47	50	50
Unemployment rate			
Below 4 percent	32	37	33
4 to 6 percent	61	53	51
Above 6 percent	46	52	47
Inflation rate			
Below 3 percent	68	64	62
3 to 6 percent	36	48	39
6 to 9 percent	33	21	25
Above 9 percent	25	0	13

Note: Unemployment and inflation are based on the average rates for the year *prior* to introduction.

N = 163 for new programs; N = 131 for large programs; N = 127 for spending programs.

SOURCE: Paul C. Light, "Passing Nonincremental Policy: Presidential Influence in Congress, Kennedy to Carter," *Congress & the Presidency* 9 (Winter 1981–82), p. 74.

fast. With more and more of the federal budget *uncontrollable*—that is, not easily subject to change on a year-to-year basis—Congress and presidents had less money to spend for new programs.

With the economy in decline by the mid-1970s, with budget deficits steadily rising, Congress became more interested in protecting old programs at the expense of new ideas. Given a choice between social security increases and Carter's welfare reform, Congress protected its constituents. Moreover, Nixon, Ford, and Carter often criticized Congress for overspending, even as they proposed major new spending programs like national health insurance and increased education funding. Though the amounts seem small in this era of trillion dollar budgets, Nixon fought to keep Congress from passing the $250 billion threshold. When Congress refused, Nixon greatly expanded the use of presidential impoundment of funds. As Allen Schick looks back,

> After he lost the spending limitation battle in 1972 but won the election, President Nixon embarked on a large-scale effort to overturn the priorities established by Congress. Far from the administration routine, Nixon's impoundments in late 1972 and 1973 were designed to rewrite national policy at the expense of congressional power and intent. Rather than the deferment of expenses, Nixon's aim was the cancellation of unwanted programs.[15]

In such a tense economic and budgetary climate, few would expect gleeful congressional support for Nixon's nonincremental requests. Rather, Congress gave Nixon the Budget and Impoundment Control Act in 1974, passing a sweeping budget reform over Nixon's veto.

Ultimately, the economic climate may have its greatest impact in shaping the range of politically acceptable programs. As the economic climate became more unpredictable during the 1970s, presidents had less operating room. With the rise of *stagflation*, a blend of unemployment and inflation, budget cuts and national sacrifice became part of the economic agenda; easy enough for Republicans, who had long advocated tight budgets, but very difficult for Democrats, who had long advocated federal spending as an economic stimulus. Higher gasoline prices, welfare reform, hospital cost containment, social security and budget cuts are not the kinds of programs to get a Democrat elected, yet there they were on Carter's agenda. In contrast to the spending programs that dominated Johnson's Great Society, Carter faced a new set of "constituentless" issues that had few advocates. Moreover, whereas Johnson pushed medicare and aid to education and model cities, Carter was forced to choose national health insurance or welfare reform or energy.

Just as the economic climate affects support for specific proposals, the fragile institutional relationship between Congress and the presidency provides a broad historical context for understanding differences in presidential eras. Carter, for example, entered the White House during a period of profound congressional assertiveness. One can scarcely imagine a more difficult moment to be president. Following the War Powers Resolution of 1973, which restricted the president's maneuverability in foreign policy, and the Budget and Impoundment Control Act of 1974, Congress pressed for an ever greater role in setting national policy. Armed with the legislative veto as a device for disciplining the executive branch, Congress was quite willing to move forward with or without presidential leadership. According to Fishel, "A Democratically controlled Congress, which had been struggling against Republican presidents for eight years, was also 'reforming' itself so as to maximize decentralized power sharing. Thus Congress inevitably would be more competitive with the presidency for agenda control in the late 1970s, even with a Democratic president. A significant increase in major, change-oriented proposals came on top of 'business as usual' in a Congress long adjusted to fewer, less sweeping proposals from the White House."[16]

This newfound independence was aided and abetted by a new kind of member. In 1974, the new generation of younger Democrats made its first appearance in Congress, bringing a new style of political leadership to Washington. As Burdett Loomis writes, that class "helped to mold, through their work and wit, a new style that has come to dominate contemporary American politics. This style emphasizes the entrepreneurial behavior of individual politicians, based in large part on the substantial resources that all members of Congress—not just top leaders—now have at their disposal."[17] The new style was, and remains, entrepreneurial. Members are willing to fight for a scarce space on the congressional agenda, even if that means dislodging a president's nonincremental request. As Lloyd Cutler, a top Carter aide, wrote of Congress at the end of the term, the legislative process had become so prone to "gridlock" that nothing short of constitutional reform would do:

> There have been the well-intended Democratic reforms of Congress, and the enormous growth of the professional legislative staff. The former ability of the president to sit down with ten or fifteen leaders in each House, and to agree on a program which those leaders could carry through Congress, has virtually disappeared. The committee chairmen and the leaders no longer have the instruments of power that once enabled them to lead. A Lyndon Johnson would have a much harder time getting his way as majority leader today than when he did hold and pull these strings of power in the 1950s.[18]

If Carter operated in an era of congressional ascendancy, Reagan inherited an entirely different climate. Within two years of his election, the Supreme Court had declared the legislative veto unconstitutional, invalidating in one sweeping decision more legislation than in the history of the United States. Moreover, congressional activism, while by no means dead, was certainly at rest (recall the difference between Carter and Reagan in the number of bills competing for agenda space).

These kinds of institutional stakes clearly make a difference for nonincremental success. They are almost impossible to measure in a statistical sense, but are important nonetheless. The more a president must compete, the lower the potential for influence. Due to congressional changes almost entirely outside his control, Carter was president at the nadir of possible influence. Though he certainly had the requisite number of Democrats in Congress, he was working against a congressional norm of independence.

The Focusing Skill

Ultimately, once a president's political resources are set, nonincremental success rests on the ability to focus congressional attention on specific requests. It is not enough merely to present the proposals to Capitol Hill. Presidents must tie their political resources to their top priorities. Presidents can ask for everything, but Congress will rarely comply; just as presidents make choices among competing claimants and priorities, so too must Congress. As one Ford congressional liaison expert said, "Congress needs time to digest what the president sends; time to come up with independent analysis; time to schedule hearings and markups. Unless the president gives some indication of what's truly important, Congress will simply put the proposals in a queue."

Thus, legislative focusing becomes a critical intervening variable in congressional influence. It can never be as important as political resources in determining outcomes—after all, by definition, focusing involves linking proposals to resources. Yet, without focusing, Congress may drift aimlessly from one presidential proposal to the next with no idea of which to concentrate on first. As such, the focusing skill is a strategic device, not a specific tactic. It involves a host of techniques—from arm-twisting to patronage to vote-trading—but sums to a strategy of gaining congressional attention.

The focusing skill has been neglected in past studies of presidential influence in Congress, mainly because political scientists prefer to focus on the separate tactics of focusing instead of the broader strategic skill. Consider Edwards' sober analysis for the impact of legislative skills:

> Presidential legislative skills do not seem to affect support for presidential policies despite what conventional wisdom leads us to expect. Sources of information about presidential-congressional relations, particularly the press, seem to have focused upon the more unique examples of these relations, implying that what they were presenting was typical.[19]

In contrast, consider former vice president and Minnesota Senator Hubert H. Humphrey's analysis of Carter's legislative problems as reported by Carl Brauer:

> You see, part of Carter's problem is that he really doesn't know the little characteristics of our colleagues up here. You've got to know what makes 'em tick, you've got to know their wives, you've go to know their families, you've got to know their backgrounds. You know, I used to say Johnson was a personal FBI [Federal Bureau of Investigation]. The son of a gun was incredible, but so was Kennedy, and so in a sense was Ford. All of the last four presidents [preceding Carter] were creatures of Congress. Kennedy, Johnson, Nixon, Ford—when they went to the White House, they had connections up here, buddy-buddy connections.[20]

So who is right? Former Senator Humphrey or political scientist Edwards? To answer that question it is necessary to define focusing as a two-part skill. The first part of focusing is timing, that is, the president's ability to set the legislative agenda early in the term, while avoiding unnecessary delays caused by overloading in key congressional committees and unproductive controversy. The ability to move quickly depends on both the president's own preparation for office and sheer luck—how much has the president's party done in the past Congresses, how fast is the new White House staff? Reagan's remarkable speed in 1981, for example, appears to reflect the impact of one highly motivated appointee, David Stockman, at that time director of the Office of Management and Budget. If the president and his appointees do not move fast, the congressional calendar will fill on its own. As Lyndon Johnson told his biographer Doris Kearns:

> A measure must be sent to the Hill at exactly the right moment and that moment depends on three things: first, on the momentum; second, on the availability of sponsors in the right place at the right time; and, third, on the opportunities for neutralizing the opposition. Timing is essential. Momentum is not a mysterious mistress. It is a controllable fact of political life that depends on nothing more exotic than preparation.[21]

As if to prove Johnson right, Carter did exactly the opposite in 1977, moving dozens of bills to Congress simultaneously, clogging the Senate Finance and House Ways and Means Committees with a series of complicated proposals, and producing little by way of success. As Carter's chief of staff Hamilton Jordan later lamented,

> I think the option would have been to set very limited goals and objectives this first year, and that was never in the cards. . . . If we had . . . we could be beating our chests now and claiming to have batted 1,000 percent. Instead, we tried to do twenty or thirty things, and it is difficult to present a coherent picture to the American people as to what you are about and why you're trying to do so many things. . . . I don't think we have presented a very coherent picture.[22]

The second part of focusing is lobbying pressure. As Johnson argued, "Merely placing a bill before Congress is not enough. Without constant attention from the administration, most legislation moves through the congressional process at the speed of a glacier."[23] As noted above, there are a number of lobbying tactics at a president's disposal. Some are carrots, others sticks. In 1981, for example, Reagan spared a Tennessee nuclear plant from his budget cuts because Senate Majority Leader Baker just happened to represent the state. OMB Director Stockman told the *Atlantic* of his frustration in not being able to cut the project: "I didn't have to get rolled. . . . I just got out of the way. It just wasn't worth fighting. This package will go nowhere without Baker, and Clinch River is just life or death to Baker."[24] Stockman eventually cut the funding, but not until after Baker had voted for the 1981 package.

The choice of one lobbying tactic over another depends on circumstances and opportunities. It also depends on a president's own skill. Johnson was very effective at bullying legislators; Carter was generally perceived as a weakling. Whatever the specific tactic, lobbying pressure is a crucial signal for staking the president's prestige and resources to specific bills. Timing and lobbying appear to make a difference in a president's nonincremental success, as Table 12–5 indicates. Timing is measured by the date on which a given proposal was cleared through OMB. Lobbying is defined as "active" if (*a*) a given proposal was mentioned in more than one State of the Union message, and (*b*) if there is at least some legislative history of presidential lobbying (for example, in newspaper reports). Obviously, these are very simple definitions of focusing. Yet, as Table 12–5 shows, even bluntly measured, focusing makes a very clear difference.

Moving quickly is important. In nonincremental policy, two themes are clearly apparent. First, presidents must "move it or lose it." There is no advantage to waiting. Second, presidents face a congressional process where "first come, first served." Reagan certainly adhered to these two themes in his presentation of budget and tax cuts to Congress. Indeed, as Stockman wrote in a transition memo, utmost speed was necessary to avoid a Republican "Economic Dunkirk":

Things could go very badly during the first year, resulting in incalculable erosion of GOP momentum, unity, and public confidence. If bold policies are not swiftly, deftly, and courageously implemented in the first six months, Washington will quickly become engulfed in political disorder commensurate with the surrounding economic disarray. A golden opportunity for permanent conservative policy revision and political realignment could be dissipated before the Reagan administration is even up to speed.[25]

More than any other person in the administration, Stockman knew how important it was to move quickly. And because Stockman controlled the budget process, he had the leverage to translate his views into tangible proposals. Stockman knew the importance of focusing.

Yet, if presidents must move quickly, they must also pay attention to the potential for delay in the congressional process. Sometimes a president must say no to one proposal in order to protect the rest of the legislative agenda. Kennedy decided to hold back on civil rights in 1961; Johnson delayed his proposal for home rule in the District of Columbia in 1965; Reagan pulled back on social security reform in 1981. Unfortunately for Carter, he held back on nothing, loading up Congress with all of his requests at once. Compared with Kennedy or Johnson, Carter did not send a particularly heavy plate of proposals in his first year. Rather, it was the *perception* of overloading that hurt.

Moreover, at a time when a Democratic Congress was struggling to work through its eight-year backlog of legislation—a backlog developed under two veto-prone Republicans, Nixon and Ford—the lack of some sense of Carter's priorities was a source of confusion and outrage on Capitol Hill. Who was

TABLE 12–5 Policy Content and Congressional Passage by Presidential Skills, Kennedy to Carter

	Percent Passage		
Variable	Spending Programs	Large Programs	New Programs
Year announced			
First	71%	64%	55%
Second	53	40	39
Third	24	28	40
Fourth	40	40	31
Lobbying			
Active	66	61	63
Passive	47	40	36

Note: N = 163 for new programs; N = 131 for large programs; N = 127 for spending programs.

SOURCE: Paul C. Light, "Passing Nonincremental Policy: Presidential Influence in Congress, Kennedy to Carter," *Congress & the Presidency* 9 (Winter 1981–82), p. 76.

this Georgia upstart who thought Congress had nothing better to do than await the president's agenda? Didn't he realize congressional Democrats had their own ideas?

If a president cannot move in the first year, it may be best to wait until the fourth. Congress may be more willing to consider large-scale and new programs in an election year, if only to take home a fuller record for the fall campaigns. Also, presidents do better when they send active signals of their priorities through lobbying. It is always possible that presidents only lobby the proposals they think will win, creating the illusion of lobbying impacts in the data. Nonetheless, lobbying and timing seem to increase the impact of political resources regardless of a president's starting point—as Table 12–6 demonstrates.[26]

As the data underpinning Table 12–6 also show, the only recent president who was not helped by lobbying was Ford. Indeed, Ford actually did better when he did not lobby Congress, reflecting the impact of his veto activity. Recall that Ford vetoed 27 bills in his first three months alone. When he returned to Congress for his own limited agenda, Congress could hardly be faulted for saying no.

CONCLUSION: WIN BIG AND LOBBY HARD

The crucial question for presidents is to determine how these various factors fit together. What comes first, political capital or institutional climate? What comes last, economic climate or focusing? A reasonable chain of rela-

TABLE 12–6   Relationship between Presidential Resources and Passage, Controlling for Skills, Kennedy to Carter (new programs only)

| | Percent Passage | | | | | |
| | Lobbying | | Year Introduced | | | |
Resource	Active	Passive	1st	2nd	3rd	4th
Public approval						
Below 50 percent	57%	26%	*	50%	44%	22%
50 to 60 percent	43	18	44%	27	14	—
Above 60 percent	69	47	57	42	—	—
Party seats in Congress						
Below 50 percent	36	23	33	10	11	—
50 to 65 percent	59	36	54	50	52	29
Above 65 percent	78	56	76	48	—	—

Note: N = 163 for new programs.

*Less than 5 cases.

source: Paul C. Light, "Passing Nonincremental Policy: Presidential Influence in Congress, Kennedy to Carter," *Congress & the Presidency* 9 (Winter 1981–82), p. 78.

FIGURE 12–1   A Model of Presidential Influence in Congress

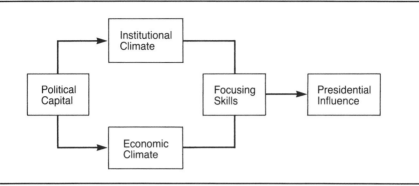

tionships between these different explanations of presidential influence in Congress is outlined in Figure 12–1.

Figure 12–1 clearly places political capital as the determinative factor in presidential success, just about where Edwards would say it belongs. The figure places economic climate, institutional climate, and focusing skills in critical mediating roles, just about where the late Senator Humphrey would say they belong. Climate and focusing can never take the place of political capital, but they can certainly act as intervening factors. Whatever the initial level of political capital, presidents will generally do better if they have a favorable climate and good focusing skills.

Unlike Edwards, who concludes that "There is little the president can do about his degree of influence in Congress" once the president's term begins, I would suggest that a president still has several options.

First, presidents can nurture a favorable institutional climate by giving members of Congress opportunities to achieve their own goals. Presidents are wise to look for ways to share the credit. The days when presidents can set the legislative agenda without consulting Congress are long over.

Second, presidents are well advised to set their agendas early in the term. There is simply no substitute for getting the top priorities to the Congress on time. Because such a strategy puts remarkable pressure on the transition into office, presidential candidates ought to give strong consideration to advance planning during their campaigns. Candidates should eschew the old notion that planning must await the election. Too much is at stake.

Third, presidents should staff their legislative liaison operations early and with top talent. Carter's choice of a relative outsider to lead his congressional liaison office was a fundamental mistake. In that regard, Senator Humphrey was absolutely right: A president must have someone in charge who knows the ins and outs of Congress.

Fourth, presidents should pay heed to the importance of personal relations in dealing with members of Congress. Whether the impact of personal favors and charm show up in the data or not, Washington is a city of political egos. While stroking members of Congress may not provide the margin of victory on specific bills, not stroking can most surely provide the margin of defeat. By itself, presidential barbecues and helicopter rides matter little, of course. As part of an overall strategy of focusing, even the smallest of favors can make a remarkable difference.

Finally and perhaps most important, presidents ought to remember that Congress is a thinking institution. Presidents may not understand quite what kind of thinking Congress does, but they should remember that Congress watches for signals of interest and intent. Congress is not a black box through which presidential proposals pass without inspection. It is a human institution with a broad array of goals and beliefs, not the least among them that presidents should provide signals and strokes.

Thus, whatever the current fashion, skills and leadership do matter. For those who enjoy the intrigue of Washington politics, the message is comforting: It still makes a difference. For those who worry about the lack of presidential-congressional cooperation, the message is more complex. Cooperation depends on far more than constitutional intent. Whether Carter would have done better in a parliamentary system is doubtful. After all, even prime ministers need focusing skills. Moreover, the Founding Fathers clearly understood they were harnessing a political *process*, a fact all too familiar to contemporary American presidents.

NOTES

Author's note: Parts of this chapter are based on my article "Passing Nonincremental Policy: Presidential Influence in Congress, Kennedy to Carter," *Congress & the Presidency* 9 (Winter 1981–82). That article benefited from the insights of the journal's editors, Susan Webb Hammond and Jeff Fishel. Unattributed quotations are from the author's interviews for this research.

1. George C. Edwards, *Presidential Influence in Congress* (San Francisco: W. H. Freeman, 1980), p. 202.
2. Lyndon Baines Johnson, *The Vantage Point: Perspective on the Presidency, 1963 to 1969* (New York: Holt, Rinehart & Winston, 1971), p. 461.
3. Paul R. Schulman, "Nonincremental Policy Making: Notes Toward an Alternative Paradigm," *American Political Science Review* 69, (December 1975), p. 1355.
4. Ibid., p. 1356.
5. Ibid., p. 1357.
6. Ibid., p. 1355.
7. John Campbell, "The Old People Boom and Japanese Policymaking," paper prepared for delivery at the annual meeting of the American Political Science Association, New York, 1978, p. 3.
8. Martin Anderson, *Welfare: The Political Economy of Welfare Reform in the United States* (Stanford, Calif.: Stanford University Press, 1978), p. 7.
9. Jeff Fishel, *Presidents and Promises* (Washington, D.C.: CQ Press, 1985), p. 94.

10. Roger H. Davidson and Thomas Kephart, "Indicators of House of Representatives Workload and Activity," Report No. 85–136S, Congressional Research Service, June 25, 1985.

11. John H. Kessel, "The Parameters of Presidential Politics," *Social Science Quarterly* 55 (June 1974), p. 9.

12. Edwards, *Presidential Influence*, p. 81.

13. Ibid., pp. 109–10.

14. Joseph Cooper and Gary Bombardier, "Presidential Leadership and Party Success," *Journal of Politics* 30 (November 1968), pp. 1014–15.

15. Allen Schick, *Congress and Money: Budgeting, Spending, and Taxing* (Washington, D.C.: Urban Institute Press, 1980), p. 46.

16. Fishel, *Presidents and Promises*, pp. 94–95; for an all encompassing study of this period in congressional history, see James L. Sundquist, *The Decline and Resurgence of Congress* (Washington, D.C.: Brookings Institution, 1981).

17. Burdett A. Loomis, *The New American Politician* (New York: Basic Books, forthcoming), draft chapter 1, p. 5.

18. Lloyd N. Cutler, "To Form a Government," *Foreign Affairs* 59 (Fall 1980), p. 132.

19. Edwards, *Presidential Influence*, p. 202.

20. Quoted in Carl M. Brauer, *Presidential Transitions: Eisenhower Through Reagan* (Cambridge, Mass.: Harvard University Press, 1986), p. 202.

21. Doris Kearns, *Lyndon Johnson and the American Dream* (New York: Harper & Row, 1976), pp. 236–38.

22. Quoted in *National Journal*, January 14, 1978, p. 46.

23. Johnson, *Perspectives*, p. 448.

24. Quoted in William Greider, "The Education of David Stockman," *Atlantic*, December 1981, p. 36.

25. Reprinted in the *Washington Post*, December 14, 1980.

26. Because of the small number of cases involved in splitting the box score by so many cuts, I have restricted the analysis to new programs only.

CHAPTER 13

Fiscal Policy and Congressional Politics

Lance T. LeLoup

President Lyndon Johnson's growing preoccupation with the war in Vietnam in 1966 did not prevent him from worrying about troubling signs in the U.S. economy. The tax cut that had been enacted in 1964 had worked as the president's economic advisors had promised—stimulating economic growth and increasing government revenues even at the lower rates. But increased government spending for the war on poverty at home and the controversial war abroad had initiated an inflationary spiral. The fiscal policy prescription was hard medicine to swallow: raise taxes while holding the line on spending. Could Congress be convinced to take such an action?

Lyndon Baines Johnson had served in Congress almost thirty years, including six years as one of the most powerful majority leaders in the history of the United States Senate. No occupant of the White House had a better feel for Congress or the dynamics of legislative politics. He well knew how difficult it was for Congress to make economic decisions:

> One major source of conflict between the legislative and executive branches is the difference in constituency. The president is concerned with the economic well-being of the entire nation. Congress, by contrast, is the product of 50 states and 435 local constituencies, each representing only one piece of the national jigsaw puzzle. Many congressmen and senators understood my concern for the economy as a whole, but each legislator had one overriding need—to make a record with the people who sent him to office. On the subject of taxes, the people were extremely vocal. Mail on the Hill was running heavily against a tax increase. On many days in 1966 one or another congressman would call me to say that he was with me in spirit—he understood my predicament and sympathized with me, but it would be political suicide for him to support a tax increase.[1]

As will be seen below, Congress finally did adopt a tax increase, but not until 1968. President Johnson, from the vantage point of the White House, identified a fundamental conflict for legislators. While they are concerned with the national economy and want to remain an equal partner with the president in formulating economic policy, these goals are often at odds with local constituency concerns.

For two hundred years, members of Congress have been concerned with promoting prosperity—doing what they could to keep the nation's economy as healthy as possible. Today, no issues in politics are consistently of greater concern to members than economic and budgetary issues. But Congress is a fragmented institution, lacking mechanisms for making coordinated economic policy decisions. Balancing local and national concerns often creates a difficult dilemma for members, causing severe strains within Congress, and testing its decision-making capability.

In this chapter, Congress's role within the larger political and economic system is examined and evaluated. In doing so a number of questions will be examined. In what ways does Congress respond to overall economic conditions? How much influence does Congress actually have in making major fiscal policy decisions? What factors serve to constrain congressional responses. To answer these questions, general patterns of congressional policy responses will be identified as well as the factors that constrain and shape those responses. Some of the most important congressional actions in the post–World War II period will then be examined.

CONGRESS AND THE ECONOMY

The early Congresses concerned themselves with issues such as trade and tariffs to protect fledgling American industries and the establishment of a national bank to promote commerce and protect the currency. In the 1980s, legislators are still concerned about these and many other economic policies. The huge trade deficits amassed in the 1980s have made trade and protectionism key issues, while Congress continues to oversee the Federal Reserve system and monetary policy. Because so many decisions made by Congress affect the economy, many must be excluded; trade, energy, monetary policy and other key aspects of economic policy lie beyond the scope of this chapter. Instead, the focus is on the dimensions of economic policy most systematically dealt with by Congress: *fiscal policy* and the *budget*. Fiscal policy encompasses decisions on taxing and spending which not only allocate money to various purposes, but determine the degree of economic stimulus to be provided by the public sector. Compared to trade and currency questions, these are relatively newer policy concerns. The federal government has had a national budget since 1921[2] and has practiced discretionary fiscal policy since the 1930s.[3] In a relatively short time, they have become some of the most important and most controversial issues that regularly come before Congress.

The Dilemma of Economic Choices

Much of the controversy inherent in budget and economic policy is attributable to the conflict between *macro-level* decision making (setting aggregate taxing and spending totals which address the goals of fiscal policy) and *micro-*

level decision making (allocating moneys to various domestic and defense programs). Sometimes characterized as "the war between the parts and the whole," this tension has never been more apparent than in the 1980s. The desire for low tax rates and high defense spending has proven inconsistent with balancing the budget. As a result, the federal government experienced historically high chronic budget deficits during the Reagan administration and the politics of taxing and spending have been highly contentious.

The tension between macro- and micro-level decisions is reflected in the organization and legislative processes within Congress. For two centuries Congress has made micro-level decisions on program authorizations, appropriations, and specific provisions of the revenue code. These decisions fall under the purview of the authorizing committees, the tax-writing committees, and the appropriations committees working primarily through their subcommittees. Until the 1970s, Congress often made important economic decisions but had no means to make separate decisions on overall levels of taxing and spending. But in 1974, as Congress became more concerned about fiscal policy, budget aggregates, and overall totals, it adopted a major reform in an attempt to improve its ability to engage in macro-level decision making. As will be examined in more detail below, the new budget process included a budget resolution to establish revenue and spending totals. This legislation became the responsibility of the newly created budget committees and the party leaders, and often pitted their interest against those of other standing committees and subcommittees.

Microbudgeting relates most closely to the goals of individual legislators in providing tangible benefits for constituents and improving reelection prospects. Macrobudgeting relates to the collective decision-making capability of Congress, its relative power compared to the president, and its overall capabilities to participate in national economic policymaking. While President Johnson was certainly correct about how difficult it is for members to vote against the wishes of their constituents, Congress often responds to the broader political and economic environment as well as to their individual districts.

Responses to the Political and Economic Environment

The cases that will be examined show that national economic conditions are a powerful stimulus spurring Congress to make macro-level economic and budget decisions. The cases will also reveal that the patterns and effectiveness of congressional actions vary considerably. Three main kinds of congressional responses can be identified:

1. Attempts to clarify economic goals.
2. Specific economic policy actions.
3. Internal reforms to improve macro-level management.

Congress reacts to general economic conditions such as a recession, high interest rates, or high inflation. But it is the political environment as well as the economic environment that shapes congressional actions. Large budget deficits, for example, may have political ramifications as severe as their economic consequences. Political parties and their positions on economic issues, the perceived impact of budget and economic issues on election results, and public opinion about the state of the economy all affect how Congress responds. Other political factors such as party control of the presidency, the House, and the Senate are also critical. As suggested earlier, congressional relationships with the president, including the president's popularity and leadership abilities, significantly affect the nature of the legislature's response to economic conditions.

Congress's response to the political and economic environment is restricted by a number of policy constraints. There are information problems: often conflicting projections and estimates of where the economy is heading and how revenues and spending will be affected. There are questions about the effectiveness of fiscal policy actions: Congress often receives inconsistent predictions on what impact certain policy actions will have. Finally, the past two decades have been characterized by growing fiscal and budgetary inflexibility. As spending and revenues have become increasingly locked in, legislative discretion has decreased. The growth of entitlements such as social security, medicare and medicaid, increasing interest payments by the federal government, and other relatively uncontrollable outlays have limited the degree to which Congress can manipulate the budget to achieve fiscal policy objectives. Some argue that the economy destabilizes the budget more than the budget is used to stabilize the economy.[4]

Political, institutional, and policy constraints create the setting within which Congress responds to overall economic conditions. The cases that follow not only reflect the three kinds of congressional responses and different degrees of effectiveness, but portray an evolving role of Congress in making fiscal and budgetary policy.

The Great Depression and the Keynesian Revolution

The Great Depression of the 1930s was the most dominant economic event of the twentieth century. The crash of the stock market in 1929 was followed by a massive downturn in the U.S. (and world) economy, ravaging the production of goods and services in the nation. By the early 1930s, industrial production had been cut nearly in half while unemployment stood at 25 percent. America was the scene of soup lines and "Hoovervilles": shanty towns of the homeless caustically named after President Herbert Hoover who still believed that government could not legitimately intervene in the private economy.

Hoover's philosophy of the role of government in the economy has long been the dominant one in America. Fiscal orthodoxy of the time demanded a balanced budget and precluded the direct creation of jobs by the federal government. That orthodoxy would soon change in the face of the economic crisis that gripped the nation. The ideas behind the change were supplied by the noted British economist, John Maynard Keynes—hence *Keynesian* economics. Keynes argued that governments could take a more activist role in promoting economic growth by engaging in deficit spending.[5] Introducing the concept of the *multiplier*, Keynes answered critics who demanded a balanced budget by noting that the increased economic growth that results produces increased tax receipts and savings.

Keynes found a willing disciple in President Franklin D. Roosevelt. Keynes' prescriptions paralleled closely the policy actions already undertaken by the Roosevelt administration, providing them with a sounder economic justification. Keynes and Roosevelt met in the late 1930s to discuss the administration's economic plans. While the U.S. economy had begun to pull itself out of the depression under FDR's stewardship, it was World War II that seemed to confirm the effectiveness of Keynes' discretionary fiscal policy. The U.S. government engaged in massive deficit spending to fight the war in Europe and the Pacific. Working through the multiplier Keynes had identified, income and investment expanded rapidly. By 1943, unemployment had fallen below 2 percent.[6]

At the conclusion of World War II, Congress prepared to make an historic change in public policy, mandating a new role for government in preventing any future depressions. The Employment Act of 1946 would be a posthumous tribute to the policies of Roosevelt, who died in 1945, and the theories of Keynes, who died in 1946. Congress was clearly responding to the economic deprivation caused by the Great Depression and to a political environment that demanded government never again let it happen. A general bipartisan consensus had emerged by the end of the war to pursue fiscal policies that would ensure full employment. A full employment plank was included in both the Republican and Democratic party platforms of 1944 and endorsed by both presidential candidates.[7] In the same year, a Roper poll reported that 68 percent of the American people believed that the federal government should provide jobs for everyone able and willing to work but not able to get a job in the private sector.[8]

Support for the concept of balanced budgets was not dead; Conservatives were still uncomfortable, but reassured by the belief that the budget would be balanced at full employment. Beneath the apparent consensus, underlying disputes about the role of government and specific policies to pursue remained. Despite the overwhelming desire to prevent future depressions, these reservations would limit the specificity of declared economic goals and the means for achieving them.

The Employment Act of 1946

The original bill submitted in 1945 was entitled the Full Employment Act, suggesting in certain terms the government's new responsibilities. The proposed legislation was the product of Senate Democrats and their allies in agriculture and organized labor.[9] It declared that "All Americans able to work and seeking work have the right to useful, remunerative, regular, and full-time employment, and it is the policy of the United States to assure the existence at all times of sufficient employment opportunities to enable all Americans . . . to exercise the right."[10] The Senate bill called for a *National Production and Employment Budget* in which the president would use all the economic tools at his disposal to create full employment. If these measures were inadequate, federal jobs were to be created directly. This National Production and Employment Budget would have expanded considerably on the federal budget, translating goals into concrete policy actions.

Despite the acceptance of government's new economic role, partisan and ideological differences remained. The Republicans looked optimistically toward the 1946 midterm elections (after fourteen years of Democratic control) and engaged in highly partisan confrontations with President Truman. From the outset, conservatives were concerned about establishing the basic "right" of all Americans to have a job. The House rejected the strongest provisions of the Senate bill, including the expanding federal budget. Despite the concern about preventing future depressions, what emerged from conference committee was a much more cautious approach. The Employment Act established as a goal of the United States, "to use all practical means" to promote "maximum employment, production, and purchasing power."[11]

The law finally enacted by Congress was much less than the sponsors originally wanted. It established the president's Council of Economic Advisors (CEA) and mandated that the president submit an economic report to Congress each year. In Congress it created the Joint Committee on the Economic Report of the President (later renamed the Joint Economic Committee), but did not give the committee any powers to make economic policies. With the removal of the National Production and Employment Budget, the goal of "maximum" rather than "full" employment was not related to any specific means for achieving the objective. The law recognized full employment as one desirable goal among many and legitimized the use of Keynesian fiscal policy. Congress had established economic goals, but it did not mandate specific policy actions nor create an institutional structure to do so.

The Humphrey-Hawkins Act of 1978

Thirty years after enacting the Employment Act, Congress once again attempted to establish economic goals for the nation. Efforts were spurred by the relatively high unemployment of the 1970s and a desire by liberal Democrats to reaffirm a commitment to civil rights and social justice. Proponents also hoped to move toward more coherent economic planning and better coordination of fiscal and monetary policy. The political and economic environment of the mid-1970s, however, was far different than that of the immediate postwar era. Serious doubts had been raised about the effectiveness of Keynesian fiscal policy because of the *stagflation* of the 1970s: simultaneously high levels of unemployment and inflation. In addition, it was a period of growing skepticism about the growth of government. The so-called *tax revolt* in the states was beginning with the passage of Proposition 13 in California: a rollback and limitation on the amount of taxes that could be collected. Other states followed suit with various statutory and constitutional limitations on the growth of government. A period of retrenchment was beginning, but the Humphrey-Hawkins Act seemed out of touch with this sentiment.

Humphrey-Hawkins was the name given to the Full Employment and Balanced Growth Act, which proposed to make it the right of every adult American to obtain employment at fair rates of compensation.[12] To a large extent, the bill was the product of the individual efforts of former vice president and 1968 Democratic presidential nominee, Senator Hubert H. Humphrey. Humphrey had been reelected to the United States Senate and dedicated himself to preserving some of the social goals of the Johnson-Humphrey administration. He first introduced a full employment bill in 1974; similar legislation was introduced in the House by Democratic Representative Augustus Hawkins from California.[13] Serious congressional consideration did not take place until after the election of Democrat Jimmy Carter as president.

Humphrey and Hawkins held a series of highly publicized public hearings across the country to dramatize the problems of joblessness and to build support for their legislation. Like the production budget of the full employment bill thirty years earlier, the new plan called for the president to submit a budget tied to concrete, quantifiable employment goals: 3 percent within four years of passage (unemployment in the mid-1970s had been as high as 10 percent).[14] Inflation was declared "a major national problem" and price increases were to be "limited and reasonable."

Despite its prominent co-sponsor, the bill languished in Congress until President Carter endorsed the legislation in late 1977.[15] Carter's economic advisors were hostile to the bill but the president was under growing pressure from the Congressional Black Caucus and organized labor. The House took up the bill in early 1978 after significant concessions had been made to conservative and moderate opponents in the Education and Labor Committee. Many of the elements of national economic planning were eliminated, but conservatives continued to attack the inflationary effects of the bill and the provisions calling for the federal government to directly create jobs.

President Carter made a final push, and the bill cleared Congress on October 15, 1978. It was signed into law two weeks later. By the time the Humphrey-Hawkins bill was enacted it no longer contained the automatic trigger mechanism to create federal jobs and it no longer contained provisions strengthening the power and responsibility of the Joint Economic Committee. Yet it remained a high priority to its supporters, for symbolic as much as for substantive reasons. It included two attractive ideas: full employment and better national economic management by which to achieve it. Humphrey-Hawkins included a wish list of desirable national economic goals spelled out in detail, but did not provide the practical means to achieve them. By 1983, the target date for full employment in the United States, unemployment was over 10 percent and budget deficits were approaching $200 billion. The specific goals established by the Humphrey-Hawkins Act were completely abandoned.

The Employment Act and the Humphrey-Hawkins Act were enacted to increase Congress's responsibility for managing the national economy, but largely failed to increase their ability to do so. Although both acts were initially intended to make full employment the primary goal, they were amended to include multiple economic objectives. The Employment Act was passed in response to pervasive public fears of another depression. It largely legitimized policies the government was already taking, but it was a response consistent with the political and economic environment of the postwar period. The Humphrey-Hawkins Act, on the other hand, seems anomalous in the political environment of the late 1970s. While citizens still supported high levels of government services and policies promoting prosperity, they were concerned with growing tax burdens and the general growth of government. Only two years after it was enacted, Republican presidential candidate Ronald Reagan would promise to sharply reduce the role of government and place greater reliance on the private sector as the means to promote full employment and prosperity.

MAKING ECONOMIC POLICY

As the role of the federal government expanded as a result of Keynesian theory and the adoption of countercyclical fiscal policies, Congress has been called on to do more than establish economic goals. The institutional Congress has often made key fiscal policy decisions. Rarely, however, has Congress been the initiator in making fiscal policy. Most frequently, Congress responds to presidential initiatives, balancing members' reading of the political and economic environment with the requests of the White House. The cases in this section demonstrate variations in patterns of executive-legislative policymaking in economic and budget policy, and suggest some of the difficulties encountered when Congress strives to make macro-level decisions.

The Tax Cut of 1948

Although most Republicans supported the Employment Act of 1946, their attention quickly turned to cutting taxes after their takeover of the Eightieth Congress in 1947. Republican leaders set out to enact a 20 percent across-the-board cut in personal income taxes.[16] While President Truman and most congressional Democrats were sympathetic to the idea of reducing taxes, they were more concerned with balancing the budget and preventing any increase in the rate of inflation. The battle over cutting taxes in 1947–48 produced a sharp partisan split over economic priorities in dramatic contrast to the general agreement over the Employment Act. Traditional conservatives were strongly in favor of the substantial tax cut, even though such a cut could potentially lead to a budget deficit. The president and congressional Democrats felt that a balanced budget was essential after massive wartime deficits. The level of conflict over economic and budget priorities was exacerbated by two factors: uncertainty in economic estimates of the impact of a tax cut, and the overall level of partisanship and animosity between the Republican Congress and the Democratic president.

The Truman administration planned to cut federal outlays from $40 billion to $25 billion, but even with this reduction in spending they believed the Republican tax cut would result in a deficit of $2 billion.[17] Republican leaders in Congress, anxious to challenge Truman and determined to take the lead in cutting taxes, passed two tax reduction bills in the summer of 1947. Both were vetoed by Truman and the Republicans were unable to muster the necessary two-thirds majorities to override.

Much of the disagreement was based on conflicting estimates of what the tax cut would achieve. Republicans claimed that even slashing taxes by as much as 20 percent would result in a budget surplus.[18] The administration, employing conservative estimates, disputed these figures. Despite agreement over the principles of the Employment Act passed the year before, the lack of certainty over the impact of macroeconomic actions led to a highly politicized process. Congressional Republicans finally got their tax cut in 1948 with the help of additional Democratic support. It was well timed since the first postwar recession occurred in 1948–49.

The tax cut battles in 1947–48 reflected the relative speed with which economic priorities can change. While unemployment was the main concern in 1945–46, cutting taxes for the Republicans and balancing the budget for the Democrats became the main objectives only a year later. The partisanship demonstrated in this period would be typical of many of the economic battles over the ensuing forty years. The case also reflects the importance of economic estimates and how uncertainty can intensify political conflict. Finally, the case is fairly atypical because of the extent to which Congress took the initiative in economic affairs in opposition to the president. More typically, the president attempts to convince Congress to adopt his proposals, as Lyndon Johnson did in the late 1960s.

The Tax Surcharge of 1968

As revealed in the opening pages of this chapter, Lyndon Johnson and his economic advisors believed that a tax increase was necessary to stem the tide of rising prices in the late 1960s. The president faced the difficult challenge of getting Congress to agree with a politically unpopular tax increase. Only a few years earlier, members had been delighted to support the president's request for a tax cut. A tax increase, of course, was a different matter. The president's advisors recommended raising taxes as early as 1966, but inflation that year did not yet appear serious enough to stimulate much congressional concern. Despite the huge Democratic majorities in the House and Senate, support for the president's proposal was nearly nonexistent. The Democrats lost a staggering 47 seats in the 1966 midterm elections, but prospects for adoption looked better in the next Congress as inflation heated up.[19]

The administration was proposing a tax surcharge—a tax on income taxes paid—in the amount of 10 percent. The key congressional actor was the powerful Chair of the House Ways and Means Committee, Wilbur Mills. At this time, Mills, an Arkansas Democrat, was at the height of his power, controlling the Ways and Means Committee through technical expertise, centralization (no subcommittees), political savvy and a legendary knowledge of the tax code.[20] Lacking any mechanism for making macro-level decisions on budget totals, fiscal policy decisions were largely controlled by the money committees: House and Senate Appropriations, House Ways and Means, and Senate Finance. Wilbur Mills was called the "second most powerful man in Washington," and his support was essential to LBJ's plan.

A fiscal conservative, Mills was concerned about balancing the anti-inflationary tax hike with reductions in federal spending, a position opposed by congressional liberals and the Johnson administration. Texan George Mahon, Democratic chair of the House Appropriations Committee, was not about to allow Mills and his committee to dictate spending cuts. Mills insisted that budget cuts be specified before any tax increase be considered. Mahon and the president wanted to wait until Congress passed the appropriations bills. A compromise on this fundamental issue was not reached until November 1967; then the work of specifying the amount of spending cuts and convincing Congress to go along began in earnest.

As 1968 began, the president attempted to sway Congress by selling the unpopular idea of a tax increase directly to the public through the State of the Union and other public addresses. Yet the tax surcharge bill remained bottled up in committee, with Mills insisting on a package of spending reductions of $6 billion. The president's cabinet felt such a cut was too severe, and would cripple the Great Society programs. Organized labor and northern Democrats in Congress also opposed the $6 billion cut. Johnson's relations with Congress had grown strained because of the war in Vietnam, causing deep splits within the Democratic party. Although, some of the divisiveness caused by the war eased when Johnson made the dramatic announcement that he would not seek reelection in 1968.

Following his speech, the Senate passed an excise bill that included the 10 percent tax surcharge but called for $6 billion in cuts. The issue would now be decided in conference committee. Despite the fact that he was opposed by the president, House leaders, and the House Appropriations Committee, Mills continued to insist on the $6 billion cut. The White House and House Democratic leaders then proposed a resolution to instruct House conferees to limit the cuts to $4 billion. But on May 29, 1968, the resolution was defeated by a vote of 259–137. The president saw the handwriting on the wall, and reluctantly agreed to support the larger cut. The administration considered the tax surcharge absolutely essential to stabilize prices, and shifted its efforts to convince the House to approve the surcharge. On June 20, the final vote came. The House adopted the conference committee report by a vote of 268–150, and the Senate adopted it the next day. The two year effort was over.

Several aspects of the tax surcharge battle are particularly notable. First, it took a lengthy period for Congress to finally adopt the president's key fiscal policy initiative. Whereas the government in a parliamentary democracy could have expected adoption of such an initiative in a matter of months, such timeliness is rarely the case in a system of separation of powers. As it turned out, the tax surcharge and budget cuts were too little, too late; they failed to check inflation in the economy. Second, the case reflected growing policy constraints: imprecision in estimates, uncertainty about the effects of countercyclical fiscal policies, and budget totals growing more rapidly than was intended or desired. Finally, the fragmentation of power in Congress made policymaking difficult. Conflict between Mills, House leaders, and the Appropriations committees reflected a clash of interests, not a coordinated effort to make fiscal policy decisions. Congress finally responded to the economic environment of the nation, but had great difficulty in making "tough" decisions that were perceived as unpopular with constituents. A somewhat different pattern of economic policymaking would emerge thirteen years later when President Ronald Reagan proposed a dramatic change in fiscal and budget policy.

The Reagan Economic Program of 1981

The 1970s were a difficult decade for the U.S. economy. The inflation that upset the Johnson administration paled in comparison to the inflation of the Ford and Carter years. Traditional Keynesian solutions no longer seemed to work, as both unemployment and inflation hit the double-digit range. Budget outlays grew rapidly in the 1970s as federal spending increasingly became composed of entitlements and other mandatory spending. As the next section will show, Congress had attempted to improve macro-level decision making on the budget and the economy by passing the Budget and Impoundment Control Act of 1974. Little did they realize at the time that the new process would be used most effectively six years later to establish a new president's priorities rather than an independent congressional plan.

Not only had the economic environment in the United States changed, but the political environment as well. Ronald Reagan capitalized on the economic frustrations of Americans during the 1980 presidential campaign by asking the question, "Are you better off today than you were four years ago?" Studies suggest that economic discontent was a major factor in Reagan's forty-four state electoral sweep.[21] The Reagan administration took office with a full head of steam determined to make dramatic changes in budget and economic policy; the administration's efforts were headed by a young former member of Congress from Michigan by the name of David Stockman.

The president's priorities included economic, national defense, and political goals. A substantial reduction in tax rates on individuals and corporations was the major economic goal. Such a tax cut was associated with *supply-side economics* as distinguished from demand-side Keynesian fiscal policy. Supply-siders advocated policies that helped the "producers" in society—entrepreneurs and wealthy investors. The second major objective of the administration was a significant increase in defense spending based on the belief that the Soviet Union had made significant advances in both strategic and conventional weapons in the 1970s. Third, the administration wanted to significantly shrink the size and the impact of the federal government. Reagan rallied conservatives with the promise to attack "big government" and return both resources and responsibilities to the private sector. The federal budget would become the engine driving the administration's economic, defense, and political agenda.

The Ninety-seventh Congress (1981–82) had a new look as well. Perhaps the most important change was the Republican majority in the Senate for the first time in a quarter century. Senate Republicans, including new Budget Committee Chair Peter Domenici from New Mexico, were ready to assist the president. On the House side, the Democratic majority had been reduced to just over fifty votes. Oklahoman Jim Jones became Democratic chair of the House Budget Committee which now included several newly appointed conservative "boll weevil" Democrats. Phil Gramm, a Democrat from Texas, would become the administration's key ally in the House.

The administration began its onslaught of Congress quickly. Within weeks of Reagan's inauguration in January 1981, the administration issued a revision of the final Carter budget. The administration requested immediate reductions in fiscal year 1981 spending and major cutbacks in domestic programs and entitlements in the budgets for fiscal years 1982–84. Defense spending was slated for annual increases of 7 percent above inflation, a buildup of $1.8 trillion over five years. A 30 percent across-the-board cut in income taxes was the keystone of the economic package.

Not only was the Reagan administration moving quickly to win adoption of its budget and economic package but it demonstrated a more sophisticated understanding of the congressional budget process than the previous administrations.[22] The *reconciliation* provisions of the 1974 Budget Act (so-called because they were intended to "reconcile" differences between the actions of the budget, tax, and appropriations committees) had been largely ignored in the 1970s. In 1981, they would be moved to the beginning of the process, allowing the packaging of a wide range of cuts into a single, *omnibus,* bill.[23] This would help overcome the usual fragmentation of congressional taxing and spending decisions that made macro-level decision making so difficult.

A lobbying blitz was launched on Congress, with David Stockman testifying before numerous committees to sell the president's program.[24] The first key battle of 1981 came in May over the fiscal year 1982 budget resolution. The Republican Senate quickly adopted the outline of the president's program. House Democrats reported a budget resolution encompassing much of what the president had requested, but it was labeled unsatisfactory by the administration. House Republicans allied with southern conservative Democrats proposed complete adoption of the president's plan in a substitute nicknamed *Gramm-Latta I* after Gramm and Ohioan Delbert Latta, the ranking Republican on the Budget Committee. With the Republicans voting as a solid bloc and joined by sixty-three Democrats, Gramm-Latta I was adopted by a vote of 253–176 on May 7, 1981. President Reagan had won the first battle.

House Democrats, led by Speaker Tip O'Neill, were not ready to concede. They intended to make some changes in the reconciliation bill needed to implement the broad outlines of the budget resolution. The key confrontation of 1981 took place in June. The Democrats planned to vote on the reconciliation plan in six parts, a divide and conquer strategy designed to let committees fight cuts in their own areas. Once again, however, the Republicans and boll weevils substituted their own plan—*Gramm-Latta II*—to win approval of the president's proposals. On June 25, the House adopted the substitute by a vote of 214–208. Gramm and 25 other "boll weevils" provided the crucial margin of victory. The Speaker and the other Democratic leaders were furious. O'Neill fumed:

> I have never seen anything like this in my life, to be perfectly truthful. What is the authority for this? Does this mean that any time the president of the United States is interested in a piece of legislation, he merely sends it over? You do not have any regard for the process, for open hearings, discussion as to who it affects, or what it does to the economy? . . . Do we have the right to legislate? Do we have the right to meet our target or can he in one package deregulate, delegislate, the things that have taken years to do?[25]

Legislative attention shifted to the tax cut, scaled back by the administration to 25 percent, the last component of the president's fiscal package. As they had twice before, the Democrats brought to the House floor an alternative similar to the president's proposals, but unacceptable to the administration. Lobbying was fierce on both sides with an unprecedented willingness to add special tax breaks to win votes. The outcome was the same; the Economic Recovery Tax Act of 1981 (ERTA) was adopted on July 29. The elements of the Reagan economic and budget plan were in place.

In the face of strong presidential leadership and a supportive political environment, Republican and conservative majorities in Congress had enacted major changes in U.S. economic policy. The plan was costly. While defense spending was slated to increase by nearly $2 trillion over the next five years, ERTA cost the Treasury $635 billion in lost revenues through lower rates and a myriad of special tax breaks. Domestic and entitlement spending cuts came far short of compensating the additional defense spending and lost revenue. As the economy plunged into a recession in 1982, the administration's rejoicing was short-lived. The results of the president's economic plan would be steady economic growth after 1983 but combined with annual budget deficits of roughly $200 billion which would double the national debt to $2 trillion by 1985. The deficit dilemma would lead Congress to adopt a radical mandatory deficit reduction plan in late 1985.

INTERNAL REFORMS TO IMPROVE MACRO-LEVEL MANAGEMENT

In the past forty years, Congress has periodically responded to the larger political and economic system by turning its attention inward—attempting to create institutions and processes to allow itself to maintain greater control of fiscal and budget policy. These attempts have most frequently been reactive rather than proactive: responses to near-breakdown, internal fragmentation, political and policy constraints, and the prevalence of individual member interests over collective interests.

Legislative Reorganization Act of 1946

Congress not only enacted the Employment Act of 1946 to institutionalize the goals of fiscal policy and prevent future depressions, but also attempted to centralize its own internal decision making to enable it to play a more equal role with the executive. Statutory changes in the federal government's responsibilities for the national budget in 1921 and for economic management in 1946 had their most dramatic impact on the presidency. Following the adoption of the Budget and Accounting Act of 1921, Congress attempted reforms to make internal decision-making processes more centralized. The interests of the established taxing and spending committees prevailed, however, and no centralization occurred.

In addition to establishing the Joint Economic Committee to receive the president's annual economic report, Congress adopted the Legislative Reorganization Act. Section 138 of the act attempted to establish a legislative budget.[26] A Joint Committee on the Budget was created to take an overview of the president's requests and evaluate overall national needs. The committee was large. It included all members of House Ways and Means, Senate Finance, and both Appropriations committees.[27] By February 15 of each year, the Joint Committee was to report a legislative budget in the form of a concurrent resolution which included a ceiling on total expenditures, a figure for total revenues, and the estimated deficit or surplus.

The attempt to establish a legislative budget took place in the same political and economic environment that characterized the Employment Act and the Republican tax cut plan. It was a reaction to congressional fragmentation, the growth of presidential power, and several years of deficit spending. With the congressional Republicans anxious to flex their political muscle, it was an attempt to centralize congressional decision making and increase legislative power vis-à-vis the president. The attempt to establish a legislative budget failed.

In 1947, the first year of the new process, Congress passed a resolution to slash President Truman's budget requests by $6 billion. A highly partisan controversy developed and the conference committee was unable to agree on any figure. No legislative budget was adopted. While an expenditure ceiling was adopted in 1948, the process lacked any enforcement mechanisms. Appropriations bills adopted by Congress that year exceeded the ceiling by $6 billion. In reaction to the disappointing performance of the previous two years, Congress moved the deadline for enacting a legislative budget to May 15. By then, most of the spending bills had already been passed and Congress did not even attempt to enact a budget resolution. The legislative budget experiment faded away quietly after only three years. Its demise and shortcomings were studied carefully when Congress again attempted to centralize its control over the budget in the early 1970s.

The Budget and Impoundment Control Act of 1974

Forces which would propel Congress to make internal changes designed to centralize macro-level management emerged in the early 1970s.[28] A vast majority of senators and representatives agreed in principal that a new budget process was essential if Congress was to retain a meaningful role in making fiscal and budget policy. Federal spending had expanded rapidly in the 1960s and Congress seemed increasingly incapable of preventing deficits. The traditional authorization-appropriations process was less able to control the growth of expenditures. Authorizing committees expanded the use of *backdoor spending*—automatic outlays that avoided the appropriations committees. Advocacy by the Appropriations committees had become more prevalent and was but one manifestation of the disintegration of the appropriation process. Fewer spending bills were enacted in a timely fashion and the executive branch increasingly operated on temporary or "stopgap" appropriations effected through *continuing resolutions* while Congress struggled to enact appropriations during the fiscal year.

Congressional procedures for dealing with taxing and spending had remained static for many decades despite major changes in economic policy and presidential power. The inability of Congress to take an overview of the budget was increasingly viewed as a fundamental flaw. It prevented Congress from controlling spending and from making responsible fiscal policy decisions by balancing total revenues with aggregate outlays. Lacking an overview mechanism, Congress was unable to debate or establish relative spending priorities. The relative priorities of defense and domestic spending could not be compared. Congress not only lacked the mechanism to make macro-level decisions, but also lacked the adequate information to do so. OMB estimates were greeted with growing skepticism as relations between Congress and the Nixon administration deteriorated. This antipathy toward Nixon, who disparaged Congress's ability to act responsibly and thwarted legislative policy actions by impounding billions of dollars of appropriated funds, finally spurred decisive congressional action. In July 1974, Congress enacted the Budget and Impoundment Control Act by overwhelming margins in both the House and Senate.

The Budget and Impoundment Control Act was an unprecedented attempt to improve macro-level management in Congress.[29] It required Congress to approve two annual *budget resolutions* that established the overall parameters of the budget: total revenues, spending, deficit or surplus, and functional subtotals. The House and Senate *Budget committees* were created to serve as macro-level managers. The *Congressional Budget Office* (CBO) was established to give Congress an independent, authoritative source of economic and budget information. A strict *timetable* was adopted in hope of making the congressional budget more timely. Finally, *impoundment controls* strictly curtailed the president's ability to unilaterally withhold appropriated funds.

Making the bold new budget process work would prove to be a difficult task. The record established between 1975 and 1980 was at best one of mixed success.[30] On the plus side, the process survived. Recognizing its critical importance, leaders emphasized the need to preserve the process at all costs, even if it did not have a dramatic impact on policy.[31] The impoundment control provisions of the act successfully limited the president's ability to thwart congressional priorities by withholding appropriated funds. The quality of congressional information on the budget and the economy increased considerably. The CBO and the House and Senate Budget Committee staffs provided Congress with better, more independent information on macro-level issues. Members became more aware of the multiyear consequences of taxing and spending decisions and the trade-offs between budget and economic priorities. In terms of the balance of power between legislative and executive branches, Congress demonstrated that it could accommodate the president, as it did in 1977, or make some independent judgments as it did in other years.

On the negative side, many problems in macro-level budgeting remained. By the end of the 1970s, deadlines were increasingly missed and waivers became more prevalent. In terms of overall priorities, relatively few major changes occurred. And despite some notable cases of increased fiscal discipline, the budget process did not significantly reduce spending or eliminate deficits. The process itself seemed to polarize Congress. Bipartisan support for the concept of budget reform in 1974 degenerated into partisan conflict over priorities in subsequent years, particularly in the House of Representatives. The new Budget committees, despite some successful challenges of the committees, remained relatively weak. The authorizing and appropriating committees were unwilling to give up their political and policy goals for the sake of macro-level management. The clashes within Congress reflected the conflicting interests of the parts against the whole, decentralized authority versus centralized control, pet programs and policies versus management of the aggregates. Nonetheless, the budget process survived its early test, even if it generally accommodated the spending goals of the standing committees and did not overcome the fragmentation inherent in congressional policymaking. The adoption of the Reagan economic plan in 1981 and the chronic deficits that followed led to another major reform in 1985; one that not only attempted to further strengthen macro-level management but established deficit reduction as the top congressional priority.

Gramm-Rudman-Hollings Mandatory Deficit Reduction Plan (1985)

A decade after the implementation of the congressional budget process and four years after President Reagan used that process to enact his sweeping economic and budget plan, Congress took a dramatic new step. In response to the deficit crisis of the 1980s and the growing deterioration of the budget process, Congress adopted the Balanced Budget and Emergency Deficit Control Act.[32] The Gramm-Rudman plan is an example of all three types of congressional responses to the political and economic environment. It established deficit reduction as the number one policy goal, it provided for a specific mechanism for making economic and budget decisions, and it attempted to once again strengthen the macro-level management capacity of Congress.

Perhaps more than any of the other cases examined, Gramm-Rudman was adopted in frustration. The tax cut and defense buildup undertaken in 1981, whatever their merits on other grounds, helped create record deficits in the 1980s. By 1985, federal debt had doubled to nearly $2 trillion. Congress was caught between an intransigent White House unwilling to raise taxes or scale back its defense plan and its own struggle to make spending reductions that seemed to always fall short of reducing the deficits. Budget inflexibility and the vulnerability of spending and revenue totals to changes in the performance of the economy caused severe strains on the congressional budget process. While a number of informal adaptations in the process took place in the 1980s such as the elimination of the second budget resolution and the institutionalization of reconciliation, the budget process was seemingly incapable of managing budget aggregates. In this context, Congress took a decisive if risky action to cut deficits and shore up its teetering budget process.

A mandatory deficit reduction process was proposed by Republican Senators Phil Gramm from Texas, Warren Rudman from New Hampshire, and Democrat Ernest "Fritz" Hollings from South Carolina in late September 1985. Within weeks it became the dominant issue in Congress. Their plan was to establish fixed deficit targets for the next five years and establish a procedure for mandatory across-the-board cuts if Congress could not reach the targets on its own. Despite reservations about such a mechanical approach to budget-cutting, the lure of deficit reduction was politically irresistible. Three months of partisan haggling produced a bill enacted and signed into law in December 1985.

The amended Gramm-Rudman plan established deficit targets beginning at $172 billion in fiscal year 1986 and dropping to zero by fiscal year 1991 in $36 billion increments. If the targets were not reached, outlays would be *sequestered*—cut across-the-board—to reach the targets. Cuts would be divided equally between defense and domestic programs but a number of programs were exempted or subject to special rules.[33] The process was applied in early 1986 when $11.7 billion was cut from the fiscal year 1986 budget.

While most of the publicity focused on the radical budget-cutting provisions, Gramm-Rudman was used by budget reformers as an opportunity to strengthen the congressional budget process. An accelerated timetable was adopted as well as enhanced enforcement procedures to make it more difficult for "budget-busting" legislation to be taken up on the House or Senate floor. Reconciliation was formally moved to the beginning of the process and the moribund second resolution was officially dropped. As they had a decade earlier, Congress adopted procedures to strengthen macro-level management, to beef up the Budget committees at the expense of the authorizing and Appropriations committees. Nonetheless, as the previous decade had demonstrated, Congress could not legislate away the inherent conflict between members' self-interest in achieving their own political and policy goals and the desire for collective responsibility.

Gramm-Rudman has been a mixed success at best. The Supreme Court struck down the mandatory sequester process and concluded that the role of the General Accounting Office (GAO) violated separation of powers, which left a fallback procedure requiring Congress to certify the cuts before they would take place.[34] The Senate adopted a revised version of the mandatory budget-cutting plan in 1986, but the House refused to go along. The enforcement mechanisms created greater constraints on the spending committees, and the deadlines in the accelerated timetable were missed: the fiscal year 1987 budget was not resolved until early October amid the threat of government shutdown and temporary stopgap spending resolutions. The target was finally reached by using an array of budgetary gimmicks and one-time asset sales, solutions that avoided the long-term deficit problem. Concentrating solely on the deficit, it appeared that Congress's ability to use the budget as a tool of economic management was reduced by the structures and fixed targets of the law. The conflicting priorities continued to clash in 1987 as Congress weighed abandoning or amending the targets versus raising taxes or further slashing both defense and domestic spending.

Despite the shortcomings, Congress succeeded in focusing attention on the deficits. Real outlay growth in the fiscal year 1987 budget was the lowest in decades and a number of major cuts were enacted. Procedural changes had strengthened the Budget committees and party leaders had tightened rules governing floor consideration of taxing and spending bills. The new requirements meant that amendments to money bills had to be "deficit neutral." Amendments reducing revenues or increasing spending had to raise revenue or lower spending somewhere else. These provisions had a profound impact on the legislative consideration of both the comprehensive tax reform of 1986 and the budget resolution.

By the end of the 1980s, Congress had come a long way in reshaping its internal processes, but had made little progress in solving the economic and budget problems themselves. The experience with Gramm-Rudman demonstrates the continued vulnerability of the budget to the economy and the limitations in Congress's ability to eliminate pervasive political and structural problems.

CONCLUSION: THE CONSTANT STRUGGLE

Despite the problems experienced in dealing with macro-level budget and economic problems in the past forty years, Congress has remained a key participant in making national policy. The picture that emerges most clearly is that Congress responds directly and indirectly to both the political and economic environment in the United States. Its responses vary with and are tempered by members' conflicting goals and motivations. Clearly, it is not sufficient to explain congressional performance solely on the basis of self-interested electorally motivated behavior, yet such motivations are essential in understanding the nature and limitation of congressional responses.

Several general conclusions can be drawn. First, macroeconomic stabilization goals are inseparable from distributive budget goals within Congress. Members make trade-offs concerning defense and domestic program goals when they take inflation, unemployment, taxes, and the deficit into consideration. Attempts to isolate goals without providing institutions or processes to achieve them, as occurred with the Humphrey-Hawkins bill, are doomed to failure. Achievement of certain priorities, as the tax cuts and defense increases in 1981, may cause other problems (deficits) which must eventually be addressed. Isolating a single goal, even providing the means for achieving it (Gramm-Rudman), is unlikely to achieve long-term success because of interconnections with other broad economic concerns.

Second, the national political environment is critical in determining both the nature and the effectiveness of congressional responses to the economy. Partisan control of the presidency and the Congress and the popularity and leadership abilities of the president are critical variables. In the 1940s, Republican majorities were eager to impose their priorities over those of President Truman and succeeded, despite his vetoes. In the 1960s, even with his large Democratic majorities and successful record with Congress, President Johnson had to bargain and make concessions to get Congress to adopt the politically unpopular tax increase. By contrast, newly elected and popular President Reagan was able to effectively marshall political resources and use Congress's own budget procedures to enact his economic and budget package in 1981. Yet, four years later, even the Reagan administration was taken by surprise by Congress's dramatic plan to force deficit reductions.

Third, in addition to political and economic factors, policy constraints limit the nature and effectiveness of congressional action. Mandatory spending for entitlements, interest on the debt, and a commitment to build up national defense predetermine outlays to a significant degree. Congress simply has fewer options: Vulnerability to changes in the economy which can increase the deficit by billions presents a sharply different picture than that of Congress using taxing and spending totals to manage the economy. These constraints have served to heighten that tension between macro- and micro-level decision making in Congress as well as heighten executive-legislative conflict.

How does Congress respond to the economy? There are no simple patterns or answers. The cases during the past forty years reveal different kinds of responses with different degrees of effectiveness. On the one hand, economic goal-setting has often been a frivolous exercise in symbolic politics in the absence of realistic means to achieve the goals. On the other hand, the establishment of inflexible methods to achieve a goal such as the Gramm-Rudman mandatory deficit reduction process may simply exacerbate other problems and threaten the health of the economy. Priorities will change, but legislators must retain the ability to respond to competing economic and budget needs.

How much influence does Congress have over economic policy? Despite the problems reflected in the cases, Congress remains a critical partner in making economic and budget decisions. Virtually no other legislative body in the world retains as much control relative to the national executive. This influence varies greatly over time, and is determined by the political and economic environment. Although Congress occasionally takes a leading role, it more frequently responds to presidential initiatives. One consequence of engaging in bargaining and negotiation with the White House is that economic decisions are often made slowly, and the crucial point in time for maximum effectiveness is often missed. This time lag in economic decision making seems an almost inevitable consequence of the American separation of powers system.

Congress not only responds to elections, public opinion, presidential leadership, and national economic conditions but struggles within itself to balance macro-level management with constituency-oriented goals. Despite disappointments with the congressional budget process, Congress has continued to play an important role in economic and budgetary decisions by revising its internal decision-making procedures. While self-interest, reelection concerns, and internal fragmentation continue to create upward spending pressures, processes to manage the whole have come in closer balance with those pressures to expand the parts. The uneasy coexistence of both motives holds the key to understanding economic and budgetary decisions in Congress. As Congress continues to deal with deficits, taxes, economic growth, and program needs, it is an internal struggle that will certainly continue for the foreseeable future.

NOTES

1. Lyndon Baines Johnson, *The Vantage Point: Perspective on the Presidency, 1963 to 1969* (New York: Holt, Rinehart & Winston, 1971), p. 440.
2. Budget and Accounting Act of 1921.
3. Herbert Stein, *Presidential Economics* (New York: Simon & Schuster, 1984). Chapter 2.
4. Allen Schick, "The Budget as an Instrument of Presidential Policy," in *The Reagan Presidency and the Governing of America*, ed. Lester M. Salamon and Michael S. Lund (Washington, D.C.: Urban Institute Press, 1985), pp. 99–102.
5. Herbert Stein, *The Fiscal Revolution in America* (Chicago: University of Chicago Press, 19), pp. 150–155.
6. Robert Gordon, *Economic Stability and Growth* (New York: Harper & Row, 1974), p. 82.
7. Steven K. Bailey, *Congress Makes a Law* (New York: Columbia University Press, 1950).
8. Elmo Roper, *You and Your Leaders* (New York: William Morris, 1957), p. 56.
9. Bailey, *Congress Makes a Law,* Chapter 5.
10. 79th Cong., 1st sess., 1945. The text of S.380 appears in Appendix A in Bailey, *Congress Makes a Law,* p. 243.
11. Bailey, *Congress Makes a Law,* p. 228.
12. Lance T. LeLoup, "Congress and the Dilemma of Economic Policy," in *Making Economic Policy in Congress,* ed. Allen Schick (Washington, D.C.: American Enterprise Institute for Public Policy Research, 1983), pp. 17–21.
13. *Congressional Quarterly Almanac* (Washington, D.C.: Congressional Quarterly, Inc., 1976), p. 371.
14. *Congressional Quarterly Almanac* (Washington, D.C.: Congressional Quarterly, Inc., 1977), pp. 175–76.
15. Ibid., pp. 273–74.
16. Stein, *Fiscal Revolution,* p. 208.
17. Ibid., p. 207.
18. Ibid., p. 211.
19. Johnson, *Vantage Point,* p. 448.
20. Catherine E. Rudder, "Tax Policy: Structure and Choice" in *Making Economic Policy in Congress,* ed. Allen Schick, pp. 196–220.
21. Gerald M. Pomper, "The 1980 Presidential Election and Its Meaning," in *Rethinking the Presidency,* ed. Thomas E. Cronin (Boston: Little, Brown, 1982), p. 22.
22. On several occasions, Presidents Ford and Carter either ignored or were unaware of certain requirements of the congressional budget. See Lance T. LeLoup, *The Fiscal Congress* (Westport, Conn.: Greenwood Press, 1980), pp. 37–46.
23. Allen Schick, *Reconciliation and the Congressional Budget Process* (Washington, D.C.: American Enterprise Institute for Public Policy Research, 1981).
24. Lance T. LeLoup, "After the Blitz: Reagan and the Congressional Budget Process," *Legislative Studies Quarterly* 7 (August 1982), pp. 321–40.
25. *Congressional Record,* June 25, 1981.
26. Jesse Burkhead, "Federal Budgetary Developments, 1947–1948." *Public Administration Review* 8 (Autumn 1948), pp. 267–74.

27. Louis Fisher, "Experience with a Legislative Budget," in *Improving Congressional Control over the Budget: A Compendium of Materials,* U.S. Senate Committee on Government Operations (March 27, 1973), p. 37.
28. See Dennis Ippolito, *Congressional Spending* (Ithaca, N.Y.: Cornell University Press, 1981); Allen Schick, *Congress and Money* (Washington D.C.: Urban Institute Press, 1980); and LeLoup, *Fiscal Congress.*
29. W. Thomas Wander, F. Ted Hebert, and Gary W. Copeland, eds., *Congressional Budgeting* (Baltimore, Md.: Johns Hopkins University Press, 1984).
30. Louis Fisher, "Reflections on the Budget Act after Ten Years: Still Searching for Controls," *Public Budgeting and Finance* 5 (Autumn 1985), pp. 3–28.
31. Lance T. LeLoup, "Process versus Policy: The U.S. House Budget Committee," *Legislative Studies Quarterly* 4, pp. 227–54.
32. Lance T. LeLoup, Barbara L. Graham, and Stacey Barwick, "Deficit Politics and Constitutional Government: The Impact of Gramm-Rudman-Hollings," *Public Budgeting and Finance* 7 (Spring 1987) pp. 83–103.
33. Harry Havens, "Gramm-Rudman-Hollings: Origins and Implementation," *Public Budgeting and Finance* 6 (Autumn 1986), pp. 4–24.
34. *Bowsher v. Synar,* 106 S.Ct. 3181 (1986).

CHAPTER 14

National Security Policy and Congress

Christopher J. Deering

In 1979, President Jimmy Carter presented to the United States Senate a treaty which had resulted from the Strategic Arms Limitation Talks (SALT II) with the Soviet Union. The controversial document, which required the Senate's consent prior to formal ratification, would have significant implications for U.S. national security policy for years to come. By long-standing tradition, treaties presented to the Senate for its consent are referred to the Foreign Relations Committee for initial review and recommendation before being considered by the whole Senate. The SALT II treaty was no exception. But the Senate Armed Services Committee, claiming the treaty had far-reaching effects on matters within its own jurisdiction, also scheduled a set of hearings. This was an exception. Political controversy between supporters and skeptics of arms control had led the more hostile Armed Services Committee to set up an alternative forum to that of the Foreign Relations Committee, a move that was applauded by opponents of the treaty and derided as a breach of tradition by supporters. But this was just the beginning of the bumpy road that would face SALT II.

After weeks of review, countless hours of lobbying, a national campaign to generate grassroots support, and comprehensive media coverage, the treaty finally made it to the floor of the Senate where another round of debate, defense, and potentially crippling amendments would occur. Doubts about the viability of the treaty were now widespread and most observers believed that had the treaty come to a vote it would have been rejected—a defeat of monumental proportions for an incumbent president seeking reelection. But no vote ever occurred because on December 27–28, 1979 the Soviet Union invaded Afghanistan, raising an international furor and prompting the administration to withdraw the treaty from consideration.

While dramatic and in many ways unusual, this series of events is indicative of the range of forces that are frequently brought into play on national security issues. Individual members of Congress staked their reputations, and in some cases their reelection, on the positions they took regarding the treaty. Internal divisions within Congress were accentuated and relations among members became strained. A Democratic president was stymied by a

Congress controlled by his own political party. And all the while, the media, interest groups, and would-be presidents jockeyed for position outside government. This was a highly salient issue that attracted a great deal of national and international attention, and as a result neither Congress nor the president could dominate the policy process.

Congress's role in national security policymaking and the policies which result are a unique blend of individual, institutional, and environmental factors. The purpose of this chapter is to map out the combination of forces which determine Congress's role in national security policymaking and the policies which emerge from that process. The argument, however, is that the central importance of the issue, the nature of our separation-of-powers system, and constitutional ambiguity conspire to guarantee that environmental factors remain the most telling.

NATIONAL SECURITY POLICY AND THE CONSTITUTION

Sharp distinctions between foreign policy and national security policy are traditionally difficult—hence the competition between the State Department and the Defense Department and between Congress's foreign policy committees and its military committees. Even so, foreign policy generally implies the broad range of relations between the United States and other nations. Since these are generally peaceful relations, foreign policy and national diplomacy are typically closely aligned. In contrast, national security policy implies a narrower focus on the physical integrity of the nation—its citizens and its varied interests. National security is, therefore, more closely linked to national defense. Ideally, the two complement each other. A successful foreign policy reduces the likelihood of war; a capable defense establishment enhances and enforces our foreign policy.

Congress has established at least a loose distinction between these two related areas by creating two different committees in each chamber to handle these issues: most foreign policy issues go to the House Foreign Affairs and the Senate Foreign Relations committees while most national security issues go to the House and Senate Armed Services committees. As will be seen, the two sets of committees contest this division on a regular basis among themselves and with other House and Senate committees as well. But for the purposes of this chapter the diplomacy-defense distinction is good enough.

While the Founding Fathers addressed both diplomatic and defense policymaking in the Constitution, they did not bother to make sharp or absolute distinctions. For the Founding Fathers, a more immediate and pressing problem had to be faced: How should, or could, a democratic nation founded upon the novel notion of citizenship conduct foreign and defense policy in a decidedly undemocratic world? The U.S. Constitution marked a radical shift in the relationship of people to their government. But the diplomatic environment of the time was decidedly old-fashioned. The Founding Fathers' solution was made up of several components.

First, the Founding Fathers adopted an approach to foreign and defense policy that can be characterized as *consolidated deterrence*. Consolidated deterrence was a means of combining our national strengths in order to deter foreign aggression. Consider, for example, the words of John Jay:

> If [foreign nations] see that our national government is efficient and well administered, our trade prudently regulated, our militia properly organized and disciplined, our resources and finances discreetly managed, our credit reestablished, our people free, contented, and united, they will be much more disposed to cultivate our friendship than provoke our resentment.[1]

For Jay, national security was best achieved through a common commercial policy, a stable and capable national government, and "discreetly" managed finances. The new, small, and indebted nation had no prospects for world domination and no appetite for international power. Separated by a vast and unexplored frontier to the west and by a wide ocean to the east, they hoped to thrive in relative isolation from the rest of the world. A strong, unified national government and an attendant strength in commerce were the two most important requirements for safety from our British, French, and Spanish rivals. A well-organized militia and a competent navy were added measures of security. At bottom, therefore, the authors of the Constitution did not express a sharp distinction between foreign and defense policy; they were closely related and jointly tied to this consolidated notion of political, economic, and military deterrence.

Second, the Founding Fathers gave to Congress, in Article I of the Constitution, an explicit and lengthy set of foreign and national security responsibilities. These responsibilities include the obvious—declaring war, establishing an army and a navy, controlling immigration, regulation of foreign commerce—and the not so obvious, such as granting letters of marque and reprisal.[2] The Constitution contains only a single explicit limitation on Congress's power in this area: "No appropriation of money to [raise and support armies] shall be for a longer term than two years."[3] In total, the Constitution offers a wide-ranging, clearcut, and explicit grant of authority to Congress where national security is concerned.

Third, the Founding Fathers provided a brief, general, and undetailed grant of authority to the president where national security policy is concerned. The only *explicit* power granted to the president consists of the following:

> The President shall be Commander and Chief of the Army and Navy of the United States, and of the Militia of the several States, when called into the actual Service of the United States . . . [4]

That is it. The president is also granted the "executive power" and admonished to "take care that the laws be faithfully executed." The Constitution does not prohibit the president from doing anything. But it does not grant him any specific authority beyond the role of commander in chief. Hence, the fourth component.

The fourth component of the Founding Fathers' solution to the problem of democratic national security was an "invitation to struggle"—namely, the separation of powers. As in other areas of policymaking, the separation of powers system invites the three branches of government to struggle over national security policy. As indicated earlier, the Constitution gives the upper hand to Congress with its explicit grants of authority, but it also leaves presidents free to carve out whatever authority they can consistent with the "take care" clause. This constitutional arrangement means that none of the three branches can accumulate, for itself, complete authority in any policy area and particularly in national security policy.

In aggregate, these constitutional arrangements ensure that national security policy is not a peculiarly congressional product. Rather, national security policy, like fiscal policy, is at the center of institutional conflict. As a result, it is as much a cause of institutional change as it is a product of institutional change. In the remainder of this chapter three aspects of national security policymaking are examined: the limited role that individual members of Congress play in making and shaping policy, the institutional traits that help determine that policy, and the environmental factors that shape policymaking. The argument presented here is that the nature of national security policy dictates that environmental factors are most important in determining how national security policymaking proceeds and what sorts of policies emerge.

MEMBERS OF CONGRESS AND NATIONAL SECURITY POLICY

It is generally accepted that changes in Congress during the past two decades have expanded the opportunities of most members to participate in policymaking. Within committees the reduced power of full committee chairs opened the way for broader participation among committee members. Likewise, a relaxed atmosphere on the floor also has opened the gates to wider participation. The most obvious indicator of this latter point is the noticeable increase in floor amendments offered by non-committee members.[5]

On balance, however, wider participation means more opportunities to share influence on policymaking rather than the ability to make policy. And this remains especially true in national security policy, an area that traditionally has been dominated by a closed circle of policy aficionados. What remains for the individual member is the ability to take a greater role in the debate of security policy, to offer "attention-getting" amendments, or to join coalitions of other members in an attempt to influence policy. And the available evidence indicates that members are doing just that. In the House, for example, the number of amendments offered and the number of hours consumed during consideration of the annual defense authorization bill has increased steadily during the last two decades.[6] (And even though statistical evidence is not available the same is apparent in the Senate.) The precise cause for this change is not absolutely clear, but broader participation in both chambers on national security issues is obvious.

Consider the following example. In 1982, just three days prior to the filing deadline, incumbent California Democrat John L. Burton announced that he would not seek a fifth term in the House of Representatives. Rather hastily, Barbara Boxer, a member of the Marin County board of supervisors and a former Burton staffer, decided she would seek the seat. Boxer's successful election campaign was based upon a liberal agenda designed to appeal to her heavily Democratic district: opposition to President Reagan's economic policies, support for arms control, environmental issues, employment programs, and women's rights. The district contains the Mare Island naval base and a modest number of constituents employed either at the base or by defense-related contractors, but it is not a classically defense-oriented district. Indeed, to the extent that security issues arise the 6th Congressional District's voters are apparently divided. For her own part, Boxer had little experience with defense issues save a brief experience with civil defense while on the county board.[7] And, upon her arrival in Congress, she was assigned to the Government Operations Committee (with emphasis on environmental issues) and to the Merchant Marine and Fisheries Committee (with emphasis on Coast Guard and other Bay area issues). So, clearly, neither by background nor by subsequent committee assignments was Boxer likely to be a key player on national security issues.

Nonetheless, during her first year in Congress, Boxer was able to persuade the Subcommittee on Military Installations and Facilities chaired by fellow-liberal Ronald V. Dellums from nearby Oakland to spend $16.6 million for Mare Island facilities. The next year, her exposure to the increasingly popular waste, fraud, and abuse issues on the Government Operations Committee led to involvement with legislation on federal government contract competition. And, in 1985, she offered legislation to substantially tighten the restrictions on government employees seeking jobs with private sector businesses with whom they do regular business—so-called revolving door issues. While this legislation was not successful, a weaker version did find its way into the annual Defense Department authorization bill. Also during 1985, Boxer dropped her membership on the Merchant Marine and Fisheries Committee in favor of the much more powerful Budget Committee. Finally, in 1987, she dropped her membership on the Government Operations Committee for a position on the Armed Services Committee.[8]

Several points are worth emphasis here. First, Boxer's ability to influence defense policy while an outsider remained clearly limited. Second, although Boxer's district and background gave her no overwhelming impetus to become involved in defense policy she was able to have an impact even in the absence of a central institutional position (for example, in the Armed Services

Committee). And, third, that lesson apparently led her to the conclusion that a position on the Armed Services Committee would be the best route to more regularized influence on such issues. In sum, while individual motivations to participate may be at work here, an individual's ability to influence legislation that has the scope and visibility of national security policy remains limited to the margins. What, then, can be said about Congress's institutional imprint on national security policy?

CONGRESS'S ROLE IN NATIONAL SECURITY

For some time, most analysts and observers of Congress have argued that Congress's role in national security policy is primarily pork barrel in nature. That is, so long as the military contracts, bases, and other goodies dispensed by the Pentagon continue to flow to the appropriate districts the executive branch can generally have its way on defense policy. National security policy, it was assumed, had become too complicated after World War II for all but a few congressional mavens to understand. Moreover, the nuclear era had necessitated presidential dominance in a policy area that had long divided the two branches. As one senior staff member of the House Armed Services Committee said some years ago, "Our committee is a real estate committee. Don't forget that. If you study our committee, you are studying real estate transactions."[9] In other words, Congress's major influence was felt on the "domestic side" of defense policy—the "real estate side," if you will—while the executive branch predominated otherwise. But how true is that assessment today? What exactly is Congress's role in national security policy today? And has it changed?

Congress's Basic Functions

Congress's role in national security policymaking centers upon two primary activities and a third more passive function: providing *program authority,* providing *budget authority,* and engaging in *oversight.*

Program authority is the legal basis, provided through acts of Congress, for defense activities performed by various agencies of the government, primarily the Department of Defense and the military services. For example, in 1947 Congress passed the National Security Act. Among other things, that act created the Department of Defense, split the U.S. Air Force off from the U.S. Army and established it as a separate military service, transformed the Office of Strategic Services (OSS) into the Central Intelligence Agency (CIA), and created the National Security Council. Authorizing bills have the additional purpose and effect of setting limits on what may later be spent for each of these defense programs. Clearly, program authority, in the form of annual Department of Defense authorization bills, covers a vast array of activities—from buying boots, shoes, and uniforms, to the purchases of multi-billion-dollar weapons systems. At least formally, this means that Congress, subject to presidential veto, may create, alter, or abolish any office, program, or activity undertaken by the Pentagon.

During the past three decades, Congress has steadily increased the number of items that must be reauthorized each year. Traditionally, Congress had been happy to grant to the Departments of the Army and Navy relatively open-ended authority to carry out their respective missions, and there is nothing in the Constitution to bar such open-ended grants. Today, the Department of Defense is not reauthorized each year, but the vast majority of its tasks are. This trend toward "annual reauthorization" began in 1959 with the *Russell Amendment*—named after the chair of the Senate Armed Services Committee, Richard Russell of Georgia—which required that virtually all major items purchased by the Defense Department be authorized or reauthorized annually. Since that time, Congress has gradually and steadily expanded the requirements for annual reauthorization. The intent of such requirements is to keep the Defense Department on a short leash to ensure that Congress has an opportunity to participate in national security policy-making, and to remind the Pentagon that they are ultimately accountable to Congress.

After authorizing various national security activities Congress must then provide the necessary funding for those activities; the process of providing budgetary authority is achieved through appropriations bills. As noted earlier, the Constitution requires that no appropriations for the army can be for a period of more than two years. This particular restriction, which did not apply to the navy, was based upon the colonists' fear of standing armies. And even though that fear is no longer prevalent, Congress has insisted on appropriating virtually all funds for defense and national security, and indeed for all other government programs, on an annual basis—either through regular appropriations bills, supplemental appropriations, or continuing resolutions. The relationship between the authorization and the appropriations process is complex and frequently misunderstood. In general, activities that are not authorized cannot be funded and, though seemingly illogical, funding need not be provided for activities that have been authorized. Hence, every national security activity performed by the executive branch requires two separate and complete legislative enactments.

Once programs have been authorized and funded Congress must also provide some oversight or review of how those programs are being run. In the case of national security programs this is a potentially vast and almost certainly impossible task. Congress's demand for annual authorizations and appropriations is one means of creating at least passive oversight. That is, while each and every aspect of defense policy cannot be reviewed each year, the Defense Department must be prepared to explain what it is up to. It also allows Congress to focus selectively upon perceived problem areas and politically sensitive issues. In recent years waste, fraud, and abuse issues have been particularly popular.

Within Congress, primary responsibility for national security activities is given to the House and Senate Armed Services committees (which write the authorization bills) and to the Defense and Military Construction subcommittees of the House and Senate Appropriations committees (which write the appropriations bills). The job they perform is highly technical, frequently mundane, and unquestionably enormous. Consider, for example, the size of the annual defense budget. For fiscal year 1987 President Reagan requested $320 billion for defense spending in a budget request that totaled $1.1 trillion. Thus, defense spending was a little under 30 percent of the president's request. In response the Congress authorized defense programs worth $291.8 billion and granted budget authority, appropriations, of just under $290 billion. Overall, Congress cut some $32 billion, approximately 10 percent, from the president's initial request.

Institutional Patterns of Policymaking

Randall Ripley and Grace Franklin have argued that there are three different kinds of defense policy—structural, strategic, and crisis—and that each is characterized by a different pattern of politics.[10] One of the chief differences among these three kinds of policy is the level of congressional involvement and its influence on the policy outcomes. Congress's role is pronounced in both *structural* policy (which involves the routine authorizations for procurement, base operations, and a wide variety of other noncontroversial activities) and *strategic* policy (which involves potentially controversial decisions about important weapons systems, the size, capabilities and missions of the various services, or major departures in defense policy). But in *crises,* the president has retained more or less exclusive authority to act along with a relative handful of close advisors.

When postwar analysts describe Congress's role in defense policy as limited to pork barrel or real estate issues it is structural issues that they have in mind. By its very nature structural policy is incremental, distributive, and noncontroversial. It is also the most resistant to change because it is the product of well established and mutually beneficial relationships between the Pentagon, the private sector (including local communities), and relevant congressional committees and subcommittees. These subgovernments, as they are called, tend to dominate discrete areas of policymaking and, as a result, offer Congress its most consistent avenue of influence in national security policy.

By contrast, strategic decisions require initiative, imply change, and are frequently controversial. While virtually all strategic initiatives originate in the executive branch they must be presented to, defended to, and passed by the Congress. Some options, such as the Strategic Defense Initiative (SDI), strike at the heart of existing military doctrine and therefore create considerable debate and controversy. Other options, such as the stealth-technology bomber (or B-2), are highly classified and are able to avoid the spotlight, at least for awhile. But they all require Congress to take new and positive steps, frequently require large sums of money, and therefore mark nonincremental departures in policy. As a result of all this, Congress's role in strategic policymaking tends to be reactive rather than formative. And its reactions can be formidable, as when it cancelled the antiballistic missile system or dramatically limited the MX missile system.

Finally, Congress's role in crisis policymaking is distinctly limited. Its size, procedures, and the limited distribution of sensitive information all militate against regular or effective participation. In spite of these limitations Congress has struggled to expand its role in what might be called "intermediate crises," for example, those that do not require an instantaneous U.S. response or which have the prospect of evolving into large-scale or long-term military actions. The War Powers Resolution of 1973 was intended to help fill the gap and assure that Congress would become a party to any U.S. military action, but in practice it has proven largely unworkable.

In sum, Congress does leave a recognizable imprint on national security policy. It insists on annual authorizations, but it does not have the time or interest to review each and every program. It retains a close (and perhaps a dominant) interest in the domestic side of military policy (e.g., appropriations for military bases). And it reserves the right to obstruct, alter, or refuse major executive initiatives without warning. The system of annual authorization and appropriation is emblematic of Congress's role. It must act positively each year, even if it does not and cannot thoroughly review every program, for the defense establishment to continue to function. In this sense, Congress sets the rules of the game. But since it does not act autonomously, as the evidence provided so far indicates, we must look to external influences that guide and shape congressional action.

CONGRESS'S NATIONAL SECURITY ENVIRONMENT

For a variety of reasons—lack of time, information, or extensive expertise, for example—Congress is in no position to dominate national security policy. Thus, environmental factors must be examined in order to fully appreciate the patterns of policymaking that exist in this area. Congress's national security environment is made up of six dominant components: the executive branch, public opinion, the media, the electoral cycle, interest groups, and the international environment. The effect of each is discussed in detail below.

Executive Branch

Without doubt, the executive branch has been and remains the most potent and important external influence on Congress's role in national security policymaking; this has been especially true since World War II. There are several reasons for this relationship. First, as commander in chief, the president has a direct stake in the defense apparatus available to carry out that role. Second, the nature of defense policy is such that there are no direct private sector consumers of the policy. That is, citizens are either successfully defended or they are not. To be sure, parts of the private sector, primarily defense contractors, benefit from large defense budgets but they do not "consume defense" directly. And third, for at least two decades after World War II the U.S.–Soviet cold war and the threat of a nuclear exchange convinced most policymakers and observers that the president needed unprecedented leeway in policymaking and management. As a result, for two decades after World War II four American presidents enjoyed rather complete cooperation from Congress in both foreign and national security policy, but that relationship ultimately also led to what historian Arthur Schlesinger has called the "imperial presidency."[11]

While the result was not an unalloyed dominance by the president over Congress the circumstances did allow a marked degree of cooperation between the two branches. One indicator of this relationship can be captured by examining the number of presidential proposals approved by Congress in domestic policy as compared to defense policy. The difference is pronounced. From 1948 to 1965, for example, the presidents' success rate in domestic policy was only 40 percent. In contrast, their success rate on defense policy was 73 percent.[12] The difference in domestic policy and foreign and defense policy were so pronounced that Aaron Wildavsky suggested that we actually had "two presidencies"—one in national security and one in domestic policy.[13] Not surprisingly, the controversy surrounding the Vietnam War lowered this success rate rather dramatically and ended the postwar era of cooperation. But even with the heightened degree of competition between the two branches, presidents' success rates in defense policy continued to run comfortably above 50 percent but below 50 percent in domestic policy.

Since the executive branch is the primary "consumer" of national security policy Congress's political environment for national security policymaking is left relatively uncluttered. One means of indicating this is to look at the types of witnesses that appear before the congressional committees and subcommittees in charge of defense policy.[14] Even a quick look at these data indicate a clear executive dominance. Since World War II fully 80 percent of the witnesses appearing before Congress's defense policy committees have been executive branch personnel. (See Table 14–1 for details.) And, while historical data are not available, information from the Ninety-first and the Ninety-sixth Congresses indicates that no committee in either chamber even approached this level and that only the House Foreign Affairs and Senate Foreign Relations committees exceeded the 50 percent level in executive branch witnesses.[15]

Thus, formally at least, Congress's primary source of input on defense policy comes from the executive branch. It is the Pentagon which prepares the defense portion of the budget and it is the Pentagon which is called on to

TABLE 14–1 National Security Witnesses by Type and Chamber: Eightieth–Ninety-eighth Congresses

| | Type of Witness | | | | | | | |
| | Executive | | Legislative | | Private | | Total | |
Congress	H	S	H	S	H	S	H	S
Eightieth (1947–48)	635	458	67	48	268	207	970	713
Eighty-second (1951–52)	1622	763	51	32	156	326	1832	1121
Eighty-fourth (1955–56)	1753	770	52	59	226	235	2031	1064
Eighty-sixth (1959–60)	1467	836	66	91	168	111	1701	1038
Eighty-eighth (1963–64)	1225	401	71	43	260	115	1556	559
Total	6702	3228	307	273	1078	994	8090	4495
(mean)	(1340)	(646)	(61)	(55)	(216)	(199)	(1618)	(899)
Ninetieth (1967–68)	1477	654	56	44	155	66	1688	764
Ninety-second (1971–72)	1763	1396	172	40	257	224	2192	1659
Ninety-fourth (1975–76)	1577	1392	149	79	255	162	1982	1633
Ninety-sixth (1979–80)	1832	1392	178	63	424	191	2440	1217
Ninety-eighth (1983–84)	1525	643	261	28	333	121	2119	793
Total	8174	5048	816	254	1424	764	10421	6066
(mean)	(1635)	(1010)	(163)	(51)	(285)	(153)	(2084)	(1213)

This sample is based on witnesses appearing before the House and Senate Armed Services committees and the Defense Appropriations and Military Construction subcommittees of the House and Senate Appropriations committees during alternate congressional sessions, Eightieth–Ninety-eighth Congresses.

SOURCE: Committee hearings.

defend that budget before Congress. And, although the total number of witnesses on defense policy appearing before Congress has risen there has been no appreciable shift in the proportion of those witnesses made up by the executive branch.

Public Opinion

The second major influence on Congress's role in national security policymaking is American public opinion. Unfortunately, while we know a great deal about public opinion—an area of research that became quite rigorous in the 1950s—we know much less about the specific connections between public opinion and public policymaking.[16] What does seem clear is that public opinion forms an important backdrop against which policymaking takes place, a backdrop which can alternately constrain or push for policy change.

The available research on public opinion about defense and foreign policy suggests that public opinion is the factor least likely to influence members of Congress on a day-to-day basis. In a classic study based on data from the 1950s, Warren Miller and Donald Stokes found that in three broad issue areas—social welfare, civil rights, and international affairs—members of Congress were likely to vote *against* their constituents' opinions in international affairs.[17] Some years later, Aage Clausen came to essentially the same conclusion in his examination of the voting behavior of members of Congress.[18] But Clausen also argued that legislators reflect the opinion of constituents within their districts who are well informed about foreign and defense policy.[19] But public opinion does play a role in national security policy; a general predisposition to support the president can be overridden by intensely held public pressure. Public opinion may not tie directly to the day-to-day decisions made by legislators but it forms a backdrop of support or opposition against which Congress makes policy.

America's two most recent wars—in Korea and Vietnam—provide useful examples of this. At the outset of the Korean War, in June 1950, a comfortable majority of the American public supported the use of American troops.[20] The entrance of the Chinese into that conflict was accompanied by an abrupt reduction in support—25 percentage points—for the use of U.S. troops. Public support for the war continued to decline throughout 1951 but reversed midway through 1952 in the lead-up to Dwight D. Eisenhower's successful election bid, his subsequent visit to Korea, and through the signing of the truce in 1953. Depending on which poll one examines, a slight majority or just less than a majority continued to support our involvement in Korea, but throughout the period a significant portion of the population opposed involvement. The U.S. role in Korea was an important issue in the 1952 elections and helped the Republicans to gain not only an Eisenhower victory but also to gain control of both the House and Senate. Eisenhower was viewed by the public as the best person to end the war and a Republican Congress was elected to support him in that effort.[21] Still, public opinion remained ambiguous, just as the end to the war was ambiguous: Korea was split in two at the 38th parallel. While the war was going badly—and relations between President Truman and General Douglas MacArthur were going sour—the Congress tended to snipe at the president. In contrast, Eisenhower's popular election and the Republican victories in Congress ushered in a renewed period of cooperation.

Our experience during the Vietnam War is much less ambiguous. Public opinion polls in the early 1960s showed a comfortable majority of Americans in support of the use of U.S. troops in Southeast Asia.[22] This support peaked at 64 percent in November 1965 but then reversed as U.S. involvement and battle deaths increased. A complementary rise in opposition to the war began at about the same time and rose steeply throughout the balance of the decade. By 1971, more than 60 percent of the American public opposed U.S. involvement in Vietnam. Congress's policy response, anchored by strong support for Presidents Lyndon Johnson and Richard Nixon, retreated slowly but inexorably. In the end, however, the House and Senate each voted to cut off all funds to support the war and ultimately even U.S. financial support for the government of South Vietnam.

In both of these cases, Congress's response to broad-scale change in public opinion was sluggish. Members of Congress only reluctantly change their minds about public opinion once they have initially made up their minds. But, as the Vietnam example makes clear, substantial change does lead to policy response by the Congress even when that change is opposed by the president.

A similarly lagged effect can be seen in Congress's response to public opinion about the level of defense spending. Throughout the 1960s, a period of rapid growth in defense spending fueled by the Vietnam War, a majority of Americans gradually came to believe that the United States was spending too much on defense.[23] From 1969 through 1975, defense spending decreased while American opinion slowly moved back in the direction of support for increased defense budgets. That sentiment appears to have continued to shift throughout the Carter administration—a period of slow growth in defense budgets—but then reversed again at the outset of the Reagan administration and continued at least through 1986.

At bottom, public opinion seems to have several indirect effects upon Congress's treatment of national security policy. First, it conditions the way Congress treats executive-branch proposals. Public opposition to presidential policies frees members of Congress to be more skeptical about executive-branch proposals. Second, public opinion can raise or lower issues on the public agenda. Absent any pronounced public concern, Congress is less likely to oppose a president or venture into untried policy territory; conversely, expressed public concern, even if indistinct, can embolden Congress. And, third, substantial changes in public opinion are followed by sluggish change in the policy positions of Congress. Sometimes additional events help to move this change along. At other times, the removal of opponents from office—

through defeat, retirement, or death—and replacement by supporters of current public opinion helps to move Congress's collective opinion along. Or, the sitting members simply "get the message" that a real change has occurred and themselves adopt altered or reversed positions.

To reemphasize, all this suggests that public opinion is generally an indirect rather than an immediate and direct influence on Congress where national security policy is concerned. Experience shows us that the public's opinion is fairly slow to change absent a crisis but that Congress's opinion changes even more slowly than that.

The Media

The national media reflect and also shape the national agenda. They reflect the agenda by providing information on the issues and events of the day. They shape the agenda by bringing issues to the attention of the public. Hence, we generally assume, without knowing systematically to what extent, that the media have an influence on public opinion. The media are, therefore, an important linkage device in the policymaking process. They report on what our political institutions are doing. They communicate information about events which occur independent of the political process. And they simultaneously inform both the public and the policymakers about the salient issues of the day.

To the extent that media coverage offers a good measure of salience it also helps to indicate what sort of environment Congress and its committees experience on a day-to-day basis. One way of looking at this is to subdivide the items which appear on the evening news into categories based on the jurisdictions of Congress's committees. This helps to show which committees get the most exposure (and perhaps pressure) and which issues are near the top of Congress's agenda from year to year. Not surprisingly, national security issues rank near the top of the list of issues most frequently covered by the news media. The two Armed Services committees consider issues of high national salience (see Table 14–2), and those two committees rank near the top of the list of committees that receive the most press attention.[24]

While interesting, it is not crucial to demonstrate here whether the media create or merely reflect the public's opinions. (Indeed, it is almost certainly safe to assume that some of each is occurring.) Rather, the point to be made here is that as a "linkage institution" the media have several distinct effects on how Congress handles national security policy. These effects can be made clearer through the use of two rather different examples.

First, the media played a central and historically novel role in the Vietnam War. Daily coverage of the war and its attendant "body counts" offered the American public unprecedented up-to-the-minute information about an ongoing war. Trends in coverage of that war, battle deaths, and public opinion were all closely related to one another during this period. And, whether the media—and in this case particularly television—reflected or created public

TABLE 14–2 House and Senate Committees Ranked by Minutes of "CBS Evening News," Devoted to Topics Falling within Their Jurisdictions (ranked by 1975–1980 standing)

House

	1969–1974	1975–1980
Foreign Affairs	2,109	4,879
Judiciary	1,216	1,299
Commerce	823	882
Armed Services	467	524
Education and Labor	333	462
Ways and Means	268	347
Public Works	180	329
Interior	249	275
Merchant Marine and Fisheries	200	216
Science and Technology	423	211
Agriculture	97	155
Banking	280	153
Government Operations	22	52
Post Office and Civil Service	52	48
Veterans' Affairs	42	44
House Administration	54	35
Small Business	5	10
District of Columbia	1	6
Rules	10	5

Senate

	1969–1974	1975–1980
Foreign Relations	2,109	4,879
Judiciary	1,518	1,299
Commerce	698	835
Labor	569	808
Energy and Natural Resources	243	772
Armed Services	467	623
Environment and Public Works	335	399
Finance	268	347
Banking	280	166
Agriculture	101	156
Governmental Affairs	22	90
Veterans' Affairs	42	44
Rules and Administration	75	35
Small Business	—	10
Committees Abolished in 1977:		
Aeronautics	387	55
Post Office and Civil Service	52	14
District of Columbia	1	0

Note: Based on a sample of newscasts excluding the Appropriations committees, and also excluding stories on energy, Vietnam, the economy, and Watergate which are either crosscutting issues or create artificially high scores for particular committees.

Source: Steven S. Smith and Christopher J. Deering, *Committees in Congress* (Washington, D.C.: CQ Press, 1984), p. 67.

opinion and concern they clearly had an effect on setting the national and therefore the congressional agenda. As the war continued, the issue of U.S. participation became more and more central to the congressional agenda.

A second and smaller-scale example concerns media coverage of a long string of horror stories about waste, fraud, and abuse in the Pentagon procurement system. Examples of poor or scandalously overpriced equipment regularly made the headlines. Some of these stories were themselves created by individual members of Congress who had uncovered various scandals. The effect of all this coverage, however, was to create a mood of cynicism about the Pentagon's operations and to produce a climate of opinion that was supportive of reform in the Defense Department establishment. And so it came to pass, in 1986, that a bipartisan group of representatives and senators fashioned the most comprehensive reorganization of the Defense Department since its creation in 1947. The Pentagon, which normally finds Congress's Armed Services committees quite supportive, was unable to stop, stall, or significantly alter the proposed changes. The coordinated forces of media coverage, supportive public opinion, President Reagan's consistent war against waste, fraud, and abuse, and bipartisan interest in Congress was an unstoppable combination.

As these two cases suggest, the media affect Congress's role in national security policy in several ways. First, they set and reflect the agenda. Second, they are a communications link between the public and the Congress. And third, they help shape and also to communicate public opinion. While some may suggest otherwise, the media almost certainly magnifies existing issues and when the underlying public mood is prepared it may serve to unify national opinion and bring it to bear on the political process.

The Electoral Cycle

One of the perennial and peculiar attributes of the American political process is the extent to which the rhythms of the *electoral cycle* affect policymaking.[25] Under our system, someone is always up for election or reelection and every four years the presidential election adds significantly to the overall importance of the electoral season. These electoral cycles are set down in the Constitution and are, therefore, part of the political facts of life in American politics. But they have a unique effect on American politics because they set down a series of two-year, four-year, six-year, and eight-year cycles which affect the willingness and the ability of the branches to engage in serious policymaking. And the cycles have a pronounced effect on the subset of national issues about which the two parties and the two branches of government are most likely to disagree. As a result, these issues are sometimes characterized as *campaign-defined issues.*

In general, two types of issues typically fall into this category: broadly based economic questions (fiscal policy) and questions of national security (defense and foreign policy). Indeed, it is rare for modern presidential elections not to have both an economic and a national security component. And in some cases these issues predominate as in the case of the alleged missile gap, an issue raised during the Kennedy-Nixon campaign, or the Vietnam War, a centerpiece for the Nixon-Humphrey and the Nixon-McGovern campaigns.

The electoral cycle affects Congress's treatment of national security in several related ways. First, every two years members of Congress must evaluate how their own positions on national security issues fit into the upcoming campaign. Few if any legislators would alter their positions, but they need to be aware of whether positions they already hold are largely congruent with or in conflict with the general trend of the upcoming campaign. For example, in 1968 sharp differences of opinion were emerging over how to deal with the Vietnam War. Most members of Congress still supported the war effort but the issue was one of several to dominate the campaign, and thus forced members to calculate how their own positions would play against the backdrop of a national campaign.

Members' judgments about how their positions will "play in Peoria" help determine their willingness to face those issues back in Washington. The more uncertain the members are about the status of the national debate—on the Vietnam issue in 1968, for example—the less willing they are to grapple with those same issues in Congress. In contrast, if the members perceive a national consensus on an issue, for example, support for expanded defense budgets—a "bipartisan" movement may emerge. In the first instance members may try to avoid taking a stand on an issue that appears to divide the electorate while in the second members may try to jump on the bandwagon of an issue that has broad national support. Hence, the electoral cycle can have the second effect of accelerating or significantly slowing the treatment of national security issues within Congress.

Finally, the electoral cycle has a significant impact upon executive-legislative relations in national security policy. Whenever Congress and the presidency are controlled by different parties—a normal state of affairs in recent decades—preelection periods are frequently characterized by posturing and stalemate on any issue that is perceived to be potentially advantageous in the coming campaigns. Moreover, since Congress is the more stable governing body—affected neither by a two-term limit or large-scale turnover—it can afford to wait out a president if necessary and see what the next administration has to offer. Hence, with each Congress and with each administration there are identifiable "windows of opportunity" when both of the branches may be ready to engage seriously in the policymaking process. To be sure, some annual business is likely to proceed regardless of the electoral cycle. But even the pace of routine business can be affected by the rhythms of electoral politics.

Interest Groups

At a simple level there are two types of interest groups at work in the national security policymaking arena. One type is made up of the direct and indirect beneficiaries of that policy; their interests are best served by a status quo or a somewhat expansionist defense budget that continues existing programs and maintains existing bases. This is the pork-barrel side of defense policy and politics and it is made up largely of private sector interests. The other type of group is more policy-oriented and seeks to influence the nature and direction of U.S. defense policy. These are generally "public interest" groups whose primary orientation and motivation is to sustain or alter various aspects of American defense policy rather than to create or to preserve some pet project, plant, or installation.

Because of their orientations these two types of groups tend to operate in quite different ways. The clientele groups typically lobby in a low-profile fashion in order to secure particular benefits from Congress. And the benefits they seek do not typically divide either the two parties or the two branches. Hence, they are most likely to work within rather than upon Congress. They are not, therefore, truly an outside influence. Examples of this sort of group include not only large defense companies and suppliers of military equipment but also local communities that benefit directly or indirectly from the presence of a military installation.

Public interest lobbies are more likely to utilize tactics that bring pressure to bear on the entire Congress. The changes they seek are likely to be controversial, frequently partisan, and the subject of interbranch disputes. Public interest lobbies almost certainly attempt to influence subcommittee and committee actions but their true "forum" is in the larger public arena.

Neither of these two types of interests is particularly new to the national security policymaking arena. Bloody riots in New York made manifest grassroots opposition to compulsory military service at the outset of the Civil War. In 1915, an American, Jane Addams, became the first president of the Women's International League for Peace and Freedom, an organization devoted to eradicating human warfare.[26] At about the same time international arms merchants such as the infamous Sir Basil Zaharoff were successfully lobbying governments around the world to purchase their innovations in weaponry.[27] The most prominent recent examples of the public interest movement include a wide variety of arms control and military reform organizations. And, of course, there is continued lobbying by defense contractors and their trade associations on behalf of the defense industry.

No one really knows how much of an effect these groups have on policymaking. A whole series of studies has indicated that the districts of members of the Armed Services committees and the Defense Appropriations subcommittees gain no unusual benefits from their members' positions on those panels.[28] Nonetheless, it is widely assumed that lobbying by defense contractors has some payoffs. By contrast, those same studies show that districts with Pentagon-dependent military and civilian payrolls are disproportionately represented on the military policy committees—suggesting that the constituency connection is stronger than the lobbying of contractors. Unfortunately, there has been virtually no systematic examination of the effectiveness of public interest lobbies. Thus, while it is clear that they shape the congressional environment for national security policymaking—indeed, that they are at least partly responsible for a marked shift in vocal support for arms control during the last decade—there is no way at present to say precisely how they do so.

The International Environment

Finally it is worth noting that events in the international environment, particularly actions by other nations, inevitably affect how Congress treats national security policy. These are truly "environmental effects." Germany's occupation of most of Europe, the Japanese attack on Pearl Harbor, or the Soviet's invasion of Afghanistan all suddenly and dramatically changed the national security policymaking environment.

In some cases, such as the onset of World War II, congressional response is immediate and unambiguous—a declaration of war. In other cases, however, such as the Soviet invasion of Afghanistan, the changes are less clearcut—increased tensions with the Soviets, an end to détente, an end to hopes for ratification of the SALT II treaty, and a spur to greater defense spending. The Soviet invasion did not by itself cause these things to occur. But it surely affected them.

International events are "wild cards." Their appearance cannot be predicted. Their effects only guessed at initially. There is no question that they change the national security environment but they can only be evaluated within the context in which they occur.

CONCLUSION: THE IMPORTANCE OF CONTEXT

Congress's role in national security policy represents a unique blend of historical factors that can be traced back to the Constitution. As with fiscal and foreign policy, national security policy and policymaking go to the heart of the U.S. separation-of-powers system. In a contemporary context, these issues also create the most problems for the American system of government since they are frequently among the most contentious, salient, and politicized. But even beyond that, issues of this kind create problems because they so frequently divide the executive and the legislative branches as to "who's in charge."

For its part, the executive branch views fiscal, foreign, and national security policy as peculiarly within its own domain. They are, presidents argue, crucial to effective governance in the twentieth century. And, because of the nature of the international system—and in particular the nature of nuclear weapons—diplomacy and defense simply cannot be left to the meddling of Congress.

But Congress is quick to point to a clear constitutional mandate, the necessities of democracy, and to frequent excesses of the executive that so worried the Founding Fathers. Except in true emergencies, Congress tends to argue, the United States should be deliberate in its actions. And, absent the democratic support that Congress can lend, the executive is too frequently in danger of adopting politically untenable policies. No matter which side you are on concerning Nicaragua, they would say, the absence of congressional oversight can lead to mistakes like the Iran-Contra initiative.

In the end, the evidence offered here suggests that individual members can and do affect national security policy. It also suggests that the institution creates the conditions for distinctive patterns of policymaking to occur. But in the end, national security policy, even if it is frequently dominated by the executive, appears as a unique blend of the forces at work throughout American politics.

NOTES

1. John Jay, "Federalist No. 4," in *The Federalist Papers,* ed. Clinton Rossiter (New York: Mentor, 1961), p. 49.
2. Letters of marque and reprisal are now obsolete. When used such "letters" or explicit authorizations granted third parties—privateers—the authority to seize property or persons unjustly captured by another nation or party. In 1856, the European powers agreed to end privateering. And, as a general practice, nations no longer authorize private third parties to "exact justice." See Louis Henkin, *Foreign Affairs and the Constitution* (New York: W. W. Norton, 1972), p. 68.
3. U.S. Constitution, Article I, Section 8, Clause 12.
4. U.S. Constitution, Article II, Section 2, Clause 1.
5. On the general patterns in the House and Senate respectively, see Steven S. Smith, "Revolution in the House: Why Don't We Do It On The Floor?" *Brookings Discussion Papers in Governmental Studies,* no. 5 (Washington, D.C.: Brookings Institution, 1986); and Barbara Sinclair, "Senate Styles and Senate Decision-Making, 1955–1980," paper prepared for delivery at the annual meeting of the American Political Science Association, New Orleans, La., August 29–31, 1985.
6. See Michael Ganley, "Near Record Number of Amendments and Floor Time Spent on DOD Bill," *Armed Forces Journal International* (July 1987), p. 8.
7. Details on Boxer's background and election are from Alan Ehrenhalt, ed., *Politics in America: Members of Congress in Washington and at Home, 1984* (Washington, D.C.: CQ Press, 1984), pp. 109–110.
8. Background on Boxer's several years in Congress comes from *Congressional Quarterly Weekly Report,* March 31, 1984, p. 731; May 26, 1984, p. 1,284; March 23, 1985, pp. 551–52; and April 6, 1985, p. 622.
9. Quoted in Lewis A. Dexter, "Congressmen and the Making of Military Policy," in *New Perspectives on the House of Representatives,* 2nd ed., ed. Robert L. Peabody and Nelson W. Polsby (Chicago: Rand McNally, 1969), p. 182.
10. Randall B. Ripley and Grace A. Franklin, *Congress, the Bureaucracy, and Public Policy* (Chicago: Dorsey Press, 1987). Ripley's and Franklin's categories are based on earlier work by Samuel P. Huntington, *The Common Defense: Strategic Programs in National Politics* (New York: Columbia University Press, 1961).
11. See Arthur M. Schlesinger, Jr., *The Imperial Presidency* (Boston: Houghton-Mifflin, 1973).

12. These data are from Lance T. LeLoup and Steven A. Shull, "Congress versus the Executive: The 'Two Presidencies' Reconsidered," *Social Science Quarterly* 59 (March 1979), p. 707.

13. Aaron Wildavsky, "The Two Presidencies," *Trans-Action* 4 (December 1966), pp. 7–14.

14. These are defined here as the Armed Services committees and the Military Construction and Defense Appropriations subcommittees of the House and Senate.

15. In fact, the data for the Ninety-first Congress indicate that both of the foreign policy committees had fewer than 50 percent executive branch witnesses, but each exceeded the 50 percent mark in the Ninety-sixth Congress. Also, largely because of the dominance in defense policy, the two Appropriations committees are dominated by executive branch witnesses. Data on the Ninety-first and Ninety-sixth Congresses appear in Appendix A–4 and A–5 of Steven S. Smith and Christopher J. Deering, *Committees in Congress* (Washington: CQ Press, 1984), pp. 278–79.

16. But see as an exception, Paul Burstein and William Freudenburg, "Changing Public Policy: The Impact of Public Opinion, Antiwar Demonstrations, and War Costs on Senate Voting on Vietnam War Motions, " *American Journal of Sociology* 84 (July 1978), pp. 99–122.

17. Warren E. Miller and Donald E. Stokes, "Constituency Influence in Congress," *American Political Science Review* 57 (March 1963), pp. 45–66.

18. Aage R. Clausen, *How Congressmen Decide: A Policy Focus* (New York: St. Martin's Press, 1973).

19. See especially Clausen's chapter 8, pp. 192–212.

20. The figures that appear here are from John E. Mueller, *War, Presidents, and Public Opinion* (New York: John Wiley & Sons, 1973), pp. 44–52.

21. On this general point see Angus Campbell, Philip E. Converse, Warren E. Miller, and Donald E. Stokes, *The American Voter* (New York: John Wiley & Sons, 1960).

22. Mueller, *War, Presidents, and Public Opinion,* pp. 52–58.

23. On public opinion regarding defense spending see John E. Rielly, "The American Mood: A Foreign Policy of Self Interest," *Foreign Policy* 34 (Spring 1979), pp. 74–86, and John E. Rielly, "American Opinion: Continuity, Not Reaganism," *Foreign Policy* 50 (Spring 1983), pp. 86–104. Defense spending figures are from Pat Towell, "Pentagon Seeks to Continue Weapons Buildup," *Congressional Quarterly Weekly Report,* February 8, 1986, p. 235.

24. For example, Stephen Hess found that the Senate Armed Services Committee ranked eighth among Senate Committees in terms of the number of network television cameras covering its activities. Stephen Hess, *The Ultimate Insiders: U.S. Senators in the National Media* (Washington, D.C.: Brookings Institution, 1986), p. 32. And, while Hess's data do not cover the House there is every reason to believe that the two chambers are comparable in this regard.

25. The best known recent exposition on this notion is Edward R. Tufte, *Political Control of the Economy* (Princeton, N.J.: Princeton University Press, 1978). Tufte credits Michael Kalecki, William D. Nordhaus, and Assar Lindbeck as being among the originators of the notion of a political economic cycle related to national elections. William B. Quandt uses the term in reference to foreign

policy in "The Electoral Cycle and the Conduct of Foreign Policy," *Political Science Quarterly* 101 (Winter 1986), pp. 825–37.

26. Jeffrey M. Berry has a case study of the Women's International League for Peace and Freedom in *Lobbying for the People: The Political Behavior of Public Interest Groups* (Princeton, N.J.: Princeton University Press, 1977), pp. 141–77.

27. See Anthony Sampson, *The Arms Bazaar* (New York: Viking Press, 1977), and George Thayer, *The War Business* (London: Weidenfeld & Nicholson, 1970).

28. See, for example, Bruce A. Ray, "Military Committee Membership in the House of Representatives and the Allocation of Defense Department Outlays," *Western Political Quarterly* 34 (June 1981), pp. 222–34; Barry S. Rundquist and David E. Griffith, "An Interrupted Time-Series Test of the Distributive Theory of Military Policymaking," *Western Political Quarterly* 29 (December 1976), pp. 620–26; Carol F. Goss, "Military Representatives," *Western Political Quarterly* 25 (June 1972), pp. 215–33; Barry S. Rundquist, "On Testing a Military Industrial Complex Theory," *American Politics Quarterly* 6 (January 1978), pp. 29–53; and Leonard G. Ritt, "Committee Position, Seniority, and the Distribution of Government Expenditures," *Public Policy* 24 (Fall 1976), pp. 463–89.

CHAPTER 15

Congress and the American People

Roger H. Davidson

The celebrated Iran-Contra hearings, which dominated the news in the summer of 1987, perfectly embodied the relationship between the United States Congress and the mass public. As the elaborate foreign policy conspiracy unravelled before the television screens, the show rivaled the soap operas for viewers' attention. The Public Broadcasting System (PBS) broadcast the sessions gavel-to-gavel, about 311 hours' worth; even the major networks turned over large chunks of their daytime programming to the event.

Congressional leaders planned the hearings to demonstrate the foreign policy blunders of the Reagan administration. The two committees, House and Senate, that conducted the hearings shaped them for the television audience, selecting witnesses and speeding up or slowing down the pace to accommodate viewers' attention spans. At the bar of public opinion, witnesses were judged by a sort of invisible applause meter, whereby the media audience assessed their credibility and human qualities. The feedback loop was complete as committee members were careful to treat the witnesses with awe or scorn, according to the public reactions as measured by opinion surveys and the volume of mail and telephone calls. Lieutenant Colonel Oliver North, a sympathetic witness who played well in front of the TV cameras, was treated gingerly by questioners, several of whom conceded that the hearings had made him a national hero. Other witnesses were treated accordingly, some (like Secretary of State George Shultz) with deference and others (like retired Air Force General Richard Secord and former National Security Advisor John Poindexter) with scorn. Members and witnesses alike were acutely aware that they were playing to the public audience, the ultimate arbiter of the proceedings; accordingly, some reputations were burnished, others tarnished, by the exposure they received.

The public's reaction to all this was predictably divided. Some people blamed Congress for the whole affair, siding with sympathetic witnesses and against the interrogators. But most people thought witnesses had been treated fairly; most thought, too, that Congress was an essential actor in foreign policy, rejecting the idea that the president should be able to conduct secret operations in foreign countries without informing top congressional leaders.[1] As an institution of government, Congress occupies a contradictory place in the hearts and minds of American citizens. On the one hand, as a popularly elected branch it enjoys wide if often begrudging public support. The role of elected legislators as tribunes of the people is embedded in political theory and practice over many centuries. Such parliamentary advocates as John Locke espoused legislative supremacy because elected lawmakers were supposed to be close to the popular will. On this side of the Atlantic, elected officials from colonial times onward have been expected to expound the causes of their neighbors and constituents. The author of Federalist Paper number 52 asserted:

> As it is essential to liberty that the government in general should have a common interest with the people, so it is particularly essential that the [House of Representatives] should have an immediate dependence on, and an intimate sympathy with, the people.[2]

This localism and particularism bothers many intellectuals and puzzles foreign observers; but it is fully consistent with the intentions of the framers of the Constitution.[3]

Yet citizens remain mystified and ambivalent about "their" branch of government. Although bathed in publicity, much of it self-generated, Congress is not well understood by most Americans. Its dual chambers, its large size, its procedural mazes, its measured pace—all conspire to cloud the average person's image of it. The average citizen can comprehend the president and even follow the careers of a few colorful cabinet secretaries and senators. But the whole Congress is another matter: to most people, it is a puzzling blur. Moreover, Congress is a constant target for public scapegoating, not just in the popular mind, but in journalistic and scholarly commentary as well. Pundits and humorists find Congress an inexhaustible source of raw material. Legislators themselves often fuel this negative image by portraying themselves as escapees from the "funny farm on the Potomac," all too often running *for* Congress by running *against* Congress, as Richard Fenno put it.[4]

THE TWO CONGRESSES

Citizens' ambivalent feelings toward the popular branch of government mirror the dual character of Congress. In the public mind there is not one but *two Congresses*. One of these two entities, the institution on Capitol Hill, is the collective maker of laws. This Congress acts as a collegial body, performing constitutional duties and handling legislative issues. It is the subject of numerous scholarly studies, and is covered by heavyweight reporters of the national media. The second Congress, every bit as important as the first one, is a collection of 540 individual senators, representatives, and delegates. They are men and women of diverse backgrounds and political careers. Their electoral careers depend not upon what Congress produces as an institution, but upon the support and goodwill of voters hundreds and even thousands of miles from Washington.

As we shall see, this notion of the two Congresses reflects public perceptions and assessments. Opinion studies suggest that citizens view the Congress in Washington through different lenses than they do their individual senators and representatives.[5]

Congress as an institution is seen mainly as a lawmaking instrument. It is judged primarily on the basis of citizens' overall attitudes about policies and the state of the union. Do we like the way things are going, or don't we? Are we bullish or bearish about the nation's future?

By contrast, citizens regard their own legislators as agents of personal or localized interests. Legislators are judged on such criteria as service to the state or district, communication with constituents, and "home style"—that is, the way the officeholder deals with the home folks. In evaluating their elected officials, voters ponder such questions as: Do I trust the legislator? Does the legislator communicate with the state or district—answering mail and helping constituents? Does the legislator listen to the state or district and its concerns? As we will see, such concerns lead people to conclusions quite different from those they reach upon looking at the collective institution of Congress.

THE COLLECTIVE CONGRESS AND PUBLIC OPINION

As an institution, Congress swims in a sea of public opinion. It dotes on news of public sentiments and responds to indicators of public whims, no matter how ephemeral. It is, in turn, an object of public attention which offers numerous opportunities for generating news and public attention.

Public attitudes—not only their direction, but also their intensity—are undoubtedly the most powerful engines propelling congressional action on legislative issues. Studying committee decision making, David E. Price found that two factors—perceived salience and conflict—determine legislative action or inaction within a policy area. Incentives for action, he concluded, are strongest in issues of high public salience and little conflict; they are weakest in issues of low salience and fierce conflict.[6] The consensus decision-making rule propounded by John W. Kingdon similarly revolves around an issue's climate of opinion: "Congressmen begin their consideration of a given bill or amendment with one overriding question: Is it controversial?"[7]

Environmental protection laws provide a dramatic example of the attitudinal backdrop for legislative action. The political climate of the early 1970s mandated congressional activism in environmental issues. Cleaning up the environment was a highly salient issue. And a series of much publicized events—the publication of Rachel Carson's *Silent Spring*, an 800-square-mile oil slick off the coast of Santa Barbara, and the banning of commercial fishing in Lake Erie because of high levels of mercury poisoning—conspired to create a mood of urgency to environmental policymaking. In 1970, 53 percent of the

American public believed pollution was the most important national problem, ranking it second only to crime in a Gallup poll which asked people to list the three problems to which they would like to see the government devote most of its attention.[8]

In those days antipollution laws were regarded as necessary public policy. According to the Harris survey, 83 percent of the American public wanted the federal government to spend more money on air and water pollution.[9] In addition to high issue salience and approval, environmental action in the early 1970s lacked serious conflict—either between political parties, between the legislative and executive branches, or between competing interest groups. In his second State of the Union Address, President Richard Nixon asserted that clear air, clean water, and open space were "the birthright of every American." The fledgling environmental lobby groups relied on public support to press their goals; there was little opposition, even from business firms that were targets of environmental laws.

Congress responded eagerly to the public consensus. By overwhelming majorities, Congress during the 1970s added thirty-seven antipollution laws to the books. A dozen of them launched comprehensive national programs: clean air, water pollution control, coastal zone management, federal regulation of pesticides, noise control, endangered species protection, safe drinking water, federal land policy and management, national forest management, toxic substances control, resource conservation and recovery of solid and hazardous wastes, and surface mining control and reclamation. The decade also saw the addition of dozens of new parks, seashores, lakeshores, historic sites, and recreation areas to the national park system—so many that several of the enactments were called "park barrel" bills.

By the 1980s, the political climate for environmental policy had chilled markedly. Public concern over pollution dropped rapidly after 1970; after 1978 the issue never reappeared in the Gallup poll's "Most Important Problem" survey. The priority the American public placed on environmental protection was unclear. A survey conducted in 1980 by the Opinion Research Corporation (ORC) indicated that citizens supported procedural amendments to environmental laws, and that many favored the proposal that air pollution control standards vary from area to area depending on the region's air quality. The ORC poll found that 78 percent of those who considered themselves "active environmentalists" supported changes which would protect the environment *at lower costs*.[10]

Environmental policymaking decisions in the 1980s moved from simple pros and cons to questions of degree. Complex, technical issues abounded; public reactions to them were difficult to measure. Legislators found themselves cross-pressured on virtually every environmental reauthorization that came up in the 1980s. Partisanship developed on several proposals; lobby groups exerted cross-pressures; legislative and executive branches found themselves at odds during the Reagan era. The first Reagan-era Congress (1981–82), facing stalemate as well as uncertain public will and sharp conflict, reauthorized only two environmental measures and enacted no new ones. As the decade proceeded, most laws were renewed, but only after prolonged and often bitter debates.

Other issues rise and fall on Capitol Hill in accord with shifts in public attitudes. The Vietnam War is perhaps the most striking example in modern times. In the war's early phases, Congress was pathetically eager to support presidential initiatives. The 1964 Gulf of Tonkin Resolution—a vague but expansive grant of authority in Southeast Asia—passed the House without dissent and the Senate with only two negative votes. The next year President Lyndon Johnson began escalating the Vietnam effort without further consulting Congress. In early 1967, citizens rejected (by a 52 percent to 32 percent margin) the notion that the United States had "made a mistake sending troops to fight in Vietnam." As the war dragged on and the casualty lists mounted, however, opinion steadily reversed. By 1968 a majority of American citizens claimed to oppose the Vietnam War. Five years later, people concluded by better than a two-to-one margin that the war had indeed been a mistake.[11]

Congressional antiwar actions lagged behind public opinion but eventually conformed with it. Increasingly, citizens supported congressional efforts to curtail the war effort. A four-to-one majority of the public supported a 1971 congressional proposal to recall all U.S. troops by the end of the year. Yet on Capitol Hill, only after 1973 could a reliable antiwar majority be mustered regularly for key House votes. The congressional reversal on the Vietnam War, striking and in the end decisive as it was, would not have occurred if it had not been for the even more dramatic turnabout in popular tolerance for the war. In the war's last stages it was Congress that tightened the pressure for curtailment; but initially Congress had been a more-than-willing partner in the venture.

More recently, Congress and the public changed their minds about the level of defense spending. When Ronald Reagan went to the White House in 1981, surveys showed firm public support for building up military strength and increasing defense spending. Such attitudes helped propel the "Reaganomics" legislative package through both chambers of Congress that year— resulting in massive military buildups at the same time that taxes were cut and domestic programs slashed. Public demand for higher military spending proved transitory, however. By the 1982 midterm elections, nearly twice as many respondents felt the government was spending too much on the military as said the government was not spending enough. Revelations of wasteful procurement and overpriced weapons, not to mention the fiscal squeeze on popular domestic programs, helped to dampen public ardor for accelerated defense funding. The shift was eventually felt on Capitol Hill: whereas military spending was a sacred cow in 1980–81, by mid-decade it was a sacrificial lamb.

Public support for a wide range of domestic programs helps explain Congress's willingness to authorize and appropriate at high levels. Congress is often faulted for spending too much on distributive-benefit programs, even at the risk of high deficits. Even so, Congress's spending proclivities are solidly grounded in public preferences. Americans typically profess to want more government spending on most programs, even though many of them complain in the same breath of government meddling and waste. The 1982 National Election Study, for example, probed respondents' views concerning sixteen categories of federal spending programs. In all but five categories, more citizens thought government was spending too little than too much to alleviate the problem. The exceptions were space exploration, military spending, foreign aid, welfare, and food stamps. For most other issues, pluralities of respondents thought that too little was being spent.[12] Such results are typical. It is little wonder, then, that members of Congress resist budget cuts and tend to allow expenditures to overrun revenues.

THE PUBLIC VIEWS CONGRESS

At the most general level, citizens give Congress only a so-so report card. Typically, Congress as an institution is rated significantly below the respondents' own representatives. In a recent survey, Congress surprisingly received a positive rating (53 to 46 percent), a striking improvement over the negative ratings recorded since the mid-1960s.[13]

Public approval of Congress rises or falls with economic conditions, wars and crises, and waves of satisfaction or cynicism. Congress's rating usually follows that for the president. Perhaps people use the more visible presidency as a handle for assessing Congress and the rest of the government. More likely, people form overall impressions of how the government is doing and rate both institutions accordingly.[14] Thus, the popularity surge of the mid-1980s occurred because people were buoyed by optimism over the government and its performance; satisfaction with the strong leadership of President Reagan especially was generalized into optimism and confidence in other sectors of federal government.

Also on the rebound has been the level of confidence people have in Congress (and, in fact, in society's other institutions). After nearly two decades of rampant skepticism, the public was by the mid-1980s relatively sanguine about their national legislature: 39 percent of those surveyed expressed "a great deal" or "quite a lot" of confidence in Congress; only 18 percent indicated "little or no confidence." While people remain less than totally enthralled by Congress, they rate it higher than newspapers, big business, television, or organized labor.[15]

Despite the mixed reviews, most Americans expect Congress to exert a strong, independent role in policymaking. This has been a consistent finding of surveys over a number of years, even in the so-called *imperial presidency* era of the 1960s. People expect Congress to check the president's initiatives, and to examine the president's proposals carefully. They even support the idea of divided government, with the White House controlled by one party and

Capitol Hill by another. In a recent survey, a huge majority (73 to 20 percent) rejected the view that the country would be "worse off" by having a Congress controlled by one party and the White House by another.[16] In other words, the notion of split control of the federal government is thought better than having one party in control. In 1986, the voters reaffirmed this view by establishing the opposition Democrats in control of both the House and Senate—after reelecting President Reagan two years earlier by a 49-state margin. Apparently the voters support the notion of divided government for much the same reason that James Madison did: they prefer that the government branches should be divided and balanced.

In certain instances, the public backs Congress over the president on specific issues. One survey taken late in the Reagan administration found people supporting the congressional position over the president's position on eight major issues, ranging from defense spending to farm subsidies to trade legislation. Margins favoring the congressional position ranged from 2–1 to more than 6–1.[17] In the midst of the Iran-Contra hearings, even after the testimony of Lt. Col. Oliver North had produced a surge of support for the Reagan administration's support of the Nicaraguan rebels, 60 percent of the respondents trusted Congress to make the right foreign policy decisions, and only 24 percent preferred the president's leadership.[18]

THE PEOPLE VIEW THEIR REPRESENTATIVES

A gap persists between the public's assessment of Congress and its satisfaction with individual senators and representatives. While a slim majority of people in the mid-1980s approved of the performance of Congress, more than two-thirds of the respondents gave a positive mark to their own member of Congress. Members achieve this status by personal service to their constituents, by building an image over time, and by positioning themselves close to the prevailing views of their voters. As a result, they are seen more as local officials than national ones.[19]

The impressive visibility that most members of Congress enjoy in their states or districts explains the support they command from potential voters. Incumbent representatives have far closer contact with their constituents than their non-incumbent challengers do (see Table 15–1). A majority of citizens report contacts with their House members by receiving mail from them, reading about them in a newspaper or magazine, or seeing them on television. Lacking the communication channels of incumbents, challengers have far fewer contacts with those whom they ask to vote for them. Incumbents, moreover, have more opportunities to do favors for their constituents. The 1982 National Election Study found that 14 percent of all respondents (or their families) had called upon their representative for assistance. Of those, four out of five were satisfied or very satisfied with the response they received.[20]

TABLE 15–1   Voter Contact with House Candidates (1982)

Forms of Contact	Incumbents	Challengers	Open Seats
Received mail	56%	18%	39%
Read about in newspaper, magazine	53	29	47
Saw on television	52	29	49
Heard on radio	30	15	25
Met personally	14	7	12
Saw at meeting	11	4	5
Talked to staff	8	3	10
Other contacts	7	4	5
(N)	(1,240)	(975)	(163)

SOURCE: American National Election Study, Center for Political Studies, *Post-Election Survey File* (IPSR 9042) (Ann Arbor, Mich.: Inter-University Consortium for Political and Social Research, 1983), pp. 131ff.

Another bond between elected officials and their voters is forged out of mutual agreement on key issues facing the constituency and the nation. The recruitment process yields congressional candidates who tend to reflect local views and prejudices. Contacts with voters throughout the campaign and while in office reinforce this convergence of views, as do representational norms adopted by a large majority of members.[21] Whatever the source, the result is a perception on the voters' part that their views are shared by their representative. In the 1982 National Election Study, people were asked whether they generally agreed or disagreed with their incumbent's votes on bills. Of those who had an opinion, only 7 percent said they generally disagreed with their representative's votes. Half of the people said they agreed sometimes and disagreed sometimes, and 42 percent reported that they mainly agreed with their representative's positions.[22]

The most persuasive evidence of public support for incumbent senators and representatives is without a doubt their success in getting reelected. If people think that elected officials as a class are rascals, they certainly do not think that way about their own elected officials. Nor do they show any eagerness to "throw the rascals out." So at the polling place, where the ultimate judgment is rendered, modern-day legislators are supported spectacularly. Since World War II, on the average 92 percent of all incumbent representatives and 75 percent of incumbent senators running for reelection have been returned to office. In 1986, the figures were 98 percent for House members and 75 percent for senators.

In sum, the public is of two minds about its national legislature. Or, to put it another way, there are really "two Congresses" that citizens perceive and judge. One of these, the collective body that holds forth on Capitol Hill, is seen dimly and at a distance; it commands lukewarm affection from a people who are accustomed to viewing politics and politicians with a mixture of respect and disdain. When it comes to individual senators and representatives, however, contacts are more direct, and they are satisfying and even cordial. Average voters hold separate views of their representatives in Washington; they cannot imagine that the person they voted for is really part of "that crowd" on the Potomac. Most citizens, in other words, see their representative as "one of us," not "one of them." Needless to add, senators and representatives take great pains to promote this dual image.

CONGRESS AND THE MEDIA

This same dualism—between Congress as an organization and its individual members—appears in media coverage. For just as there are two Congresses in the public mind, so these two entities are covered differently by the press. In fact, they are covered by a different press—*national* in the case of the institutional Congress and its work, *local* and *regional* in the case of individual senators and representatives. It is no accident that these two very different media channels yield two quite different pictures of Congress, that in turn produce divergent judgments of Congress's work.

Reporting about the Institution

Although extensively reported in the media, Congress is not well understood by the average American. Partly to blame are the size and complexity of the institution. There are 535 lawmakers (plus four delegates and one resident commissioner who vote in committee but not on the floor) organized into more than 50 committees and 250 subcommittees. The twists and turns in the legislative process add to the sense of buzzing confusion, even for veteran observers of the congressional scene. A vote taken one day may be modified or nullified the next day. "It ain't over till it's over" is an understatement when applied to congressional decision making. Even decisive enactments may include so many amendments that the effect of congressional action is merely to transfer policy conflict to executive or judicial arenas.

Reporting such a disparate and complex mechanism is no small challenge. Despite the presence of a large press corps containing many of the nation's best journalists (Capitol Hill is, after all, the best beat in Washington), neither reporters nor their editors/producers are able to convey in the mass media the internal subtleties and external linkages that characterize the lawmaking process. True, such subtleties abound in the other branches of government. But the complexities of the vast executive establishment are disguised in the mass media by the personage of the president, who speaks or acts with what seems to be unity and simplicity. Judicial deliberations are equally complex, but courts hand down rulings that typically declare winners and losers—a surefire way of simplifying action for public understanding. In contrast, the complexities and indeterminacies of the legislative branch are on display for all to see, and for reporters to try to put in order.

The contrast between Congress and the presidency as a news source could not be more striking. With its multifaceted organization and relatively weak leadership, Congress cannot exert strict control over how it is presented to the media. Its leaders may be the chief sources of news, but they cannot protect themselves against the outbreak of news from other sources within the institution. In the White House, news is managed more tightly: most of the White House press corps spend their time following the president's movements or waiting for statements or handouts from the president's press secretary. Press conferences are staged affairs, and other opportunities for free exchanges with the president are very scarce. The president's schedule is skillfully manipulated to provide news events and visual "opportunities" nearly every day which, it is hoped, will translate into lead stories. There is little time to seek out meaningful stories by interviewing widely in and out of the White House. Thus, the president tends to be portrayed in the media as he and his advisors arrange for him to be portrayed.

News about the institutional Congress is recorded and disseminated by the national press corps, a large and diverse group of journalists who cover events in the nation's capital. The *inner circle* of this corps is composed of reporters who work for the two wire services (Associated Press, United Press International), the major radio and television networks (CBS, NBC, ABC, PBS, CNN), the national news magazines (*Time, Newsweek,* and *U.S. News & World Report*), and a few of the major daily papers of national reputation (including *The New York Times, Washington Post, The Wall Street Journal, Los Angeles Times,* and *Boston Globe*). These outlets not only cover national news regularly and sometimes in depth; some of them help policy-makers keep in touch with each other. In addition to these general circulation outlets, specialized publications and news services disseminate stories of interest to a given industry, profession, trade union, or ideological grouping.

It is not my purpose to outline in detail how the Washington press corps works, what its news judgments are, and whether it serves the citizenry adequately or not. For purposes of the argument here, it is important to make only two points about the press corps.[23] First, most of them *specialize* in the subjects they are reporting. Either they are assigned exclusively to cover Congress, or the House or Senate, or they cover stories about a specific topic, for example, labor relations or higher education or the aerospace industry. Thus, they are well prepared to handle their assignments, and to deal with Capitol Hill news sources on the basis of more or less equal status. Second, they retain some distance from their news sources. With many sources to choose from, they are not dependent on the goodwill of a single senator or representative. If they write an unflattering story about one of their sources, they are not likely to be boycotted, for senators and representatives need reporters as much as or more than the reporters need them. And in any event reporters are unlikely to be boycotted: if one source dries up, another can usually be called upon.

So these national reporters can afford to maintain a cool, neutral stance toward their news sources on Capitol Hill. Following the canons of investigative journalism, many are on the lookout for scandals or evidence of wrongdoing. To the extent that they reveal bias in their work, it is the bias of the suspicious adversary. Thus, most close observers believe that reporters are "tough" on Congress, especially in in-depth or interpretive analyses. Ethical problems, congressional pay and perquisites, and junkets abroad are frequent subjects for such stories. This is perhaps as it should be, but it has the effect of reinforcing popular negative stereotypes about Congress as an institution.

Local Coverage of Members

If Congress as an institution is reported mainly by the national press corps, individual members of Congress are publicized primarily by local media outlets. One of the great anomalies of American society is the fact that, despite its impressive technological sophistication, its mechanisms for gathering and disseminating the news are highly decentralized. More than 9,000 newspapers are published in this country, 1,700 of them dailies. More than 10,000 periodicals are put out, and the number is rapidly rising. More than 9,300 radio stations and 1,150 television stations are operating; their numbers, too, are increasing. The number and variety of these media outlets is based on the continuing vitality of local issues and local advertising, and on the proliferation of what historian Daniel Boorstin calls "consumption communities"—people connected by what they buy or do or believe in, rather than where they live.[24]

Most local media outlets rely on national news channels—wire services, radio and TV networks, and chain or syndicated services—for their coverage of national news, including news that emanates from Capitol Hill. But for local stories, or for local or specialized angles on national news, these outlets must look elsewhere. Sometimes the outlet can persuade a news service or wire service to provide special coverage with a local angle. For example, a paper owned by a chain may be able to call on someone from the chain's Washington bureau to write such a story.

More often, local newspapers or radio and television stations desiring specialized treatment of a story will turn to the local representative or senator to give the needed "local angle." For the elected official, this is the ideal way to gain publicity: it is targeted to constituents, it displays the source's knowledge of and concern for local problems, and it portrays the legislator in an informational rather than a confrontational role.

Members and their staffs accordingly devote great attention to the care and feeding of the press corps back home. Most legislators have at least one staff member who serves as press aide; most of them regularly use the House and Senate radio and television studios, where audio or video programs or excerpts can be produced for a fraction of their commercial cost. With the advent of low-cost technology for television transmissions by tape or satellite, local stations are no longer content to rely simply on network coverage of major events. They can cover specialized aspects of the story for local news programs, often simply by getting a statement on tape from their senator or representative. The elected official will never say no to such as request. Few lawmakers would trade such exposure in the hometown media for a few seconds on "CBS Evening News" or a brief mention in *The New York Times*. "I am never too busy to talk to local TV," said Democratic Representative's Dan Glickman from Kansas. "Period. Exclamation point."[25]

There is another advantage of such appearances for incumbent lawmakers. Unlike their counterparts in the Washington press corps, local reporters approach a senator or representative from a position of weakness, not equality. Local reporters, especially for the electronic media, are likely to be on general assignment, which means that they are often ill prepared to question the lawmaker in detail. Moreover, local reporters are inclined to treat members of Congress with deference and respect because of their prominence and experience. Unlike the national reporter, the local newsgatherer has little choice in news sources; the primary goal, then, is just to get the legislator on tape.[26] For incumbent legislators, such a situation is ideal: it lets them express their views in their own words with a minimum of editing and no challenge from the reporter.

As a result, individual members of Congress are presented to the public very differently from Congress as an institution. Individual legislators are portrayed in a more favorable light, often getting a "free ride" from ill-prepared reporters eager simply for a good quote or "news bite." Or they are presented to their constituents through their own efforts, in press releases, newsletters, targeted mailings, or prepared radio or television appearances. Whatever the mechanism, the result is that individual members receive a large measure of free, uncritical publicity. It is little wonder, then, that their public image is measurably more favorable than that of Congress as a whole.

TELEVISING THE CONGRESS

If there is ever to be a convergence in the public view of the two Congresses—the institutional and the individual Congress—it is likely to occur through the direct broadcasting and telecasting of legislative sessions. Congress's television presence on a continuing basis is of recent origin. But is has changed the two houses in ways that are both subtle and obvious, and it has brought congressional deliberations to the attention of millions of citizens in an unprecedented way.

Television, of course, came to Capitol Hill very early. Indeed, some of TV's most memorable moments occurred during the infrequent coverage of congressional hearings. The Kefauver crime hearings of 1951, the Army-McCarthy hearings of 1954, the Senate Foreign Relations Committee's Vietnam inquiry of 1966, the Watergate investigations chaired by Senator Sam

Ervin, a Democrat from North Carolina, in 1973, and the Nixon impeachment hearings of the next year—all these riveted public attention on Congress and produced an awareness and appreciation of the institution that could not have occurred otherwise. Yet the daily deliberations of the House and Senate and of their committees took place largely outside of camera range. Meanwhile, modern presidents were exploiting the power of television to capture attention and dramatize issues. Indeed, the imbalance in television coverage of Congress and the presidency may well explain the post–World War II rise of the imperial presidency and the eclipse of the legislative branch.

Eventually, Congress decided that its image and public support would be enhanced by live television coverage. The House acted first in 1979, the Senate not until 1986. The House select committee that examined the matter concluded that television coverage of floor deliberations would help members and staff carry out their duties, provide a more accurate record of proceedings, and contribute to public understanding of the House. When the Senate followed suit after protracted debate, the unstated reason was the perceived need to catch up to the House in public media attention.

In both chambers, studio technicians use remote-control cameras mounted unobtrusively in the chambers themselves. In the House, cameras normally focus on the Speaker's dais, two lecterns at the front of the chamber, and the majority and minority floor managers' tables. Because senators speak from their individual seats, cameras pan to many different points around the chamber. In both chambers, coverage is unedited and gavel-to-gavel.

Signals from both chambers are relayed by closed circuit to Capitol Hill offices, so that members and staffs can follow the deliberations, going to the chamber to cast votes or to participate in debates. The signals are also available to radio and television networks, which can broadcast the proceedings live or can tape excerpts for news programs. Excerpts are widely used not only by networks but also by individual stations.

The complete proceedings are relayed also by the Cable Satellite Public Affairs Network (C-SPAN), which in turn relays House proceedings on C-SPAN I and Senate proceedings on C-SPAN II. The House proceedings are available to cable television systems in 50 states, with some 29 million potential viewers. Senate coverage is available to approximately 9 million homes in 45 states (some cable firms carry the House channel but have no channel available for C-SPAN II).[27]

By all accounts, television has been a smashing success on Capitol Hill. Although it has brought about few disruptions or alterations in parliamentary procedure, it has sharpened debate and made members more aware of their audience—not only in the chamber, but in the nation as a whole. Members are preparing their remarks more carefully, adhering to tighter time limits, and paying more attention to their wardrobes.

In the House, two long-standing customs have been adapted for the television cameras: *one-minute speeches* and *special orders*. An established informal practice, the brief remarks called "one minutes" are ideal vehicles for brief, personal commentary at the outset of each legislative day. Since the television era dawned in the House, the use of one minutes has increased three-fold. At the end of the day, during lulls in legislative business, members can ask unanimous consent for "special orders" to speak on a particular subject. Members use this procedure to raise and publicize issues they feel are being ignored in other forums.

The Senate has altered its procedures hardly at all to accommodate the television cameras. One exception is special-order speeches, in which senators seek unanimous consent to speak on any subject. With the advent of television, senators decided to limit such speeches to five minutes—the Senate's only formal accommodation to television. During the 1986 TV trial period, such speeches increased five-fold.

The most important effect of televised proceedings will no doubt lie in enhanced public understanding and approval of Congress. In addition to providing citizens a window on their representatives in action, television coverage assists schools and colleges in teaching about citizenship, law, politics, history, and journalism. Some members have become celebrities on the tube; all are aware of its presence. From all accounts, there is a core audience of C-SPAN fanatics around the country, relatively small in numbers (at least compared with the network audiences) but loyal and well informed. In a 1986 study, 27 percent of those surveyed reported having watched televised sessions of Congress. By a landslide, the people endorsed the idea of live telecasts of congressional sessions.[28] It is not farfetched to assume that the upsurge in popular support for Congress is related to television broadcasts of its proceedings.

CONCLUSION: THE TWO FACES OF CONGRESS

The two Congresses turn different faces toward the public. Congress as an institution is a policymaking machine, covered heavily by the national press corps—correspondents for the TV networks, wire services, and leading newspapers. Their basic stance is distant and their prevailing mood is cynical. Individual lawmakers, in contrast, are heavily indulged by the local press. In most cases, local media outlets that pay any attention at all to legislators give them respectful coverage. Understaffed and underprepared, they quote the member's words, rely on office press releases, or give unimpeded play to the member's statements.

Public perceptions of Congress display a parallel dualism. The institutional Congress is viewed in terms of general impressions of the state of the nation, in recent years ranging from skeptical to cautious. Individual lawmakers, in contrast, are seen in brighter hues. Unlike the institution, one's own representatives tend to be well known, favorably judged, and—most important—reelected. This is the essence of the argument about the existence of two Congresses: that they are viewed through different lenses, reported by different channels of communication, and judged by different criteria. Of course, the paradox is that, despite these disparities in communication and public perception, the two Congresses are interlocked and interdependent. The well-being of one rests on the well-being of the other, even though the average citizen may be unaware of that fact.

NOTES

1. Richard J. Meisling, "Majority in New Poll Still Think Reagan Lied on Iran-Contra Issue," *The New York Times,* July 18, 1987, p. 7.
2. Alexander Hamilton or James Madison, in *The Federalist,* ed. Edward M. Earle (New York: Modern Library, n.d.), p. 343.
3. Michael J. Malbin, "Factions and Incentives in Congress," *Public Interest* 86 (Winter 1987), pp. 91–108.
4. Richard F. Fenno, Jr., *Home Style: House Members in Their Districts* (Boston: Little, Brown, 1978), p. 168.
5. Glenn R. Parker and Roger H. Davidson, "Why Do Americans Love Their Congressmen So Much More than Their Congress?" *Legislative Studies Quarterly* 4 (February 1979), pp. 53–61.
6. David E. Price, "Policymaking in Congressional Committees: The Impact of Environmental Factors," *American Political Science Review* 72 (June 1978), pp. 568–69.
7. John W. Kingdon, *Congressmen's Voting Decisions* (New York: Harper & Row, 1981), p. 243.
8. American Institute for Public Opinion (The Gallup Poll), *Public Opinion, 1935–1971* (New York: Random House, 1972), pp. 2248–49.
9. Louis Harris, *Harris Survey Yearbook of Public Opinion, 1970* (New York: Louis Harris & Associates, 1971), p. 48.
10. Everett Carl Ladd, "Clearing the Air: Public Opinion and Public Policy on the Environment," *Public Opinion* 5 (1982), pp. 16–20.
11. George H. Gallup, *The Gallup Poll: Public Opinions, 1972–77* (Wilmington, Del.: Scholarly Resources, Inc., 1978), p. 87.
12. Warren E. Miller and the National Election Studies, *American National Election Study, 1982: Post-Election Survey File,* IPSR 9042 (Ann Arbor, Mich.: Inter-University Consortium for Political and Social Research, 1983), pp. 184–90, question F–13.
13. Louis Harris, "Overall Job Rating for Congress Nears Marks for Individual Members," *The Harris Survey* 47 (June 13, 1985).
14. Glenn R. Parker, "Some Themes in Congressional Unpopularity," *American Journal of Political Science* 21 (February 1977), pp. 93–109; Roger H. Davidson, David M. Kovenock, and Michael J. O'Leary, *Congress in Crisis* (North Scituate, Mass.: Duxbury Press, 1966), pp. 59–62.
15. *The Gallup Report,* No. 238 (July 1985), p. 3.
16. Louis Harris, "Voters Convinced Better to Have Divided Federal Government," *The Harris Survey* 59 (November 3, 1986).
17. Louis Harris, "Public Backs Congress over President on Key Issues," *The Harris Survey* 7 (February 9, 1987).
18. Linda Greenhouse, "How the Democrats Are Kept on the Defensive," *The New York Times,* August 9, 1987, p. E1.

19. Timothy E. Cook, "Legislature vs. Legislator: A Note on the Paradox of Congressional Support," *Legislative Studies Quarterly* 4 (February 1979) pp. 43–52; also in the same volume see Glenn R. Parker and Roger H. Davidson, "Why Do Americans Love Their Congressmen So Much More than Their Congress?" pp. 53–62.

20. Miller, *American National Election Study, 1982,* p. 131, (question E-13).

21. See Roger H. Davidson, *The Role of the Congressman* (Indianapolis, Ind.: Bobbs-Merrill, 1969).

22. *American National Election Study, 1982,* pp. 136–37.

23. This argument is made in greater detail in Roger H. Davidson and Walter J. Oleszek, *Congress and Its Members,* 2nd ed. (Washington, D.C.: CQ Press, 1985), and Michael J. Robinson, "Three Faces of Congressional Media," in *The New Congress,* ed. Thomas E. Mann and Norman J. Ornstein (Washington, D.C.: American Enterprise Institute for Public Policy Research, 1981), pp. 55–96.

24. For a succinct statement of this technological pluralism, see Robert J. Samuelson, "Computer Communities," *Newsweek,* December 15, 1986, p. 66.

25. Bob Benenson, "Savvy 'Stars' Making Local TV a Potent Tool," *Congressional Quarterly Weekly Report,* July 18, 1987, pp. 1551–55.

26. Peter Clarke and Susan H. Evans, *Covering Campaigns: Journalism in Congressional Elections* (Stanford, Calif.: Stanford University Press, 1983); and Charles M. Tidmarch and Brad S. Karp, "The Missing Beat: Press Coverage of Congressional Elections in Eight Metropolitan Areas," *Congress & the Presidency* 10 (Spring 1983), pp. 47–61.

27. See Senate Majority Leader Robert C. Byrd's discussion of radio/TV coverage of the Senate, *Congressional Record* (June 2, 1987, daily edition), S7394, S7401.

28. Louis Harris, "Congress in Action Should Stay on Live TV," *The Harris Survey* (July 7, 1986).

CHAPTER 16

Congress and the Constitutional Balance of Power

Charles O. Jones

> *Of all the powers with which the people have invested the Government, that of legislation is undoubtedly the chief . . . the Legislature is the only power which can create other powers. . . . The members of the House of Representatives are the special delegates and agents of the people in this high trust. They, and they alone, proceed immediately from the suffrage of the people. They, and they alone, can touch the mainspring of the public prosperity. They are elected to be the guardians of the public rights and liberties.*[1]

This well-stated and forceful theory of legislative primacy is to be found in a report on raising the compensation of members of Congress, dated December 18, 1816. Note that the rationale for congressional dominance is two-fold: the significance of the lawmaking function itself and the legitimacy of legislators as having electoral connections to the people. The theory of legislative primacy was even more elegantly outlined by Representative John C. Calhoun from South Carolina in the ensuing debate over the congressional pay bill. Calhoun was determined to show that members of Congress deserved better pay. Indeed, he argued that compensation was "intimately connected with the very essense of our liberty." Surely their pay ought to be commensurate with the duties and the station of their position. Here is what Calhoun had to say on January 17, 1817:

> This House [of Representatives] is the foundation of the fabric of our liberty. . . . If . . . understood correctly the structure of our Government, the prevailing principle is not so much a balance of power as a *well-connected chain of responsibility.* That responsibility commenced here, and this House is the centre of its operation. The members are elected for two years only; and at the end of that period are responsible to their constituents for the faithful discharge of their public duties. Besides, the very structure of the House is admirably calculated to unite interest and duty. The members of Congress have in their individual capacity no power or prerogative. These attach to the entire body assembled here. . . . We then as individuals are . . . not less amenable to the laws which we enact, than the humblest citizen. Such is the responsibility, such the structure, such the sure foundation of our liberty.
>
> This, then is the essence of our liberty; *Congress is responsible to the people immediately, and the other branches of Government are responsible to it. . . .*[2]

Nowhere do we find a more articulate expression of the institutional linkage within the separation of powers. Nor is one likely to find clearer argument on the important point that separated powers, or institutions, are not necessarily equal and independent. Calhoun's position should be modified to account for the popular election of the Senate and the president. But it remains a forceful theory of democratic accountability.

This chapter examines the role of Congress in the constitutional system. It will identify the constitutional, political, and policy contexts within which the three branches competitively coexist and change. It is organized to consider the original constitutional design, the emergence of counter theories of institutional balance, various periods of congressional and presidential dominance, Congress and the courts, and the ever-present reform mood to alter whatever balance happens to exist at any one time. Final comments direct attention to the policy context within which the issues of balance and competition among institutions have practical significance for the ongoing political system.

The central thesis of this chapter is very close to that of Calhoun: that Congress is the centerpiece of democracy. The democratic connections are of three types: senators individually representing states, House members representing districts, and the institution collectively representing the nation. Institutional legitimacy is conferred by these three forms of agency and therefore Congress is justified in overseeing and checking the other branches. Of course, the greatest challenge is to control the executive since a growing government naturally enhances the power of that branch. Much of the history of the modern Congress is a study of efforts to preserve a constitutional balance that maintains representational ties to the people through an effective legislature.

In what has become my favorite definition of the term, E. E. Schattschneider claims that "Democracy is a competitive political system in which competing leaders and organizations define the alternatives of public policy in such a way that the public can participate in the decision-making process."[3] Surely for national-level policy matters, Congress is the principal institution for accomplishing Schattschneider's functions. Presidents come and go, bureaucracies and courts stay but hardly promote participation in their decision making. Congress structures itself to be competitive within policy issues and in so doing encourages public participation. As Calhoun argues, then, Congress is base camp; it is the first and most important institutional link in the chain of responsibility.

THE ORIGINAL DESIGN

The Congress under our first constitution, the Articles of Confederation, was the dominant institution but it was part of a weak national government. The states entered into what was called "a firm league of friendship." Congressional delegates were annually appointed "in such manner as the legislature of each state shall direct." They could be recalled, they could serve no more than three years out of six, and though the number of delegates from states varied from two to seven, each state had only one vote "in determining questions." "A Committee of the States" was appointed by Congress "to sit in the recess of Congress"—thus serving one function of an executive. One member of the Committee of the States served as president, but no more than "one year in any term of three years." Other committees, too, could be appointed by Congress "for managing the general affairs of the United States."

Since Congress appointed this weak, interim executive, government under the Articles of Confederation was not characterized by separation of powers. At the very least, the legislature and executive must be independently elected for the political system to qualify as separationist. And though we think of the separation of powers as a central feature of our government today, the fact is that it was not a part of either of the two major plans considered in Philadelphia. The Virginia Plan served as a basis for the deliberations and provided that the "National Executive" and the "National Judiciary" both were "to be chosen by the National Legislature." One can hardly label any such plan "separationist." The New Jersey Plan (offered as an alternative to the Virginia Plan) likewise provided that "the United States in Congress be authorized to elect a federal Executive." Had either plan been adopted, we presumably would have developed exactly the parliamentary system so admired by many modern day reformers. That is, the majority party in Congress would have selected its leadership to serve in the executive—as a president or prime minister and a cabinet.

The mode of selection of the executive was debated at length during the convention. Election of the president by Congress "was in fact adopted three times, and was incorporated into the penultimate draft."[4] Many of the delegates feared legislative dominance of the executive branch, however, and supported some form of popular election. Even James Madison, who had been instrumental in preparing the Virginia Plan, came to support the separationist plan of independent elections for the two branches. As William H. Riker points out, one concern among the separationists was that parliamentary cabals might form in Congress that would lead to "intrigue." "By 'intrigue' the Framers probably meant no more than maneuvering to form cabinets in fragmented parliamentary systems."[5]

At the very last moment, the delegates approved a rather strange electoral process—one with no precedent and one that has been heavily criticized since. Viewed in the context of the debate in Philadelphia, however, the plan satisfied many fears that had been expressed. Riker summarizes the advantages of this new, Electoral College system as follows:

> The committee [on postponed matters] tailored a plan to satisfy all those who might oppose legislative election. For distant states, electors were to meet in the states, thereby saving a trip to the capital. For those in favor of popular

election, electors were to be chosen in the manner prescribed by state legislatures, which allowed for popular election. For the separationists, the college avoided the legislature entirely, if any candidate got a majority. For the small state interest, there were two provisions: First, each state was to have as many electors as representatives and senators, which gave the small states an edge [due to the equality of representation in the Senate]. Second, if no candidate had a majority of electoral votes, the [House, with each state having just one vote] . . . was to choose from the five highest.[6]

Here was a classic compromise. Every worry was addressed and legislative institutions were involved without actually controlling the outcome (except in unusual circumstances). However odd it may appear today, the provision for electing the president was at the time the result of old-fashioned bargaining.

One might well argue that the resolution of this debate was in the direction of a weakened legislature. I urge a somewhat different interpretation. Above all the delegates were determined to prevent tyranny. They were, however, anxious to establish a viable government. Creating a government is no simple task for those who believe in the corruptibility of power and its bad effects. Republicanism, in the form of a representative legislature, is a natural remedy. But legislatures too can tyrannize, and so they must be checked. Here is how the argument was stated in *The Federalist*:

- In republican government, the legislative authority necessarily predominates. [No. 51]
- [The legislature's] constitutional powers being at once more extensive, and less susceptible of precise limits, it can, with the greater facility, mask, under complicated and indirect measures, the encroachments which it makes on the coordinate departments. [No. 48]
- We have seen that the tendency of republican governments is to an aggrandizement of the legislative at the expense of the other departments. [No. 49][7]

Legislative primacy was accepted as inevitable, yet absolute power in a legislature could lead to tyranny. Indeed, the encroachment might well be masked by the representative nature of the institution. Possible excesses were therefore to be guarded against. This view is not contrary to that of Calhoun's stated above. Rather, it establishes the rationale for a chain of responsibility and for "still further precautions" [No. 51] to prevent the chain from becoming a whip.

It is also interesting to contemplate whether having approved legislative selection of the executive would have in fact led to even greater congressional power. Based on the parliamentary experience in Great Britain, it seems an unlikely outcome. Indeed, Congress today compares favorably with parliaments around the world in terms of its independent authority. The means devised for selecting presidents also preserved the separateness of the legislative branch and in so doing permitted Congress to make its own adaptations to changing circumstances—including those favoring an imperial presidency. It would have been difficult for Congress as a parliament to withstand growth of executive power in the twentieth century. Separation permitted the members to justify resistance as reflecting their individual and collective mandates from the people.

THE UNRESOLVED DEBATE

A debate so fundamental as that involving the relative power of the executive and the legislature is unlikely ever to be resolved. Indeed, the growth of national government functions may be expected to intensify the debate. One can identify at least four perspectives of the balance of power: legislative primacy, presidential primacy, cooperative mixed government, and adversarial mixed government.

The perspective of *legislative primacy* has already been described as dominant at the Constitutional Convention; Calhoun's statement exemplifies the rationale of those who cling to this outlook. Does it exist today among members of Congress? Unquestionably, it does. A day hardly passes on Capitol Hill without a member of Congress expressing the theory of legislative primacy. Members do not doubt the important role played by the president, but they are stubbornly protective of their prerogatives. Indeed, not even his own party members will support the president if it is judged that he has exceeded his authority and thwarted the will of Congress. Thus, for example, the Budget and Impoundment Control Act of 1974, which was, in large part, a response to what was judged to be President Nixon's excesses in the exercise of budget authority, passed both houses by huge margins. In a more recent example, Congress overwhelmingly overrode President Reagan's veto of a clean water bill in early 1987; a large majority of his own party voted against him in both chambers. Reagan had used the "pocket veto" to defeat the bill in 1986 after the bill had passed with no dissenting votes in either house. Speaker Jim Wright, of Texas, suggested that the issue was less a dispute between Republicans and Democrats than between Congress and the White House.[8]

Whereas the legislative primacy perspective has had advocates throughout our history, the *presidential primacy* perspective is of more recent vintage. Woodrow Wilson's book, *Congressional Government*, contains a classic statement regarding the rationale for presidential power. Having spotted what he judged to be exactly the encroachments that worried the Founding Fathers, Wilson concluded that it was time for a change:

> [The presidency] has fallen from its first estate of dignity because its power has waned; and its power has waned because the power of Congress has become predominant. . . .
>
> Congress is (to adopt Mr. Bagehot's description of Parliament) "nothing less than a big meeting of more or less idle people." In proportion as you give it

power it will inquire into everything, settle everything, meddle in everything. . . . Accordingly it has entered more and more into the details of administration, until it has virtually taken into its own hands all the substantial powers of government.[9]

Wilson judged that presidential dignity and power had to be reestablished. Among other things, he worried about accountability with a predominant Congress. *"Somebody must be trusted,* in order that when things go wrong it may be quite plain who should be punished."[10] That somebody, in his judgment, should be the president since he was a single individual, elected by the nation.

It is not certain that Wilson would be pleased with developments subsequent to his presidency. On the one hand, presidential responsibilities have grown enormously; on the other hand, it is doubtful that trust has increased that much. Wars and sizable increases in the role of the federal government in the domestic sphere have resulted in a greater reliance on the executive branch. Media attention, too, has naturally tended to focus on the White House. Thomas Cronin speaks of the "primetime presidency" and the "television-magnified presidency." Unquestionably, this attention enhances the role of the chief executive, and yet the authority of the office is still rather limited. The president may thus be held accountable for actions which he may not fully control. And as Cronin observes, "Television has helped to make [presidents] more important but less popular."[11]

The greatest increment in presidential power undoubtedly occurred during Franklin D. Roosevelt's administration, when the combination of domestic policy breakthroughs and wartime responsibilities contributed to executive-centered government. Post–World War II presidents have had to meet grand expectations. According to Richard Neustadt, "A President may retain liberty, in Woodrow Wilson's phrase, 'to be as big a man as he can.' But nowadays he cannot be as small as he might be." With the growth of government, Neustadt observes, "Everybody now expects the man inside the White House to do something about everything."[12]

Yet this designated primacy of the executive branch is accompanied by the same suspicions that were expressed at the Constitutional Convention. Thus, the realization that all presidents were powerful—even those less likely to be entrepreneurial—led scholars and others to examine critically the constitutional balance of power. In 1965, James MacGregor Burns published *Presidential Government,* in counterpoint to Woodrow Wilson's *Congressional Government,* written decades earlier.[13] Then, in 1973, Arthur M. Schlesinger, Jr., published *The Imperial Presidency.* Schlesinger found the presidency to be "resurgent" in World War II, "ascendant" in the Korean War, and "rampant" in the Vietnam War. He found Richard Nixon's presidency to be a particular threat to the system—a "revolutionary presidency."[14] The Watergate scandal had a profound effect on those advocating presidential primacy. Unquestionably the status of the office was badly damaged by that incident and by the first resignation of a president in history. Still, as Neustadt correctly observes, it is difficult nowadays to manage the government with a "small" chief executive.

Equality of the branches is central to the third and fourth perspectives. They differ in the style or manner of relationship that is advocated. I label these *mixed government* perspectives. The notion of balanced strength rather than primacy for one institution clearly has advocates—at least among members of Congress if not among presidents. In fact, for many members the reform efforts during the 1970s were directed toward coequality, not congressional primacy. Former Texas Democratic Representative Barbara Jordan argued that the "revitalization of Congress need not result in a weak presidency." And as James Sundquist points out, Democratic Representative from Indiana, Lee Hamilton, even doubted that Congress could or should achieve co-equality. Sundquist quotes Hamilton as stating that:

> The effort of the Congress to reassert itself should not be misunderstood to mean that the Congress can truly become an equal branch of government. It is simply too difficult for 535 strong-minded aggressive persons "to get it all together" on all the issues on the nation's agenda. . . . No one advocates a weakened presidency . . . a shackled presidency would not be wise. Our system requires a strong presidency, but a strong president *under* the Constitution.[15]

In considering mixed or balanced government, a useful distinction can be made between a *cooperative* and an *adversarial* style. Cooperative mixed government depends on harmony between the branches, which normally can be achieved only if the same party is in control of both. We never expect full cooperation, of course, but there are instances when the president and Congress have worked effectively together. Furthermore, there are definite advocates of cooperative mixed government. These tend to be the so-called *party responsibility* advocates who promote changes that will encourage unified government through the political parties. The classic statement in favor of this position was that prepared by the Committee on Political Parties of the American Political Science Association. Quoting from their report:

> The president could gain much when party leaders in and out of Congress are working together with him closely in matters concerning the party program. As party head, the president could then expect more widespread and more consistent support from the congressional leaders of his party. These, in turn, would present a more united front. As a result, on issues where the party as a party could be expected to have a program, the program of the party, of the party leaders in each house of Congress, and of the president would be the same program, not four different programs.[16]

For this outcome to be realized, political parties would have to be greatly strengthened—they would have to somehow overcome all of the roadblocks built into the system by the Founders. Otherwise, realizing cooperative mixed government will continue to be circumstantial—that is, merely a con-

TABLE 16–1   Variations in the Constitutional Balance of Power (twentieth century)

Variations	Periods When Dominant
1. Congressional primacy	1903–1911 (the Cannon era); 1921–1933 (weak president era)
2. Presidential primacy	1933–1945 (Roosevelt); 1964–1966 (Johnson)
3. Mixed government– cooperative	1913–1917 (Wilson); 1945–1947 (Truman); 1953–1955 (Eisenhower); 1981–1983 (Reagan)
4. Mixed government– adversarial	1919–1921 (Wilson); 1947–1953 (Truman); 1955–1961 (Eisenhower); 1961–1963 (Kennedy); 1967–1969 (Johnson); 1969–1977 (Nixon-Ford); 1977– 1981 (Carter); 1983–1989 (Reagan)

SOURCE: Compiled by the author.

sequence of a particular set of electoral conditions or of a special relationship between a president and congressional leaders (note its infrequency in Table 16–1).

Adversarial mixed government has occurred more frequently and, indeed, one might even conclude that it has come to be the dominant mode of presidential-congressional relations in the post–World War II era. In this view, the two branches are co-equal and highly competitive. Most often the adversarial posture is a consequence of divided government, where one party controls the White House and the other party has a majority in one or both houses of Congress. Note, in Table 16–2, how exceptional that condition was during the first forty-six years of this century. In only one Congress—the second Congress following Woodrow Wilson's reelection—were both houses under the control of the other party. Divided control has occurred a majority

TABLE 16–2   Divided Government in the Twentieth Century

Time Period	Form		As a Percentage of the Total Period
	President and Congress (no. of years)	President and House (no. of years)	
1901–1947	2	4	13%
1947–1989	18	6	57
(1969–1989)	(10)	(6)	(80)

SOURCE: Compiled by the author.

of the time since the war and, remarkably, 80 percent of the time in the past 20 years.

The argument for adversarial mixed government is simply that good policy is the result of competition between the institutions. Although I know of few advocates of such a position, the American voters are responsible for frequently producing such outcomes in recent decades. Many Americans appear to support the idea of this further check on government, even doing James Madison one better by adding partisan divisions to the Madison design for separation. In 1980, the voters went to the extent of providing split partisan control of the House and Senate—an outcome then repeated in 1982 and 1984.

It should be noted that split party control does not necessarily result in an adversarial relationship. During his first Congress (1981–82), President Reagan can be said to have had cooperative mixed government despite the fact that the Democrats were a majority in the House. Republican congressional leaders cooperated with him in enacting his program and there were sufficient Democrats as well who were willing to vote with the president. Furthermore, same-party control of Congress and the White House does not ensure cooperation. President Carter experienced tense relationships with the Democratic party leaders in Congress. The special circumstances of his election (taking office in the post-Watergate mood) encouraged him to separate himself from his own party.

The four perspectives on the constitutional balance of power between the president and Congress have been discussed (a) as a set of *preferences* by students and other observers of our national political system, and (b) as a set of *characteristics* of particular eras in the twentieth century. Table 16–1 gives examples of the periods when each perspective has been dominant, although no perspective can be said to be "pure." Also, there may be variations in which perspective or set of characteristics is dominant even within one administration. Nevertheless, Table 16–1 illustrates the variations in institutional balance in this century.

CONGRESS AND THE COURTS

The largest portion of this discussion has focused on the constitutional balance between the president and Congress because policy relationships between the two branches are continuous, whereas the issue of balance between Congress and the federal courts is less immediate and more episodic. William Keefe and Morris Ogul observed that "Legislative-judicial relations in the United States are ordinarily marked by harmony and mutual indifference."[17] The courts unquestionably decide important policy matters, and the power of the Supreme Court to judge the constitutionality of congressional acts was settled early in our history, in *Marbury* v. *Madison* (1803). But the process of policymaking by the Court is less direct than in the case of either the president or the Congress. Typically, the Court's influence comes either as a consequence of objections to policy solutions by the other branches or because of the failure of those branches to act on an important issue. To be sure, conflicts do arise between the Congress and the Courts, but they do not actively compete in the on-going national policy process because their agendas differ in kind and by source.

As in relationships with the president, the potential for imbalance is two-directional—the Court over Congress and vice versa. Two types of interaction characterize both: that which is more institutional or procedural in nature and that which is more substantive in nature. In regard to the first type, the Court occasionally makes judgments about congressional elections and the authority of Congress in relationship to the executive. Important recent examples include:

- *Wesberry* v. *Sanders* (1964)—a decision stating that Article I, Section 2 of the Constitution is to be read as requiring that congressional districts must be as equal in population as possible.

- *Immigration and Naturalization Service* v. *Chadha* (1983)—a decision that invalidated the so-called *legislative veto,* an increasingly common practice by which Congress (or one of its organizational entities) reserved the right to disapprove of executive actions.

Of course, any such institutional or procedural actions by the Court have important substantive policy implications. Such decisions are directed to the broader constitutional issue of congressional structure and authority and less to the range of substantive policy matters that might be affected.

In regard to the second type of interaction—Court rejection of a substantive policy solution by Congress—the actual issue involved may be relatively minor. Also, the Court is often reluctant to use constitutional grounds in substituting its judgment for that of Congress (in fact, the actual number of congressional acts held unconstitutional is quite small—approximately 130). The range of issues that the Court may choose to act on is quite considerable, given the authority of Congress itself to act on so many policy issues. The following are examples illustrating different substantive policy issues:

- *United States* v. *Romano* (1965)—invalidated a provision of the Internal Revenue Service that presence at an unregistered still (unless otherwise explained to the jury) was sufficient for conviction.

- *Frontiero* v. *Richardson* (1973)—held that statutory differentiation between male and female spouses of members of the armed forces for certain dependents' benefits violated equal protection, as guaranteed by the Fifth Amendment.

- *Jimenez* v. *Weinberger* (1974)—held that statutory differentiation among illegitimate dependents for disability insurance benefits under the Social Security Act violated equal protection, as guaranteed by the Fifth Amendment.

- *National League of Cities* v. *Usery* (1976)—held that sections of the Fair Labor Standards Act extending wage and hour coverage to state and local government employees are invalid as beyond congressional authority under the commerce clause of the Constitution.

As these illustrations suggest, the Court's decisions do not necessarily pose a major threat to congressional power. Still, there have been periods, as with the development of Roosevelt's New Deal program, when Court actions were interpreted as interfering with the national policy process and both the president and Congress threatened actions to limit the Court's role.

Congress is by no means helpless in the face of Court decisions. And, indeed, it has constitutional authority regarding the structure and makeup of the federal courts. Article III is brief. In fact, as one observer noted, "the convention . . . only crayoned in the outlines. It is left to Congress to fill up and colour the canvas."[18] Congress can create inferior courts, determine the number of judges, and regulate the appellate jurisdiction of the Supreme Court. Appointments to the federal courts must be made "by and with the advice and consent of the Senate." The Judiciary Act of 1789, one of the first acts by the new Congress, set forth the basic structure of the federal court system. Many acts have been passed subsequently. And, of course, congressional influence in appointments has been important in shaping the courts. Few Supreme Court nominees have been rejected (only four in this century) but the hearings on appointments may be influential in projecting congressional expectations.

Congressional reaction to Court decisions regarding its authority or its policy decisions may take several forms. Congress may seek to accomplish its goal by enacting new legislation that avoids the constitutional issue raised by the Court. Or an effort may be launched to change the constitution through amendment. Several unsuccessful attempts to do so have been made in recent years in reaction to Court decisions on topics including the rights of criminal suspects, abortion, school prayer, redistricting in the states, and school busing, suggesting that the Court definitely has power on policy issues. One successful effort was in response to a Court decision in *Oregon* v. *Mitchell* (1970). The Court held that a provision of the Voting Rights Act of 1970 setting the minimum voting age at 18 could not be applied to state and local elections. Congress responded by passing a constitutional amendment, which was then quickly ratified by the requisite number of states (now the Twenty-sixth Amendment).

There are always a few issues which lead to conflict between the Supreme Court and members of Congress. Walter Murphy observes a pattern associated with these differences. First is the decision on a controversial issue of public policy. Next is "severe criticism of the Court coupled with threats of remedial and/or retaliatory legislative action." And the third step "has usually been a judicial retreat."[19] Even at its most serious, however (as with conflicts between Congress and the Warren Court), the competition pales in comparison to that between Congress and the executive. Thus, in regard to the Warren Court, Murphy concludes that "the crisis . . . passed without serious injury to the prestige or power of either institution.[20] The same cannot be said about the Watergate crisis and other conflicts during the Nixon administration.

Members of Congress will complain bitterly about a particular Court decision, even to the point of expressing concern about constitutional imbalance. Further, they will frequently criticize the Court "because it doesn't cost anything."[21] But they worry daily about the growth of presidential power and act frequently to curb it. The difference in congressional attitudes is traceable to the nature of the power struggle within each branch. As David O'Brien observed, "On major issues of public policy, Congress is likely to prevail or, at least, temper the impact of the Court's rulings."[22] The same cannot always be said in the matter of competition with the president.

REFORM AND THE BALANCE OF POWER

As Roger Davidson, David Kovenock, and Michael O'Leary taught us more than twenty years ago, the "pathways to reform" are heavily influenced by the preferences of the reformers.[23] Thus, for example, those preferring a strong executive will propose changes that increase the president's authority and protect his prerogatives from congressional encroachment. Those favoring congressional preeminence will suggest greater resources for the legislative branch and restrictions on the exercise of presidential power. It is useful for purposes of this essay to review congressional reforms because of what they reveal about the balance of power between the branches. Particularly relevant are the many reforms enacted during the 1970s. At no other time in its history did Congress make such important changes. And as compared to other reform eras, many of these changes were designed to reestablish congressional preeminence in national policymaking.

There have been four major reform eras in this century. The first occurred in 1910–11 in response to the significant growth in the power of the Speaker of the House and specifically to the exercise of that power by Joseph Cannon. The issue at the time was less the balance of power between Congress and the other branches, however, and more the concentration of power in the hands of one man. The reforms enacted at that time decentralized authority to the committees and to political party units.

The second set of reforms (1945–46) was stimulated by a perceived imbalance in the roles played by the president and Congress. Presidential power increased markedly during World War II. In part, this development was to be expected given the need for centralized leadership. It was also the case, however, that Congress was poorly organized.[24] Burdened with too many committees and cumbersome procedures, it was ill equipped to participate actively and constructively in the war effort. A first priority following the war was to modernize the Congress. The Legislative Reorganization Act of

1946 sought to accomplish that goal: committees were abolished, staffing increased, new budget procedures introduced, and oversight capability enhanced.

The third important reform occurred in 1961 with the enlargement of the House Rules Committee. This reform can also be classified as having been stimulated by a perceived imbalance between the two branches. In this case the president, John F. Kennedy, expressed concern that his program might be stalled by the powerful Rules Committee. The twelve-member committee was then controlled by an "unholy alliance" among Chairman Howard W. Smith, a Virginian, the next ranking Democrat, William Colmer from Mississippi, and the four Republicans. The president won and the committee was increased by two Democrats (to ten) and one Republican (to five)—a change that gave liberals a slim 8 to 7 working majority.[25] Here was an opening salvo in the battle against arbitrary committee chairs, a battle fought out in the 1970s for the benefit not of presidents, but of junior members.

The fourth and most dramatic period of reform started in hearings before the Joint Committee on the Organization of Congress in 1965 and ended in 1979. Before it was over, reform proposals had emanated from three joint committees, two major party groups in the House (plus several minor ones), three House committees or commissions, and two Senate committees or commissions.

The reforms enacted were responses to perceived threats to institutional authority and prestige from the following sources: (1) an aggressive president (Richard Nixon); (2) the arbitrary exercise of power by committee chairs; (3) weakened political parties and leadership; (4) limited policy analytical capabilities (particularly in competition with the executive); (5) cumbersome procedures; and (6) public and press criticism of the institution.

Little was left untouched by the reform advocates. Actions were taken to curb presidential power, disperse committee leadership, enhance party leadership, provide greater policy analytical support, and improve congressional standing with the public. Unquestionably these changes were motivated by the perspectives of legislative primacy and mixed or balanced government. Fearing loss of prerogatives due as much to congressional inadequacies as to presidential aggrandizement, members supported actions to reconnect the "chain of responsibility" and to equip themselves to meet the associated challenges.

Table 16–3 categorizes reforms of the 1970s as responses to the threats cited above. One has to be impressed with the scope of the reforms, as well as their audaciousness (as with the War Powers Act and the Budget and Impoundment Control Act). It is still too early to judge the full effects of these changes, but we can confidently assert that they have not led to "congressional government." A balance, however, has been restored: one which encourages Congress to restrain the executive, not substitute for it.

Speaking to a conference in 1975 on the role of Congress, Democratic Senator Edmund S. Muskie from Maine warned against efforts to make Con-

TABLE 16–3   The Reforms of the 1970s: Seeking to Restore the Balance

Response to Threats	*Specific Reforms Enacted*
1. Curbing presidential power	War Powers Act (1973); Budget and Impoundment Control Act (1974)
2. Curbing the power of committee chairs	More power for members (1970, 1976, 1977); seniority system modified (1970, 1971, 1973, 1975, 1977); subcommittee bill of rights (1973); greater role for Speaker and Democratic Steering and Policy Committee (1973, 1974)
3. Strengthening political parties	Reestablish Democratic Steering and Policy Committee (1973); increase in Speaker's powers (1973, 1974, 1975, 1977); Steering and Policy Committee nominates committees (1975); minority party rights (1970, 1975)
4. Increasing congressional capabilities	Staff increases (1973, 1975, 1977); enhancement of CRS and GAO (1970); creation of OTA (1972) and CBO (1974); computer services (1971); Budget and Impoundment Control Act (1974)
5. Reorganizing and improving procedures	Committee reorganizations (1974, 1975, 1977); committee appointments (throughout 1970s); electronic voting in House (1972); procedural modifications (throughout 1970s)
6. Reducing criticism from outside	Campaign regulation (1972, 1974); adoption of ethics codes (1977); opening committee deliberations (1973, 1975, 1977); televising the House (1978)

SOURCE: Compiled from information in Charles O. Jones, *The United States Congress: People, Place, and Policy* (Homewood, Ill.: Dorsey Press, 1982), p. 429; and Leroy N. Rieselbach, *Congressional Reform* (Washington, D.C.: Congressional Quarterly Press, 1986), pp. 155–58.

gress the whole government. In so doing, he also defined congressional responsibilities.

> Let me say this about Congress, incidentally. A Congress is not a President. A Congress, thank God, cannot be a President. A Congress should be nothing more, nothing less, than what it is: a reflection of the will of our people and the problems that disturb them and the actions they want taken. The Congress ought to improve its ability to serve that function, and the Congress ought not to try to become a President.[26]

CONCLUSION: THE CONSTITUTIONAL BALANCE IN PERSPECTIVE

In an article on "The Legislator as Educator," former Arkansas Senator J. William Fulbright offered this wise counsel:

Our proper objective is neither a dominant presidency nor an aggressive Congress but, within the strict limits of what the Constitution mandates, a shifting of the emphasis according to the needs of the time and the requirements of public policy.[27]

Often the debate regarding the balance of power among the branches is abstract and based on generalizations about the motives and exercise of power. Reforms are typically structural, organizational, or procedural in nature and assume changes in policy outcomes that are not at all guaranteed by the new structure.

Policy issues, meanwhile, continue to be fed into a system of separated institutions with variable constitutional prerogatives and policy-making capacities. In other words, competitive coexistence among the branches occurs within the continuing policy agenda of a working government. As Sundquist documents, "The balance between president and Congress [has] gone through nearly two centuries of ups and downs." He observes that "in the third century the seesaw would continue."[28] Personal quest for power surely plays a role in this competition, but it cannot explain the full extent of the shifts (nor should it under the terms of the original constitutional design); more important are the policy demands and how they change over time. The policy context also helps to explain the unanticipated consequences of reforms, for whatever the structural alteration may be, one can expect adjustments among those who want government to act on policy problems. Seldom are these adjustments predictable in advance (nor do most reformers even take them fully into account).

What, then, are we to say in conclusion about Congress and the constitutional balance of power? Most notably, that the issue is primarily rhetorical—associated with varying perspectives of the relative status, prestige, and power of the three branches. Saying that the issue is rhetorical is not to downplay its importance. It is, rather, to point out that the ongoing debate brackets the roles of and relationships among the branches, providing a rough measure of where we are and announcing the worries of those who spot excesses in the exercise of power. Much of the debate over the setting of boundaries will take place in Congress. That is as it should be, given the representational responsibilities of that body. It is in this sense that Calhoun's chain of responsibility theory has contemporary application. Congress must continue to be the primary forum for the debate on the balance of power. Should it abdicate that function, then the constitutional balance truly would have shifted and democracy would be threatened. "A Congress," as Senator Muskie said, "should not be a President." But in reflecting "the will of our people" it must monitor trends in the exercise of political power.

NOTES

1. Quoted in Charles S. Hyneman and George W. Carey, eds., *A Second Federalist* (New York: Appleton-Century-Crofts, 1967), pp. 148–49.

2. Quoted in Hyneman and Carey, pp. 150–51. Emphasis added.

3. E. E. Schattschneider, *The Semisovereign People* (New York: Holt, Rinehart & Winston, 1960), p. 141.

4. William H. Riker, "The Heresthetics of Constitution-Making: The Presidency in 1787, with Comments on Determinism and Rational Choice," *American Political Science Review* 78 (March 1984), p. 3.

5. Ibid., p. 7.

6. Ibid., p. 13.

7. James Madison, *The Federalist*, nos. 51, 48, and 49 (New York: Mentor, 1961), pp. 322, 310, and 315–16 respectively.

8. Joseph A. Davis, "House Rejects Reagan's Offer; Passes Clean Water Bill Again," *Congressional Quarterly Weekly Report,* January 10, 1987, p. 91.

9. Woodrow Wilson, *Congressional Government* (Boston: Houghton Mifflin, 1885), pp. 43–45.

10. Ibid., p. 283.

11. Thomas E. Cronin, *The State of the Presidency,* 2nd ed. (Boston: Little, Brown, 1980), p. 97.

12. Richard E. Neustadt, *Presidential Power* (New York: John Wiley & Sons, 1960), pp. 5–6.

13. James MacGregor Burns, *Presidential Government* (Boston: Houghton Mifflin, 1965).

14. Arthur Schlesinger, Jr., *The Imperial Presidency* (Boston: Houghton Mifflin, 1973), chapters 5–8.

15. Both quoted in James L. Sundquist, *The Decline and Resurgence of Congress* (Washington, D.C.: Brookings Institution, 1981), p. 460, emphasis added.

16. E. E. Schattschneider et al., "Toward a More Responsible Two-Party System," *American Political Science Review* 44, (September 1950), supplement, p. 89.

17. William J. Keefe and Morris S. Ogul, *The American Legislative Process: Congress and the States,* 6th ed. (Englewood Cliffs, N.J.: Prentice-Hall, 1985), p. 377.

18. As quoted in Congressional Quarterly's, *Guide to the U.S. Supreme Court* (Washington, D.C.: Congressional Quarterly, Inc., 1979), p. 6.

19. Walter F. Murphy, *Congress and the Court* (Chicago: University of Chicago Press, 1962), p. 247.

20. Ibid., p. 268.

21. David M. O'Brien, *Storm Center: The Supreme Court in American Politics* (New York: W. W. Norton, 1986), p. 309.

22. Ibid., p. 316.

23. Roger H. Davidson, David M. Kovenock, and Michael K. O'Leary, *Congress in Crisis: Politics and Congressional Reform* (Belmont, Calif.: Wadsworth Publishing, 1966), chapter 2.

24. For details see Roland Young, *Congressional Politics in the Second World War* (New York: Columbia University Press, 1956).

25. For details see Douglas Price, "Race, Religion, and the Rules Committee," in *The Uses of Power,* ed. Alan Westin (New York: Harcourt Brace Jovanovich, 1962).

26. Edmund S. Muskie, "Dinner Speech," in *The Role of Congress II* (New York: Time, Inc., 1975). (Editorial project by the editors of Time, Inc.; not paginated.)

27. As quoted in Sundquist, *Decline and Resurgence of Congress,* p. 461.

28. Ibid.

Further Reading

Rather than an exhaustive bibliography, the following list of readings is intended to suggest the types of books that might reasonably fall into each of the three levels of analysis. The reader will note that the materials generally fall into the traditional members-institution-system organizing scheme but that that is not always the case. Hence, some works (e.g., Shepsle's *Giant Jigsaw Puzzle*) will appear "out of place" relative to their normal topical location. It should also be recognized that, because authors' purposes differ they might not agree with the placement I use here. I apologize to them in advance. And, clearly, some works (such as West's *Congress and Economic Policymaking* which explicitly addresses all three levels) simply do not fall neatly into a single category.

I. GENERAL TREATMENTS

The fact that there are many fine textbooks on Congress is suggestive of the wide variety of factors that guide instructors in choosing their texts. I believe that instructors will find *Congressional Politics* an excellent companion for whatever text they assign—or even in the absence of a basic text. But the plethora of texts also suggests that offering recommendations can be a perilous business. Hence, for illustrative purposes, and also because they happen to be excellent books, I list three other Dorsey publications on congressional politics that make an excellent Congress package.

Jones, Charles O. *The United States Congress: People, Place, and Policy.* Homewood, Ill.: Dorsey Press, 1982.

Kozak, David C., and John D. Macartney. *Congress and Public Policy: A Source Book of Documents and Readings.* Homewood, Ill.: Dorsey Press, 1987.

Ripley, Randall B., and Grace A. Franklin. *Congress, the Bureaucracy, and Public Policy.* Homewood, Ill.: Dorsey Press, 1987.

II. MEMBERS OF CONGRESS

The following studies, which generally can be described as rationalist or purposive in approach, view individual members as the primary unit of analysis, as "rational actors," and therefore as the primary explanation for congressional politics.

Arnold, R. Douglas. *Congress and the Bureaucracy: A Theory of Influence.* New Haven, Conn.: Yale University Press, 1979.

Baker, Ross K. *Friend and Foe in the U.S. Senate.* New York: Free Press, 1980.

Bibby, John F., ed. *Congress Off the Record.* Washington, D.C.: American Enterprise Institute for Public Policy Research, 1983.

Clapp, Charles L. *The Congressman: His Work As He Sees It.* Washington, D.C.: Brookings Institution, 1963.

Clausen, Aage R. *How Congressmen Decide: A Policy Focus.* New York: St. Martin's Press, 1973.

Clem, Alan L. *The Making of Congressmen: Seven Campaigns in 1974.* North Scituate, Mass.: Duxbury Press, 1976.

Fenno, Richard F., Jr. *Home Style: House Members in Their Districts.* Boston: Little, Brown, 1978.

Ferejohn, John A. *Pork Barrel Politics.* Stanford, Calif.: Stanford University Press, 1974.

Fiorina, Morris P. *Congress: Keystone of the Washington Establishment.* New Haven, Conn.: Yale University Press, 1977.

_____. *Representatives, Roll Calls, and Constituencies.* Lexington, Mass.: D. C. Heath, 1974.

Jacobson, Gary C. *The Politics of Congressional Elections.* 2nd ed. Boston: Little, Brown, 1987.

Jacobson, Gary C., and Samuel Kernell. *Strategy and Choice in Congressional Elections.* New Haven, Conn.: Yale University Press, 1981.

Johannes, John R. *To Serve the People: Congress and Constituency Service.* Lincoln: University of Nebraska Press, 1984.

Jones, Rochelle, and Peter Woll. *The Private World of Congress.* New York: Free Press, 1979.

Kingdon, John W. *Congressmen's Voting Decisions.* 2nd ed. New York: Harper & Row, 1981.

_____. *Candidates for Office: Beliefs and Strategies.* New York: Random House, 1967.

Maisel, Louis Sandy. *From Obscurity to Oblivion: Running in the Congressional Primary.* Knoxville: University of Tennessee Press, 1982.

Malbin, Michael J. *Unelected Representatives: Congressional Staff and the Future of Representative Government.* New York: Basic Books, 1980.

Mann, Thomas E. *Unsafe at Any Margin.* Washington, D.C.: American Enterprise Institute for Public Policy Research, 1978.

Mayhew, David R. *Congress: The Electoral Connection.* New Haven, Conn.: Yale University Press, 1974.

Olson, Mancur. *The Logic of Collective Action: Public Goods and the Theory of Groups.* Cambridge, Mass.: Harvard University Press, 1965.

Parker, Glenn R. *Homeward Bound: Explaining Changes in Congressional Behavior.* Pittsburgh, Penn.: University of Pittsburgh Press, 1986.

Shepsle, Kenneth A. *The Giant Jigsaw Puzzle: Democratic Committee Assignments in the Modern House.* Chicago: University of Chicago Press, 1978.

Tacheron, Donald G., and Morris K. Udall. *The Job of the Congressman.* Indianapolis, Ind.: Bobbs-Merrill, 1970.

III. THE INSTITUTIONAL CONGRESS

The following works, which generally can be described as sociological or institutional in approach, view the component parts or structural attributes of Congress as the basic unit of analysis. They tend to see congressional politics, and the behavior of its members, either as the product of a variety of institutional structures and procedures or as patterns of behavior exhibited by identifiable groups or coalitions.

Bauer, Raymond A., Ithiel de Sola Pool, and Lewis Anthony Dexter. *American Business and Public Policy: The Politics of Foreign Trade.* New York: Atherton Press, 1964.

Clark, Joseph S. *The Senate Establishment.* New York: Hill & Wang, 1963.

Cooper, Joseph, and G. Calvin Mackenzie, eds. *The House at Work.* Austin: University of Texas Press, 1981.

Davidson, Roger H. *The Role of the Congressman.* New York: Pegasus, 1969.

Davidson, Roger H., David M. Kovenock, and Michael K. O'Leary. *Congress in Crisis: Politics and Congressional Reform.* Belmont, Calif.: Wadsworth Publishing, 1966.

Davidson, Roger H., and Walter J. Oleszek. *Congress Against Itself.* Bloomington: Indiana University Press, 1977.

Dexter, Lewis Anthony. *The Sociology and Politics of Congress.* Chicago: Rand McNally, 1969.

Fenno, Richard F., Jr. *The Power of the Purse: Appropriations Politics in Congress.* Boston: Little, Brown, 1966.

––––––. *Congressmen in Committees.* Boston: Little, Brown, 1973.

Follett, Mary Parker. *The Speaker of the House of Representatives.* New York: Longmans, Green & Co., 1896.

Fox, Harrison W., Jr., and Susan Webb Hammond. *Congressional Staffs: The Invisible Force in American Lawmaking.* New York: Free Press, 1977.

Froman, Lewis A., Jr. *The Congressional Process: Strategies, Rules, and Procedures.* Boston: Little, Brown, 1967.

Goodwin, George. *The Little Legislatures.* Amherst: University of Massachusetts Press, 1970.

Hess, Stephen. *The Ultimate Insiders: U.S. Senators in the National Media.* Washington, D.C.: Brookings Institution, 1986.

Hinckley, Barbara. *The Seniority System in Congress.* Bloomington: Indiana University Press, 1971.

Jones, Charles O. *The Minority Party in Congress.* Boston: Little, Brown, 1970.

LeLoup, Lance T. *The Fiscal Congress.* Westport, Conn.: Greenwood Press, 1980.

Manley, John F. *The Politics of Finance: The House Committee on Ways and Means.* Boston: Little, Brown, 1970.

Matsunaga, Spark M., and Ping Chen. *Rulemakers of the House.* Urbana: University of Illinois Press, 1976.

Matthews, Donald R. *U.S. Senators and Their World.* New York: Vintage Books, 1960.

Oleszek, Walter J. *Congressional Procedures and the Policy Process.* 3rd ed. Washington, D.C.: CQ Press, 1988.

Orfield, Gary. *Congressional Power: Congress and Social Change.* New York: Harcourt Brace Jovanovich, 1974.

Parker, Glenn R., and Suzanne L. Parker. *Factions in House Committees.* Knoxville: University of Tennessee Press, 1985.

Peabody, Robert L. *Leadership in Congress.* Boston: Little, Brown, 1976.

Price, David E. *Who Makes the Laws? Creativity and Power in the Senate.* Cambridge, Mass.: Schenkman Publishing, 1972.

Ripley, Randall B. *Power in the Senate.* New York: St. Martin's Press, 1969.

Schick, Allen. *Congress and Money: Budgeting, Spending, and Taxing.* Washington, D.C.: Urban Institute Press, 1980.

Schneider, Jerrold E. *Ideological Coalitions in Congress.* Westport, Conn.: Greenwood Press, 1979.

Sinclair, Barbara. *Majority Leadership in the U.S. House.* Baltimore, Md.: Johns Hopkins University Press, 1983.

_____. *Congressional Realignment, 1925–1978.* Austin: University of Texas Press, 1982.

Wahlke, John C., Heinz Eulau, William Buchanan, and LeRoy C. Ferguson. *The Legislative System: Explorations in Legislative Behavior.* New York: John Wiley & Sons, 1962.

White, William S. *Citadel: The Story of the U.S. Senate.* New York: Harper & Row, 1956.

Wilson, Woodrow. *Congressional Government.* Boston: Houghton-Mifflin, 1885.

Young, James Sterling. *The Washington Community, 1800–1828.* New York: Columbia University Press, 1966.

IV. CONGRESS IN THE POLITICAL SYSTEM

The following works, which generally can be described as systemic in their approach, tend to view Congress as the basic unit of analysis, frequently feature longitudinal examination of institutional relationships, and see congressional politics as the product of a variety of environmental forces.

Binkley, Wilfred. *President and Congress.* New York: Alfred A. Knopf, 1947.

Blanchard, Robert O., ed. *Congress and the News Media.* New York: Hastings House, 1974.

Brenner, Philip. *The Limits and Possibilities of Congress.* New York: St. Martin's Press, 1983.

Cater, Douglass. *Power in Washington.* New York: Random House, 1964.

Crabb, Cecil V., Jr., and Pat M. Holt. *Invitation to Struggle: Congress, the President, and Foreign Policy.* 3rd ed. Washington, D.C.: CQ Press, 1988.

Dodd, Lawrence C., and Richard L. Schott. *Congress and the Administrative State.* New York: John Wiley & Sons, 1979.

Edwards, George C. III. *Presidential Influence in Congress.* San Francisco: W. H. Freeman, 1980.

Fenno, Richard F., Jr. *The United States Senate: A Bicameral Perspective.* Washington, D.C.: American Enterprise Institute for Public Policy Research, 1982.

Fisher, Louis. *The Constitution Between Friends: Congress, the President, and the Law.* New York: St. Martin's Press, 1978.

_____. *The Politics of Shared Power: Congress and the Executive.* Washington, D.C.: CQ Press, 1981.

Follett, Mary Parker. *The New State: Group Organization the Solution of Popular Government.* New York: Longmans, Green & Co., 1918.

Freeman, J. Leiper. *The Political Process: Executive Bureau–Legislative Committee Relations.* Rev. ed. New York: Random House, 1965.

Frye, Alton. *A Responsible Congress: The Politics of National Security.* New York: McGraw-Hill, 1975.

Griffith, Ernest F. *The Impasse of Democracy.* New York: Harrison-Milton Books, 1939.

Hamilton, Alexander, James Madison, and John Jay. *The Federalist Papers.* Ed. Clinton Rossiter, originally published in 1788. New York: Mentor, 1961.

Huntington, Samuel P. *The Common Defense: Strategic Programs in National Politics.* New York: Columbia University Press, 1961.

King, Anthony, ed. *Both Ends of the Avenue.* Washington, D.C.: American Enterprise Institute for Public Policy Research, 1983.

LeLoup, Lance T. *Budgetary Politics.* 4th ed. Brunswick, Ohio: King's Court Press, 1988.

Light, Paul C. *The President's Agenda.* Baltimore, Md.: Johns Hopkins University Press, 1982.

_____. *Artful Work: The Politics of Social Security Reform.* New York: Random House, 1985.

Ogul, Morris S. *Congress Oversees the Bureaucracy: Studies in Legislative Supervision.* Pittsburgh, Penn.: University of Pittsburgh Press, 1976.

Olson, Mancur. *The Rise and Decline of Nations.* New Haven, Conn.: Yale University Press, 1982.

Price, David E. *Policymaking in Congressional Committees: The Impact of Environmental Factors.* Tucson: University of Arizona Press, 1979.

Sabato, Larry J. *PAC Power: Inside the World of Political Action Committees.* New York: W. W. Norton, 1984.

Saloma, John S. III. *Congress and the New Politics.* Boston: Little, Brown, 1969.

Schattschneider, E. E. *The Semisovereign People: A Realist's View of Democracy in America.* New York: Holt, Rinehart & Winston, 1960.

Schlesinger, Arthur M., Jr. *The Imperial Presidency.* Boston: Little, Brown, 1973.

Schlozman, Kay Lehman, and John T. Tierney. *Organized Interests and American Democracy.* New York: Harper & Row, 1986.

Shuman, Howard E. *Politics and the Budget: The Struggle Between the President and Congress.* 2nd ed. Englewood Cliffs, N.J.: Prentice-Hall, 1988.

Sundquist, James L. *The Decline and Resurgence of Congress.* Washington, D.C.: Brookings Institution, 1981.

_____. *Politics and Policy: The Eisenhower, Kennedy, and Johnson Years.* Washington, D.C.: Brookings Institution, 1968.

Truman, David B. *The Governmental Process: Political Interests and Public Opinion.* New York: Alfred A. Knopf, 1951.

Wayne, Steven J. *The Legislative Presidency.* New York: Harper & Row, 1978.

West, Darrell M. *Congress and Economic Policymaking.* Pittsburgh, Penn.: University of Pittsburgh Press, 1987.

Index

A Note on the Type

The text of this book was set 10/12 Palatino using a film version of the face designed by Hërmann Zapf that was first released in 1950 by Germany's Stempel Foundry. The face is named after Giovanni Battista Palatino, a famous penman of the sixteenth century. In its calligraphic quality, Palatino is reminiscent of the Italian Renaissance type designs, yet with its wide, open letters and unique proportions it still retains a modern feel. Palatino is considered one of the most important faces from one of Europe's most influential type designers.

Composed by Weimer Typesetting Co., Inc., Indianapolis, Indiana.

Printed and bound by R. R. Donnelley & Sons Company, Crawfordsville, Indiana.